RING OF DECEIT

RING OF DECEIT

INSIDE THE BIGGEST SPORTS AND BANKING SCANDAL IN HISTORY

BRUCE HENDERSON
AND DEAN ALLISON

Ring of Deceit: Inside the Biggest Sports and Banking Scandal in History
Copyright © 2014 by Bruce Henderson and Dean Allison

Published by: BruceHendersonBooks, Menlo Park, CA

www.BruceHendersonBooks.com

ISBN-13: 978-0989467537
ISBN-10: 0989467538

To the men and women of the Federal Bureau of Investigation and the United States Attorney's Office in Los Angeles, California.

PART ONE

CHAPTER ONE

January 23, 1981, started out to be a typical Friday morning at the bank. But it wasn't to stay that way for long.

Lloyd Benjamin Lewis sat at his desk in the Operations Department, trying to get through a stack of paperwork. For Lewis and the other forty or so employees of Wells Fargo Bank in Beverly Hills, California, the end of the workweek was in sight. No one was looking for new problems. In fact, given that it was Friday, most of them wanted to avoid fresh entanglements. Monday would be the beginning of a new week. Everything that could wait until then would just have to wait. Ben Lewis felt the same way.

A veteran of twelve years with Wells Fargo, Lewis was adept at coping with the ceaseless flow of paperwork that characterized bank operations. He was a survivor. He had learned how to maneuver around difficulties and keep the paperwork under control. He concentrated on priorities, working his way down a mental list from the most pressing to the least important matters. Unfortunately, the priorities had a way of changing without notice.

A compact black man with a quick smile and friendly nature, Lewis was a lieutenant in the small army of middle-management personnel needed to keep things running smoothly at Wells Fargo Bank, the nation's eleventh largest and California's oldest bank. His job was not glamorous. But then Lewis was not a glamorous man, although he wanted to be.

He disdained the conservative banker's three-piece suit. Instead, he was wearing a blue blazer, a designer shirt open at the neck, wool slacks, soft Italian loafers and gold jewelry. A carnation was pinned to his shirt. Two years shy of fifty, he had thinning hair and horn-rimmed glasses with tinted lenses. Proud of his heritage, he wore a small gold pin with a black center shaped like the continent of Africa on his jacket lapel. In earlier years, Lewis had been a serious athlete, playing competitive basketball and some semipro baseball. Still an avid sports fan, his hero was Muhammad Ali.

Lewis noticed his boss, branch Operations Manager Brian Feeley, heading his way. It probably meant more work. It would have to be damn important to not wait until Monday. He looked up when Feeley reached his desk.

"Take a look at this when you get a chance," Feeley said as he handed over a piece of paper. Feeley was a tall, slender Irishman in his mid forties. He smiled infrequently, possessed a quiet, somewhat nervous nature and favored the predictable banker's gray suits.

Despite their outward differences, Feeley and Lewis worked extremely well together. Each knew he could rely on the other to get the necessary tasks done efficiently and to follow up on any loose ends. Feeley delegated to Lewis almost complete responsibility for handling the mechanical details of day-to-day operations work at the branch, while Feeley handled personnel, administrative and general supervisory problems. Although they did not spend much time together outside the bank, their close working relationship had led Lewis and Feeley to become the best of friends. Each man trusted the other implicitly.

"Sure." Lewis saw that the piece of paper was a branch settlement tracer. He recognized the $250,000 transaction it reflected and felt a sudden rush of adrenaline.

"I got a call yesterday from Judy MacLardie at Miracle Mile," Feeley said. "She got this tracer and figures we screwed up." The tracer had obviously resulted from some sort of clerical mistake or foul-up by the bank's computer in misinterpreting programmed information. That was what Feeley thought and that was what he had told MacLardie.

"No problem, Brian."

Lewis stared down at the tracer as Feeley walked away. His pulse quickened. So harmless-looking unless you knew what the tracer meant. It concerned a transaction he had put through a month earlier. He remembered because it had been Christmas Eve. He had been in a rush to leave the office.

The tracer originated from a computer—housed in the bank's San Francisco headquarters—which kept track of thousands of daily money transfers among the bank's three hundred branch offices in California. Since it wasn't practical to transport actual cash from one branch to another, the computerized system enabled the bank to keep track of these interbranch transactions through a bookkeeping procedure based on credits and debits. Every major financial institution involved in branch-banking operations had a similar system. At Wells Fargo it was called the branch settlement system. It had been operating smoothly for several years. Or so bank officials thought.

The system was fairly simple. For example, if a customer walked into the Beverly Drive branch and asked to withdraw money from an account he had at the Miracle Mile branch, his account balance was verified electronically and then he was given the money. A Beverly Drive officer filled out the debit half of a branch settlement ticket, a two-part form with carbon paper in the middle, and placed it in his office's outgoing-mail bag. This debit ticket, when it reached San Francisco, told the computer, in effect, to charge the branch settlement system for the money paid out to the customer. Meanwhile the Beverly Drive officer was supposed to send the credit half of the same branch settlement ticket in the interbranch mail to the Miracle Mile office, alerting officers there to the transaction and notifying them to charge the customer's account for the money. After charging the customer's account, the Miracle Mile office then put the money back into the branch settlement system by sending the credit half of the ticket in to the computer. This brought the transaction full circle: money had been paid out of the branch settlement system at the Beverly Drive end and put back into the system at the Miracle Mile end.

The key to the system, as in most computerized verification operations, lay in giving the computer what it wanted. So long as the computer received both the debit and credit halves of the same branch settlement ticket within ten business days of each other, it treated the transaction as complete and correct, provided the tickets were properly encoded. The encoding procedure, verified by the computer as well, required that the two halves of a branch settlement ticket bear the code numbers of two different Wells Fargo branches to ensure that the transaction in question was really an *interbranch* transfer of funds. The system was never supposed to be used for transactions carried out by one branch alone. Keeping the computer happy, therefore, required that both halves of a branch settlement ticket be sent in within ten working days, each bearing a different branch code number. If one half of a ticket did not get to the computer in time, or if the proper code numbers were not used on both of the two halves, the computer would send out an inquiry notice, known as a tracer.

Lewis sat immobilized. He was sure he had sent in both halves of the ticket for this transaction in plenty of time. For two years he had been careful, making sure that he was never away from the bank for too long a period. Even when he was sick with pneumonia, he had dragged himself to the office in order to feed the necessary paperwork into the computer. Forsaking extended holidays, he had disregarded a bank policy that required employees to take an annual two-week vacation. The rule had been designed with security in mind. Something might be wrong if an employee couldn't be away from the bank for two weeks and have his job covered by another employee. For two years Lewis had taken no more than ten days' vacation at a time, but no one had noticed.

He began to sweat. He wiped his forehead; slick and clammy. He had to watch it. Perspiration meant nervousness, since the office was air-conditioned. The last thing he needed was someone coming over to ask what was wrong. He must remain outwardly cool.

Friday or not, this was a new urgent priority. Nothing else on his desk mattered now. His reputation, his career, hell, his *life* depended on his actions now. He was good at unraveling other people's problems. There had to be a way to explain this one. But both Feeley and that MacLardie woman over at Miracle Mile were aware of the tracer. Lewis tried to review his options. He looked up the phone number for the Miracle Mile office and called Judy MacLardie. When she answered, he made an effort to sound relaxed.

"Hello, Judy, this is Ben Lewis over at Beverly Drive."

"Hi, Ben. How you doing?"

"Fine." He had decided to try a bluff. "Say, I've got the tracer that you sent over to Brian. I'm familiar with the transaction. Do me a favor and just make up a substitute branch settlement. Process the credit and send me the debit. That ought to clear it up."

"You think so?"

"Sure," he said. "That'll get Branch Settlement Control off our backs. I know all about this one and it's okay, believe me."

He tried to be casual and not sound like he was pleading. If he could convince her to send in a new credit half of the ticket, the computer would never know the difference. He only wished he knew MacLardie better because he was asking a big favor. He was pretending that the tracer was nothing more than a clerical foul-up and that she could save him some added work by clearing it up with a new credit. It was the kind of administrative "covering" that one banker would sometimes do for another as a professional courtesy. But once in a while, you'd run into some tight-ass who refused to bend the rules. Even to help a fellow banker. He just hoped MacLardie was the bending kind.

"Well—okay, if you say so."

"Thanks, Judy."

He was so relieved he didn't notice the edge in her voice.

✳ ✳ ✳

Four days later, Judy MacLardie received another telephone call from Lewis. He sounded better than he had on Friday, when she had agreed to draft the substitute branch settlement form. Actually, she had no intention of doing so. Immediately after Lewis's first call, she had phoned Brian Feeley to tell him she thought something might be wrong. She had sensed it in Ben Lewis's voice. Feeley had said he was sure there was an explanation and promised to look into it. After that, MacLardie had shelved the matter, turning her attention to other business. She had expected to hear back from Feeley, not Lewis.

"I didn't get that duplicate branch settlement yet," Lewis said. "Did you make it up?"

"Gee, no," she said. "I forgot. I've been really busy. I'll try to get to it right away."

"Yeah, we really oughtta take care of it."

Something still bothered her about Lewis's behavior. If it had been an honest mistake, an operations officer in his position should be trying to get to the bottom of the problem, if for no other reason than to make sure it wouldn't happen again. But Lewis seemed interested only in a quick solution.

"I'll get to it today," she said, not knowing what else to say. She didn't like to fib, but this whole situation was getting her worried.

When they hung up, she replayed the conversation in her mind. A full-bodied, spunky woman in her forties, MacLardie's first inclination was usually to look at the funny side of a situation. While she conscientiously applied herself to her job, she was willing to give someone the benefit of a doubt. This easygoing attitude, complemented by an earthy sense of humor, had not stopped her from reaching the responsible post of assistant vice president. Now her well-trained instincts were telling her that something was not right about this transaction.

It was more than Lewis's not wanting to take the time to find out why the computer had issued the tracer. He wouldn't have bothered to call a second time if that was the case. No, Lewis was concerned—*too* concerned. She was picking up the warning signal that all bankers hope they will never have to face. To suspect that a colleague has gone bad is dreadfully awkward for all. In almost two decades of banking—the last thirteen years with Wells Fargo—she had never come across a larcenous bank officer.

The tracer had posed a mystery for MacLardie from the beginning. When it had first arrived at her office a week earlier, she had searched through Miracle Mile's records for the credit ticket but could not find it. Then she reviewed the microfilm of every electronic transfer transaction her branch had processed during the previous month. The credit record wasn't there. This struck her as odd. If Miracle Mile had charged a customer's account and credited the branch settlement system—as the tracer indicated it had—then the branch should have a record of that action. And if it was a mistake—maybe another branch had charged one of its customers and the tracer had been sent to Miracle Mile incorrectly—then why was the Miracle Mile branch settlement code number on the bottom of the ticket? Employees of one branch were not even supposed to *know* the code number of another branch, let alone *use* it.

Puzzled, she had telephoned the bank's Difference Research Department. Located in the East Los Angeles suburb of El Monte,

Difference Research served as the bank's troubleshooting bureau, reviewing all irregular transactions, rechecking such things as addition and subtraction and correcting any errors. Through its reports, journals and microfilm records, Difference Research could determine the underlying transactions corresponding to specific branch settlement debit and credit tickets. Since MacLardie couldn't identify the second half of the transaction that involved the charging of a customer's account at her branch, she wanted to know more about the first half.

A day or two later, a clerk in Difference Research called to tell MacLardie that the transaction underlying this tracer apparently involved money paid out to a customer at the Beverly Drive branch. At that point, MacLardie went to her boss, Gene Kawakami, the Japanese-American manager of the Miracle Mile office, and told him of her findings. "Oh shit," Kawakami had said, "it looks like someone screwed up over at Beverly Drive."

That was when MacLardie had first called Brian Feeley and told him about the tracer. He had asked that she send him a copy, which she did that same day by interbranch mail. Attached to the tracer was a note, typical of MacLardie's irreverent humor:

My Dear Brian, I grew 4,927 gray hairs, hit my nails to the elbow, wet my pants twice, had three fainting spells, tried (unsuccessfully) to swallow my tongue and am on the verge of a nervous breakdown, because I got this tracer. I am currently in enough trouble with R-E-G-I-O-N (and others) to last a lifetime PLUS. This type of thing makes me sweat a lot and my teeth shake. I would appreciate any help you can give me, because if I don't get this cleared quick, God and others will be out to get me … I just don't understand it.

In a funny way, the note was meant to show MacLardie's genuine concern with the tracer. Her comment about "trouble with Region" alluded to past episodes in which she had been called on the carpet before staid bank administrators who wanted to know why she was rocking the boat over some bureaucratic procedure she thought unnecessary.

Now, after the second telephone call from Lewis about the tracer, MacLardie decided it was time to speak to Feeley again. Determined to convey her sense of foreboding, she pulled no punches when he came on the line. "You remember that branch settlement tracer I sent over a few days ago? I'm sure there's something wrong with it. I can't find any record of the transaction on our microfilm, and Ben has called me twice about it. He's acting very strange."

"Really, Judy, I'm sure there's nothing to worry about," Feeley said. "Someone probably just put the wrong branch code on the ticket. The volume has been pretty heavy here lately, and Ben's been under a lot of pressure. I'm sure it's nothing to be worried about, but I'll look into it right away."

This time, however, Feeley's assurances alone weren't enough to satisfy MacLardie.

"I think you should do that right away, Brian. In the meantime, I'm going to ask Difference Research to pull the documentation on the transaction. I hope you're right about it just being a screwup somewhere, but I really think something's wrong here."

After hanging up on a somewhat chastened Brian Feeley, MacLardie called Difference Research. She asked them to pull all the paperwork that had been attached to both halves of the branch settlement ticket involved in the tracer. This would tell her who had processed the mysterious Miracle Mile credit half, as well as the identity of the officer at Beverly Drive who had authorized the original $250,000 payment.

On Friday morning, January 23, 1981—three days after she requested this documentation—MacLardie received photocopies of the original branch settlement tickets. The debit half, sent in to the computer from Beverly Drive, carried this handwritten explanation: "As per your, instructions, we have issued our cashier's check." It was signed by Ben Lewis. The credit half bore a similar handwritten note, stating "As per instructions, we have charged our customer's account." According to the branch settlement code number it bore, the credit half appeared to have been sent in to the computer from Miracle Mile, where it supposedly originated. But the handwriting on the debit and credit halves of the ticket was the same.

Now MacLardie was convinced her hunch had been right. She would give Feeley the first opportunity to bring the auditing and security forces down on his own branch. Professional courtesy dictated that. But if he wavered at all, then MacLardie, a boat rocker from way back, was fully prepared to blow the whistle on Ben Lewis.

***

"We seem to have a problem here," Brian Feeley said in a tone of voice that betrayed his discomfort. His eyes purposefully avoided Lewis sitting across from him, as if looking at his friend was too painful. They were at a small booth in The Red Onion, a Mexican restaurant across the street from the Beverly Drive branch. They were not eating lunch. This was a private meeting that Feeley had sought, away from prying eyes at the office. A glass of wine sat in front of each man, barely touched.

"You know that tracer Judy sent over?" Feeley continued. "Well, it hasn't been cleared and Judy is raising hell. She ordered the offsets and something doesn't look right. The signature on the credit doesn't appear to be yours, but the writing does. She's called me about it several times, and now she's threatening to call Auditing. What do you know about this?"

Feeley waited for an explanation. The impropriety MacLardie suspected wasn't the sort of thing that Ben Lewis would be involved in. It had been less than an hour since Feeley had received the disturbing call from MacLardie, and the possibility of wrongdoing didn't appear any more real to him now than it had then. There *had* to be an explanation. He just needed to hear it from Ben.

Lewis said nothing at first. Staring out the front window of the restaurant at the passersby on the street, his mind reeled. What could he tell Brian—Brian of all people! For two years he had feared some foul-up like this, something over which he had no control, like a branch settlement ticket being misplaced by a clerk or getting lost in the mail. Now the computer had caught up with him. That damn tracer was forcing his hand.

"Well," Lewis began softly, "you know the big fight Harold Smith has coming up in Madison Square Garden next month? He figures to make at least fifty million on it." Lewis took a breath. "He needed some money on a short-term basis to cover expenses involved in putting the show together. He had money coming in from one of the TV networks, but he was a little short. So, I gave him an advance."

"You used a branch settlement for that?" Feeley asked, incredulous.

"Uh-huh. It was a real short-term thing, just an accommodation, really, so I figured that was the easiest way to handle it."

Feeley's heart sank. Harold Smith was a boxing promoter with a dozen or so personal and business accounts at Beverly Drive. His companies, Muhammad Ali Professional Sports (MAPS) and Muhammad Ali Amateur Sports (MAAS), were well known both locally and nationally. Feeley was aware that Lewis had worked closely with the flashy promoter and his boxing enterprises. There was certainly nothing wrong with that. To the contrary, as in any other service business, it was good for the bank officers to develop a personal rapport with the branch's clients. But this was something else again. What Lewis had done, however well-meaning his motives, amounted to a misappropriation of the bank's funds.

"Did you use Miracle Mile's number on the credit half to clear it?"

"Yeah." Although Lewis did his best to make the whole situation sound routine, it fell flat. "There's no loss involved, Brian—it was paid back. When Harold's TV check came in, I cleared the branch settlement. Like I said, it was just a short-term advance."

"Ben, you know that's improper."

"I know."

"Were there any other *advances?*"

"No, just that one."

There was a long silence at the table as Feeley seemed to be studying his wine glass.

"You know that you've put your job in jeopardy," Feeley finally said, leveling a hard look at Ben. "We're going to have to tell Bob Smith. And we'll have to let Auditing know about it."

Lewis was numbed by the thought. Now the branch manager and the bank's Auditing Department were getting involved. His troubles were growing. His friend Brian was not going to give him any more time to clear things up. Struggling to hold back a flood of emotions, Ben feared he would lose control. "What do you think's going to happen?" he asked.

"I don't know," Feeley said stiffly. His eyes carried no glint of friendship or understanding. They were clouded by hurt and disappointment.

***

In the conference room at the Beverly Drive branch, Lewis sat across from Feeley and Bob Smith, the branch manager, who was about to hear of the "advance" for the first time.

"Bob, a problem has arisen with a tracer on a branch settlement that Ben handled," Feeley explained. "Ben issued a branch settlement ticket to advance two hundred and fifty thousand dollars to one of our major customers, Harold Smith, as a—favor."

Smith sat stonelike, watching his operations officer struggle with the difficult explanation.

"Ben processed both halves of the settlement himself. He tells me that the advance was paid back and that there is no loss involved. But obviously we have a deviation from proper procedure here."

Smith looked coldly at Lewis. "You know this is grounds for termination?"

"Yes, Bob, I know."

"I think we had better call Auditing right now," Smith said.

Feeley picked up the phone. He soon had the supervisor for the bank's Southern California auditing operations on the line. Upon hearing the parameters of the problem, the supervisor said, "I'll have to call San Francisco and get back to you. In the meantime, have Ben sit down and write out a statement."

Feeley took Lewis back to the Operations Department, instructing him to write out a description of the transaction. Taking out a pad of paper from his desk, Lewis found a pencil and stared at the blank sheet before him. He breathed deeply, trying to calm his jangled nerves. What should he write? He silently cursed the computer and the tracer that had put him in this position. As if the tracer itself weren't bad enough, it had been just his damn luck for the thing to land on the desk of that busybody Judy MacLardie. But he couldn't waste time dwelling on his lousy luck. And he couldn't possibly sit here and write out a statement. Apart from the problem of keeping his hand steady, a written account—if accurate—would enable them to unravel everything.

For the Christmas Eve withdrawal now plaguing Lewis was typical of the hundreds of one-sided branch settlement transactions he had carried out since 1978. He had known from the start that using Miracle Mile's branch settlement code number, to make it appear that the credit tickets he was generating at Beverly Drive had been sent in to the computer from Miracle Mile instead, was absolutely forbidden under the bank's normal operating procedures. He was not even supposed to know the Miracle Mile code number, much less use it for transactions handled exclusively at Beverly Drive. The number had been supplied to him long ago by a friend who had worked at Miracle Mile, just before that friend left his job with the bank.

Lewis's trance was broken when he heard a secretary tell Feeley that Lloyd Gasway from Auditing was on the line. Lewis had met Gasway. Although they had always been cordial when work had brought them together in the past, Lewis knew that Gasway was a tough ex-policeman and an experienced internal auditor. As Lewis approached Feeley's desk, the latter picked up the phone and once again described the discovery. He concluded with "All right, Lloyd, I'll make sure Ben is here to meet you after lunch."

Lewis motioned to Feeley, who asked Gasway to hold on.

"It would be pretty embarrassing for me to meet him here in the branch in front of everyone."

Feeley nodded understandingly. "Could Ben possibly meet you somewhere outside the bank? One o'clock at your office? Fine."

Lewis felt trapped. He had to get out of the bank. He knew it would only be a matter of time before the other discrepancies were uncovered.

"Brian, I'm feeling shaky," Lewis said when Feeley was off the phone. "I'd like to get some fresh air."

"Okay. But this has to be cleared up today."

Lewis felt the need to say something more. To reassure the friend he had let down so badly.

"I just want you to know how sorry I am about this."

"So am I," said a grim Feeley.

***

Lewis was trembling so badly he was hardly able to steer his car. He managed somehow to drive the ten miles to his house. Later, he had no memory of the trip.

He lived in a split-level house in Baldwin Hills, a residential neighborhood that was home to many black professionals and their families. He had come home out of a natural instinct to be in secure surroundings so he could concentrate on the best course of action. But once inside the house, he felt more trapped than ever by the outside world. He had still not gotten over his separation from his wife, Gladys, and having to live alone in the home they had once shared. Now, as he sat in the kitchen and dialed a Santa Monica number, it seemed emptier than ever.

"Muhammad Ali Sports," answered a woman's voice with a pronounced Southern accent. "May I help you?" The voice belonged to Teri Key, an attractive brunette in her late twenties who was Harold Smith's executive secretary.

"Teri, this is Ben. Let me talk to Harold."

"Sorry, he's not here."

"Where the hell is he? I've got to talk to him."

"He's at the track."

Great, Ben thought, *the whole world is falling in on me at the bank and Harold is off at the racetrack.*

"Can you page him?"

"Not at the track." Key had gotten bawled out for doing that once before. Smith complained that the security guards had come for him, making it look like he was in trouble with the authorities.

"It's urgent," Lewis said.

"He took a limo to the track. I guess I could try and have the limo company page the car."

"I'll do it myself. Give me the number."

A few minutes later, the limousine company operator informed Lewis that she was unable to reach anyone in the car, a luxurious stretch Lincoln limo with dark windows and a fully stocked bar that Smith had rented earlier that day.

No wife. No Brian. No Harold. The frustration was too much. Lewis broke down as he had only a few times before in his life. Afterward, taking deep breaths to regain his self-control, he was limp and exhausted. There was no way he could show up at Auditing in this shape. He called Gasway and told him he wasn't feeling well. It didn't take any acting on his part to sound like a man who was in no condition to drive. Gasway agreed to reschedule their appointment for 3 p.m. that day and told Lewis to see a doctor in the meantime.

Delaying the inevitable was little relief. In a mental fog, Lewis got into his car and headed for the MAPS offices. He had no other place to go.

* * *

"What are you doing here?" asked a surprised Teri Key when Lewis walked into her office. The banker never came to MAPS headquarters at this time of day.

"I gotta talk to Harold."

"I still haven't heard from him. What's wrong, Ben? You look—"

Lewis had already disappeared down a corridor. He passed the gallery of framed pictures on the wall opposite the door, memorable scenes from track meets and boxing matches frozen in time. Athletes like Houston McTear and Olympic boxing champ Leo Randolph caught in the midst of extraordinary performances. Hung in a prominent place was the king of the sports world himself, Muhammad Ali, ready to deliver a blow with raised gloved fists. Lewis found no solace in their company now. He strode down the corridor, glancing quickly into the empty office suites he passed, like a caged animal looking for a way out.

Lewis found himself alone in a spacious office in the back of the building. The lettering on the door said "Lewis and Smith Enterprises." He was the Lewis.

The entertainment promotions firm had been Lewis's pet project. He had been proud and felt so satisfied when they had put on a concert with Shirley Bassey. A picture of Lewis with the celebrity was proudly displayed atop the desk at which he now sat. The man in the picture, his open shirt revealing a tangle of gold neck chains, his arm around Shirley Bassey, smiled at him uncomprehendingly. Lewis didn't know whether to laugh at himself or cry. They had made lots of big plans, like the candlelight dinner show at the Waldorf scheduled for next month. None of those plans was even worth thinking about now, not unless something could be done about the problem at the bank.

Various possibilities raced through his mind. Was it still possible to contain the problem? How much time did he have before everything was discovered? Would the bank call the FBI or would it treat the problem as an internal matter?

But that was all there were—questions. There were no answers, at least none that he wanted to think about.

For the first time in his life, Ben Lewis began to seriously consider the prospect of going to jail.

CHAPTER TWO

arold Smith arrived at the MAPS offices in a somber mood. At six feet two, with the body of an ex-athlete now running to fat, he was a big man, dressed in his usual attire of blue jeans, cotton workshirt, cowboy boots and Stetson hat.

From Smith's restrained demeanor, Teri Key guessed he had not picked many winners at the track. When he won, everyone within shouting distance knew it. That happened a fair amount of the time. But Harold could lose big, too, since it was not unusual for him to bet $10,000 on a single race. On a good day, he was known to slip each of the women around him several hundred dollars, telling each he had placed a special bet for her that had come in a winner. His gambling was not limited to the track. Teri had personally seen him put $25,000 on a roll of the dice at Vegas. He also claimed to have won $250,000 on the first Leonard-Duran fight by betting on Duran. He became stoked at the prospect of getting something for nothing, enjoying the rush of having so much more than he had a moment before and the attention, particularly female, that a big winner and his money always attract. Smith treated losing as only a momentary delay. He always acted confident of getting it back—and then some—on another day soon. He was a promoter in every way, and first and foremost, Harold Smith promoted himself.

Key's intense personal loyalty to Smith had more than a financial dimension. He had helped her at a desperate time in her life, when she first came to Los Angeles from North Carolina, broke and ostracized as a white woman traveling with her black musician lover. Not one to forget such favors, she had good-naturedly put up with Smith's tireless efforts to get her into bed. Fortunately, Smith was easy to fend off since he got plenty of action elsewhere. Harold could be a pain in the neck, Teri knew, but as far as she was concerned he had a heart of gold.

"Ben's here," she said. "He needs to see you."

"Any other calls?" Smith asked.

"Nothing that can't wait."

When he reached his office in the back corner of the building, Smith had taken off his Stetson.

"Where the hell have you been?" Ben asked.

Smith closed the door. Lewis looked awful. His mouth sagged and his eyes were reddened.

"What's the matter with you, man?"

"There's trouble at the bank."

Smith replied casually. "What kind of trouble?"

"Remember I told you a few days ago that the computer had sent out a tracer and it went to the wrong branch?"

"Yeah. I thought you took care of that."

"Judy MacLardie at Miracle Mile was supposed to issue a duplicate to clear the tracer but she didn't. She's raising hell."

"How bad is it?"

"Real bad. Brian called in the branch manager. They called Auditing. I was supposed to meet with the auditor this afternoon but I didn't go. It looks like the whole damn thing is going to be exposed."

With his eyes hidden behind dark glasses and most of his face covered with a bushy beard, Smith wasn't easy to read. "It's Ali's people," he said. "I bet one of his attorneys went to the bank."

Several months earlier, in late 1980, Muhammad Ali's representatives had begun asking to see the financial books and records of the companies that bore the Champ's name, Muhammad Ali Amateur Sports and Muhammad Ali Professional Sports. The inquiry had been initiated by Ali's lawyers. Thereafter, the request had been pursued by the Los Angeles office of Arthur Andersen and Company, the Big Eight accounting firm that watched over details of Ali's financial empire. On Harold Smith's instructions, the Arthur Andersen representatives had been told that such an audit would not be possible until early 1981 because the in-house bookkeepers at MAPS and MAAS would need until then to bring all the records up to date and complete the companies' year-end financial statements for fiscal 1980.

Apart from his other motives for resisting the intrusion, Smith also clearly resented it. The Champ trusted him as a black brother and had no reason to be poking around in his books. For the last several years, he had never asked the Champ for a dime. In fact, the cash flow went the other way. A cut of his profit in exchange for the use of Ali's name. Besides that, he had given the Champ money whenever he asked for it and often when he didn't. Wasn't that proof enough that he was taking care of finances just fine? It had to be the people in Ali's entourage, either some of his white business advisors or members of the Muslim faction, who resented how close he was to the Champ and were always trying to drive a wedge of mistrust between them. Smith knew the technique well, since he used similar devisive tactics himself to keep his subordinates where he wanted them: loyal to him alone.

"It's gotta be them Muslims—you know they're out to get me," Smith continued. "Herbert Muhammad's worried 'cause I'm so close to the Champ. They probably went directly to the bank and started causing trouble for us. They know you and me are tight."

Lewis didn't think Ali's camp had contacted the bank. He knew most of them well enough to recognize them if they had come around. The computer had sent out the tracer for its own reasons. This paranoid rambling by Smith solved nothing.

"What am I going to *do*, Harold? The bank wants answers."

Smith reached for his cowboy hat and buzzed for his Cadillac to be brought around to the back door of the office complex. "I think we better go somewhere else and talk," he told Lewis. "Take your car and follow me."

***

Smith's home was located in the rolling hills above the famous Sunset Strip. For the high-priced neighborhood in which it was situated, it looked relatively modest from the outside, despite the Mercedes and Cadillac in the driveway. The house and the one next door where the "live-in" maid resided were leased and paid for out of the company checking accounts.

Tens of thousands of dollars had been spent decorating and furnishing the interior. Smith's wife had supervised the work, which was done by a professional decorator. The den was equipped with a floor-to-ceiling stereo system. The master bedroom featured a sunken bath and king-sized platform bed. There was a well-appointed formal dining room. Hardwood floors and Oriental rugs. Expensive fabric on all the walls and cushioned furniture. A pool and patio. And an elaborate home security system.

They were in the living room. Lewis was standing in front of the fireplace, taking long gulps from a tall Scotch and soda. Barbara Lee Smith, Harold's blond wife, who was only a couple of inches shy of six feet, had put the drink in Lewis's hand soon after he walked in the door because he looked so shaky. Smith was sipping a drink too. He was trying to get Lewis calmed down and assess the problem at the bank. He had made his friend start at the beginning, reciting the developments following the issuance of the tracer and various conversations with Feeley and MacLardie at the bank.

"How did Judy sound?" Smith asked.

"I haven't talked with her for a while. She called Brian this morning."

"Why don't you give her a call and find out? Lee, get Ben another drink."

Smith picked up the receiver of an extension phone and put his palm over the mouthpiece as Lewis placed the call. When MacLardie came on the line, Lewis could think of nothing to say except to apologize for the trouble he had caused her.

"It's really out of my hands now," she said warily.

"I just want you to no there will be no loss to the bank," Lewis offered and then said good-bye.

After the conversation, Smith came over and shrugged. "I don't know, she didn't sound that mad. You'd better call Brian and see what's going on."

Lewis dialed again.

Feeley was even cooler. "Where are you?" he asked.

"I'm over at Harold's—he's right here with me."

"Have you been to see Lloyd Gasway yet?"

"No, I just wasn't feeling well, so I called him and postponed it. I probably won't be able to make it out there till Monday."

"Try to pull yourself together and get out there. It's important that you get this resolved today. Things won't get any better by putting it off."

"Listen, Brian, I just called to tell you how sorry I am about this thing," Lewis said. When Feeley remained silent, he continued, reaching awkwardly for something—anything—to say that would make things better.

"Please don't think too badly of me," Lewis said. "Like I told you, Harold repaid the one advance I made him, so there's no loss to the bank."

"Ben, were there any other transactions like that?" Feeley asked.

"No. That's the only one."

Feeley put him on hold, then came back on the line. "Come on, Ben, level with me. Gasway is on the other line. He's already found another one for two hundred and fifty thousand. We're going to have to freeze all the accounts."

"Oh, yeah, I forgot that one. I'll tell you about it later."

"You've got to go see Lloyd today, *please*. If you don't, it'll only make things worse for you."

Lewis looked confused as he put the receiver down. He was having a difficult time accepting what was happening to him. "It's all over. They're freezing all the accounts. There's no concealing it now."

He suddenly turned on Smith. "This never should have happened! It *wouldn't* have happened if things had been taken care of the way they were supposed to be." His eyes bulged in anger. "It's ridiculous to think that something like this could be concealed in any banking system for more than two years."

"Hey man," Smith said soothingly, "calm down or you're gonna have a stroke."

Lewis fell back heavily onto the sectional.

"No use puttin' money in frozen accounts," Smith mused aloud. He picked up the phone and made a quick call. Then he sat quietly.

Moving over to sit in front of Lewis, Smith leaned forward and looked into Lewis's eyes, measuring him.

"Okay, Ben, what do you want to do?"

"I don't know, but I sure don't want to stick around and go to jail."

Smith looked at him somberly. "Let me tell you somethin', brother. Runnin' is a hard life," he said knowingly. "A real hard life."

* * *

"How much cash you got?" Smith asked.

"Almost fifty thousand," Lewis said.

The money was the first thing he had stuffed into his shoulder bag at home. Lewis normally didn't keep that much cash around the house; it was recent winnings from trips to the track and Las Vegas with Smith. Lucky break. With all the accounts frozen, he wasn't going to be able to write any checks. He had also tossed some clothes and belongings into a garment bag. He wasn't sure what to bring and what to leave behind. Was he going away for a weekend, a few months or a lifetime?

They had rendezvoused at the Queen Mary, the former luxury ocean liner permanently docked at a Long Beach pier where it serves as a tourist attraction, restaurant and hotel. When the Smiths pulled into the parking lot, the backseat of their Mercedes 450SL was heaped with clothes still on hangers. When Lewis's Cadillac Seville arrived, Gladys was behind the wheel. Their separation had been long enough that it was now amicable, and they still had deep feelings for one another. Ben had called Gladys and pleaded with her to come with him because he was in trouble.

At Smith's suggestion, Lewis had Gladys register in her name for the two-bedroom, two-bath Henry VIII Suite. The two couples had separated to freshen up in their own quarters, agreeing to meet in the common living room. Lewis waited there now, the noises coming through the wall telling him that Smith was still on the phone, as he had been for at least twenty minutes.

So much was still unresolved in Ben's mind. My God—had it only been nine hours since Brian Feeley confronted him? This had been the longest day of his life, and it still wasn't over. Every moment had been agonizing. He was still searching desperately for solutions when Smith emerged from his bedroom.

"Maybe we could try to make a deal with the bank," Lewis said. "They could get back all the money if they let us go ahead with the fight."

"It'll take another ten million dollars to put on that fight," Smith replied. "You really think them people at the bank gonna give two black dudes like us that kind of money after what's happened?"

"I don't know, man, but it could be worth asking," Lewis said. "They might go for it if they realize that letting the fight go on is the only way they can get paid back."

The fight the two men had in mind was to be an event unprecedented in professional boxing history. It was entitled "This Is It," in accordance with a trend requiring promoters to give their fight cards grandiose titles. Smith had been telling everyone, including Lewis, for weeks that it would gross somewhere between $50 and $100 million. Scheduled for Madison Square Garden on February 23, 1981, less than five weeks away, the MAPS event featured eight championship or championship unification fights. The fighters' names were among the most recognizable in the business. A formal dinner show was to be held the night before, sponsored by Lewis and Smith Enterprises. Tony Orlando would be the headliner at no cost to the promoters. (When Orlando was depressed at the death of his friend Freddie Prinze, Smith had Ali call the singer. The Champ ruminated about the ups and downs of life and cheered Orlando up. It was a call and a favor the singer had not forgotten.)

"Who would be the guy to talk to at the bank about lettin' the fight go on—this man Gasway?" Smith asked, showing apparent interest in Lewis's idea.

"No, Gasway is just a security man. He doesn't have any loan authority. We'd have to go pretty high up to get the okay for something that big."

"Who's the top man, then? I'll talk to him myself."

"The chairman of the board is Richard Cooley," Lewis said. "You'd probably have to get his approval on something like this." As he said it, Lewis dimly realized that the idea of Smith persuading the chairman of the board of Wells Fargo Bank to lend him $10 million was preposterous, but in his desperation to find some way out of the problem, he could think of no alternative.

"I'll talk to him as soon as I've figured out the best way to approach it," Smith said reassuringly. "But it'd be best if you stayed out of sight for a while as things are getting worked out. You're the one they're out to get, so your being around is just gonna make it harder to get them to listen."

Lewis nodded dumbly as Smith outlined the plan in more detail. At this point, he was too confused, too frightened and too tired to be analytical. He just wanted to get away and felt almost thankful that Smith was arranging for his escape from Los Angeles. At least that was what he thought Smith was arranging.

Lewis and Smith split up the next day. Although neither would have guessed it, they would not see each other for a long time. Their partnership, and friendship, forged out of financial necessity for one and deeper psychological reasons for the other, were nearly finished.

***

Teri Key was frightened and confused. She was waiting in a darkened Pioneer Chicken parking lot in Venice with a briefcase full of cash. Things obviously weren't right at MAPS.

The day before, an hour or so after Smith and Lewis had left the office, Harold had telephoned with an urgent request for her to check all the Wells Fargo accounts and if there were any overdrafts to cover them from the Harold J. Smith Productions account at Beverly Drive. He told her to prepare the checks and said he would be in to sign them so that they could be deposited before the bank closed at six o'clock.

The Harold J. Smith Productions checking account, known to Teri and everyone else around the offices simply as "the Production account," was almost always the source Smith used when he needed ready funds or when the regular MAPS and MAAS checking accounts needed replenishing. At times, the Productions account seemed like a bottomless pit. She was never really sure where the money in the account came from, since there was no separate business being conducted under the name Harold J. Smith Productions. But she had ceased to question the source of the money soon after she started keeping the company checkbooks. This was partly the product of her Southern upbringing and an instinct for her proper place as a secretary and partly because she was just too busy trying to keep up with Harold to worry about such things. She had never received a good answer from Smith anyway, the few times she had asked. Sometimes Smith would say, "It's my money, I know what I'm doing." Other times he indicated that the money came from television contracts. Since it was Teri's job to pay the bills, her main concern was simply that there was enough money in the MAPS and MAAS accounts to cover the checks she wrote. When there wasn't, she told Smith, and he always took care of it.

After she had finished writing the checks to cover the negative balances in four different accounts, she received another call from Smith. In a complete reversal, Smith said it wasn't important to make the deposits after all.

"Listen," he continued, "something much bigger has come up. The word is out that the Muslims around Ali are gonna try to break into our offices this weekend. I want you to take all the records home with you tonight. Be sure and get the checkbooks and my personal files. And don't let anyone see you."

"What about Larry's stuff?" Teri asked, referring to the papers that Larry Jones, the accountant for MAPS and MAAS, had spread all over the conference room table to help him prepare the companies' year-end financial statements for 1980.

"Take them too," Smith replied. "I'll call you later at home to make sure everything's all right."

This hurried message from Harold, who obviously was upset, scared Teri. Based on what she'd heard, the Muslims played for real. As far as she knew, Ali had little control over them; if anything, *they* controlled him. She was also aware that many of Ali's "people" had little love for Smith and went along with what he did only because of his close relationship to the Champ. Muslims disliked Smith not only due to his flashy, hedonistic life-style, but because he was not one of them and because he represented a growing area of Ali's business activities that was not under their influence or control. Some were simply jealous of Smith's ability to talk the Champ into seeing things his way. Others in Ali's entourage were displeased because of Smith's repeated postponements of the audit of his companies' books. Teri knew this because every time Smith would cancel a scheduled review of the books she was the one who had to call Ali's advisors with the news.

For the past couple of weeks, Smith had been talking constantly about rumored death threats leveled at him by the Muslims. "One of the Muslims is the guy who shot Malcolm X," Smith claimed. He had also reported hearing gunshots near his home. One morning he suspected that a bomb had been put in his car and had the car thoroughly searched, but nothing was found.

Under these circumstances, Smith's professed concern to safeguard the company records did not surprise Teri. While she did not appreciate their true significance, she only had to use common sense to realize that the loss of its chief financial records would create chaos at MAPS. They would be a logical target for someone out to damage her employer's business.

She found it difficult to believe that Ali would know about any Muslim threat to MAPS, much less that he had approved of one. But then the Champ was a unique man. He was so many poses and moods that most people were unsure of his true feelings about them. One thing was certain, though: if the Muslims managed to discredit or embarrass Harold so that Ali pulled away from MAPS, everything they had worked so hard to accomplish would be lost. The Ali name was crucial. Without it they would lose much of the credibility they had with fighters, TV network officials and other promoters. They could be ruined.

Teri waited until after six o'clock, when Tony Key came to pick her up. Everyone thought they were married, but they weren't. She had used Tony's last name for several years to legitimize the relationship. It was difficult enough for an interracial couple to get housing and jobs, and Tony was not only black but, as a jazz musician, mostly unemployed. They had found a bit more acceptance when people thought they were married. The appearance of being married was also a good way to keep men at bay. Fighters, she had learned, were the horniest guys around. They all seemed out to disprove the old theory that sex was bad for an athlete's legs.

Teri carefully executed Harold's instructions about the records. She gathered up all the checkbooks and canceled checks for MAPS, MAAS and Harold J. Smith Productions accounts at Wells Fargo. Folders full of fight contracts, advertising records, revenue sheets and bills also went into several cardboard cartons she had found in the office. Because Harold had made special mention of it, she took particular care to clean his personal files out of the credenza behind the desk in his office: separate folders pertaining to his boat, the automobiles he had acquired for himself and other members of the MAPS entourage, and his stables of racehorses. All of it had to be protected against the expected intruders, and Teri was more than willing to be the protectress.

When she went to gather up the accountant's papers from the conference room, though, Teri had to improvise. Even though it was Friday evening, Larry Jones had stayed late to finish some of the schedules he was working on. The accountant was still sitting at the big table, poring over the wave of papers that seemed to wash over the surface in front of him. Thinking fast, Teri made a decision. Larry was trustworthy, and there was no telling how long he might stay if she tried to wait him out. Given that she had no way of knowing when the expected intruders might come and no way of reaching Harold, the risk of taking Larry into her confidence seemed less than that of waiting until it was too late to save the records.

Without mentioning the reasons behind it, she told the accountant of Harold's belief that trouble was imminent and his instructions to her to remove the records. Honestly believing that everything would be back in place Monday, she suggested that Jones leave his papers behind and go home for the weekend. Adding these records to the others made four full cardboard boxes. She and Tony stacked the cartons in their car and drove home to their Santa Monica apartment, where the boxes were placed in a corner of the living room. Harold had told her to take them there for safekeeping and wait for further word.

Instructions came the next morning in a phone call from Smith, who would not say where he was calling from. Harold reminded Teri that he had recently sent his horse trainer, Hal King, to the Florida Breeders Auction with $100,000 cash. King had bought two horses to add to Smith's thoroughbred racing stable at a cost of $74,000. The $26,000 in change and other funds, chiefly from Harold's track winnings, were in a horseman's account at Santa Anita in the name of Michael Blake, a crony of Smith's who also had some of Harold's horses registered in his name. It was an open secret at the track that the horses and the account were Smith's. Harold told Teri he needed some cash and that she should withdraw whatever balance remained in the horseman's account, including the $26,000 left over from the trainer's Florida trip. He needed to go to Vegas to pay a fighter, he explained. She was to bring the money and meet him in this parking lot. Smith suddenly needing cash was nothing new. Today being Saturday, he obviously couldn't go to the bank to get the money. Still, she had never known him to take money from the horseman's account for a boxing deal.

Smith was now an hour late for the rendezvous. He was often late. But how safe was it for her to wait in this seedy area? She had already begun to draw the attention of a few unsavory types. She checked again to make sure that the car doors were locked. How long should she wait? Smith had made it clear that it was important for him to have the money.

Finally she spotted him. Harold was on foot, crossing the street toward her. Someone must have dropped him off. She unlocked the passenger door and he slid in.

"You brought the money?" he asked.

"Yeah. It's in the briefcase."

"Good girl. Let's take a ride. You wanna drive?"

"No, I'm too nervous."

They switched seats, and he headed toward Marina Del Rey.

"Are the records safe?" he asked.

"They're all at my place."

Smith fell silent. He obviously had things on his mind. She knew better than to try to push him into talking. He talked only when he wanted to talk. And at those times he could talk nonstop.

"Teri, you know how much I care about you," he finally said. "I'm going to tell you some things that may not be necessary for you to know. Everything might work out okay. But in case they don't, I want you to know what's going on. I want you to have heard it from me."

She nodded. She had a feeling that what she was about to hear wasn't going to make her feel any better. But at least she would know what was happening.

"When I went into this business, I went to the bank for a loan. The bank gave me a line of credit for eight million dollars. When I used that up, I went back for more. The people in the bank's regional office turned me down. But Ben and some other people at the bank who believe in us decided to give me the extra money anyway. You know, give it to us on the local level, without the bigshots knowing anything about it. Now, I'm not exactly sure how it happened, but it looks like one of the guys involved had a fight with his girlfriend and the chick called bank headquarters and blew the whistle. We're gonna negotiate with the bank to let us go on with 'This Is It.' But if they turn us down, things could get real bad ..." His voice trailed off.

Teri was stunned by the latest news. First the trouble with Ali. Now the bank and maybe the law. What was going on?

Smith pulled in at the Amfac Hotel on Lincoln Boulevard. He said that Lee was upstairs. "Do you have any ID in another name?" he asked.

She did, an old Virginia driver's license identifying her by her maiden name, Terisa Godwin. She registered in that name, paying with cash Smith gave her from the briefcase she had brought from the racetrack. He accompanied her to the room.

"Do you trust Tony?" he asked when they were inside.

She was startled by the question. "Of course I do."

"Call him," he said. "Tell him to bring enough clothes for both of you for a few days. Have him meet us in this room. Get another room in his name and one for Kathy Stewart. She's on her way."

Katherine Stewart, an attractive Hawaiian-looking woman, was the ex-wife of musician Sly Stone of Sly and the Family Stone. Teri knew that Kathy and Harold had been seeing each other for several months.

"Where's Lee?" Key asked.

"In our room with John."

Of course, John, their four-year-old son and Harold's pride and joy, had to be with them under the circumstances.

When Tony Key arrived a half hour or so later, Smith repeated for his benefit the story he had told Teri about the unauthorized line of credit at Wells Fargo.

"They might try to put Ben and me in jail for this," Smith said.

"*Jail?*" Teri was shocked by the word.

"I might have to leave the country for a while," Smith said. "I'm not going to jail for *nobody.*"

He sent Tony out to buy Asti Spumante. Tony returned with three bottles of the sweet champagne—Smith's favorite—and plenty of potato chips, peanuts and other munchies. A vial of cocaine appeared. They all did a few lines. The depression in the room soon lifted.

Smith handed Teri a check for $10,000. It was drawn on the Lewis and Smith Enterprises account. "Take this," he said. "If anything goes wrong, I want you to be taken care of." He gave her several checks for other MAPS employees—including one for $25,000 for MAPS President Sammie

Marshall—that he and Lewis had written while holed up on the Queen Mary the night before. "But hang on to everyone else's check until we find out what the bank is going to do. Ben and I are going to lay low for a while. We may even have to get out of the country. If I do that, I'm going to have to put my assets in the names of other people. Friends like you who I can trust to give it back to me when this all blows over."

Teri was trying to think of what property Smith meant. He had rented or leased everything. Even his racehorses were in someone else's name. It didn't seem to her that hiding assets was going to be a major problem.

Smith sent Tony to deliver the briefcase of cash to Lee in another room. Lee returned with Tony and joined them briefly. She made the mistake of asking her husband a question he didn't want to answer.

"You're getting on my nerves," he yelled.

"You're getting on mine too," she said.

"Go back to the room, then. Make sure John's all right."

It struck Teri, who knew Harold well, that he wasn't really upset at what Lee had said but had something else in mind. She knew she was right when, a few minutes after Lee left, Kathy Stewart arrived. After some more wine, cocaine and talk, she and Smith retired to another room.

Key didn't sleep well that night. She figured Harold could take care of himself. But she was worried about Ben Lewis. Apparently he had done all the paperwork at the bank for the line of credit. Clearly his neck was on the line. He was too nice a guy to get into such a jam.

At the same time, she was proud that Smith had put so much trust in her when the going got rough. Protecting the records. Gathering money. Handing out big checks. He had given her so many important tasks to perform. It was time for her to start paying him back for all those past favors. She didn't mind one bit. She felt a glow of loyalty and secretarial pride.

The next morning, Smith showed up at the door to the Keys' room around 9:30 a.m. "Lee's still sleeping and I need to use the phone," he explained. He dialed a long distance number and asked for a room number.

Teri guessed he was calling Ben, and her hunch was quickly confirmed.

"Listen, now, Ben," he said, "I'll have Tony pick you up. Go to San Diego and you'll be right across the border from Tijuana—just in case." Smith paused, evidently while Lewis spoke.

"Okay, now relax, man, and I'll talk to you tomorrow."

Smith turned to Tony Key. "Tony, I want you to pick Ben up in front of the TraveLodge by the airport. Take him to San Diego and get a hotel room."

Kathy Stewart stopped by to say she was leaving, that her sister was picking her up downstairs. A few moments after the door closed behind her, Smith picked up the phone to make another call.

Robin Grant, the woman he called, was another "friend." She was Australian, and Teri had been told by Smith that he had helped get Robin into the country illegally. She soon arrived at the hotel. Smith told her, almost tearfully, that he was leaving, perhaps for a long time. The two of them went into the bathroom. From the sounds they could not help but hear through the bathroom door, Teri and Tony knew that the "good-byes" being exchanged were intimate ones.

Thirty minutes later, Smith had new marching orders for Key. He wanted her to take all the records back to the office except the Productions account check register, the fighters' contracts and a few other specific documents. He told her to show up for work the next morning as if it were any other Monday.

After Tony left to pick up Ben, Teri dropped Smith off at an apartment he kept as a love nest.

Before getting out of the car, he hugged and kissed Teri. "I may not see you again," he said, his eyes watering.

Key sobbed. "Take care of yourself, Harold. Please stay in touch." Tears ran down her cheeks. "We all need you."

That evening, she returned to the office, carrying out her instructions from Smith. She put the MAPS and MAAS checkbooks back, transferring the Productions account records, Harold's personal files and Larry Jones's records to the trunk of the Seville. The office looked fine. No one had broken in. She turned out the light and decided to go back to the hotel. She was too nervous to stay home alone. She kept thinking about the Muslim death threats. Her home address would be easy to find. What would happen tomorrow? And the next day? How long could they keep operating without Harold?

The following morning she showed up at the MAPS office at nine o'clock sharp. She remembered Smith's last words to her: "Be sure you get to the office on time like nothing is happening. Tell everyone I had to go out of town."

A few minutes after nine, Sammie Marshall walked in. A heavyset black man almost six feet tall with a potbelly, Marshall was the president of MAPS but, like everyone else, he took his orders from Smith.

The first thing Marshall said was "Where's Harold?"

"He had to go out of town," Teri answered matter-of-factly. She didn't particularly like Marshall, and the feeling was obviously mutual.

"Where?"

"New York."

Marshall went back to his office, located across the hall from Smith's.

Funny, even though Marshall knew Ben Lewis well and had an intimate knowledge of banking, he had obviously not been taken into Harold's full confidence regarding the latest difficulties. Key approved, as she considered Marshall a bumbler. She knew Marshall would be angry when he finally found out about all the trouble with the bank. He would probably feel that he had a right to know. After all, he had introduced Smith and Lewis. Back when Marshall was an officer at Wells Fargo's Miracle Mile branch.

* * *

Ben Lewis didn't like the sound of Mexico. He didn't know anyone there. He would be a black man in a brown country. He didn't know the language. The natives were poor, and he was carrying a lot of cash. It was not a place he wanted to spend any time. But he could think of nothing else to do. Nowhere else to go.

After seeing Gladys off in his car from the Queen Mary that morning, he had gone to the TraveLodge near the Los Angeles International Airport. He slept little, less than an hour. By the time evening came, he was depressed, exhausted and lonely to the point of desperation. He had called Bruce Barrett at home. A skinny man in his late twenties, Barrett was the only full-time employee of Lewis and Smith Enterprises. Lewis told Barrett he was in trouble and needed to talk to him. "Please come over," Lewis pleaded. "Make sure you're not followed."

Barrett was a hyperkinetic entertainment industry hanger-on. He had worked at Motown Records and bragged of rubbing shoulders with Diana Ross, Marvin Gaye, Smokey Robinson, the Temptations and the Jackson Five. He had also worked for actor Billy Dee Williams before launching his own unsuccessful record company. After meeting Smith at Hollywood Park— Smith was always interested in anyone who knew celebrities—he worked his way into Smith's entourage and ultimately was hired for $350 a week plus 20 percent of the net revenues from the shows he produced. His job was to help line up talent and handle the production chores for the schedule of concerts and other entertainment promotions which were planned.

Barrett immediately heard the dread in Lewis's voice. He was calling from a motel? He was in trouble? What kind of trouble could it be? Not one to take unnecessary chances, Barrett armed himself with a revolver he kept in his apartment.

At the motel, Lewis opened the door a crack, then quickly ushered Barrett into the room.

"We're finished," Lewis said, sitting down on the bed. He looked nothing like the dapper banker normally proud of his appearance. He was rumpled and haggard, like a defeated man who knew it was no use kidding people. He was beaten, and everyone might as well know it.

"What do you mean finished?" Barrett asked.

"All of us. You. Me. Harold. The fight. The Orlando show."

"What are you talking about? I'm supposed to leave for New York this week to set things up."

"Forget New York." Lewis wiped the tears away with the back of a hand. His nose was running. "Everything's over. Forget about the company. All our deals are off. All the money was stolen. I embezzled it from the bank."

Barrett's eyes widened in fear. "You did *what?*" It was more a high-pitched scream than a rational question.

"It's all over, Bruce. All the money for MAPS, MAAS, Lewis and Smith—everything—it was embezzled from Wells Fargo."

Barrett jumped out of a chair and stood as if poised to run. "I don't believe it." But one look at Lewis told him that this was no joke.

"It's—true." Lewis's crying was uncontrollable now.

Barrett went into a frenzy. "I'm running a legitimate business!—ready to have all these concerts in the next six weeks!—ready to sign a major artist who just got nominated for a Tony!—maybe do a movie!—and you steal money from the bank?"

"Yeah."

What about the credit line Harold has?"

"That's bullshit."

"Why did you do it?"

"I'm going to tell you everything, Bruce. I need to tell someone."

Barrett sat back down. He appeared to be in a state of shock.

The explanation took hours.

In the wee hours of Sunday, an exhausted Lewis voiced a new fear that had arisen since his last talk with Smith. "Harold could have me killed in Mexico." Eliminate the chief witness. It would be no problem. If Smith was desperate enough and felt as if he was going to be taken down for the fall, it was conceivable. Wasn't it? Lewis no longer knew what made sense.

A few hours later, Lewis and a shaken Barrett parted downstairs, where Tony Key waited out in front of the hotel. Lewis got into the car with Tony, who got on the southbound San Diego Freeway, heading toward San Diego and the Mexican border. No way Tony would be the hit man. If he was going to be killed, Lewis knew it would be in some ratty hotel room in Mexico. At the hands of some punk, maybe someone recruited through Smith's cronies in the Latin fight game. His neck would be snapped. His face battered beyond recognition. His body thrown into a sewage-filled river. He would have no ID and never be identified. Ben Lewis would just vanish and some stiff would later float up, his broken body covered with shit.

Lewis sat in stony silence. He was past exhaustion. He was beyond reason. He was in the most terrible state of his life. Nothing compared to it. Not marital separation. Not the death of a loved one. Nothing. He was even afraid to call his wife again for fear of getting her involved in his messy crimes. He had no one. He was burned out from the cocaine he had been using for the last forty-eight hours to keep going. He needed rest and food but couldn't stand the thought of either.

Ben Lewis knew that he had lost control of his life.

CHAPTER THREE

It had been a busy five days for Lloyd Gasway since he had first talked to Brian Feeley about Ben Lewis. Feeley had not sounded too concerned in that first phone call as he told of Lewis advancing money to a customer named Harold Smith. Gasway had never heard of the promoter. This guy Smith's apparent connections to Muhammad Ali had Gasway intrigued— and worried. It would sure be a messy situation if he had to investigate the most popular sports figure in America. But Feeley had assured Gasway that there was no loss to the bank. "Ben says it only happened once and was paid back," Feeley said. "We're just calling to report it like we're supposed to."

Yet a red light had gone off in Gasway's mind. As a senior loss investigator for Wells Fargo, trouble was his job. And, despite Feeley's explanation, this sounded like it had all the potential for big trouble. Gasway was paid $35,000 a year to investigate internal frauds; being suspicious and cautious came with the turf. He had investigated a number of cases that had resulted in bank personnel being convicted. Wells Fargo had $24 billion in assets. With the stakes so high, no one was above suspicion.

Gasway did not fit the stereotype of a bank auditor. There was nothing studious or bookish in his appearance, though like any good investigator he was meticulous in his work. A police officer for twelve years before joining the bank a decade earlier, Gasway still looked like a cop. A bulky man weighing two hundred and fifty pounds, he had pawlike hands and thick forearms. He had the suspicious nature and cynical humor of a career cop who had seen it all and was shocked by little.

He had worked virtually every type of internal bank fraud. He approached each one with the same self-assured fatalism. He was a pay-me-now-or-pay-me-later guy. When Gasway got on a case, he was like a bear tracking a wounded deer through the woods. He followed the scent, never wavered in his determination and understood that he would eventually catch up with his troubled prey. Like all good investigators, he knew that time was on his side.

Gasway's strategy on this case would be to use the reported irregular branch settlement as a starting point. He would trace through the records and scrutinize virtually every transaction involving Lewis and this particular customer. If Gasway found nothing more, only then would he be satisfied that it had "happened only once." Regardless of what Gasway discovered, Lewis would undoubtedly lose his job. Although he knew and liked Ben Lewis, Gasway could feel no sympathy for the man. Once bank officers went bad in any way, it was impossible to keep them around. One day they would be skirting regulations to help a friend—a seemingly minor infraction—and the next day slipping money into their briefcases.

Gasway often wondered how many customers would guess that banks lose many times more money from internal embezzlements than from robberies. He knew the public had no idea of the high incidence of bank embezzlements. But a prudent bank like Wells Fargo was careful to protect its image. Letting word leak out about internal thievery was no way to foster public confidence. Gasway had personally investigated embezzlements that totaled in the many hundreds of thousands of dollars. None of them had made headlines. The biggest problem with embezzlements was that they were seldom one-shot deals. Usually, the employee stole over a long period, often getting bolder—and more careless—as time went on. The challenge of the bank's Auditing Department and its investigators was to discover the source of the embezzlements, identify the culprit and stop further loss as soon as possible. Then came the task of ascertaining how bad the damage was, tracing the embezzlement back to its origins and estimating the total loss. That was why Gas-way had swung into action so quickly.

Gasway worked straight through the weekend at his Spartan office in the bank's El Monte service center. His first priority was to determine whether or not there was any loss to the bank and, if so, what the total exposure might be. He needed to be able to tell his superiors as soon as possible. This manipulation of the branch settlement system was clever. And so simple that it was frightening. Everyone had thought the system was secure with all the backup and tracing procedures built into it. But Gasway understood more than some bank officials that nothing was entirely safe. Any lock or system built or devised by man could be breached by man. That was what was so frightening about a bank officer gone amuck. They knew all the procedures. They had the codes and keys. They knew where—and how—the money was kept.

Hunched over a microfilm viewer, Gasway soon came to suspect that his worst fears were true. The first $250,000 "advance" Lewis had made to one of Harold Smith's accounts was not the only one. In trying to trace it through the system, he came across a second $250,000 transaction. He carefully studied the signatures on the tickets. Same signature. Lewis had done it at least twice. It didn't look good. Lewis was not telling the truth. The money had clearly not been paid back. The exposure for the bank then stood at half a million dollars. But how much further did it go?

He called Feeley immediately and asked him about the second $250,000 transaction. Feeley said he knew nothing about it but that Lewis happened to be on another line and he would ask him. Feeley put him on hold. A minute or so later, he came back to say that Lewis had "forgotten" about the second one but did not want to talk about it.

"Did he say anything else?" Gasway asked.

"No. He got off the line pretty quickly. But I told him we had frozen all the accounts."

"We sure don't want any more money leaving the bank. Brian, make me a list of big deposits for the last month or six weeks and call me back with it as soon as possible."

"You think there's more?" Feeley asked worriedly.

"We have two now. That's one more than we knew about this morning. Ben isn't being straight with us. Who knows how many we still don't know about?"

The cop in Gasway hungered to get to Lewis, sit him down and begin the questioning. Lewis sounded so remorseful, Gasway thought that perhaps he could get to the bottom of the scheme in fairly short order. A guilty person was often willing to tell the truth while still in a state of shock at being caught in the act. But when they had time to calm down and rationally think things over, they often realized that it might be best to keep quiet and talk to a lawyer first. That inevitably led them to withhold further information.

In their last conversation, Lewis had been crying hysterically. Gasway thought that a bad sign. The cancellation of their meeting and Lewis's overwhelming emotions made it appear as if Lewis was a guilty man with *more* transgressions to hide. Lewis had said he had taken a sedative and was unable to discuss anything. "I'm just so glad there's no loss to the bank," Lewis had sobbed. Gasway had agreed to postpone their meeting until Monday, but even as he did so he knew the chances of the meeting taking place were slim to none. Gasway's instincts told him that he was going to have to make this case without any help from Lewis.

For Gasway, the information that lay buried in the reels of microfilm was far more riveting than any murder mystery novel. He stayed with it nearly nonstop, pausing only long enough for Cokes, cigarettes and rest for his eyes.

He pulled the offsets to the list of deposits Feeley had given him late Friday, deposits made to four accounts controlled by Harold Smith. He backtracked to check the source of each deposit. Were they checks? Cash? Transfers from other accounts? No, each and every one was offset by a branch settlement ticket. While checking the offset to one of these transactions, he stumbled across an entire string of alternating debit and credit branch settlement tickets, all dated the same day and entered into the system in one batch. In all, there were twenty-four transactions. Most unnerving was that each of them appeared to be the tip of still another series. And all the branch settlement tickets appeared to be in the same handwriting.

Momentarily overwhelmed by the magnitude of what he was looking at, Gasway sat back from the viewer and lit a cigarette. How far back did all this go? He would have to begin to painstakingly work his way down the string in order to get to the bottom. It would take weeks. And if he found additional strings of debits and credits, maybe even months. He took off his glasses and massaged his stiff neck before resuming his tedious task. Thankless investigations like these were his job.

Starting with the first of the new string of twenty-four tickets, he worked it as a regression, beginning at the end and moving down the line of earlier transactions. He noticed that each prior debit was no more than ten days apart from the credit, so that the computer had not been triggered to put out a tracer. Concentrating so as to not lose his place, he found the previous offset for each item. He couldn't skip one without breaking the chain. Interestingly, the first few transactions in this string were for the same amounts as on the preceding tickets in each series. When, several hours later, he had worked his way down until there were no other offsets, he found himself at the beginning of that particular chain.

He reviewed his findings. What somebody had evidently done was to work the series of debits and credits up to a certain figure, then "rolled over" that amount so that the computer wouldn't catch on. The "roll over" was accomplished by sending a credit in for the total amount, then a debit, then another credit and so forth. Why did the chains stop at a certain dollar amount? Was the culprit worried about the total getting too high and attracting attention?

There was a revealing pattern. Each debit ticket was coded with a number ending in "607," which was the confidential Beverly Drive branch settlement code number. And each credit ticket was encoded with a number ending in "609," the corresponding Miracle Mile number. Most curious was that the recipient line was not filled in on any of the credit tickets supposedly sent in from Miracle Mile. To Gasway, this indicated that the credit tickets had not been received by anyone at the Miracle Mile office, acknowledging receipt of the documents supposedly sent there from Beverly Drive. This effectively short-circuited the branch settlement system's method of justifying the debits. All the tickets—both credit and debit—apparently had been put into the branch settlement system at one branch: Beverly Drive. Again, that was not the way the program was designed to work. But by using Miracle Mile's code number, it had been made possible. Just one man had signed all the tickets. As Gasway suspected, the handwriting appeared to belong to Lewis. The total for the first string was just short of—*one million dollars*. My God, thought Gasway, I still have *twenty-three to go*.

He would have to trace back through the microfilm for each series of tickets in the same manner. Some of them turned out to be offset by only a few branch settlement tickets. Others involved many dozens of debits and credits. The total number of unauthorized transactions initiated by Lewis would end up at nearly one thousand. Although it would be six weeks before he would sort all this out and have an exact total, Gasway knew on Sunday that the bank's loss was climbing into millions of dollars.

On Monday morning, after breaking the bad news to his superiors, a weary Gasway picked up the phone to call the Los Angeles division of the Federal Bureau of Investigation. It was time to involve the feds. Laws had been broken, crimes committed and money stolen by a banker who had taken enough to fill dozens of briefcases.

Lewis, of course, had not reported for work that day or showed up for his appointment with Gasway. There was no doubt in Gasway's mind: Ben Lewis had to be found, and fast.

As he waited to be connected with a special agent so he could begin the long story, Gasway wondered just what Lewis had done with all that money.

CHAPTER FOUR

To Teri Key's relief, nothing unusual happened on Monday. If she hadn't known of all the trouble brewing, she would have considered everything normal.

Smith telephoned several times. Although Key had no way of knowing it, he had left town and was calling from a hotel room some four hundred miles away. Each time he began with the same uneasy question: "Heard anything?" Each time she was able to report it quiet on the MAPS front.

Thankfully, her worst fear of FBI agents descending on the office with search warrants did not materialize. Second to that was a scenario involving a Muslim takeover. But there were no agents, no Muslims and no calls from the bank either. She was kept busy answering the phone and dealing with routine matters.

Still thinking about the records in Key's possession, Smith had arranged to have them picked up and brought to him by one of his gofers. Key would not find out until days later that the errand had taken the driver all the way to Sacramento, the state capital.

Her only special assignment for Monday was to secure passports for the Smiths and Lewis. But that had posed a problem. Once the logistics were solved and recent pictures of all three had arrived, she ran into problems with the passport office in downtown Los Angeles. The listed destinations of Colombia and Venezuela were acceptable. But the passport official—an accommodating Japanese-American man whom MAPS had used before on rush applications for various athletes traveling abroad for sports events—refused to renew Harold Smith's outdated passport. The official had previously issued a temporary passport even though Smith had not presented a birth certificate at the time. Smith's "sworn" statement about his birthplace had been enough. That passport had been renewed once, though Smith had still not come up with a birth certificate. The official chose today to put his foot down. No birth certificate, no renewal. When she passed the word to Smith, he had said, "I can't get my birth certificate. It was destroyed in a fire. Forget the passports."

That meant that Harold Smith could not legally leave the country—other than to go to Mexico or Canada. And it meant that Lewis was in the same boat.

Tuesday passed. Smith and Lewis were now communicating through Key. Smith passed messages for the banker to "hang in there," and Lewis left panicky messages for Smith to call him in San Diego. But Smith did not call that day.

Lewis finally heard from Smith on Wednesday.

"Why haven't you called before this?" Lewis said, perturbed that he had been isolated in a San Diego hotel room all this time. He felt as if he'd been living in a pressure cooker.

"It's been hell, brother. I had to run through freezing woods with my little baby in my arms. They were shooting at me. Gunfire filled the air."

"Who was shooting?"

"Plainclothes cops. I hitchhiked and got a ride with an old guy in a truck. Things are getting rough."

"Jesus." Lewis knew that Smith was prone to exaggeration. But would he make up such an outrageous story? The cops could certainly be onto them by now. It had been five days since the bank found out about the unauthorized transactions. If a full-scale manhunt was underway, the authorities would undoubtedly be looking for him too.

"Mexico is our only way out," Smith reiterated.

"I don't want to cross the border at Tijuana," Lewis said. "It's too dangerous."

"You can go to Houston and cross there."

"Houston?" Houston wasn't anywhere near the Mexico border. What was Harold thinking?

"I'm gonna talk to Cooley at the bank about our loan," Smith said.

Now Lewis was inclined to think it wouldn't work. He just couldn't see Cooley receiving Harold Smith right at this time. Too much money had been misappropriated over too long a period of time.

"Ben, there's something I gotta know."

"What?"

"How much money we talkin' about?"

Lewis had the totals on a slip of paper in his pocket. He had kept a running tally since the first day, two years ago, when he had used the branch settlement system to cover three MAPS checks totaling $14,000. At the time, Smith had played on his sympathy. "I'm trying to do something for amateur sports and the kids," the promoter had said. "Athletics is the only thing these little brothers have going for them." Lewis had done it for the kids that day. Later, he had done it for other reasons. To get into sports promotions. To break into the entertainment business. To help other black people. To be important. To be close to Ali. But he had planned, all along, for the money to be repaid.

The MAPS bottom line had never been good. The company consistently lost many thousands of dollars on fight after fight. Smith justified the expenses to Lewis and others as seed money needed to secure the loyalty of boxers, their managers and TV network officials who bought the rights to sports events. Looking at it as objectively as he could, Lewis thought that Smith had great prospects in the boxing business because he had signed the world champions and top contenders in nearly every weight class. It was a powerful argument, for when Smith finally achieved monopolistic control over the sport, MAPS stood to reap enormous benefits. In the meantime, Lewis had to keep financing Smith and MAPS because unless they succeeded the money would never be paid back and Lewis would be exposed and ruined.

Lewis had given Smith the new total almost weekly and reminded him regularly of the need for repayment. Smith kept putting him off, telling him not to worry; they would get it back on the next event they put on.

Lewis had kept each daisy chain of branch settlement credits and debits under seven figures because he didn't want a clerk or teller making a mistake on the amount. The more figures, the more chance of an error. Each chain—once it reached the high six figures—kept getting rolled over and the total not increased. To generate additional monies, Lewis would simply start a new chain.

"You want each chain separately?" Lewis asked.

"Yeah, give me a total on each one."

"The first one is nine hundred, forty-six thousand—"

"Wait, wait. Give me each number. Go slow."

"Nine, four, six, comma ..."

Smith had a difficult time getting the amounts down accurately. He had never been good with numbers. Lewis had to repeat each one several times. Finally they came to the total.

Smith didn't sound surprised or concerned. "If I can convince them bankers to go along with us for our big fight," he said, "then we're home free, brother."

***

Smith never did call the office of Wells Fargo Bank Chairman Richard Cooley. Later in the day, though, he telephoned Teri Key and told her to reach Lewis at his hotel in San Diego.

"Tell Ben I'll be in touch," he said.

She rang the hotel, but Lewis had checked out. Desperate, she checked with the front desk to see if he had left any messages. He hadn't.

Ben Lewis was gone.

***

Bruce Barrett also made a call on Wednesday afternoon. To the Long Beach *Press-Telegram*. He told a reporter in the sports department everything Ben Lewis had told him at the motel during their marathon discussion Saturday night.

The Thursday morning paper carried the banner headline, HUGE BANK EMBEZZLEMENT ... MUHAMMAD ALI INVOLVED?

The chase was officially on.

CHAPTER FIVE

Since the days of J. Edgar Hoover, the Federal Bureau of Investigation has disliked the media poking about in its business. The FBI feels pressure anytime a story is written about an ongoing investigation. The Bureau is convinced that publicity makes its job more difficult, and perhaps justly so. Witnesses are sometimes less inclined to talk. Suspects have a way of disappearing. Agents in the field don't like reporters looking over their shoulders. Supervisors get worried about the image of the Bureau. If the Bureau breaks the case and makes arrests, it's perceived as doing only what's expected. If it does anything less, then it has failed. It's close to a no-win situation.

When the Long Beach newspaper, quoting an unnamed source, had more information about the Wells Fargo embezzlement case than the Bureau after four days, the mood at the FBI's Los Angeles division was made even edgier. The Bureau's press spokesman was directed to make the same two-word statement to any and all inquiring reporters. "No comment." The calls started coming in fast. From the Los Angeles *Times*. The New York *Times*. *The Wall Street Journal*. The London *Times*. All the wire services. The TV news organizations. It was frustrating for Bureau personnel. Most bank embezzlements were kept quiet, and no one knew about them until grand jury indictments were handed down. Yet here they were working what could easily end up as the biggest bank embezzlement in United States history, and it was being splashed all over the front pages of newspapers throughout the country.

FBI Special Agents Joe Woodall and Chuck Jones, who were assigned the Wells Fargo case, were doing their best to identify all the players and figure out exactly how the crime had been committed. It wasn't easy. Neither of them had ever heard of the branch settlement system. But thankfully they were quick learners. They had received the case on Monday, following Gasway's call to the Bureau.

Woodall and Jones were the most experienced members of the Bureau's Bank Fraud and Embezzlement squad. Working with them from the start was Dale Taulbee, a former U.S. Army intelligence officer skilled at tracking down fugitives. The squad, fifteen agents strong, was headed by Supervisory Special Agent Jim Nielsen and was part of the contingent of four hundred and fifty agents assigned to the Los Angeles division in the seventeen-story federal building located a mile south of the UCLA campus in Westwood. While Taulbee and numerous other agents went into the field to find out more about Ben Lewis and Harold Smith, their associates and businesses, Woodall and Jones made it their mission to learn all about the Wells Fargo branch settlement system and figure out exactly how the money was stolen and where it went.

Most of their colleagues considered Woodall and Jones, both trained accountants, among the best at their jobs. Their area of expertise was solving complex financial crimes. The white-collar beat required a different type of agent than was needed to capture dangerous kidnappers, bank robbers or fugitives. Macho agents who preferred action and physical danger were unflatteringly referred to by prosecutors, defense lawyers and even their own colleagues as "cowboys." Woodall and Jones found infinitely more interesting the challenge of uncovering financial frauds and making a case against the cynical and sophisticated con men who were behind the schemes. It was not uncommon for them to spend many months on one case, filling rooms and hallways with boxes of evidence.

In working street crimes like bank robberies and kidnappings, an agent's main problem was not figuring out what had happened but rather *who* had done it. For Woodall and Jones, the problem was usually the exact opposite. They generally had a suspect but didn't know exactly *what* had happened. They had to be able to figure out what might be a complex flow of funds from one bank account or corporate entity to another, often through a deliberate maze of financial activities.

Many of the white-collar crooks running around nowadays are every bit as intelligent as the agents whose mission it is to stop them. In most cases, no charges can even be filed—let alone convictions gained—unless the government can show where the money went. Con men and securities swindlers, of course, know this too and do everything they can to obscure their activities and hide the incriminating evidence. Hot money moving from a Beverly Hills bank account to an offshore bank in the Bahamas to a Swiss account belonging to a European commodities broker who exchanged the money for valuable goods could be a difficult trail to follow. It would take a knowledge of accounting, a touch for details and a sophisticated understanding of financial matters. Woodall and Jones possessed all of these.

Their job was not finished after concluding an exhaustive investigation and writing sheaves of reports. They were then required to give accurate and articulate testimony in court while avoiding ambush by bright defense attorneys. The agents might sit for weeks in a courtroom, listening to testimony and helping the Assistant U.S. Attorney in prosecuting the case while waiting to be called to the stand themselves. But this was what they wanted to be doing. For them, the satisfaction in seeing a smart criminal who had stolen millions of dollars being put behind bars was one of life's sweetest victories.

When Gasway called late Monday, Jones took the call in the "bull pen," a large room filled with dozens of desk-bound agents hard at work.

After introducing himself and explaining his job at the bank, Gasway got right to the point. "We have a branch that may have lost twenty million dollars," he said.

Jones's first thought was that no branch kept that kind of money lying around. He asked Gasway a few questions and started taking notes on the branch settlement procedures. He had never before seen an interbranch embezzlement. Was it actually possible that Wells Fargo had lost that much money?

"Where do you want to meet us?" Jones asked.

"We're out at the El Monte service center," Gasway said. "All our microfilm is out here."

"You want to meet today?"

"It's pretty late in the day," Gasway said. "There'll be lots of traffic. Why don't you come out tomorrow."

Jones wondered how serious this could be if the auditor didn't want to meet that day. Still, after the conversation, he went in and told the supervisor, Nielsen, about the call. Nielsen assigned him Woodall, who was due back at work the next day after being out for minor surgery. Interestingly, Jones and Woodall had never worked together before. They made an ideal team, though. Woodall was admittedly obsessed with the most minute details, while Jones liked to stand back and consider the big picture, mull over motives and plan strategy. Neither man was any slouch in the other's area, either.

The two agents drove out to El Monte the next day—Tuesday, January 27, 1981. Gasway took about two hours explaining the ins and outs of the bank's branch settlement system to them. By then, Gasway had identified twenty-one chains and thought he knew how much money was missing. His total: $21,300,000. One of the agents whistled softly.

The money, Gasway told them, apparently had gone into accounts controlled by a customer named Harold Smith.

"Who is Harold Smith?" Jones asked.

"He's a boxing promoter," Gasway explained.

"I'm not a boxing fan," Jones admitted.

"He runs two organizations using Muhammad Ali's name," Gasway said.

"Muhammad Ali?"

The agents looked at each other. Even Jones recognized *that* boxing name. Was it possible that Ali had benefited from the embezzlement?

Gasway, of course, didn't have any idea who benefited. All he knew for sure was that Wells Fargo was out the money, Ben Lewis apparently had orchestrated the embezzlement, and the funds had gone into those accounts.

"Tell us about Lewis," Woodall said.

Gasway filled them in on their prime suspect. Lloyd Benjamin Lewis was a male Negro, born on September 27, 1933. He lived at 3725 Clyde Avenue, Los Angeles. He was separated from his wife, Gladys A. Lewis, who lived in an apartment at 8310 South Van Ness. He was assistant operations officer at the Beverly Drive branch of Wells Fargo Bank, at 265 North Beverly Drive, Beverly Hills. He was hired on September 15, 1969. His salary was $1,750 per month.

The agents well appreciated how a man in Lewis's position could do untold damage to a bank. While robberies were the more dramatic crime, embezzlements accounted for a far greater loss to financial institutions. In Los Angeles in 1980, for example, there had been a reported loss of $2,847,000 from bank stickups. The same year, there were $14,619,000 worth of bank embezzlements reported to the FBI. It was easy to see why banks took internal security so seriously.

Back at the office, Jones went to his desk and dialed the number for the U.S. Attorney's office. He had a good idea which prosecutor he would soon be telling about the Wells Fargo theft. This was clearly a Special Prosecutions case, an elite unit in that office staffed by personal selection of the U.S. Attorney only.

At his own desk, Woodall began writing out a long Teletype message to be sent to the FBI director's office in Washington, D.C. Any crime this big had to be immediately reported to the top. Woodall described in as much detail as he could how the money was taken through a manipulation of the branch settlement system, then had the wire sent highest priority. Soon a message came back from Washington, D.C. *Rewrite message. Director does not understand.*

"Don't get too technical," Jones told Woodall. "Just tell him that it looks like twenty-one million dollars has been embezzled through a kiting-like operation from one branch of Wells Fargo to another."

As Woodall went back to write another message, Nielsen came over and told Jones the entire Bank Fraud and Embezzlement squad was at his disposal.

At that moment, no case at the FBI office had a higher priority.

* * *

On Friday—exactly one week after the bank had discovered the money missing—Dale Taulbee finally resorted to trickery in order to get through to Gladys Lewis. He had tried calling her numerous times, always identifying himself as an FBI agent and asking for Mrs. Lewis. The woman who answered the phone—it sounded like the same person each time—said Mrs. Lewis wasn't home. Taulbee had become suspicious.

This time when the woman answered, he said casually, "Hi, Gladys?"

"Yes," she responded.

"Dale Taulbee. FBI. There have been some serious allegations made against Ben. We have to talk to you."

She reluctantly invited him to come over to her apartment.

Once there, Taulbee stressed the importance of her husband voluntarily coming in and talking to the FBI. That was an easier way to go, the agent said, than being arrested on sight.

Gladys, who looked as if she had been crying, nodded her head in agreement. "He should come in. But I haven't heard from Ben in days. I'm so worried about him."

CHAPTER SIX

Assistant U.S. Attorney Dean Allison received the telephone call from the FBI because, as Chief of the U.S. Attorney's Special Prosecutions Unit, he was in charge of assigning all major financial fraud cases. Sitting in his office on the twelfth floor of the federal court-house in downtown Los Angeles, Allison listened and didn't interrupt Chuck Jones's dispassionate briefing that had begun with the personalized teaser "I think I've got a case for you, Dean. It involves boxing."

Those acquainted with Allison couldn't help but know that he was a fanatic boxing fan. The conference table in his office was piled with ragged copies of *Ring* and *Sports Illustrated* instead of the standard legal periodicals. Still possessing a welterweight's build, Allison had boxed in college. Well, sort of. The only member of the Brown University boxing team, his sole workout partner had been the coach, a German professor who happened to be a six-foot six-inch heavyweight. "Do you know how to hook, son?" the coach asked Allison his first day at practice. "No," Allison replied innocently. The coach floored Allison with a looping swing that began somewhere in Connecticut and then patiently pointed out, "Dat is a hook." Years later, Allison's only boxing outlet was jabbing and hooking tall indoor plants, a habit that often sent friends fleeing with favored plants whenever he walked into a room.

The Wells Fargo case—which, according to Jones, appeared somehow to involve people around Muhammad Ali—seemed well suited for Allison. And it didn't take him long to determine what the top priority should be.

"Our major concern at the moment," Allison told Jones, "should be to get our hands on the MAPS records. We can't afford to have them turn up 'missing.' It may already be too late." Allison knew from experience how important documents were when it came to putting together a complex fraud case. If this evidence was unavailable, the government might have embarrassing and insurmountable gaps later in court when it attempted to reconstruct the flow of embezzled funds.

"I'll start drafting the grand jury subpoenas now," Allison said. "They'll be ready for you later."

Once off the phone, Allison went to see his boss. United States Attorney Andrea Ordin was a Jimmy Carter appointee who had been in the top federal prosecutorial job west of Manhattan since 1979. A compassionate, polished administrator who worked hard at maintaining good morale on her staff and keeping smooth relations between the U.S. Attorney's office and the various agencies it worked with, Ordin took a *laissez-faire* approach to individual cases. She allowed the experienced attorneys in her office to handle their own areas of responsibility. Ordin had a large corner office, and her door was always open for her colleagues.

"Andrea, have you heard about the twenty-one million dollar embezzlement at Wells Fargo and the boxing promoter?" Allison asked.

"No, not yet."

"We're onto it. I've just talked to the Bureau. We've already got subpoenas out for the records of the boxing business, and the bank will be cooperative. After all, it's their ox that got gored. I just wanted to let you know in case you start getting calls."

"Let me know if there's anything I can do," she said. "Good luck."

Allison appreciated the leeway Ordin gave her subordinates. And he wasn't afraid to take his best shot and live with the consequences. So far, so good. Although he never bragged about his undefeated trial record—in his view, that was what they were paying him for, and a goodly number of his colleagues were also undefeated—he was proud of *why* he had never lost. It was simple: fanatical trial preparation. He always tried to make sure that before trial began there was no question about the evidence or the law in the case that he didn't know the answer to. He immersed himself in the witness reports and tried to know the documents better than his opponents. At trial, he believed in cross-examination by misdirection—leading an unfriendly witness in an apparently unthreatening direction for ten boring minutes, only to suddenly and dramatically change direction and catch the witness off guard. Done right, the witness and the defense counsel didn't know where Allison was headed until it was too late. And by then he had already made the damaging point or, even better, had caught the witness in a contradiction or backed him into an important concession.

To be a success in court, any federal prosecutor needed the strong support of the investigating agency. If it didn't put a priority on a case and supply the necessary manpower, a prosecutor could have a difficult time preparing a case for trial. Sometimes what the agency considered a top priority the prosecutors didn't, and vice versa.

Allison pushed to have the more dedicated and experienced agents assigned to the difficult investigations and complex cases handled by his seven-person Special Prosecutions Unit. In drawing Joe Woodall and Chuck Jones, he had lucked out. Although they had never worked directly together before, Allison had heard from his colleagues (prosecutors traded information on agents just like agents swapped stories about prosecutors) that Woodall and Jones were among the best. They would be an asset to the prosecution team, of that Allison was sure.

Allison had been with the U.S. Attorney's Office since 1977. He had focused his search for a prosecutor's job on big cities because that was where the big cases were. In Los Angeles, he found the type of cases and people he wanted to work with. This was where some of the biggest and most complex financial crimes in the country were committed. He threw all his belongings and his motorcycle into a rented truck and drove cross-country from New York, taking a cut in pay from $38,000 with a big private law firm to $23,000 a year to become a prosecutor.

From the beginning of his legal career, Allison had tried to steer clear of office politics and gossip. He wished to be judged solely on performance. Extra aggressive like many smaller men, Allison preferred taking on the best, whether it was the sharpest con men or the shrewdest defense attorneys. He found plenty of both in Los Angeles.

California had become fertile ground for white-collar criminals—and L.A. a field for particularly ripe pickings—largely because there was so much loose money around. Unlike the more traditional Eastern seaboard, where sophistication, background and breeding were accorded more emphasis, in Los Angeles deference was often given to the high roller. Sudden wealth and instant celebrity were commonplace. Mercedes and Rolls, one after the other and often leased, lined the roadways. Fancy yachts and sleek sailboats filled the marinas. If you talked the game, dropped the right names and played the part well, you could go far. Whether the field was entertainment, sports, banking or crime, stars were made overnight.

A longtime boxing fan, Allison had heard of Muhammad Ali Professional Sports. They had put on some of the biggest fights in the business during the last couple of years. Allison doubted that Ali himself was involved in this embezzlement. He certainly hoped not because he had always admired Ali's ring skills and what he had done for the sport. *The Champ had made far too much money to be tied up in anything crooked,* Allison thought, *and had plenty of professional advisors to safeguard his investments.* But, like any conscientious prosecutor, he was willing to let the chips fall where they may.

Allison drafted a subpoena for the vital records at the MAPS-MAAS offices. On Friday morning, FBI agents served the subpoena at Smith's office. It directed the firms' "custodians of records" to gather the records and turn them over to the grand jury.

Allison's biggest fear was that key records would show up missing. This was not uncommon in white-collar crimes. Records are evidence and can be just as damning as a robber being caught with the goods. What he was most interested in were the general ledger and the cash receipts and disbursements journals—some of the most revealing financial documents for any business—as well as check registers and other records pertaining to banking activities of MAPS. Until those records were obtained and reviewed, he had to play a waiting game.

The prosecutor and agents considered their predicament. They knew a large bank embezzlement had taken place involving many millions of dollars. How much of the money was left? Was it now in an offshore bank account? Ben Lewis, the "inside" man, was gone. Harold Smith, the customer into whose accounts the money went, was also missing, which fed suspicions of his intimate involvement in the crime. But what exactly was Smith's role? Was he guilty of complicity? Or was he a dupe for a crooked banker? Maybe Lewis had simply used Smith's account numbers to fool the computer and had stashed the money in a Swiss bank account.

As a standard preliminary step, the agents entered Smith's name in the law enforcement computer network but found no arrest record or outstanding warrants. He appeared to be clean. So did Ben Lewis. It was not uncommon, in white-collar crimes, for the perpetrators to be first-timers. They are often people who gave in to the fantasies that many people have about committing one juicy score—maybe at their place of employment—and getting away scot-free.

Everything else aside, it was clear that Ben Lewis was the main suspect. How long had he been embezzling bank money? Did he do it alone, or were other bankers involved? There were so many questions that needed answering.

Bank embezzlements were nothing new to Allison. He also had experience dealing with computerized financial systems. All major banks these days rely on computers. While they are certainly needed for the volume of transactions that banks handle, computers aren't the panacea that many people think. They are only as good as the people who operate them.

Allison figured that getting access to all of Wells Fargo's records relating to the theft would be no problem. Since the bank itself was a victim, it would cooperate in every way. Banks were not nearly as helpful when they were in the position of being a third-party witness. If it was a matter of assisting the government in documenting a financial crime which had not resulted in any loss to them, banks could drag their heels. In fact, they were infamously slow when it came to complying with grand jury subpoenas for voluminous account records. Federal bank privacy laws, of course, were designed to prevent willy-nilly dissemination of customers' financial information. They certainly served a noble purpose. But unfortunately, they also protected criminals by slowing down the investigators.

The top priority now was locating Ben Lewis while continuing the financial investigation to find out exactly where all the money had gone. Also, they needed to determine whether there were any other bankers involved and Harold Smith's true role. The only suspect at the present time was Lewis, and he was among the missing.

The prosecutor knew that the government needed a break, and soon.

CHAPTER SEVEN

Teri Key's worst fear finally came true.

When the FBI agents descended on the MAPS offices with a subpoena on Friday, January 30, it was like a scene right out of a Hollywood movie. As if having to brush off a score of reporters as a result of the Long Beach newspaper article wasn't bad enough ("I don't know where Mr. Smith is but I'll let him know you called"), then the feds arrived in force. When she saw the unsmiling men dressed in suits walk into, the office, she guessed their occupation instantly.

"Chuck Jones, FBI," the agent said, flipping open a black leather wallet to reveal a badge and identity card. The other two agents did likewise.

"We have a subpoena for your records," Jones said.

She gulped hard, trying to keep calm. Harold had told her what to say. "I'm sorry but I'm not authorized to accept service," she said.

"Who can accept service?"

"Sammie—Sam Marshall. He's our president. But he just left for lunch."

"We'll wait."

And wait they did, for two long hours. They seemed to stare at her most of the time, though it could have been her imagination. In any case, by the time Marshall returned she was a nervous wreck. It was one of the few times in her life that she had actually been pleased to see Sammie Marshall.

Marshall took the agents into his office. A heavyset man, Marshall had been president of MAPS since leaving Wells Fargo in 1978. Most people considered him Smith's "front man," and rightly so.

"You're the president of MAPS?" asked an agent.

"Yes, I am."

"We're serving you with a subpoena for your records. You can gather them together, turn them over to us, and we'll take them to the grand jury so you don't have to appear personally. Otherwise, you can bring them down to the grand jury yourself. Attempts by you or any of your employees to hide or destroy any records could be considered an obstruction of justice."

"I understand. I have to speak to the company attorney. It'll take us a few days."

On the way out of the MAPS office, one of the FBI agents made the same thinly veiled threat to Key regarding obstruction of justice. The words made her stomach churn. Would they consider it obstruction of justice if they found out she had helped send the records away? What if they asked her about that? And while she had returned some of those documents, others were still gone. She *knew* that. If they asked her about the missing records—like the ledgers and journals—she had two choices: tell the truth or lie. Lying was really not an alternative. That was something she had been raised not to do. She wasn't sure she could lie successfully even if she wanted to. The truth was always best. Anyway, she was sure that once all the real facts came out, Harold could not be guilty of any wrongdoing. Sure, they had spent a lot of money, but they were not thieves. They had all worked hard to make the business a success. Still, for the time being, though, she hoped that no one would ask her about that crazy weekend when she had carted the records away.

***

Most of the problems swirling around MAPS and its business commitments to various fights—including the upcoming "This Is It" fight in Madison Square Garden and other less ambitious affairs—landed squarely on Sammie Marshall's shoulders during those first confusing days. The day that the FBI agents served the subpoena on him, Marshall met later with MAPS attorney Ed Franklin.

Marshall had been tipped off to a problem at the bank even before the FBI agents confronted him. A MAPS employee had told him of going down to the bank to cash his paycheck and being informed that the

MAPS payroll account was frozen. The employee asked to speak to Ben Lewis, thinking that the officer who was so close to their operation could straighten out whatever foul-up had occurred. But he was told that Lewis no longer worked there. The teller suggested that the employee go back to the MAPS office and talk to his boss. Hearing this, Marshall had called Feeley immediately.

"What's going on?" Marshall had asked. "Where is Ben?"

"He's gone," Feeley had answered sadly. "There was a problem with a $250,000 loan Ben made to Harold on a branch settlement. Another office detected it. Ben had an appointment to meet with the auditors, and we never saw him again. We had no choice."

"Did Harold pay the money back?" Marshall asked.

"Ben told me the money was paid back."

"So, what's the problem?"

"I don't know," Feeley said, sounding confused. "I've been trying to find Ben. Do you have a phone number for him?"

Marshall looked it up and read a number to Feeley.

"I have that number," Feeley said. "There's no answer. I've gone over to his house, but no one comes to the door."

"Where the hell is everybody?" Marshall said angrily, venting his frustration. "Harold isn't here either. He hasn't been here all week. What's the situation with our accounts?"

"They've all been frozen," Feeley said.

That left MAPS and Marshall—who found himself in the uncomfortable position of being left alone at the helm—in a predicament. Most urgent was a routine fight scheduled for that weekend in Philadelphia. MAPS was the promoter and had to put up the purse money for the boxers before the fight. Without the advance payment, there would be no fight. And if there was no fight, MAPS would not earn the network television money it was to receive for TV rights to the fights.

Marshall and Franklin huddled over the problem. Franklin called and spoke to the bank's lawyers, who told him the freeze would not be lifted, fight or no fight.

"I don't see where there is anything we can do," Franklin told Marshall. "Our funds are tied up."

Marshall had an idea. He picked up the phone and called a television executive involved in the deal. "We have a problem out here," Marshall explained, "and we may not be able to fulfill our obligation with the bout unless you can help. Will you be able to pay me the TV money up front so I can use it for the purse."

The TV man answered him in a single word: "No."

"Well, if that's the case, there's nothing we can do."

The next phone call Marshall made was to a Philadelphia boxing promoter whom Marshall thought might be willing to take over the fight. MAPS wouldn't make any money—it wouldn't lose any either—but that way the fight and coverage could go ahead as scheduled. Marshall felt it was better to allow someone else to move in than to cancel the fight at this late date, which would cause ill will among the fighters and TV people.

The Philadelphia promoter agreed, and the next day Marshall and Franklin flew back East and signed the necessary papers to transfer the fight to him. Franklin returned home—he had to take possession of the MAPS records and turn them into the FBI the following week—but Marshall stayed over and watched the fight. Though his mind wasn't entirely on the fight, it was a good show between WBA Bantamweight Champion Jeff Chandler and challenger Jorge Lujan. Chandler, one of the first champions MAPS had signed, won in a decision.

MAPS, meanwhile, appeared to be going down for the count.

CHAPTER EIGHT

Behind the guarded gates of Fremont Place, an exclusive enclave of mansions with seven-figure price tags near the mid-Wilshire district of Los Angeles, Muhammad Ali sat waiting for the press. He had decided to go public.

Since news of the embezzlement first surfaced, speculation had been rampant in the media that the former heavyweight champion was somehow involved in the scandal surrounding MAPS and Wells Fargo. At one point, Ali had a microphone thrust in his face by a TV newsman as he stepped off a plane on the East Coast and was asked pointblank whether he had benefited from the alleged bank embezzlement. Ali's off-the-cuff denial of any wrongdoing had not been enough. So he had decided to set the record straight. He would invite the press into his home and use them to tell the people the truth. He trusted his fans to believe him.

The uniformed guard at the Wilshire gate allowed the cars and TV-equipped vans of the press representatives to pass. It wasn't often that Fremont Place residents allowed such visitors. In fact, they usually went to great lengths to keep media visitors out. That's why they had gate guards on duty around the clock. But this morning the guard had different orders. *Let the reporters in. All of them.* If the Champ wanted to have a press conference, then he would have a press conference.

The story had become a contest between some of the leading news organizations in the world, including *Newsweek,* the London *Times,* CBS, ABC, NBC and the BBC, the New York *Times,* Reuters and, locally, the Los Angeles *Times* and *Herald-Examiner.* More than a hundred reporters were beating the bushes to find out what had *really* happened at Wells

Fargo. It was too good a story to ignore. It was the kind of story that sold papers and hooked viewers.

Even if Ali revealed little new information, a visit with the ex-champion would be worthwhile and entertaining. In the vernacular of the business, Ali was good copy. That's why there were dozens of reporters and photographers surrounding the ex-champion in his den.

The room was tastefully done in richly ornate furnishings. The Champ sat in a high-back chair behind a small desk. He was wearing an expensive pin-striped suit that failed to hide his still-powerful arms and chest. A pastel-colored tie was loosened at the neck. Heavy electrical cords were underfoot from the TV equipment. Portable spotlights bathed Ali in a bright glare.

"The FBI is calling me," Ali said, sounding somewhat hoarse. "The CIA is guarding the house. Everything's on me. I got to be protected by Allah. If I didn't believe in god—Allah—I probably would have cracked up long ago."

Just then the phone on the table rang, and Ali quickly grabbed it. Without waiting to find out who was on the line, Ali deadpanned into the receiver, "City morgue. Is he dead?" To what was probably a confused response on the other end, Ali persisted, "This is the city morgue, man."

After a short banter, Ali had no sooner put the phone down than it rang again. He was sailing now—a would-be comedian before a captive audience. "Yeah, the White House? You calling from the White House? Hey, Ronald, how are you doing? Glad you called."

Several reporters looked at each other and shrugged. The boxing great was cutting up and enjoying the event like a big kid. He obviously liked all the attention. Even though many of the reporters present had never met Ali before, they knew from watching televised interviews with the Champ over the years that once he got going he could be difficult to contain even for the most tenacious interrogator. But what could they do? Ali was not going to change now and become a quiet and thoughtful man willing to sit and give serious answers to serious questions.

Ali hung up. "You know," he said, "I changed my number a week ago and now everybody's got it." He said it almost as if he couldn't understand *why* he was getting so many calls.

"Champ," one reporter asked, "can you tell us the extent of your financial arrangements with Harold Smith?"

Ali raised an eyebrow, looking at the reporter suspiciously. Ali seemed to be trying to control his emotions. "What are you trying to say?" he demanded. "You asking did I steal it? If I needed money, I wouldn't rob no bank. If I was a bank robber, they'd rate me bigger than Jesse James."

Ali was not going to sit here and tell these reporters everything about his arrangement with Smith. No way. They just wouldn't understand. Sure he had gotten money. Their deal called for Ali to receive 25 percent of the net profits from all MAPS-sponsored events. So far it had not amounted to a fortune. He had received several payments in the range of $10,000 to $15,000. Twice he had received payments of several hundred thousand dollars, once for an Australian tour and another time for an appearance at a MAPS fight in Detroit. Ali subsequently gave his wife $100,000 of the money to use for decorating their home and sent most of the rest to his attorneys to put aside for his tax liability. Smith had promised bigger paydays in the future. Ali didn't want to tell the reporters all this for fear that they might think he was guilty of something he didn't do.

The phone rang again. "I've got the press surrounding the house and surrounding me," he said into the phone, widening his eyes in mock fear. "It's like I'm Jesse James."

Off the phone again, he looked up into the glaring TV lights and said wistfully, "Sometimes I wish Howard Cosell is a fireplug and I'm a dog."

One reporter present, Dave Palermo of the Los Angeles *Herald-Examiner*, decided the rumors he had heard about Ali were true. The Champ had answered the bell too often. Ali's voice was sometimes slurred. His attention span was short. His face was puffy. It was sad and strangely embarrassing to see him like this. But really, it shouldn't have been. Everyone grows old, even former great athletes. And boxers take more punishment than most. There was still something special about Ali, something that the man would probably take to his grave with him: that charismatic personality that could be both charming and alarming.

"Have you seen Harold Smith lately?" someone asked.

Ali shook his head.

"Do you have plans to meet with him?"

The famous head kept shaking.

"*Would* you if Smith asked for a meeting?"

Ali's head stopped.

The airwaves had been filled the previous day with reports of Smith calling various people in the news media saying that he was back in the country after having to flee to Europe and that he was anxious to meet with Ali to clear his name. It was Smith's first public utterance since news of the scandal had broken the week before. Smith vehemently denied that he had bilked Wells Fargo out of millions, and charged that bank officials were trying to kill him. He vowed to return and present certain documents to Ali that would establish his innocence.

"I'd tell Harold to meet with the FBI," Ali said slowly. "I wouldn't meet with him alone. They'd say I stole the money and helped him."

Ali honestly couldn't recall exactly when he had first met Smith. It was, he thought, during his exile from boxing for refusing to be drafted into the Army, maybe around 1969 or 1970. Smith approached Ali on a movie set and explained that he had this successful amateur track program going in Los Angeles. He was working with young black kids, like the talented Houston McTear, who was breaking national high school records in the sprint races while his family lived in virtual squalor in Florida. Smith's proposal was for Ali to allow his name to be used for the track program. It would be good for the kids and good for the Champ, he explained. They would call themselves the Muhammad Ali Track Club. If there ever was any profit—such as TV contract money—then Ali would get a piece of it. But primarily it was a humanitarian gesture for Ali, and it sounded like a fine idea to the softhearted boxer. It wasn't long before Ali even bought the McTear family a new home, a charitable act that made news throughout the country.

What Ali mainly felt was disappointment, not anger. He had trusted Smith one hundred percent. He was a black brother and he had seemed honest. AH had certainly approved of the way Smith promoted the track program. He had been surprised and delighted to see Smith put together a nationally televised track meet carrying his name. Ali even ran in a celebrity race. He was flattered by all the attention. It looked like a miniature Olympics with his name on the team uniforms. Maybe someday, Smith had suggested to him, there might be a whole U.S. Olympic team with his name on it. Ali was also proud of all the young boys and girls who were competing—many of them involved in organized sports for the first time. In addition to working with track athletes, Smith had a busy amateur boxing program underway. Later, Smith had approached Ali with a plan to expand into pro boxing. It sounded like a good idea to Ali, and he again gave permission for his name to be used.

Ali did not tell the assembled reporters all of this. It would sound silly for him to say that he knew nothing about the legal problems, the business deals, the banking connections, the fighters' contracts. Though it was the truth, it probably wouldn't ring true to the reporters and the public. *If Ali's name was on the business, then he must be involved.* Sure, his name had been used. But that was it. How could he possibly explain his embarrassment over the scandalous rumors circulating about Smith and MAPS?

Ali was not ready to throw Harold to the dogs. Maybe Smith had been set up by rival promoters. Boxing was a cruel business, and Ali, of all people, knew it. Or maybe Smith was being used as a scapegoat by the white bankers. Ali didn't always trust those kind of people himself.

"People who know him say that Smith was a big spender," said a reporter. "Did you ever wonder where he got all his money?"

"I saw him with all those beautiful girls, planes, boats," Ali said. "I used to say, 'You sure everything's okay, Harold?' He always said everything was fine. I believed him."

Ali had given almost the exact same answer to the same question just a few weeks earlier in a legal deposition. He had been served with a subpoena in a lawsuit between MAPS and ABC Sports concerning the breach of a contract for the television rights to a boxing event. On the appointed day, he had shown up at the Century City law offices of the ABC lawyers. Ali had brought his own attorney with him. Also sitting in for the session had been Ed Franklin, the MAPS attorney. Over Franklin's objection, the ABC lawyer spent nearly two hours asking Ali questions about Smith's background and financial resources.

"What do you know about the source of MAPS and Mr. Harold Smith's financing for professional boxing?" the ABC lawyer had asked.

"Not one thing," Ali said. "Not the least little bitty thing … I still don't know where he gets his money. I'm still wondering. The more you ask the question, the more I wonder."

Ali's advisors had known for some time that most of the fights MAPS had promoted had lost money. The purses to the fighters were always higher than what other promoters paid for equivalent bouts—sometimes three and four times more. Smith was getting money from somewhere to keep throwing in the pot. But where was it coming from? That's what Ali's lawyers and accountants wanted to know, and that was why they had been pressuring Smith for a review of the MAPS books.

But Ali would share none of this with the reporters at the press conference. He wanted them to simply take him at his word that he had nothing to do with ripping off Wells Fargo. That *was* the truth. He had earned his money—and lots of it—the hard way and was proud of it.

"Are you mad at Smith?" a reporter asked.

"I'm not mad at all. I'm sorry for his family, his nice little boy and wife. I trusted him. He was a heavyweight, mentally. You see, being Muhammad Ali, *everybody* wants to use my name."

PART TWO

CHAPTER NINE

The air is usually cool and clean in Marina Del Rey, except on rare occasions when the easterly Santa Ana winds—dubbed by popular crime writers an evil manifestation—blow the inland air pollution toward the beach communities and out to sea.

There was no such irksome wind one day in 1976 when a casually dressed black man strolled into the Wells Fargo Bank branch at Marina Del Rey, looking to speak to a bank officer. Wind or no wind, this random meeting would lead to the largest bank theft in the annals of American crime.

Working at the Marina Del Rey office was considered good duty for bank employees. The view from the office was of countless sailboats moored at nearby docks and modern condominiums ringing the man-made harbor. Life, as well as dress, was casual here. More customers came into the bank dressed in beach attire than in business suits. The loan activity centered around automobiles, a main-stay of the California good life, and there was little real estate or commercial business.

The customer immediately spotted the officer he wanted to deal with and approached him. He was a black man. The sign on his desk read "Sammie Marshall."

The banker looked up at the new customer. "What can I do for you?" he asked.

"My name is Smith," the man said, sitting down in the chair. "Harold Smith. I've just moved into the area, and I need to have a check cashed."

Smith handed the check to Marshall, who looked it over.

Marshall had been in banking for six years, starting at Wells Fargo in 1969 as a lowly clerical employee after three years of college and military service, during which he attended the U.S. Army School of Financing. In

1972, he had joined the bank's management training program and learned the duties of a loan officer—called a "banking services officer" at Wells Fargo. The following year, thanks to the intervention of an old friend, he was assigned to the Marina Del Rey office.

In the four years Marshall had been a bank officer, he had come to recognize a problem check when he saw one. It looked just like the one he was now holding. The fact that it was a third-party check was bad enough, considering that he didn't know this Smith fellow. But when he saw it was out of state, Marshall knew there was nothing he could do for the man.

"I'm a track promoter," Smith explained.

"Is that so?"

"Yeah. I ran track in college. Back East. I was in the civil rights movement too. I worked with Muhammad Ali and got to be friends with him. He's behind me. I'm trying to put together a track team for poor black kids who don't have the grades to get into college."

"That right?" Marshall said. "I like sports myself. There's a lot of young brothers out there who need help."

"What I want to do is gather all those kids and put them in a situation where they can compete on a national and international level. You know, give them an opportunity they wouldn't get no other way."

Marshall's interest in the customer had picked up at the mention of Ali. This guy might develop into a good customer after all. Still, there was no way he would cash this check. Smith might be genuine, but the party who wrote the check might not have any money in his account. Marshall was not going to stick his branch with an out-of-state NSF (nonsufficient funds) check.

"What you're doing sounds good," Marshall said. "But I'm sorry, I just can't cash this for you. It's a third-party check and out of state. I'd have to hold it for collection. It might be a while before the funds come in."

Smith was disappointed. "I need this money to go back to New York for a meet. I have identification."

"That wouldn't tell me if there are any funds to back up the check. I suggest you open an account so that in the future I might be able to help you." Like all bankers, Marshall was always on the lookout for a new customer. Particularly ones who were well connected.

But Smith wasn't interested in opening an account.

Smith appeared at the Marina Del Rey branch two weeks later. This time he was accompanied by a muscular young black man who walked in short, almost dancelike steps.

"Sammie," Smith said proudly as he approached Marshall's desk, "I'd like you to meet Houston McTear, the fastest human alive."

Houston McTear the track man, of course. The 100-yard dash was his specialty, and he ran the distance about as rapidly as anyone in the world. He had been considered a candidate for an Olympic gold medal, but McTear had suffered an injury and had to stay home when the U.S. Olympic team traveled to Montreal. McTear was built like a human gazelle, with huge thighs, muscular calves, a large chest that housed powerful lungs, a thin waist and sinewy arms. He was considered by some experts to be the most gifted natural Sprinter since Jesse Owens. Marshall remembered reading newspaper stories about the kid. He was apparently down on his luck. Something about financial and family difficulties back home in Florida.

"Pleasure to meet you," Marshall said, offering a handshake.

McTear nodded and awkwardly took the banker's hand. He seemed unsure of himself and painfully shy.

"You're from Florida, aren't you, Houston."

"Yep."

"Houston's my main man," Smith put in. "He's gonna smash all the records there's to smash. The Champ's behind him too."

"That's great."

"We got to get to a meet in Philadelphia," Smith said, handing Marshall a check.

This one was made out to both McTear and Smith and drawn off a Philadelphia bank.

"Out of state," the banker said.

Smith nodded.

It was the exact same situation Marshall had faced previously. And since the first day Smith showed up in the branch, the promoter had done nothing to form an account relationship with the bank. Marshall probably should have turned him down again. But having an athlete like Houston

McTear appear and all this talk of Ali had its effect on him. Marshall felt good vibes from Smith. The guy seemed to be a mover and a shaker. Marshall thought over all the ramifications and made his decision.

"Tell you what," he said. "I'll call the bank in Philly, and if there's enough money in the account, I'll cash it for you."

He made the phone call and talked to a bank officer who assured him the check was good. The East Coast banker volunteered that there was a big track meet coming up, and Houston McTear was expected to be there. Everything sounded on the up-and-up. Marshall cashed the check, and McTear and Smith left.

A short time later, Smith came back in alone with still another check. He was in a mood to talk at length about his track club and McTear. "I got Ali to take an interest in Houston," he said. "The kid's father had a stroke, and this huge family with eight kids were all living in a two-room house. We went down to Florida and bought a new house for the family."

"Yeah," Marshall said. "I read about that."

"Now I'm trying to get a private tutor for Houston so he can get into junior college."

Marshall called the other bank and once again found that there was money to pay the check. So he cashed it.

For a year, the contacts between Marshall and Smith were limited to occasional meetings like these. As long as Marshall could verify that a check was good, he provided the cashing service to the track promoter.

Late in 1976, Marshall decided to leave the Marina Del Rey branch in order to further his management career at the bank. It was time for him to get experience in real estate and commercial loans, something he couldn't do at the small community branch in the laid-back beach locale. The busy Beverly Drive branch had an opening for a commercial loan officer. Marshall took the job. An added bonus was that his best friend at Wells Fargo, Ben Lewis—with whom he had briefly crossed paths at Marina Del Rey—was now at Beverly Drive.

Marshall and Ben Lewis had joined Wells Fargo the same year— 1969—and met the following year while both were working at the Pershing Square branch in downtown Los Angeles. They were introduced by Marshall's sister, a Wells Fargo clerk. She had thought the two men might hit it off, and they did. For a time, they were both assigned to the bank's El Monte service center to gain experience in the Proof of Deposit Department. They learned how the computer system caught mistakes in branch settlement transactions and what the process was for correcting them. They had both been attentive students. Over the years, as their respective careers took them to different offices, the two friends had kept in touch and regularly got together for drinks, to attend Los Angeles Lakers games and to watch televised football games. Both played on the Wells Fargo basketball team.

Lewis had been responsible for Marshall being assigned to Marina Del Rey. When the office became too busy for the number of personnel working there, Lewis had called the bank's Personnel Department to see if Marshall could be assigned to his office, which he was, on a temporary basis. Later, before Lewis departed from the branch in May 1973, he called Personnel again and managed to get Marshall assigned to the branch as a permanent employee. While working together, the two friends went out to lunch together nearly every day.

Harold Smith began to visit Marshall regularly in Beverly Hills, bringing checks, as usual, which he wanted cashed. Even though it was out of the way to drive the fifteen miles from Marina Del Rey to Beverly Drive, Smith wanted to deal with Marshall rather than some banker closer to home who didn't know him.

One day Smith came into the bank all excited. He told Marshall about a big outdoor track meet he was organizing, which was going to be held at a junior college near Long Beach. He invited the banker to come to the meet and help out as a volunteer. Smith told him his club, the Muhammad Ali Track Club, was helping a lot of young athletes.

Marshall agreed to help. Wells Fargo encouraged its officers to find worthy community projects to which they could donate some of their off-hours. The bank figured that such volunteerism was good for its image and, not incidentally, that it might lead to development of future business.

Marshall went to the event—tabbed the First Annual Muhammad Ali Invitational Track Meet—and assisted with some administrative chores. One job that his superiors at the bank would undoubtedly have frowned upon had him standing outside the locker room handing out envelopes full of cash to some of the *amateur* athletes who had competed. The bigger the name, the thicker the envelope. It was surprising to see how many athletes were openly accepting money.

The banker was duly impressed by the whole scene. Ali was there and so were the TV cameras. Marshall was proud of his association with Harold Smith. The bank had been emphasizing to its loan officers that they should court solid people who had good prospects for success. Smith certainly seemed to qualify. His business looked sound. Marshall could see that Smith was well on his way to putting together a strong organization, thanks to his own initiative and the backing of that magical name: Ali.

Marshall felt so positive about Smith that when the promoter came to him for a loan of $3500 the banker didn't flinch. Smith explained that he needed the loan for expense money to put on an amateur boxing show. This struck Marshall as just the sort of "business development" the bank had in mind. A profitable bank had to lend out money at a higher interest rate than it was paying depositors. The "spread" of three to six percentage points involved—de-pending on how well the bank was run—represented the bulk of a bank's profits. The trick, though, was to not lend money out just to be unloading it. A bad loan was worse than no loan at all. The idea was for both the interest and principal to be paid to the bank on time. Then even more money was available to lend.

Despite his optimism about making a loan to Smith, Marshall went to his immediate supervisor and discussed the request. His boss was not in favor of the unsecured loan. It did not seem prudent because all Smith had going at the time was a network television contract. The loan was a "performance-type contract," the supervisor pointed out, meaning that unless Smith performed successfully as promised (by staging a successful show), there would be no revenue to repay the loan.

"But Sammie, you're a loan officer and you have to use your own discretion," his boss said. "Make the loan or don't make it based on the information you have at hand."

Marshall knew the television contract was valid because he had personally called the TV people and spoken with them about the terms of the deal. Marshall believed in Smith more than ever. He regularly carried his new friend's overdrafts, allowing time for revenue or advances to reach Smith.

"I'm inclined to make the loan," Marshall said.

Thanks to the support and growing friendship of loan officer Sammie Marshall, Harold Smith was well on his way to becoming a regular customer of Wells Fargo. Marshall figured that one day he would get a lot of credit for bringing Smith to the bank.

CHAPTER TEN

When Ben Lewis came to work at Beverly Drive in the fall of 1976, he moved right into the position he would hold for the next four years until his world collapsed that Friday in January 1981.

Lewis settled in quickly as operations officer at the active branch. Operations was the backbone of any branch. Pull the managers out and everything could run okay. Pull operations out and things would go downhill fast. Unfortunately, bank supervisors did not always seem to appreciate everything that he—and other operations officers—did to keep the well-oiled machine running smoothly. His job responsibilities were many and included carrying out a physical security check of the premises each morning, making sure the surveillance cameras were loaded and operative, and opening the night depository. What took up most of his time, though, was overseeing the daily paper flow in the operational area of the bank. All the clerks and tellers were subordinate to him, and it was his job to make sure they were doing their jobs right.

Ben approved all large-item deposits and checks over one thousand dollars and decided whether or not to approve for payment checks written on accounts that held insufficient funds. Paying NSF checks was a privilege afforded to some customers at the discretion of bank officers, not a right given to all. It was, essentially, a free and unsecured loan. Lewis had to be familiar with the customer and have a belief in his or her ability to make good on the deficit promptly before he would grant such a favor.

From day one his immediate supervisor was Brian Feeley, who had been in charge of the Beverly Drive Operations Department since 1974. The branch manager at the time was Joel Ziskind. Lewis's friend, Sammie Marshall, sat not far away on the other side of the long counter that separated the tellers and operations personnel from the public side of the bank. Marshall and the other employees who sat on that side of the bank were part of "platform" operations, which consisted of the manager, loan officers, and those handling new accounts and Master Charge, Visa and "Express Window" activities for customers.

Lewis shared with Feeley the responsibility for reviewing all branch settlement transactions conducted at the branch, though it was Lewis who followed up on the majority of tracers that came to the branch arising out of such transactions. From the beginning, Feeley made it clear that he would give Lewis whatever leeway he needed to carry out his job. It made Lewis feel good that Brian trusted him to do his work properly without close supervision.

In the three years since leaving Marina Del Rey, Lewis had harbored deep resentment because of the way the bank had treated him while working at the beach office. The work load there had been overwhelming. Even after he had been able to get Marshall assigned to the branch to help with platform operations, they were still short several employees. Lewis kept pestering his superiors for additional help, but his cries seemed to fall on deaf ears. It was only *after* he left Marina Del Rey that Region apparently decided he had been correct in asking for assistance and assigned more people to work at the branch. Lewis never forgave Wells Fargo for what he saw as bureaucratic insensitivity which forced him to shoulder an unnecessarily heavy burden for nearly a year. The honeymoon was over as of then. For the first time, Lewis came to see the bank as an uncaring institution that would use and discard people at will.

From Marina Del Rey, Lewis went to the Vernon Industrial Center office and found himself in still another difficult situation. The branch was without an operations officer when he arrived, and it had a poor performance record as a result. He worked hard for the next two years, trying valiantly to push back his growing ill feelings toward Wells Fargo. In April 1975, Lewis was sent back to Pershing Square as operations officer in charge of the daily operations. It was a full circle for him, since this was where he had started with the bank six years earlier. But he was a different man now. He was no longer optimistic about his career. He wondered if he would ever achieve higher administrative positions and better pay. To top it off, his personal life had taken a turn for the worse when his marriage to his first wife, Dorothy, broke up. He knew she was fed up with the long hours he was putting in at the bank. And, in all honesty, he couldn't blame her.

Things hadn't gotten better at his next assignment, although he went off to it with great expectations following a big going-away party given him by his Vernon coworkers. His next duty station was the Westwood branch—a westside community with a village atmosphere known best as the home of UCLA. It didn't take long for Ben to feel that the operations department there was a shambles.

Lewis couldn't believe it when he saw that the manager had paid a $30,000 overdraft for a company that was on the kiting list. Customers so listed were suspect of manipulating funds between two or more banks. In this case, the firm had an East Coast bank too, and it appeared that it was purposely setting up a "free float" period—giving the customer free money during the time it took checks to clear each bank. Instead of scrutinizing all deposits and checks to make sure that the customer wasn't engaged in manipulating funds as bank officers were supposed to do, the manager was allowing the overdraft situation to worsen. At one point, the total exposure to the bank was $1.5 million. Lewis figured out a way to protect the bank's interest. When he asked for a deposit to cover an overdraft, he asked for more than what was actually needed. When he had accumulated enough excess funds to cover all overdrafts, he closed the account and saw that the bank was paid back what the customer owed.

Changing existing procedures wasn't always that easy, though. When Lewis tried to institute what he thought were improved methods, he was criticized—often behind his back—by fellow employees loyal to his popular predecessor. Lewis rankled at the thought that his predecessor, who had fostered the errant procedures and was the source of all this employee resistance, had been promoted to Region. This made him even more resentful toward the bank and its management.

Soon reports of staff dissension reached his immediate supervisor at Region, which, as bad luck would have it, was the person he had replaced at the branch. The guy from Region kept coming out and telling him to put things back like they were. Lewis's frustration reached a peak one afternoon when the manager criticized him for taking a long lunch, despite the fact that he was working all hours of the day and night plus weekends and holidays, trying to straighten out the problems in Operations. Once again his department was woefully short of help. The confrontation with his boss quickly turned nasty, and their working relationship was never the same. Lewis found himself ostracized by the rest of the staff. His situation was not enhanced by an audit in September 1976 which showed that the branch had failed to solve many of its difficulties.

As his resentment grew, Lewis became disgusted by the entire situation at Westwood. He felt he wasn't being allowed to do his job and was encumbered by what he regarded as ineptitude on the part of others. He had to get out. Unconcerned about how it might look on his record, Lewis called Region and requested a transfer. It came through the following month, when he was assigned to Beverly Drive.

His attitude toward Wells Fargo was not improved when—once again shortly after his departure from a branch—additional personnel were brought in. It had happened at Marina Del Rey and now again at Westwood. Was he destined to have such bad luck throughout his banking career? Or was it more sinister? Were certain people at higher levels trying to sabotage him? He thought about the possibility that it might be racial. He doubted he would have had as much trouble getting what he needed—more people and better support from his superiors—if he had been white.

Of course, there was another side to the story. "I heard that Ben was over his head at Westwood," an officer who worked with him would say later. "The bank felt if they put him in a secondary position [under Feeley] at Beverly Drive, he wouldn't get in too much trouble."

Regardless of which was true—and the truth probably lay somewhere in the middle—the undeniable fact was that Lewis *believed* he was being persecuted by Wells Fargo. That did not make for a healthy situation. In fact, it would become quite unhealthy for all concerned—especially the bank.

***

Ben Lewis liked Harold Smith as soon as he met him.

The introduction took place in early 1977. One afternoon Marshall appeared in the Operations Department and asked Lewis to come over to his desk because there was someone he wanted him to meet.

"Ben, I'd like you to meet my friend Harold Smith of Muhammad Ali Amateur Sports," Marshall said proudly. "Harold, Ben Lewis, our operations officer."

Lewis recognized the name immediately. An avid reader of the sports page, he had followed some of Smith's exploits involving the track and field club. A couple of months earlier, Marshall had given Lewis tickets for the First Muhammad Ali Invitational Track Meet in Long Beach, an event sponsored by Smith's organization. Ben had taken his son, Tony, to the meet, and they enjoyed seeing some of the biggest names in track and field competing.

Lewis shook Smith's beefy hand. "Glad to meet you," Lewis said. "Sam talks a lot about you." The promoter acted sheepish, almost embarrassed. But under the bill of a baseball cap, Ben saw two bright eyes watching him intently. It was as if Smith was measuring his reaction.

"Harold and I go back a ways," Marshall explained. "He's trainin' Houston McTear."

"I went to your Long Beach meet," Lewis told Smith, who sat in a chair with his long legs stretched out and his face covered by a shaggy beard.

McTear had won the sixty-yard dash against a strong field. He exploded down the track dressed in a white running suit with the words "Muhammad Ali Track" blazed in black letters across his chest and went on to set a world's record. There was even a celebrity sprint race in which Ali came in sixth but received the loudest applause of the night for his distant finish.

"So you work with Ali," Lewis said. It was more a statement than a question. He hoped that his hero worship of Ali wasn't too obvious.

"The Champ and I are tight," Smith said. "He's committed to what we're doin' for the kids."

"Those kids need all the help we can give them," Lewis said. "This world is a tough place to grow up in."

Marshall told Lewis that Smith had been living near the beach but had recently moved closer to Beverly Hills and now wanted to open accounts at Beverly Drive. Smith's business was expanding into amateur boxing, Marshall explained. Lewis was proud of his friend Sam—the sports promoter was clearly a good catch for the bank. Who knew, they might even attract Ali himself as a customer.

The first checking account opened by Smith at Wells Fargo—in October 1977—was called the Muhammad Ali Invitational Track Meet account. It was trouble from the beginning. The account kept popping up on the overdraft list, which disturbed Lewis. It was his job to review the list regularly with the loan officers and discuss the status of accounts which they were supervising. He discussed the MAAS account problems with Marshall many times during such meetings. The condition of the account was putting Marshall under substantial pressure. Branch manager Joel Ziskind was constantly after him to get the overdrafts cleared, which he tried to do on a regular basis. With Lewis sitting across from him, Marshall would call Smith regularly and ask him for funds to cover the overdrafts.

"I'm trying to work with Harold," Marshall would explain privately to Lewis. "He's trying to get his program started and I want to help him. He'll be overdrawn once in a while, but he's okay."

What was happening, apparently, was that Smith's first priority in handing out money was to the athletes. Their loyalty was what he sought most. He was regularly spending $60,000 to $80,000 per meet. He thought nothing of flying top athletes in from all over the country, setting them up in fancy hotels and having them chauf-feured around town in style. It was tough for an amateur runner, not used to such extravagancies, to turn down. They all said, "Sure, count me in, I'll run," when Harold called them. He was the most exciting thing to happen in track and field in a long time. The fact that Smith might only gross $40,000 on a meet if he was lucky—leaving a sizable deficit—didn't seem to faze him. There was often no money left over to pay the support personnel who had helped with a meet, like the caterers, limo companies, printers and others. Sometimes he would write them bad checks. Other times he would simply avoid them.

Like Marshall, Lewis was inclined to do what he could to help the promoter build his business. First and foremost, he trusted Marshall's judgment. His friend Sammie thought Harold was a good risk, so Ben gave him the benefit of the doubt. But Lewis was his own man. He made his own decisions and stuck by them. From where he stood, Smith's future looked bright. The promoter was putting on impressive events—*real* happenings and not just idle talk—which Lewis had seen with his own eyes.

If Smith was running a little hand-to-mouth right now, well, we all have hard times now and then. He was a black man trying to get ahead, and Lewis empathized with him. From a business standpoint, the important thing as far as Lewis was concerned was Smith's association with one of the biggest names in the sports world. The name of Muhammad Ali carried clout around the world and opened all kinds of doors. Lewis knew such influence could be highly profitable.

Around this time, Lewis and Marshall formed an unofficial partnership. They always tried to talk to each other first about any problems involving Harold Smith. Hopefully, between the two of them, they could iron out the difficulties without having to get other bank personnel involved. They wanted to give Smith every break they could so that the promoter in turn could give every possible break to all those black athletes who were trying to live up to their talent and promise in an uncompromising world. The beneficiaries of Smith's efforts were mostly young people who had stunning natural ability, but for a lack of education and the color of their skin had the odds stacked against them. This was an effort Lewis would support anyway he could. For him, it was not simply charity; it was a natural thing to do.

This comfortable rationalization was not difficult for Lewis to make. He gave no thought to the long-term consequences of his actions. Besides, he had overcome the odds in his own life to achieve a position of respect in the community. He was certainly willing to help other black people who were less fortunate.

CHAPTER ELEVEN

It was a circuitous route which brought Harold Smith to California in 1975. Few people knew its true course, and most of them weren't talking. Ben Lewis certainly had no idea that Harold Smith was not the promoter's real name. Neither did Sammie Marshall. The same went for Muhammad Ali.

Harold's common-law wife, Barbara, who liked to be called Lee, knew the score. But then, her real name was not Barbara or Lee. It was Alice. Like her husband, she was running and hiding too. Wittingly and with more than a degree of pride, she became a partner in his big dreams and bold schemes.

He had been born to Eddie Fields and Nancy Taylor at Hillman Hospital in Birmingham, Alabama, during the late evening hours of April 21, 1943. He was named Ross Fields. His mother was thirty-two years old, and he was her eighth but not last child. Four other births had been stillborn. His father was a thirty-eight-year-old steel-worker. Both parents listed their race on the birth certificate as "colored." Both had themselves been born in Alabama.

When Ross was ten, the Fields family moved ninety miles north to Huntsville. Raised mostly by an older brother and sister, he grew into a tall, thin kid who was a gifted runner. Later in life, he would joke that he learned to run fast so that he could get to the table faster than all his hungry brothers and sisters.

Running was what he did best in junior high school and later at Councill High School. Like the rest of the South during those years, Huntsville schools were segregated. The all-black high school didn't even have its own track. So almost every morning at daybreak, Ross climbed over the fence surrounding the cinder track at all-white Huntsville High, laced up his worn track shoes and ran in long, graceful strides around the track. Other times he ran in the open countryside outside of town, lost in his own private world and alone because few could stay up with his relentless pace. He never seemed to tire. He ran until the other kids thought he was crazy. He ran when his feet hurt. He ran in the rain. He ran when he was hungry and thirsty. He ran because he loved the freedom that speed gave him. Running was to be his ticket out of Huntsville.

In 1962 he won a track scholarship to Tennessee State. But his dreams of stardom at the school that had developed so many famous black runners were derailed when he suffered a stress fracture his freshman year. The sad day that he returned to the dorm and packed his bags to return to Huntsville turned out to be a lucky one for him. A recruiter for American University in Washington, DC, had heard about the promising young runner and chose that day to come talk to Fields about switching schools. The following year, Fields won a full track scholarship to American University.

His new coaches saw his best potential in the mile, a distance that few of his fellow black competitors were interested in. He worked hard, improved his time to 4:10 and anchored a record-setting four-man mile relay team that college officials still fondly remember as the best in the history of their school. Two other black runners on that relay team were Bob Campbell and Hilton Nicholson, a sprinter from Trinidad. Both Campbell and Nicholson would reappear in California a decade later and go to work for the man who no longer called himself Ross Fields. They were two of only a few people who knew the true roots of one "Harold Smith." But both were fiercely loyal to their old teammate and both would keep quiet.

It was while traveling with the track team that Fields had his first taste of the good life. While in New York for a track meet, he and Campbell checked into a midtown Manhattan hotel. Up in their room, Ross picked up the phone and ordered room service for the first time in his life. The Alabamian asked what kind of steaks they had, and when told the fare was filet mignon, he ordered two dinners, complete with champagne. The "down home 'Bama" youth and his buddy ran up a $200 food bill and charged it to the American University athletic department. Once he had seen the lights of the big city, it would prove impossible to keep the rural kid "down on the farm." Steak and champagne would remain his favorite meal.

Fields shone in indoor competition and was as brilliant a tactical runner on "the boards" as his coaches had ever seen. On the wooden tracks of indoor stadiums, victory often was the result of the best strategy and uncontained desire instead of the swiftest pair of legs. He possessed an ability—some called it a cunning—that enabled him to find and exploit weaknesses in other runners and somehow turn them to his advantage.

Outside of athletics, Fields was learning how to turn things to his advantage too. A psychology major, he went into the concert promotion business and organized tours of black colleges for some well-known singers. It didn't take him long to discover how much he enjoyed rubbing elbows with celebrities. From the beginning, he seemed to have a knack for getting them to like him. It was an uncanny ability that would follow him in life—and out to California. The small-town boy felt like a big-time success when someone famous knew his name.

In his junior year (1966) of college, Fields encountered what school officials later termed "academic problems" and left the university. With his withdrawal, Fields lost any chance of achieving his dream of making the U.S. Olympic team. He would have to become famous some other way.

Not long after he left college, he met an attractive black student nurse while recuperating from an illness in a Maryland hospital and married her. In 1969, Harriet Fields gave birth to a boy, Ross Fields, Jr.

Although there were frequent visits to Huntsville, Ross and his new family stayed in the nation's capital, where he established Ross Fields Productions and became a concert promoter, working with such stars as Roberta Flack and Jerry Butler. Life was going well for him. He was making more money than ever before while mingling with the famous. He had a loving wife and a young son. He was the pride and joy of the extended Fields clan in Alabama. He was hot. "He would sell the world," recalled one friend from that era. "He could get money out of a lamppost," said another. "He had the quickest mind I've ever seen, and he worked all the angles," said a third. "Sharp. Very sharp." Ross even took his flashy show home, staging concerts in Huntsville, donating proceeds to needy high school athletes and giving interviews to the local newspaper. "A lot of people helped me over the years," a humble Fields told the *Huntsville Times* in a 1967 interview. "I feel I owe them something." (He may still owe them something back in Alabama. Authorities there subsequently filed fraudulent check charges against him.)

Fields also became involved in small-time boxing promotions, organizing bouts and selling rights to local television.

One day in 1971 a thin, well-dressed man walked into the New York offices of big-time boxing promoter Bob Arum's Top Rank, Inc., and introduced himself as Ross Fields. Arum had never met Fields before, but he listened to the smooth talker's plan for handling closed-circuit telecasts of the Muhammad Ali-Jimmy Ellis fight, which Arum was promoting. He was impressed by Fields. The guy proposed concentrating on the markets in such medium-sized cities as Memphis, Tennessee, and Winston-Salem, North Carolina, a feasible plan which made sense. There seemed to be a way for everyone to make money. Arum signed a deal for Fields to sell certain regional telecasts in exchange for a piece of the action. After the fight, Arum had a difficult time finding Fields and collecting his money, though he did end up getting most of it. Several months later, Fields was back with a plausible explanation as to the payment delay and a plan for making a similar arrangement for Ali's June 27, 1972, fight with Jerry Quarry. Arum made another deal with him, but after that fight Fields never made good on the money he owed Arum—something in the range of $10,000 to $20,000, according to Arum's estimates.

Around the same time, Fields was sidling up to one of the biggest entertainers in the business: singer, actor and Sinatra crony Sammy Davis, Jr. While still attending American University, Ross had organized a big dance at the local DAR Constitution Hall and somehow hooked Davis to serve as emcee. From then on, Ross didn't let Davis forget him. Some people close to the entertainer thought Fields was a nuisance the way he hung around Davis. But Ross could be charming, and it was difficult to say no to a devoted fan. He kept pestering Davis to allow him to open a nightclub in the capital named after the entertainer. It would be good for Davis's image in the largely black community and could be highly profitable, Fields insisted. Finally, Davis gave his permission.

The "Sammy Davis Jr. Nightclub" discotheque opened at 13th and E streets NW under the sole ownership of Ross Fields, who did not always make an effort to tell employees, customers, entertainers or the landlord to whom he owed money that the famous entertainer did not have a piece of the action. Business did not go well, and in 1972, after only fifteen months, the club was shut down. Rent and other bills totaling thousands of dollars went unpaid. Some creditors called Davis in an effort to get their money and learned for the first time that he had nothing to do with the club. About the same time, Ross Fields Productions went broke.

In the summer of 1973, Fields met a tall, leggy blonde named Alice Vicki Darrow, who had grown up in nearby Maryland. After two years at the University of Maryland and two more years at the National Academy of Art, she went to work for a sales promotions firm. Like Fields, she was a dreamer. Their chance meeting was the beginning of a long partnership and the beginning of the end for Ross and Harriet Fields's marriage. Harold and Alice knew there had to be more to life for both of them, and together they set out to find it.

That same year, Fields found himself in trouble with the law. He was convicted of a bad check charge in Montgomery County (Maryland) District Court and received an eighteen-month suspended jail sentence and three years probation. But he didn't hang around to meet with his probation officer many times. Instead, he disappeared, leaving behind his wife and a small son named after him.

Ross and Alice moved briefly to New York City. Soon back on the road, they embarked on a nationwide check-passing spree, leaving over a hundred bad checks strewn across thirty states from coast to coast. In 1975 alone, federal warrants were issued for their arrests in Chicago, North Carolina, Alabama and New Orleans. The salt and pepper couple appeared on post office walls in their first wanted posters that year. But they were never captured because they managed to stay ahead of the law by moving quickly. Ross Fields was running again.

The FBI circulars that warned about the couple described their scam. He would get a phony corporate check and give it to her. She would take it to a bank, fill out a deposit slip with a fictitious account number and go up to the teller. Upon seeing that part of the check was being deposited, the teller would assume that the customer had written down her right account number. But actually she was only going through the charade of a deposit, so that she could walk away with the rest of the check in cash.

They used numerous aliases. At various times, Ross Fields became Gerald Fidelman, Gerald Fiedlman and Gerald Tishman. Alice Vicki Darrow passed herself off as Ellen Burke, Margaret Chadwick, Jeanne Collins, Lynn Evans and Anne Kelly, among other names. By the time they reached California late in 1975, he had become Harold J. Smith and she was Barbara Newman Smith. Later, when a fair-skinned son was born to the union in 1977, he was named John Smith.

Once in Southern California, the couple settled into an apartment on Tahiti Way in Marina Del Rey, where the hedonistic singles life flourished. Residents indulged themselves with plenty of sun rays and casual sex. There were a lot of promoter types in the Marina in those days, full of big ideas, with big mouths to match, and all carrying ravenous pocketbooks. The "new" Harold Smith and his tall blond girlfriend fit right in. He liked to boast about the important people he knew, and she liked to party. He dabbled in rock promotions that weren't successful and waited for his big break.

One day Smith saw a newspaper story telling about the financial plight of Houston McTear, who had just missed the Olympics. He saw an angle here. He must have known that this was a kid he could get to relate to him because of his own hard times growing up in Alabama. It was a perfect match. He picked up the telephone and called McTear. He spoke to him as one brother to another, one track man to another, one failed Olympian to another. Whatever he said, it worked. McTear agreed to a meeting to discuss some promotional ideas of Smith's. When they met, each apparently thought that the other could do something for him. Both were prophetic.

McTear would get some mileage—both on and off the track—out of the partnership with Harold Smith. While he would never become an Olympic gold medal winner or ruler of the cinders for any length of time, he would make money and have some fun in the process. It was a sign of what was in store for him when—shortly after meeting Smith—the promoter had him picked up at the airport in a long black limousine. It sure beat being dirt poor.

But as always seemed to be the case, Harold Smith would get the better of the deal. McTear was his entree to the legitimate sports world. It was the calling card he so desperately sought. McTear was a star—not a *big* Star, but still a *star.* Together, they would attract attention. McTear would bring Smith notoriety. He would bring him Muhammad Ali.

And Ali would give Smith the world.

CHAPTER TWELVE

"**H**arold's still here," Ben Lewis said when he came to the familiar account number.

"I know," Sammie Marshall said with a sigh.

The two bankers were seated at Marshall's desk in the Beverly Drive branch, reviewing the list of accounts on the overdraft list, as they did most days. It was not good business to allow an account to remain overdraft for long. Computerized overdraft notices were sent out automatically, and, when necessary, customers were telephoned and asked to make the necessary desposits. Banks couldn't do business any other way.

"Joel's on me all the time," Lewis said. "I'm not supposed to pay these any more."

"Yeah," Marshall said, "he wants these cleared up. It's just that I'm trying to work with Harold. I keep telling Joel that Harold's getting this program started—he needs a little time."

Lewis nodded understandingly.

Marshall picked up the telephone and dialed a number from memory. "This is Sam Marshall," he said. "Let me talk to Harold."

The overdrafts had started soon after Smith opened those first accounts at Beverly Drive in late 1977. In no time the accounts of Smith, his Muhammad Ali Track Club and sprinter Houston McTear showed up overdrawn. As a courtesy, their checks were being paid instead of returned unpaid. Marshall and Lewis were doing so strictly on their own authority.

It didn't take an experienced banker to realize that the problem was not a temporary cash flow problem, as Marshall and Lewis wanted to believe, but rather a chronic shortage of money. When branch manager Joel Ziskind noticed the pattern, he became impatient. Though Ziskind preferred to avoid confrontations with his employees, he began complaining aloud about the overdraft activity. Most of the heat fell on Sammie Marshall—after all, he had brought Smith to the bank. Ziskind told him to keep a tighter rein on "his" customer.

"Hey, Harold," Marshall said into the phone. "We've got to have a deposit to cover overdrafts. Ben and I are sitting here—yeah, I know. Tomorrow morning? Well, okay."

It was always the same, with Harold promising he'd be in "tomorrow" with a deposit. Unfortunately, there were lots of tomorrows and woefully few deposits.

The fallout from all the NSF checks affected other branch employees. Loan officer Judith Nordahl, a thin brunette with a friendly disposition, had immediate responsibility for overdrafts at the branch. She still remembers the difficulties she used to have getting Smith's accounts out of the red. "I would see Harold and Houston in the bank and call them over. I'd tell them in a friendly way that they were overdraft again and ask what they could do to work things out. Harold would always say something like 'Don't worry, Ali is taking care of everything.' All we ever heard was Ali this and Ali that. So many people were impressed with the connection that they overlooked things."

Smith obviously didn't let little annoyances like having no money to cover his checks deter him. When he walked into the branch, he did so with a confident swagger. He wandered at will behind the tellers' counter (where Lewis worked) and made himself comfortable in the platform management area (where Marshall was stationed), all the while behaving like a man who had friends in high places. "Although he probably wouldn't do well on an IQ test, Harold was smart," one officer said. "He was a manipulator and quick as a cat." Houston McTear, however, was another matter. "We showed him over and over how to balance his checkbook, but he still couldn't seem to figure it out."

As Ziskind continued to gripe about the bad accounts, Marshall complained about the manager's racial "prejudice." The standoff escalated into a battle between some white and black employees. During one staff meeting held to try to iron out some of the difficulties, Ziskind ended a short speech with "Now what are we going to do about these problems?"

Marshall stood up heatedly and said, "This is all a bunch of bullshit. I'm not going to do anything." With that, Marshall turned and stalked from the room.

With the friction too great to suit anyone, Marshall took a transfer to the Miracle Mile branch in February 1978, leaving Lewis alone to "service" Smith's accounts. Not long after that Ziskind delivered the ultimatum which had been long coming. "I want these Smith accounts out of here," the manager told Lewis. "They stink. Close them all."

On the day of the ultimatum, Smith's balance was a negative $5,769.25. Lewis had to do something about the debt. He didn't have time to wait on Harold anymore. If he couldn't figure anything out, it would be charged off against the branch's profit and loss and he would get the blame now that Marshall was gone. Ben called his old friend at Miracle Mile for help.

"Joel's had it," Lewis reported. "I've got to close Harold's accounts. What should I do with the overdraft balance?"

"Go ahead and zero out the account," Marshall said. "Send the charge to me."

Lewis was relieved. It meant that the loss could be taken off the books at Beverly Drive; it would be Miracle Mile's problem now. He typed up a branch settlement ticket and used the debit half to bring the account to zero. Then he sent the credit half—which had to be paid off—attention to Marshall in the interoffice mail pouch. The next day, Smith's Beverly Drive account appeared on the overdraft list again, showing $8.00 still owed for a service charge. Lewis did the same thing with this relatively small amount. He wanted it all off his books and gone.

As of June 23, 1978, Harold Smith no longer had accounts at Beverly Drive. Officially, he was no longer a customer of the branch. But that was only officially. Ben Lewis would be seeing a lot more of him.

* * *

Lewis had surprised his girlfriend, Gladys, with a marriage proposal during a trip to Las Vegas. In fact, it had been on April Fools' Day, and Gladys thought the whole thing a practical joke until Ben put the money on the counter for a marriage license. Back at work a few days later, Lewis had told Marshall how much he wanted to take his new bride on a "really nice" honeymoon. But, as usual, money was tight on his salary. Marshall, who had opened some new accounts for Smith at Miracle Mile, said he thought the promoter might be able to help Ben get a good deal.

Everything was set up a few days later. All travel arrangements were handled by a friend of Smith's: Tom Bole of Continental Travel Agency. The best part was that Ben and Gladys got a "twofer"—both traveling for the price of one—which made the trip affordable. Lewis accepted the explanation that this perk was possible because Smith had given the agent so much business. It was done as a favor to the promoter, who turned it into a favor to the banker.

Upon his return from Europe, Lewis discovered that the trip had some short strings attached to it. It wasn't long before Smith showed up at the branch with a check for $3,000 that he wanted cashed. (Ironically, this check was drawn on Beverly Hills-based American City Bank, which would be declared insolvent and taken over by federal regulators five years later.) It was written on the account of Thomas and Christina Bole and made out to the travel agent. On the back, it had been signed over to Harold J. Smith.

"Is this Tom Bole the travel agent?" Lewis asked.

"Yeah," Smith said. "I'm doing this as a favor for him."

Lewis had no business cashing the check. Smith was no longer a customer at Beverly Drive. Worse yet, he had been booted out of the branch for passing bad checks. Ben knew he should send the promoter to Sam Marshall over at Miracle Mile. He would be sticking his neck out on this one. But a favor was a favor. He and his bride had just returned from the trip of a lifetime made possible by Smith. Ben initialed the check and went to a teller to get the cash. Back in a few minutes, he counted out a stack of greenbacks.

Lewis was mistaken in thinking that he had adequately repaid the favor. Three weeks later, Smith was back with another check, this one written by a sports equipment firm and made out to him for $5,600. Lewis cashed the check once again, only this time it was returned unpaid to the bank a few days later. A stop payment order had been issued, and the originating bank refused to pay the check. Lewis called Marshall right away and told him what had happened.

"Harold mentioned that a new check is being issued," Marshall said.

"I guess I'll have to put it in accounts receivable until the replacement check arrives," Lewis said, thinking aloud.

An account where the bank put payment pending items was where the check belonged. Lewis had done the right thing at the time. The trick was that checks were not to stay "parked" there for long. In some cases, the bank was already out the money and needed to collect as quickly as possible, which was the situation with the Bole check. Ben told Brian Feeley that he had put the check in accounts receivable and was awaiting issuance of a new check. Feeley voiced no objection. Though Lewis had clearly extended a courtesy to a former customer, nothing improper had been done.

Lewis received a shock when, in early September 1978, the $3,000 Thomas Bole check was returned unpaid too. It had bounced around in limbo for several weeks since he had cashed it, and the bank had made numerous attempts to collect. Four days in a row he called American City Bank to see if there was enough money in Bole's account to cover the check. There never was. Since it was clear that Wells Fargo was not going to get payment on it, Lewis couldn't in good conscience put it in accounts receivable. Instead, he decided to send it over to Marshall as a branch settlement transaction—like he had done with the earlier over-draft charges. Ben had done all he could. Sammie would have to charge it to one of Harold's accounts at that branch. That was all there was to it. He placed it in the interbranch mail pouch without bothering to tell Sammie that it was coming.

Three days later, much to Ben's surprise, the Bole check came back from Miracle Mile. Marshall had not charged it off to any of Smith's accounts and instead wrote on the ticket that since the item had been cashed at Beverly Drive, Beverly Drive was where it belonged. Lewis was flabbergasted. Marshall had thrown the bad check back to him like a hot potato.

This time, Lewis called Harold Smith directly. "We haven't been able to collect on either the Bole or Mitre Sports checks," he explained. "They're no good."

"I'll make 'em good," Smith said. "The Bole check was a favor to Tommy. The Mitre people are writing me a new check."

"Right now, the bank is out nine grand."

"Hey, Ben, I'm having some problems right now. Do me a favor and hold them for a little while."

Both the checks went into Lewis's "in" basket on his desk. This was where he kept items that needed immediate attention. It was also where he put letters to answer and bills to pay. He did not tell Brian Feeley that he put the wrinkled, often-stamped check here. In the strictest sense, he was not following proper bank procedure. He was giving Harold Smith free money. It was their secret—between him and Harold. Smith had already done a lot for him. What had Wells Fargo ever done? Work him unmercifully hard at relatively low pay for years, that's what. Harold would come through. He always did. Sammie thought the world of the man. And besides, the greatest heavyweight champion in history trusted Harold Smith. If Harold was okay in Ali's book, he was okay in Ben's.

Smith called Ben several days later and vindicated his decision.

"How would you like to go to the Ali-Spinks fight in New Orleans?" Smith asked. "As my guest."

"Hell yes," Lewis said. He knew that Smith was making ambitious plans with his move into amateur boxing. It would be fun going to the fight with Smith. It would probably be a heck of a fight, with Ali attempting to win back the heavyweight crown for an unprecedented third time.

"Okay, my man," Smith said exuberantly. "I'll take care of everything. Airplane fare, tickets to the fight, hotel reservations, the works."

Lewis was now more sure than ever: Harold Smith was a good man to know.

***

Meanwhile, across town at the Miracle Mile branch, Sammie Marshall had welcomed his old Beverly Drive customer with open arms. He had introduced Smith to branch manager Gene Kawakami in the summer of 1978. Marshall explained to his boss that he wanted to bring Smith and his MAAS accounts to Miracle Mile because it would be "good business" for the branch. Kawakami readily agreed, privately hoping that Smith might convince Ali to give Wells Fargo some of his banking business too.

So, Smith's bad record at Beverly Drive did not follow him to Miracle Mile, thanks largely to the positive image that Marshall created of the promoter. No one at Miracle Mile was the wiser. It was as if the two branches did not belong to the same bank.

By the end of that summer, Smith was stopping by Kawakami's desk to chat. Kawakami saw enormous potential—for himself and the bank—in Smith's enviable association with Ali. Smith's announced intention to go into boxing was seen as a shrewd move by the branch manager. Even though Kawakami thought little of Marshall's abilities as a banker—the manager had already given his assistant a poor evaluation and suggested he "reconsider" his banking career—the nisei officer was pleased with this new customer, who usually appeared at the bank wearing a baseball cap and jeans. Kawakami had been around long enough to know that dress meant very little in this town. Often the more casual the attire, the more successful the wearer.

Harold Smith was well into courting his third Wells Fargo banker. He understood how important the bankers were to him; without them and their money, his business would have quickly folded. It wouldn't be long before his efforts at keeping the bankers in his corner started paying off in a big way. Bigger than Smith would even have dared think.

CHAPTER THIRTEEN

New Orleans was hot and humid, but the weather would be no factor. The championship bout was held indoors on September 15, 1978, at the huge air-conditioned Superdome. Ali-Spinks II was a fight that would go down in history for more than one reason.

Seven months earlier to the day, Ali had lost the heavyweight championship title in the ring for the first time when Leon Spinks, a former street fighter from the ghetto of St. Louis, outpointed him in fifteen rounds in Las Vegas. More than a decade Ali's junior at age twenty-five, Spinks wreaked havoc on Ali's clever rope-a-dope ring strategy that had worked so well against George Foreman and Ken Norton. The plan was simple: Ali, covering up, would rest against the ropes while his opponent tired himself hammering away ineffectively at a shield of forearms and gloves, then Ali would uncoil an assault of his own in time to win the fight. The trouble was that Spinks never tired and kept slugging away. Only Ali wearied of the action; eventually he dropped his guard and exposed his body to further punishment. When the split decision was announced to a cheering, pro-Spinks crowd, Ali sat slumped in his corner, staring down at the floor. Later, in the quiet sadness of his room, Ali shook his fist defiantly at a TV news camera, stuck his swollen face into the lens and promised hoarsely, "I shall return."

Memories of the first Ali-Spinks fight were going through Ben Lewis's mind a few days before the rematch as he stepped off a commercial plane at New Orleans International Airport with his twenty-four-year-old son, Tony. Both of them were determined to enjoy the pageantry of the rematch even if the unspeakable happened and Ali lost. But Ben knew he would feel cheated if his hero was not victorious. It just wouldn't be fair to

Ali, either. The Champ *had* to win the title back. Lewis was even carrying a special present for Ali. Harold had promised that he would get to deliver it personally before the fight.

Harold Smith's entourage was sizable—some two dozen people came as his guests, including two other Wells Fargo bankers: Sammie Marshall and Gene Kawakami. They had a block of rooms at a fancy hotel in the French Quarter.

Ben and Tony mostly went their own way, sticking together like a father and son who didn't get enough time together. They roamed the hotel in their brown and tan warm-up suits that had their first names and "Superdome 1978" on the front and "Muhammad Ali" on the back. They felt a part of history and proud to be associated with Muhammad Ali, however tenuously.

The day before the big fight Smith escorted Ben and Tony to Ali's hotel suite. Ben carried in a neat bundle under one arm a fighter's robe made by a friend. Done in lavender and white silk, it was lined in terry cloth. Smith knocked softly on the door. Someone he knew opened the door, and they exchanged brief pleasantries. Smith said they had a little present for the Champ and asked if he could possibly come to the door. The second told them to wait at an adjacent door and disappeared back into the suite, which was filled with a horde of people. Soon the other door opened. Looming in the bedroom doorway, larger than life, stood Muhammad Ali, dressed in a well-tailored suit with sports shirt open at the collar. He was a big man, a genuine heavyweight. Ben was struck by how old and tired he looked. So wrung out. Could this man possibly climb into a ring tomorrow night and take on the young, tough ex-Marine who was now heavyweight champion of the world? It didn't seem possible.

What Lewis didn't know at the time and only read about later was the existence of a closely guarded medical problem that had shown up in Ali just four days earlier. Complaining of unnatural weariness after a workout, he had been rushed to a doctor, who administered a blood test and discovered an alarming shortage of salt, iron and potassium in the fighter's system. He had been taking a dozen pills a day to make up for the deficiency. He had trained hard for the fight at a rented brick house near Lake Pontchartrain, just outside New Orleans, suffering mightily on a green rubbing table, doing exercises and stretching his body to the limits. Now it was a question of whether or not he had trained too hard. The answer would come in the ring.

"Sorry to disturb you, Champ," Smith said. "This is my friend and personal banker, Ben Lewis. And his son, Tony."

Ali whispered something under his breath. He didn't offer to shake hands. His hands were worth too much money to use for such niceties.

"They have a present for you, Champ."

Ben handed him the robe. He felt awkward. "A friend of mine made this for you, Champ. She did some research and found out these are your favorite colors."

Ali took the robe. "Thanks very much." His mind was obviously a million miles away. Or maybe just a few miles away—at the ring in the Superdome, where he would soon be risking his life, limb and reputation.

A lump had grown in Lewis's throat. He had a hard time believing that, thanks to Harold Smith, he was standing in the company of the most famous boxer of all time. "All of us hope—wish you luck," he managed.

"I'm so tired," Ali said. "All these people." He looked back into the room with dulled eyes.

Lewis could see past the Champ. Through the opened door to the living room he saw a crowd of people standing in a cloud of smoke.

"After the weigh-in, I'm going out to the house to get away. Get some rest."

"Good idea, Champ," Smith said, smiling humbly. "Good idea."

There was a streak in Harold's personality that Ben now saw for the first but not the last time. While Smith always acted so confident and important around other people, in the company of Ali he became a patronizer.

"Take care," Ben said softly as the door closed.

At the weigh-in, the entire entourage was there to see Ali and Spinks meet face-to-face. Ben, Tony, Harold, Marshall, Kawakami, all the rest. It was the first act of the spectacular show. Spinks tipped the scales at 201 pounds. A subdued Ali came in at 221 pounds, eleven pounds heavier than when he took the title away from Sonny Liston in 1965, five pounds heavier than when he dethroned George Foreman four years earlier. Ali was carrying a new aura of seriousness too, some observers thought. To Ben, standing on his tiptoes to see over the crowd, Spinks seemed nervous and had a wild look in his eyes, as if he knew he was in over his head. Since the new champ's pro ring record was then only seven wins and one draw as opposed to Ali's five hundred and thirty rounds of professional fighting—almost half that number in title defenses—it was justifiable for him to feel apprehensive.

For the first time, Ben began to feel confident instead of just wishful. "I think Spinks knows he's in trouble," he said. He didn't say but thought *I hope Ali gets a good night's sleep.*

The crowd belonged to Ali. At the weigh-in. In the hotel corridors. In the bars and restaurants. On the streets and in the jazz clubs. At the coffee shop counters. There were fight souvenirs for sale everywhere. Many of them carried Ali's name alone, and these were the hottest items. None had Spinks's name alone. The odds makers called the fight two to one in favor of Ali. Some of the fight experts in the media were not so sure. *Time* magazine suggested that Ali's legs would go; Dick Young of the New York *Daily News* didn't think the former champ could come back against the young dynamo. Of course, the press had doubted Ali in earlier fights against Liston, Foreman and Frazier. Somehow, as if a mystical force were guiding him, Ali had always found a way. Spinks had youth and the title. But Ali was Ali.

The next day Ben and Tony, dressed in their official-looking warm-up suits, did some sight-seeing before the fight. There were quite a few sights to see. A hookers' convention was going on in town. Ladies of the night had come in from all over the country, usually in the company of their outlandishly dressed pimps. Together with the fight crowd, they made the streets look like a human zoo to Ben.

On Bourbon Street, Ben and Tony were waiting for a light when a car pulled over to the curb. A young black man leaned toward the open window and said, "Hey, you know who I am?"

Lewis, the devout fight fan, recognized the man immediately.

"Yeah, sure," Lewis answered. "You're Matt Franklin."

"You got it. I'm going to be champ someday."

Ben smiled. "You sound like you believe it."

"I do," Franklin said confidently. "I do."

"See you there, brother."

(Determination is as much a part of the fight game as solid fists and good legs. Seven months after this chance encounter, Franklin stopped Marvin Johnson in the eighth round to win the WBC light-heavyweight championship. Subsequently changing his name to Matthew Saad Muhammad, he reigned until losing to Dwight Braxton on December 19, 1981.)

That night the Superdome was filled with more than 65,000 paying spectators. The gate was a whopping $4.8 million, then the biggest in boxing history. Of course, that dollar figure did not include revenue from television and other ancillary rights—which took the total income into the tens of millions of dollars.

The fight wasn't great in anyone's book. But Ali fought a much better fight this time around against Spinks. From the first bell, he made it clear that he had a new strategy. He was abandoning the ropes and planting himself in the center of the ring. He couldn't float like a butterfly any more, but he proved that he could still sting like a bee once in a while.

In the first round, Spinks came out with the reckless disregard of youth and won the round. Ali established control over the fight in the next round, bobbing and backpedaling, jabbing and clinching, keeping Spinks confused and out of synch. It looked like an old pro against a rank amateur, a wily veteran against an aggressive upstart. If Ali's combinations weren't as powerful as yesteryear, they were scoring the necessary points. In truth, he was but a shell of the bronze young warrior who stood over a fallen Liston long ago and taunted the bearlike figure to get up and fight. Still, he had enough left to handle Spinks. At the end, Ali was still dancing and Spinks was still trying to find him. Ali's aged legs carried him the full fifteen rounds, and he won a lopsided decision. To Lewis, Ali looked as if he could have gone another five rounds.

Any victory, however lackluster in appearance, was a turn-on for Ali's delirious fans. Lewis clapped as hard and cheered as loud as anyone. His hero had carved another notch in boxing history. He had done what no one else had been able to do—win the heavy-weight championship crown a *third* time.

It was all heady stuff for Ben and his son, caught up in the whirlwind that encircled the Muhammad Ali Amateur Sports crowd. At the hotel, there was an open house in Smith's suite. Drinks and food were shared by all and toasts to victory abounded.

For Ben it was a special time, and they were all special people with special destinies. This was what he wanted out of life. To feel important and successful. And above all, appreciated. He was part of the glamour team. It made him feel important.

He sat back on the edge of a bed, sipping champagne and taking it all in. There was no doubt about it: Harold Smith was going places and was exciting to be around. He had gone from being a hanger-on around Ali to having his own entourage. He was important because everyone knew how close he was to the Champ. Anyone associated with Ali could count on having lots of people around him. That came with the turf.

Harold was telling a group of admirers who had formed around him about the scene in Ali's dressing room. Ben loved it all. At this moment in time there was no other place he would rather have been than here with all these successful and famous brothers. He had reached a pinnacle, he knew. After years of struggling as an anonymous bank officer for what he considered a heartless and sometimes racist institution, he now had it within his grasp to *be* somebody. To reach for fame and glory. A crucial crossroads in his life was approaching. He could sense it. It could well be one of those radical change of directions which may only come once in a lifetime if you're lucky—or never at all if you're not. The kind of opportunity that one has to act on quickly before it passes forever.

Lewis was confident that when the time came he would choose the right path. He had been waiting too long to do anything less.

CHAPTER FOURTEEN

A month after the New Orleans fight, Sammie Marshall had a problem at the bank.

Actually, it had started as Harold Smith's problem. The promoter owed Telstar Travel a sizable chunk of change—$19,007.52, to be exact. The New Orleans trip had not come cheap, and the owner of the agency had been badgering Smith for payment. The problem was that Smith didn't have the money to pay the bill.

On October 4, Marshall issued a cashier's check payable to Telstar. A cashier's check was supposed to be justified by a cash payment or withdrawal from a customer's account. As a favor to Smith, the banker initiated a branch settlement transaction, transferring the charge for the cashier's check to another branch. Under ordinary bank procedures, this would merely have required that the funds for the cashier's check be withdrawn from the customer's account at that branch. But in this instance, Marshall planned to hold the debit half of the ticket as long as possible; hopefully, Harold would come up with the money to clear the transaction before the ten-day deadline. If he did, then Marshall would simply deposit the money and clear the branch settlement transaction. If Smith was unable to come up with the money, making it impossible for Marshall to clear the item in time, then the banker planned to send it over to Beverly Drive, where Smith had no account but rather a growing pile of bad checks. Of course, Marshall was building a stack of Smith's bad checks at Miracle Mile too. By holding on to the credit half of the settlement ticket, rather than sending it to another branch promptly, Marshall would give Smith additional time to pay for the cashier's check—and a free loan of the money in the meantime.

Not long after the Telstar transaction, Marshall submitted a request for an indefinite leave of absence to Gene Kawakami. Instead of resigning, Marshall was hedging his bet. He might be able to come back to Wells Fargo should the boxing business not work out as planned. The request was quickly approved by Kawakami and his superiors. No one at Miracle Mile tried to talk Marshall out of leaving, and no one was particularly sorry to see him go.

For his part, Kawakami was more than willing to inherit Harold Smith as a customer at Miracle Mile. He was pleased that Muhammad Ali, at Smith's urging, had opened two personal accounts at the branch. Having Ali show up at the branch had been a thrill. It was the second time he had met the Champ. The first time was in New Orleans, when Smith had taken him up to Ali's hotel room and introduced them. Ali was lying on the bed, his head propped up by a pillow, and he remained in that position for the short visit.

As far as Kawakami was concerned, Smith was sitting on a gold mine in his connection to Ali. Kawakami had told the promoter more than once that he could make a lot of money if he played his hand right. The banker was determined to get a piece of the profits for himself.

Ben Lewis wasn't at all happy with Marshall's departure from the bank. In fact, he was confused and worried—for good reason. The growing snowball of Smith's rubber checks would soon be his problem alone. How was he going to continue juggling between Beverly Drive and Miracle Mile all these bad checks for Harold if there was no Sammie Marshall on the other end? Shortly after they all had returned from New Orleans, Lewis, Sammie and Harold had talked together and worked out a system to give Harold even more time on his checks. It was agreed that he would cash checks written on his Miracle Mile accounts at Beverly Drive and not at Miracle Mile. At first Harold didn't understand the advantage. Ben and Sammie explained to him that interoffice transactions take a few days longer to clear. "That will give you some extra time," Ben told Harold. When he got the point, Smith heartily approved. Lewis was happy to help with this plan to aid the promoter. Ever since the Ali fight, Lewis had felt much closer to Smith. But now with Sammie leaving, how in the world was he going to manage all this by himself?

Even with Marshall's help, it had not been easy. When Lewis was out sick for a few days, Brian Feeley had opened the metal file drawer containing the accounts receivable items and had come across several uncollected or overdraft checks of Smith's that Ben had parked there to give Smith more time. Feeley recognized them for what they were: checks that Lewis had paid but which had proved to be no good. The customer who received the money was the same on all of them: Harold Smith. Knowing that Smith had accounts at Miracle Mile that could be charged for the losses, Feeley shipped them over to Marshall. Why should Beverly Drive suffer the losses when Smith wasn't even its customer? When Ben returned, Feeley explained what he had done and added, "There's no reason why we should get stuck for those checks." This was the type of trouble Lewis now feared even more. He was limited in terms of what he could openly do for Smith at Beverly Drive. After all, the man was hardly a valued customer there. Anything but: everyone knew that he had been kicked out of the branch. That didn't buy him any favors—at least official ones.

Lewis knew that Smith was trying to stay on the good side of Gene Kawakami by bringing him along to New Orleans. He wasn't sure what, if anything, Smith was getting out of Kawakami. Lewis couldn't imagine that the Miracle Mile branch manager was doing the same kind of things for Harold that he and Marshall were doing. Harold was probably just trying to impress Kawakami because he was Sammie's boss. Lewis was not close to Kawakami. They were two different types of men with only one thing in common: an association with a customer named Harold Smith. Each of them, in the realm of his influence and responsibilities at his branch, kept his relationship with the promoter to himself and did not share it with the other. Though they would occasionally continue to cross paths at boxing events and on trips as Smith's guests, Lewis and Kawakami would never find the opportunity or have the desire to discuss the banking business of Harold Smith.

The crunch day came on Friday, October 27, Marshall's last day as an employee of Wells Fargo. Lewis received an unpleasant surprise when he opened his interbranch mail that day. In the stack of paperwork was a $19,007.52 settlement ticket offsetting the Telstar cashier's check Marshall had issued for Smith's benefit. Lewis didn't even recognize the payee's name.

Marshall had made it appear on the branch settlement ticket that the check had been paid for. Lewis briefly considered his options. There were only two things he could do: sit on the ticket until ten days passed and let the computer spit out a tracer, or bounce it back to Marshall like he had done numerous times before. Both options were bad; the first would cause auditors to ask questions, and the latter was impossible because, come Monday, Marshall would be gone. Ben picked up the phone and called Miracle Mile. It was one of the last times he could ask Sammie for help.

"What's this settlement ticket for nineteen grand?" he said when Marshall came on the phone.

"It's an item I put through to help Harold," Marshall explained. "I couldn't clear it over here in time. Do me a favor, Ben, and carry it for a while. Harold and I'll make it good."

"What am I going to do with it?"

"Encode the ticket with our number." Marshall had lowered his voice. "Just keep rolling over the amount every seven or eight days until it's paid off. When Harold gives you the money, put it in as a credit. Everything will be cool."

Lewis wasn't sure. At first he said nothing. "But we're not supposed to do that." Several things which could go wrong had already occurred to him. At the top of the list was alerting the computer by using the wrong code number for Miracle Mile. "I don't even know the number."

"I can give it to you."

"I don't think it's going to work," Ben said worriedly. He honestly didn't know if the procedure was foolproof.

"Don't worry, it'll work," Sammie said. He gave Ben the number.

On Monday, Lewis received another surprise in the mail. It was still another branch settlement ticket from Miracle Mile. Sammie had also sent him a batch of Harold's bad checks he couldn't leave behind when he cleaned out his desk. The total was $5,348. Lewis was annoyed. A call to Marshall that morning—his first day at work in Smith's office—elicited a promise to have Harold pay off the additional amount just as soon as possible.

With mixed feelings, Lewis did what Marshall had taught him. He issued another branch settlement ticket with the Beverly Drive code on it and encoded the credit half with the secret Miracle Mile number Marshall had given him. Ben had done the same thing on Friday for the Telstar cashier's check. While the total debt to the bank had quickly escalated to $25,000, it still seemed manageable to Lewis. One single event which brought in $60,000 could repay the loan, with money left over. In bank terminology, it was a "work out" situation—meaning that the bank was working with the customer instead of putting him out of business. In the ordinary delinquent loan situation, these decisions were made not out of sympathy but rather on a pragmatic basis. Even if it meant lending more money to a strapped customer, a bank often had to do so in order to eventually receive repayment of all outstanding debts. But of course this was not a normal delinquent loan situation. Lewis was not a loan officer and did not have the prerogative to advance money to any customer. And it certainly wasn't his job to give "free" loans to a favorite customer. He could pay overdraft checks, sure, but his line of authority was only one thousand dollars. For emotional rather than fiscal reasons, Lewis was keeping Harold Smith in business with Wells Fargo money without Wells Fargo's knowledge. It was the most devious thing he had done in his life.

Lewis had inherited Sammie Marshall's problem at the bank in full.

The following weekend, Ben made his first visit to Smith's new offices on Montana Avenue in Santa Monica. The rented space wasn't yet furnished, and moving boxes were stacked along the walls. Nonetheless, the place already was a beehive of activity, with people dropping by and the telephones ringing incessantly. Harold and Lee made him feel at home. Ben pitched right in, helping to unload boxes and answer the phones.

During the previous week, the two men had talked daily on the phone. Harold usually initiated the calls, warning Ben that he had written a check which was on its way to the bank and asking Ben to cash it even though there wasn't enough money in his account to cover it. Several such NSF checks had come through that week, and Ben had cleared them in what was becoming a repeated and very risky manipulation of the branch settlement system. Though one part of Lewis wanted to disassociate himself from Smith and his exciting but hazardous ventures, the pragmatist in him knew that it was too late to stop doing these special favors. It was in his best interest for Smith to be successful and get his business to the point where it was profitable. That was the only way the money would be paid back.

"Harold, the debt to the bank is thirty-five thousand dollars as of Friday," Lewis said, reading from a piece of paper. At the bank, he hid the list of "advances" under his green desk blotter. He had already lied to Brian Feeley, just a few days earlier, when his boss asked him if Smith's overdraft checks had been paid and Ben told him they had.

"That's just what I thought," Smith said nonchalantly, flipping through a sheaf of papers. "After the track meet, we'll have enough money to pay it back."

Lewis saw no reason why the Second Annual Muhammad Ali Invitational Track Meet—scheduled for January 6, 1979—shouldn't be a success. There would be money from the live gate and additional revenue from TV rights. If it were run properly with expenses kept down, it could make much more than $35,000.

The offices of Muhammad Ali Amateur Sports became a second home to Lewis. Though it was too far to travel to during his lunch hour, he began stopping off after work and nearly every Saturday. During his visits, Ben discussed with Harold upcoming events and new ideas to make more money.

"We could do well in entertainment," Smith said one day. "I used to be a concert promoter, you know. Worked out of my car and traveled a lot. I did shows for Jerry Butler and some other guys. I might be able to get Marvin Gaye to do a concert for us. Maybe in January. Between that and the meet we'd have more than enough to pay the bank back."

"Sounds good," Ben said. "Another idea I've got is for a line of Ali souvenirs. Remember how well they sold in New Orleans? This friend of mine, Connie Robinson—you know, she's the one who made the robe for Ali—wants to sell Ali T-shirts."

"We can talk to the Champ about it when we go to Vegas next week for the Holmes-Evangelista fight."

To Ali loyalists, Holmes was the "other" heavyweight champion, owning the World Boxing Council (WBC) title. His title defense against Alfredo Evangelista, scheduled for November 10, 1978, was already being criticized by the media as a borderline nonevent. In agreeing to fight

Evangelista, who was considered little more than a club fighter, Holmes was overlooking such worthy challengers as Earnie Shavers and Mike Weaver.

Lousy fight or not, Ben didn't care. *They were flying to Vegas to talk to the Champ.* Problems at the bank notwithstanding, he was liking this boxing business more all the time.

***

Gene Kawakami had his own Harold Smith problem, though he was confident that in the end things would work out as he had planned. The Miracle Mile manager had become a fan. Smith had spoken to him at length about the boxing business, and, after the all–expenses-paid trip to New Orleans, Kawakami was hooked, not as much on the glamour of the fight game as on the prospects for financial gain. There were fortunes to be made, and Kawakami saw himself reaping his fair share. Money, not friendship, was his driving force.

Shortly after the New Orleans trip and not long after Sammie Marshall had left the bank, Smith came into the Miracle Mile office to see Kawakami. He boasted of a lucrative three-year contract he had with NBC Sports to telecast five amateur boxing events each year. The promoter was guaranteed $40,000 per event, making the contract worth a minimum of $600,000. Those sounded like good figures to Kawakami. Smith said his goal was to produce the best amateur boxing team this country had ever seen in time for the 1980 Olympics in Moscow. The only thing, Smith explained, was that he needed some money to help promote the amateur event he had planned. There was nothing chancy about it because the event was guaranteed to make money with the TV contract.

Kawakami knew that Smith wouldn't qualify for a bank loan. There was no collateral. But he believed so much in Smith's ability to make money with his important connections that he volunteered to invest some of his own money.

"How much?" Smith asked.

"Twenty-five thousand for now, maybe more later."

"That would help. I could have the money back to you in a year."

The next day, Smith came to the bank, and Kawakami took him outside. The banker gave him $25,000 in cash. Kawakami didn't want to make the delivery inside the bank for fear his co-workers would see it. Bankers were not allowed to engage in financial transactions with customers for their own account. Kawakami didn't tell this to Smith, nor did he mention that the money came from recent gambling winnings. Despite his conservative appearance, Kawakami enjoyed taking a risk now and then.

"I want to put your skills to work," Smith said, slipping the money into a briefcase. "I want to get you involved in the organization. I trust you, Gene. You're a real friend."

A few weeks later, Smith came back to Kawakami and said he needed more money for the upcoming boxing show. It was important that this first one be done right. He wanted to keep the network happy. Kawakami had no more personal funds, so he went to his father. The elder Kawakami took a second trust deed on his house so his son could make another loan—this one for $30,000. Kawakami deposited some of the money directly into Smith's checking accounts to clear overdrafts. The boxing event was held as planned, but the only real money that came in was the $40,000 from NBC. The live gate was a disappointment, with fewer than two thousand people attending. The expenses were greater than the TV money so there was nothing left to pay off the $55,000 in loans from Kawakami. Smith told the banker not to worry. This event was only a small part of his overall plan. Money would be coming in soon. He already had plans for another boxing show in November. Shortly thereafter, Smith was back asking Kawakami for another loan, supposedly to pay agents and vendors in advance for their services.

At this point Kawakami decided to make a bank loan. It was in his own best interests that Smith succeed. His own money was at stake. But Kawakami tried to be more prudent this time. He contacted NBC to verify the $40,000 per event contract. He then suggested to the TV people that he would make the promoter a loan for necessary expenses if the network would agree to tie the loan to the NBC contract. The producer of NBC Sports was shrewder: he would not agree to assign the contract to Wells Fargo unless the bank was willing to guarantee that the November boxing show would, in fact, be held. Kawakami immediately figured out what the network was trying to do. If the boxing event did not come off as planned, the bank would owe NBC $40,000. That was an unacceptable role for the bank. It could not be in the business of guaranteeing a sporting event. Kawakami signed the papers for a $25,000 unsecured Wells Fargo loan to Smith. That seemed safer. It was a ninety-day loan to be repaid after the track meet.

Overdrafts were now occurring regularly in Smith's personal and business accounts at Miracle Mile. At one point the total was $50,000. To cover them—Smith was of course unable to—Kawakami made another bank loan, this time in the name of Muhammad Ali Amateur Boxing Club. The amount: $50,000, also unsecured. Kawakami disbursed the funds directly into Smith's accounts to clear the overdrafts.

Like the October show, the November event was not a financial success. Worsening matters this time was the fact that the $40,000 due from NBC for televising the event was tied up in litigation. Some vendors had been paid only part in advance, while others had not been paid *period*. Once again, Smith emerged from his latest promotion deeper in debt.

Kawakami recognized that he was at a crossroads. He had lent the promoter $75,000 in bank money, $25,000 of his own money and $30,000 of his father's money in order to stage these events. Yet not only was the profit nonexistent, the overdrafts in Smith's accounts were larger than ever. But if he didn't lend additional monies now to keep Smith afloat, Kawakami knew there was a chance that the imprudent bank loans he had made and the overdrafts he had allowed might be spotted by his superiors and the auditors. He might lose his job, and his banking career would surely be jeopardized. He and his father would also be out $55,000. The risk was too great. He had to keep Smith in business. He confronted the promoter over the debt problems. Tightening the reins, Kawakami said he would make no more loans unless Smith agreed not to pay his expenses with checks. Instead, Kawakami would pay them directly with cashier's checks, which would give him control over how any new monies were spent. It was too bad he hadn't done this sooner.

Realizing he had to go along with this plan, Smith agreed. Then he told Kawakami about his newest idea. "I'm gonna produce a New Year's Eve party starring Marvin Gaye."

"How much do you think it will cost to put on?" Kawakami asked. He was getting more cautious now in his dealings with Smith.

"Twenty thousand," said Smith. "Plus a fifteen-thousand-dollar retainer for Gaye. He won't agree to do it unless I pay him up front."

Marvin Gaye was a potentially big draw. If the event was staged right, the chances seemed good for a big gate. Kawakami upped the ante. He wrote another unsecured loan for $25,000. It brought the total to $100,000—his loan authorization limit for any one customer. Fifteen thousand of the new loan went for a cashier's check made out to Gaye.

The snowball of Harold Smith's debts at Wells Fargo was well on its way to becoming an avalanche.

CHAPTER FIFTEEN

The last time Ben Lewis was in Las Vegas he had married Gladys. She was staying home this trip. It was ironic that he was going to be in the company of one of the few people in the world she didn't like. Gladys had told him after meeting Harold Smith for the first time that she didn't trust the man. Ben had just smiled. He could understand quiet, religious Gladys not taking to the fast-talking, hustling Harold. It didn't bother him. They both had their places in his life.

From the airport, Lewis took a cab directly to the hotel and hurried through the lobby. Ben knew that Connie Robinson had taken an earlier flight. Harold was supposed to have arrived in town last night. He hoped he hadn't missed the meeting with Ali.

When he got out of the elevator, Ben saw them heading his way down the hallway. Ali was in the middle. His arm was around Connie, an attractive, light-complexioned black woman in her early thirties. Harold was walking on the other side of the Champ. They were laughing. Obviously, the meeting had just concluded.

"Take your arm off that lady, Champ," Lewis said, making sure his smile was apparent. "This is supposed to be business."

Ali stopped and looked at him in wide-eyed surprise. "You think she's your girlfriend?" He threw both his powerful arms around Connie in a bear hug. "She's mine. You ain't pretty enough."

"Let's see who's the prettiest," Ben said. He had spotted a full-length wall mirror next to the elevator. "Come on. The prettiest one gets to keep her." It was all in good fun. Even though Ben had met Connie when he was single and lonely, they had never been more than platonic friends.

"Ben, you're crazy, man," Smith said, laughing.

A playful grin spread across Ali's face. "Don't worry," he told Connie, "I'll win."

Looking at himself in the reflection of the mirror standing next to Ali, Ben felt miniature. Harold and Connie cracked up at the sight of the two men, who acted like old friends comparing mugs and taunting each other.

The teasing continued down in the elevator and across the lobby. In front of the hotel, a chauffeur and long black limousine awaited Ali.

"Aren't you staying for the fight?" Smith asked.

"Naw," Ali said. "It don't mean nothing to me."

As the driver held the door open for him, Ali turned to Connie. "I gotta go. What you gonna do? Stay with him or come with me?"

The joking was over. This sounded like a real proposition. It was vintage Ali all the way.

Connie smiled and shrugged. "I'm going to stay with Ben."

"You can do better than that," Ali muttered as he climbed into the plush backseat.

The three of them stood watching as the limo pulled away. Ali quickly turned around and looked out the rear window. He was biting his lower lip and baring white teeth in a menacing grimace as he shook his fist at Ben. It was an exaggerated I'll-get-you-for-this gesture. They all had a good laugh at the Champ's antics.

"He said okay, Ben," Connie said, almost squealing with delight. "I can design and market the official Ali T-shirt."

"That's great."

"He liked my ideas," she said proudly.

"You financing the project yourself?"

She nodded. "I don't mind as long as I have his permission."

Naturally, both Ben and Connie were novices when it came to dealing with Muhammad Ali. They would both learn their lesson. For Connie, it would come the hard way. The Champ had a disturbing tendency to agree with whomever he was with at the time. He was particularly likely to accede to any proposal suggested by a charming woman. But, unfortunately, what he had agreed to in person would often not materialize. It wasn't that Ali was dishonest. Rather, he had a generous heart and wanted to make people happy. When put on the spot, he had a difficult time saying no to anyone. There was something else at work here too. Luckily for Ali's financial security, he had hooked up with the prestigious Chicago law firm of Hopkins, Sutter, Mulroy, Davis and Cromartie. Senior partner Michael E. Phenner personally watched over the Champ's business interests. Ali knew better than to enter into any deal without the approval of his lawyers. In fact, the lawyers eventually nixed the T-shirt deal, but by then Connie had invested several thousand dollars of her own money developing a product line.

On that November day in 1978, though, life looked promising for all concerned. The heavyweight champion of the world had met with them, joked, teased and played with them, flirted with Connie and okayed her business proposal. They would stay in town and go to the fight that night, where Holmes would do what the experts expected him to do and eliminate a club fighter in the seventh round on a technical knockout.

Ben thought he would dally at a casino or two while here. Take in some blackjack and maybe even the slot machines. He was feeling so lucky these days.

* * *

The Second Annual Muhammad Ali Invitational Track Meet was held January 6, 1979, in Long Beach. Smith took rooms for himself, Ben Lewis, Sammie Marshall, some of the MAAS amateur boxers and the entire Muhammad Ali Track Club at the Queen Mary luxury liner hotel. By then, Lewis was fully involved in Harold's business and was helping to organize the meet. He handed out assignments for rooms and helped with the logistics of meals, equipment, travel arrangements and scheduling of events. He had also provided needed funds at the bank by covering continued overdrafts. His justification was simple: it was a necessary evil so that they could all get their heads back above water. Ben did his best to keep a handle on the outgoing money. One expense he did not approve: sending rented limos to Palm Springs to pick up Marvin Gaye and friends. Smith had invited Gaye to run in the celebrity race, but since then the singer had canceled the planned New Year's Eve concert, claiming he was having too many problems with the bankruptcy court. Lewis had seen all those $50 and $100 tickets they had planned to sell flying right out the window. "Gaye didn't do us any favors," Ben told Harold, "so why should we do something for him? If he comes and runs in the race, I'll trip him as he comes around the track." The limos were not sent, and Gaye did not attend the meet.

It was exciting for Ben to be working in the meet instead of just being a spectator like last year. He was sure this was what the bank had in mind when it encouraged its officers to get involved in community activity. What better cause than amateur athletics? Most of the same athletes competed, including Ali, who once again received a nice round of applause for losing the celebrity sprint race in a field that included heavyweight boxers Ken Norton, Mike Weaver and Joe Bugner and singer Tony Orlando. Several thousand people were in attendance, and an NBC Sports film crew recorded the meet for future airing. By the festive atmosphere that surrounded the activities and the celebrations afterward at the hotel, Ben was sure it had been a financial success. That was important, real important.

A week later, as had become his custom, Lewis showed up at Smith's Montana Avenue office after work. That night he had planned to work out with Harold a speedy arrangement to funnel the profits from the track meet into the bank in order to repay the debt without anyone catching on. He hoped that the proceeds from the gate and TV rights would cover the entire debt he was carrying at Beverly Drive. It was what Harold had been promising all along.

Behind a portable partition that was being used to separate Harold's desk from the other activity in the office, Lewis laid it out to his friend. "Here's the total right now," he said, handing Smith a tally.

"That looks about right," Smith said, quickly handing back the slip of paper.

The figure written in ink was $156,000.

"Now, how should—"

"We didn't make that much, Ben."

"What? How much did we make?"

"I'm not sure. I know it cost more than I figured. Anyway, there's a lien on the NBC money." Smith went on to explain that the Canadian manufacturer of the indoor track had filed a lien, claiming additional money was owed them. It was now being worked out by the lawyers.

"Let's make a partial payment," Lewis said, his voice trembling.

"We can't, man. We're short as it is."

"I can't believe it."

"Look, we got a bunch of other things coming up. Money's gonna be coming in to take care of it. Don't worry."

Lewis had been looking forward to this meet as his salvation. Was it really possible that it had made *nothing*? After all Harold's talk? Bitterly disappointed and angry to boot, he quizzed Smith hard for a breakdown of expenses. An hour later, Ben left the office demoralized. The meet had been nothing more than an expensive sideshow which had garnered plenty of publicity but no profit. Something was not right in this business.

It took Lewis several days to get over his depression. He avoided Smith during this time. It was easy for *Harold* to say "don't worry." All he was doing was spending the money. Ben hated having to keep hiding the rising debt total at the bank and remembering to make the crucial rollovers in time. He was living in the shadow of a computerized sword of Damocles ready to come down on him at any second. And all those people—the branch manager, the auditors, Brian Feeley—any of them could stumble across his indiscretions any day. One slip was all it would take. One ticket that didn't get returned in time. A one-digit mistake on an amount. Trouble with the code number. Suppose Miracle Mile changed its code number? He would have no way of knowing it. The pressure was getting to him. He was beginning to crack. He was sleeping fitfully and suffering from stomach pains and headaches. Day by day, he was feeling more isolated at the bank. His loyalty to Wells Fargo had evaporated at an alarming speed, though he still had immense pride in his abilities on the job. The paradox of being a stern taskmaster who counted the tellers' monies while himself misappropriating sizable sums of money was beginning to catch up with his psyche. At work, he felt like the fraud he was. Personally and professionally, he was throwing in his lot with Harold. At an all-important junction in life, he had chosen this path. His plan was to eventually join Harold in the promotions business. He had always been interested in entertainment and was glad to see Harold beginning to move in that direction. If Lewis and Smith Enterprises could make a bundle while allowing him to work in a field he enjoyed, he would have the best of both worlds. But first the embezzled money had to be repaid. He hoped he had taken the right path. If he hadn't, it was already too late.

One question played and replayed in his mind: when would Harold pay back the money?

***

Sitting behind his desk at Miracle Mile, Gene Kawakami also wondered how long it would take Harold to pay him back. First the Gaye concert was canceled—the singer did *not* return the $15,000 advance payment, according to Smith—and then the track meet failed to show a profit. Kawakami was in a real jam. He couldn't stop carrying Smith now. The roof would come down on him the moment he did. He was still convinced that there was money to be made here. But in order for Smith to make it, he needed even more funding, this time for a January 1979 boxing show that was guaranteed the usual $40,000 in TV money. Kawakami was backed into a corner. He had no more personal money to lend. And if any more loans to Smith or his businesses appeared on the branch's books, he could get caught exceeding his loan limit. He was in a dilemma.

There was only one way out, even though actually it would put him in even deeper. He reached into a drawer and took out a printed card for opening a new checking account. Casually looking around to see that no one was watching, he filled it out. Under customer's name he wrote "Ken Kato" and signed on the signature line. A few days later, he approved an unsecured $50,000 loan to L. O. Banks. Like Kato, Banks was a phony name. Kawakami knew how to prepare the loan document so that it looked good and would not be questioned by the auditors. The L. O. Banks loan was disbursed to the Kato account. The next step was simple: from the Kato account he purchased several cashier's checks. The money eventually found its way to clear some of Harold Smith's debts.

Kawakami was too smart to let Smith know the truth about where the latest $50,000 had come from. He did not want Smith to know that he had compromised himself for fear that Smith might never repay the loan. After all, what kind of trouble could Smith be in for falling delinquent on an illegal loan? And how could Kawakami possibly report him? So Kawakami made everything look as legitimate as possible. He told Smith the new money came from several "outside investors" he had lined up. Kawakami said these people were willing to loan Smith money for a 20 percent return on their investment. Smith thought this was just fine. Kawakami saw it as a way to accomplish two things: to achieve continued financing for Smith and to make money himself. He planned to keep the 20 percent interest in return for all his own time and trouble when Smith made repayment.

Late in January, Smith brought Kawakami $15,000 cash. Smith said it was money from the November fight which had finally been released after the squabble with the vendors had been ironed out. Kawakami deposited the money into the Kato account and used it to make interest-only payments on all the outstanding loans in various names. But now the January track meet proceeds were tied up. The money that came in was always too little and too late. They just kept slipping deeper into a bottomless pit.

It did not take a financial wizard to see that there wasn't much profit potential in amateur boxing or track meets. Gates were sparse and the fees for TV rights not enough to cover expenses. One show after another had failed to turn a profit. Smith was spending more money than he was taking in. By now, Kawakami had closed all Smith's business checking accounts in order to halt the endless overdrafts. He allowed just one personal account in the names of Harold and Barbara Smith to remain open in order for the couple to pay personal bills.

Kawakami was positive that promoting professional fights would prove much more lucrative. No doubt people would be more willing to shell out money to see two capable pros slugging it out for a title or the right to meet the division champion than would be to see unknown amateurs chase each other around the ring, even if Ali was there to make a ringside appearance (something Smith constantly tried to get the Champ to do). But Smith was not quite ready to make the jump to the pros yet and do battle with the likes of Don King, then the preeminent promoter of big-time boxing events. That would come soon, but first Smith needed to attract more quality boxers and season those amateurs he already had fighting for him. In the meantime, what was needed immediately was a major money-making event.

When Smith approached Kawakami with the plan for a tour of Australia with the amateur boxing team, the banker liked the sound of it immediately. All but guaranteeing its success was the participation of Ali. Smith said the Champ had promised to fight an exhibition bout in Sydney. They were now lining up Joe Bugner, the British Commonwealth champion, as his opponent. It would be a nontitle fight, say six rounds, fought in sweats and headgear. Putting the U.S. and British champs in the same ring in Australia even for an exhibition seemed to hold promise for a good gate. The rest of the card would be filled out with the Muhammad Ali Boxing Club taking on an Australian team, with national pride at stake. If the "Down Under" tour was successful, a world tour could follow.

"We'll cover four cities," Smith explained. "I've got a $200,000 letter of credit from an Australian promoter, and NBC has said they'll pay a hundred and twenty thousand for the TV rights."

"You've got a contract with NBC?"

"No, it's a verbal agreement. I need a loan of fifty grand to make this work."

Kawakami shook his head. There was no way. That was too much money. He couldn't possibly swing it. "I can't give you any more money," he said. "I'm at the limit with the bank's funds and my own." There was a limit even to the phony loans he would allow.

Smith nodded understandingly. "I'll get it somewhere else. No problem."

But Kawakami had an idea for saving Smith some money. "You should incorporate as a nonprofit corporation so you won't have to pay taxes. Otherwise, you'll get hit by the U.S. and Australia. I'll talk to some tax attorneys if you want."

"That's a good idea. Go ahead. Realistically, I think we can make a million on the tour."

"That'll clear the boards," Kawakami said. He could pay off the $150,000 in outstanding loans and pocket $10,000. And there'd be plenty of money left over to finance other promotions. Yes, this was just the kind of event they needed.

On January 15, 1979, Muhammad Ali Amateur Sports, Inc., was incorporated as a nonprofit organization under California State law. The president of the new firm was Harold J. Smith. The vice president was Gene Kawakami. The secretary/treasurer was Barbara Smith. The corporate attorney was Ed Franklin—Harold had met him six or seven months ago through travel agent Tom Bole. At the time Franklin had been a member of a large Los Angeles law firm. Now, starting his own practice, Franklin was hired by Smith to handle the necessary legal documentation for the incorporation.

Ironically, at the same time he was officially joining Smith's team, Kawakami closed the last remaining account of Smith's at Miracle Mile. It was a bold move, but he had little choice. Trying to control Harold's expenditures, professional and personal, had become an impossible task. It was like trying to ride the surf away from the beach. He expected Smith to be mad at him, but, surprisingly, the promoter wasn't. In fact, he even invited Kawakami to Australia—all expenses paid, of course. Kawakami was surprised by the invitation and was not sure whether or not it was a genuine one.

"Can I bring another couple along?" he asked, half jokingly, testing Smith.

"Sure, no problem."

As soon as the boxing business started making money, everything would be better. Smith and Kawakami were in agreement on that. The banker felt he was acting with more fiscal prudence. He had put a lid on the debts—all of them—and stopped the bad check writing. Though it was clearly a potential conflict for Kawakami to serve on the board of a company that was a loan customer, such an indiscretion was the least of his worries right now. Foremost in his mind was helping Smith become successful and getting some money back into the coffers of Wells Fargo Bank—not to mention his own pockets.

He hoped the Australia tour would be their redemption.

* * *

Ben Lewis was looking forward to the "Down Under" tour for his own not dissimilar reasons. Smith had kept him from getting into a deeper funk over the escalating debt by selling him on the big tour that would include New Zealand in addition to Australia. One January night when Ben stopped at the MAAS office after work, Harold invited him to come along on the tour.

"How long will it be?" Lewis asked.

"About two weeks."

"I can't be away from the bank that long. If I don't keep rolling over all those branch settlement tickets, the computer will put out a tracer. I can't be gone more than ten days."

"Yeah, we sure can't let that happen," Smith said, scratching his head. "Why don't you come just for the Australia swing. Skip New Zealand. We'll make sure you're back in a week."

Lewis said he thought he could do that without causing any damage at the bank. It would be his first vacation since the rollovers had started. He really didn't like leaving the bank now, but he didn't want to miss this trip. It was going to be great for the amateur team, Smith had said, and the two of them could make some extra money producing and selling souvenirs through Lewis and Smith Enterprises. That sounded fine with Ben. He came up with a list of proposed items, including pens, balloons and caps, all carrying the Ali name. He wasn't opposed to making some money for himself. But the expectation that the tour would bring in a potful to finally repay the bank was really what kept him going.

Ben was relieved that the debt total had not risen much since the track meet. Sure, he'd cashed a few checks for Harold and his associates—$500 here, $150 there, $360 to buy carpeting—but it was pretty much nickel-and-dime stuff. Toward the end of January, Smith came in and said he needed a new bank account. He was going to use it to hold all the money for the Australian tour, Harold explained. There was some of the money he didn't want in his name or MAAS's name for tax reasons. Ben thought there was no problem opening an account now. Beverly Drive had a new manager—Bob Smith had replaced Joel Ziskind—and it had been long enough that several other employees who might have recalled Smith's overdraft problems had been assigned to new offices. The new account was not in Harold's name but was called Bodak Promotions. Though he named the account after Chuck Bodak—a former Ali trainer now employed at Smith's Santa Monica gym training amateur fighters—Smith was the real signatory on the account.

Also in January, Sammie Marshall came into the branch for a visit. Ben spotted him standing at the customer service window chatting with some bank employees. He went over to say hello and find out how the boxing business was treating him.

"By the way," Marshall said in passing, "has Harold taken care of that stuff?"

Ben knew what he was talking about and couldn't believe it. Didn't Sammie know that he was carrying Harold for nearly $200,000? Wasn't Harold keeping Sammie informed about the growing debt? Wasn't Sammie asking Harold for details? Ben had assumed all along that Sammie knew how things had escalated since he had left the bank. The thought had made him feel better about what he was doing because he trusted Sammie's judgment. Sammie wouldn't let him do anything that would get him in trouble. Now it worried Ben that Sammie obviously *didn't* know. But it was not the time or place to brief him on the extent of the deep hole that had been dug at Beverly Drive.

"No," Ben said with concern.

The next time he saw Marshall was on Tuesday, February 13, 1979—a few weeks before the Australia tour was scheduled to begin. For Ben it would prove a strange meeting. Ben had just returned from lunch when the telephone on his desk rang.

"Operations, Lewis."

"Ben, this is Harold. I'm with Sammie. We need to talk to you. We're out in the parking lot."

The parking lot? Ben could picture Harold standing at the pay phone located on a concrete post about thirty feet from the bank's side door, with Sammie next to him. Behind the phone was a pay parking lot used by bank employees and visitors. Why the parking lot? What could be so important or secret that they couldn't discuss it inside the bank?

Lewis knew better than to ask. "I'll be right out," he said.

He nodded to the guard, let himself out the door and locked it behind him. As he approached the two men still standing by the pay phone, Lewis knew from their downcast expressions that this was not going to be pleasant.

"Hey, Ben," Sammie said softly.

"We've got a big problem," Harold said dejectedly. "We need a favor."

Ben shrugged. There was nothing new about that. He'd been doing favors for Smith for a long time.

"Everything we've worked for is about to go down the tubes," Harold said.

Lewis wasn't sure he'd ever seen Harold so depressed. His voice was lowered, his shoulders slumped. He looked like a man who had lost his best friend. "What do you mean?"

"I mean Australia," Harold said. "Everything we've worked so hard for. Ali's people are threatening to cancel if we don't pay him in advance. Without Ali—if Ali doesn't come—"

"But I thought you arranged for a letter of credit with the Australian promoter," Ben said.

"Not good enough," Smith said. "If we don't pay up front, Ali don't fly."

"How much you need?"

"Two hundred twenty-three thousand."

"Damn, how did you let this happen?" Ben fumed.

"His lawyers got into the act," Smith said, holding his hands palm up in a gesture of helplessness.

Lewis was trying to stay calm, but the panic he felt when he heard the dollar amount wouldn't let him. They wanted him to come up with the money. That's why they were here. The debt to the bank would more than double from $200,000 to almost half a million dollars.

"Goddamn," Ben said softly, more to himself than to the other men. He had no problem completing Harold's unfinished sentences. *Without Ali* the tour would be lost. The amateur fighters alone would not carry the necessary drawing power at the gate. The television people would lose interest. *If Ali doesn't come,* the whole show would have to be canceled. Without Australia—without all the money that could be made down there—Ben could see no way that the bank could be paid off in the immediate future. Maybe never. If he didn't come up with the money for Ali, he'd be stuck carrying $200,000 indefinitely. Whereas if he doubled the ante and got the money, he would have to carry the new total only until the Australia money came in. Repayment would be more sure. But God, how he hated getting in any deeper.

"We really need it," Sammie said.

The fact that Sammie was here asking for the money meant something to Ben. It meant that this was darn serious. Harold alone, well, he might exaggerate about how bad things were. But Sammie was backing him up all the way. Ben knew he had no choice.

"I'll go inside and see what I can do," Ben finally said.

"We'll wait out here," Harold said. His voice had picked up.

Lewis let himself back into the bank and went behind the counter to the operations area. One good thing about such a large branch was that everyone was too busy to notice what anyone else was doing. He took a blank cashier's check out of a drawer and rolled it into a typewriter. He typed out the amount: $223,000. The payee: Muhammad Ali. He slipped the bank copy of the check into the pending file on his desk. He would have to deal with that later, when he would start another chain in the branch settlement system and put through a debit to offset the cashier's check. What difference did one more make? He put the cashier's check in a blank envelope and went back outside.

It had taken all of ten minutes. He had crossed another line. He was committed to the embezzlements for the duration. There would be no backing out now.

Harold was just hanging up the pay phone. Ben handed him the envelope. He wished that Ali and some of the other people could know that it was he—Benjamin Lewis—who was financing this big tour. Not Harold Smith. But that was silly. There was no way they could be told.

"You really saved us," Harold said. "Thanks a lot."

"Thanks," Sammie echoed. "I'm leaving for Australia. Got all kinds of advance work to do. See you there, Ben."

"Yeah," Ben said.

They had turned the tables on him. Now they were feeling good, and he was depressed.

* * *

In Chicago, Mike Phenner replaced the phone receiver. That had been an odd call. He knew that Harold Smith was concerned by the threat of

Ali pulling out of the Australian tour if the Champ's front money wasn't forthcoming. And he could understand why Smith would want to notify him that the money was finally on its way. Phenner had expected the payment to be in the form of a bank letter of credit wired to the Champ's commercial account at the First National Bank of Chicago. That was what he had suggested to Smith. He certainly didn't expect Smith to be personally delivering a *cashier's check*. That was most unusual, yet that's what Smith was doing. The promoter had told him that he had just taken out a loan at Wells Fargo Bank, received a cashier's check and was getting on a plane first thing tomorrow morning. Smith said he would be in Phenner's office late in the afternoon Chicago time.

Phenner had gotten tough with Smith after putting up with several delays. And they had meant what they said: no money in advance, no heavyweight champion of the world. Ali's time and name were too valuable to allow anything else. The payment was considered "earnest money." If Smith canceled the tour, Ali could keep the money. If Ali pulled out of the tour of his own volition, the money would be returned to Smith.

But this flying east with a cashier's check was strange stuff. Was Smith stalling for another twenty-four hours? Before Phenner made a report to Ali, he wanted to be sure. He had asked for the name and phone number of Smith's banker in case verification was necessary. He decided it was. Phenner dialed the Los Angeles number. When a woman answered "Wells Fargo Beverly Drive," Phenner asked to speak to Ben Lewis.

When Lewis came on the line, Phenner identified himself. "Harold Smith just called and told me you had issued a cashier's check to him."

"Yes, that's correct."

"The amount?"

"Two hundred and twenty-three thousand dollars."

"Made out to Muhammad Ali?"

"That's right."

"Will you give me the number, please?"

Lewis put him on hold and then came back with the number of the cashier's check: 45375.

It was the same number Smith had given Phenner on the phone. Everything seemed in order.

"I'm curious, Mr. Lewis, as to why you didn't just wire the money."

"Harold said you wanted cash." On the other end of the line, Lewis was squirming. Wiring the money would have been the logical way. But a wire would have caused too much attention in other departments of the bank and would have required too much justification. He had come up with the money through his familiar branch settlement manipulation. By issuing a cashier's check, the payment stayed in his own arena, where he had better control.

"Well, wired funds are entirely acceptable," Phenner said.

"I just did what my customer wanted."

"Of course. Fine. Thank you, sir."

When Phenner hung up he still was perplexed. But actually, it wasn't his problem. If Harold Smith wanted to waste his time spending a day or two getting on and off planes and delivering money that could have been wired cross-country in a matter of minutes, that was his business. Maybe he was looking for an excuse to come to Chicago.

Phenner was a busy man and had scores of other matters competing for his attention. So after Smith delivered the cashier's check the next day, the lawyer forgot about the curious method of payment. He wouldn't remember it until much later. In the meantime, Phenner called Ali and told him the money was in the bank. Australia was on.

Ali didn't sound surprised. In fact, an excited Veronica had already started packing. After all, Harold Smith had always come through in the past.

CHAPTER SIXTEEN

The "Down Under" tour began on Wednesday, March 13, 1979.

It was Ben Lewis's first trip to Australia, and he was going in style, seated in the first-class compartment of a jumbo jet with a host of celebrities. Muhammad and Veronica Ali. The Champ's corner man Bundini Brown and his lady friend. Heavyweight Joe Bugner and his wife Marlene. Harold and Lee Smith. Actress Cicely Tyson, who had nothing to do with the tour but was headed to Melbourne for the Australian Academy Awards. During the fourteen-hour flight they all became acquainted. Ben got Tyson's autograph, and the actress invited Muhammad and Veronica to attend the awards presentation. Ben was running in fast company.

Traveling in coach class were several other MAAS guests. Gene Kawakami, his wife and the other couple Harold had generously allowed him to bring along. Hilton Nicholson, the former American University sprinter now working as a trainer for MAAS. Tom Peters, a pleasant black man employed as Harold's driver. Dr. Tom Burns, a Michigan physician who served as a sports medicine consultant to MAAS. C. B. Atkins, a longtime hanger-on of Ali's now on the MAAS payroll as a gofer. In all, MAAS was paying the freight for a supporting cast of sixty. Some of them—like "advance man" Sammie Marshall, former Ali sparring partner and ex-WBA World Heavyweight Champion Jimmy Ellis (now a MAAS trainer) and the amateur boxers—were already in Australia awaiting the arrival of the rest of the group.

The day before at the bank Ben had done what he had to do. He rolled over all the branch settlement chains, now totaling nearly half a million dollars. He planned to miss eight banking days and return to work just in time to roll them over again before the computer sent out the dreaded tracers. He was cutting it close but, damn it, he needed a break. Also, he wanted to do whatever he could to see that the Australia tour was a success. A lot was riding on it.

When they arrived at the King's Cross Hotel in Sydney, everyone was in high spirits. As the luggage was being taken to the room and Smith was checking in with his team, Ali asked for company and headed for a limousine. Ben went along; there were six or seven of them in all. Ali told the local driver he wanted something to eat, and the limo pulled away from the hotel.

"I want to go to a place where they won't feed us," Ali said.

"They'll feed you anywhere, Mr. Ali," the helpful driver said.

"Just certain of us. Like the famous ones. But I hear some places don't feed ordinary black folk."

"Well—" The driver cleared his throat. "There are a few places—like that." He was stammering now. "But—they're just dumps and—"

"Let's go there."

The driver waited before he answered. He waited so long Ben wondered if he was going to refuse the order. Perhaps he was just hoping that someone would tell him the Champ was pulling his leg. When no one did, he finally said, "Yes, sir."

Ali told everyone his plan. Once they got to the restaurant, a couple of them would go inside and try to get service. He would wait in the car. Who wanted to go inside?

Ben volunteered without thinking. Then he realized that this could be real trouble. At the very least it could develop into a major controversy that would certainly be exploited by the local press. At the worst, one or more of them might get shot by some redneck who had an aversion to pushy blacks, whether or not they were in the company of the heavyweight champion of the world. Hell, Ali himself might get blown away. They could touch off a major race war. Ben silently chastised himself for not trying to talk the Champ out of it. Like it or not, he was now along for the ride.

Ali continued excitedly, explaining that when the "inside men" were refused service they were to come out and get him. He would then stroll in, surprise everyone and set the place straight. He'd been waiting a long time to do something like this.

The driver kept looking back in the rearview mirror at his passengers in the backseat, obviously worried about the predicament he found himself in.

Several minutes later, as they reached the outskirts of town and the city lights dimmed in the background, Ali suddenly became quiet. Ben looked over and saw that he had fallen asleep. It struck him as odd because the Champ had been so hyper and talkative just a minute or so ago. Of course, it had been a long trip on the plane. Maybe that was it.

Ali stirred. "Not now," he said, his words slurred by fatigue. "Take me back. I want to sleep."

The release of tension in the car was felt by all as the driver made an immediate U-turn and headed back to the hotel.

Early the next morning, Ben went jogging in the rain with some of the MAAS boxers. He enjoyed the comradeship among the young men. They all had high hopes and big dreams to go along with their strong bodies. They wanted to be just like their mentor and revered champion: Muhammad Ali. They wanted to have money to buy homes for their parents. They wanted to make it to the top, marry their sweethearts and show other young brothers from the poor side of town that it could still be done. Some of them would make it and some wouldn't. But they were all being given a fighting chance by Muhammad Ali Amateur Sports, by Harold Smith and, yes, by Benjamin Lewis. If it hadn't been for Ben's help at the bank, MAAS would have shut its doors months ago. These young men would have been back home standing in unemployment lines instead of preparing for fights in faraway Australia. That thought allowed Ben to feel important and needed. He liked that. A mile down the road, he pulled a leg muscle and hitched a ride back to the hotel with two attractive women. Ben had learned a long time ago that in every defeat there were small victories.

Walking through the lobby, Ben was stopped by a radio news reporter who spotted his "Ali" warm-up suit. Anxious to interview someone, *anyone,* in the Champ's retinue, the reporter corralled him. Ben agreed to answer a few questions into a tape recorder. Harold usually did this sort of thing, but he evidently was still sleeping and, anyway, it was all for the common good. Bundini Brown had even appeared on a late-night talk show last night, though he was obviously tipsy from all the free drinks on the flight.

The reporter flipped on the tape recorder. "Is Muhammad Ali in good shape?" he asked.

"The Champ's ready to go six rounds with Bugner," Ben said, trying to be as diplomatic as possible. Truthfully, Ali was heavy. His weight always shot up when he wasn't on a rigid training schedule and diet. But this wasn't a title fight. It was only an exhibition.

"What do you think your fighters' chances are against the Australian team?"

"The Ali Boxing Team is expertly trained and coached. We've got some hungry young men."

"Thank you, Mr.—" The reporter had forgotten to ask his name before they began.

"Lewis. Benjamin Lewis."

"And your position?"

"Friend and—advisor to the team."

At the elevator, Ben was surprised to see Ali step out alone. He was suited up for jogging and looked like any other boxer ready for road-work. A bath towel was wrapped around his neck and stuck inside his sweatshirt. A wool cap was pulled down over his ears. He had already started bouncing on the balls of his feet and jabbing at imaginary targets in the air.

"Did you see Bundini on TV last night?" the Champ asked. "I heard he was on."

"Yeah, I did."

"I told him not to do it 'cause he'd been drinking. How did he do?"

"He wasn't that bad. The host kept baiting him. Bundini asked for a glass of water, so they got him one. There was this big dog on the set, and it started drinking out of his glass. Bundini pretended not to see it and kept drinking from the glass. The TV guy said, 'You know my dog drank out of your glass?' Bundini came right back with, 'Dog spelled backwards is God. God just drank out of there.' "

Ben laughed, but Ali seemed to get angrier.

"Wait till I see him," the Champ hollered, his eyes flashing in anger and his fists now cutting through the air so fast that they were lost in blurs. "I told him not to go on! I told him!" He trotted away, mumbling to himself.

Ben had never seen Ali so perturbed. No way would he want to be in Bundini's shoes. He watched the Champ hit the street, shadow-box momentarily, then start out in the rain, running to an inner beat that needed no accompaniment.

Lewis now had a new worry: the rain.

The Sydney boxing show, with the main event of the tour—the Ali-Bugner exhibition—was slated to be held at an outdoor stadium.

***

It did not let up. Not for an hour or a single minute. It was one of the heaviest rains in recent memory. The ring was covered by a make-shift canvas roof, but the winds blew the downpour underneath it. Everything was soaked. Because the tour was on such a tight schedule here and in several other cities, there could be no rain delays. The show must go on.

Advance ticket sales had been a disappointment. In fact, most of the advance work was a letdown. Logistics were a mess, local business and banking contacts almost nonexistent. Adding to the problems on the Australian end were the usual woes resulting from Harold Smith's inability to plan ahead. He always put everything off until the last minute, a bothersome trait that was to plague him throughout his career as a boxing promoter. As a matter of necessity because so many of its people had failed to do their jobs, MAAS was relying heavily on local Sydney-based promoters to carry off this tour.

The hope was that the real money would come from the people who showed up at the gate on the night of the fight. But the large crowd did not materialize in the inclement weather. Ben thought there were no more than three or four thousand hardy souls sitting under umbrellas in the downpour. Marshall later claimed there were as many as ten thousand paid spectators. Maybe the embarrassed Sammie, trying to save face, counted each head more than once. Whichever number was right, there were tens of thousands of empty seats in the stadium—seats which Harold Smith had hoped would be filled by screaming Aussies rooting on Bugner, the long-inactive British Commonwealth Champ, and their own national team. But the cheering horde was too smart. It stayed home out of the rain that night.

Ben noticed from under his own umbrella that there were no television cameras around. He had not bothered to ask Harold for specifics about the TV deal. He had assumed it would include both Australia and U.S. coverage. But now he wondered whether there was going to be any coverage at all. How much would it cost them in lost revenue if the TV people stayed home too? The expenses incurred in bringing the entourage over here had to be more than the money collected from this sparse audience. Where was all the profit going to come from? The first amateur bout had already started with two bantamweights going at each other for three rounds. The plan was to present all the amateurs first, saving the stars for last. Glancing nervously at the endless rows of empty seats, Ben went looking for Harold.

"Are we in trouble?" he asked when he found Harold.

"We'll be okay," Smith said.

After three bouts, the rain was coming down heavier than ever, and the ring was waterlogged. Fearful that if they put off the main event the weather might force its cancellation altogether, it was decided to bring on Ali and Bugner. If they didn't show these soaked spectators the big guns, they might see a riot—albeit a small one.

Wearing headgear and a plastic warm-up suit, Ali looked fat. The only person who moved slower in the ring that day was Joe Bugner. They played patty-cake with the oversized gloves for three rounds before the show was stopped.

The promoters wisely left it up to the local police to be the spoilsports. But it was obvious to all how dangerous it was for the fighters to be performing in the slippery ring. There were no protests from the crowd. In fact, everyone seemed grateful to be able to get in out of the rain.

Cold and wet, Ben still felt a nagging uneasiness as he headed back to the hotel to take a hot shower. For the sake of them all—Harold, MAAS, Wells Fargo, himself—he dearly hoped things would get better after Sydney.

* * *

"Here, hold this for me," Harold Smith said as he handed Ben the unsealed white envelope.

"What is it?"

"Cash. I'm carrying too much."

"How much is it?"

"Ten grand."

"What am I supposed to do with it?"

"Put it in your pocket and don't say nothin."

Ben pocketed the envelope. The other passengers on the flight from Australia began standing and reaching in the overhead compartments for their baggage. The plane had just touched down at Honolulu International Airport and pulled up at the international terminal. It was March 22. Harold was coming home a week early, leaving the rest of the MAAS team to carry out the remainder of the tour. The last eight days had been grueling, and Ben was looking forward to making the connection to Los Angeles and arriving home in time for a late dinner and needed shut-eye. He had some important work to do at the bank the next day.

At U.S. Customs, Ben filled out the standard declaration and handed it to Customs Inspector Sharon A. Knee. The "No" box was checked next to Question #11: "Are you or any family member carrying over $5,000 in monetary instruments ... ?"

As part of the usual questioning, the inspector reiterated the query. "Are you carrying more than five thousand dollars?" she asked.

"No," Ben said.

He had lied on the form, and he had just lied again. Why? It was a standard declaration, simple and to the point. He might have had to pay a duty on the funds, but, primarily, he knew it was designed to notify law enforcement agencies in case the person was a major criminal. Why should he feel guilty? Why had he lied? *Don't declare it,* Harold had advised. Harold must have had his reasons.

"Exactly how much do you have, sir?"

Ben hesitated. He felt the customs inspector boring into him with an icy stare. She undoubtedly saw his discomfort, sensed his nervousness. She *knew* that he was lying. "Five thousand dollars," he said. He couldn't very well say five dollars when he had an envelope stuffed full of money in his pants' pocket.

Harold walked by as if he didn't know Ben.

The inspector gave him another form to fill. Form #4790: "Report of International Transportation of Currency or Monetary Instruments." He filled out the first section, name and address and so forth. But he froze when he got to the bottom section. It asked exactly how much money he was carrying. He put the pen down on the counter.

"Look, I don't know *exactly* how much I have," he said. He reached into his pocket and took out the envelope. "Here, you count it."

Inspector Knee was surprised to see the large stack of bills. "Is this less than five thousand dollars?" she asked automatically.

Ben shrugged.

She flipped through the bills. They were all hundreds. No way was this under $5,000. The inspector activated the red light above her station to summon a supervisor.

My God, Ben thought, they've caught me lying.

When the supervisor arrived, Lewis and his luggage were taken into a search room. He was frisked, and his bags were opened and thoroughly inspected.

"Listen, I'm a banker," he said in desperation. He wanted them to know he wasn't a crook. He wanted them to know he was a law-abiding citizen. "I'm a bank operations officer in Beverly Hills for Wells Fargo."

"Then you should be familiar with the currency reporting laws of the Treasury Department," the inspector replied coolly.

"Yes, I am," he said, his voice barely audible. "I just didn't have time to count the money." Why the hell did he tell them he worked for Wells Fargo? Now the government might notify the bank, and he could lose his job. If he lost his job now and those rollovers were discovered—he couldn't even form the next thought. It was too painful.

The money was counted and confiscated. It was exactly $10,000.

Ben started telling the truth. He explained that he was returning from a business trip to Australia, where he and his partner had engaged in a promotional venture. His business partner, Harold Smith—"that guy right over there"—had just handed him this money as they were getting off the plane. It had caught him off guard. It was all a big mistake. He was sorry.

He was relieved to see the inspectors handling this as a bureaucratic matter rather than slapping handcuffs on him as a smuggler. He was finally instructed to fill out two more forms. On one he was told to write in his own hand "I, Benjamin Lewis, hereby accept responsibility for not properly declaring currency which I was carrying." He gladly did so. The other pertained to a penalty he would have to pay for failing to disclose the money. It amounted to $1,075 and was subtracted from the $10,000 before it was returned to him. No problem, take all you want. Next he was advised that the U.S. Attorney in Honolulu would be notified of his act, and it would be up to that office as to whether or not he would be criminally prosecuted.

The words *"criminally prosecuted"* hit him with the impact of a sledge-hammer. Would they actually file charges? As Ben finally cleared customs, he realized what a mess Harold had gotten him into.

(Prosecution was eventually declined by an Assistant U.S. Attorney in Honolulu because "the circumstances of the case failed to disclose any evidence of criminal activity or intent." Ben never heard anything more about the incident.)

* * *

The bad news came the following weekend.

"I just got a call from Sydney," Harold told Ben. "One of the local promoters took off with two hundred grand of our money."

"What?"

"That's right. Just disappeared."

"Where'd he go?"

Harold shrugged. "Who knows."

"Where's the rest of our money?"

"That was it."

"That was our entire profit? I don't believe it. How much did we make in ticket sales total?"

"Don't know. The guy had the figures."

"There's—no profit?"

"That was it. Hey, two hundred grand wasn't bad."

"Wasn't bad? We don't have anything."

"Not our fault."

Ben lowered his head. "It never is."

CHAPTER SEVENTEEN

Teri Godwin Key and her lover, Tony Key, arrived in Los Angeles during the opening days of 1979. Driving out from their native North Carolina, they were determined to make a go of it in the big city. Tony wanted to pursue his music career, and Teri just wanted to be happy and have enough money to feel secure. Traveling with them was Teri's young daughter from a previous marriage.

They had more than one rude awakening. The cost of living was higher than they had expected. The job market was much tighter than they had figured. The housing situation was almost intolerable—sky-high rents for what could only be classified as urban dumps. They had expected so much more. California was supposed to be the land of opportunity. The prejudice they encountered as an interracial couple was nothing new, but they had hoped it would be less than in the South. Again they were disappointed. The little money Teri had managed to put aside for the move dwindled at a frightening rate. They stayed in a motel while trying to find jobs and a moderately priced apartment that would take children. They failed on both counts and, rapidly running out of money, Teri decided to send her daughter back to North Carolina to live with her parents and finish out the school year. If things didn't improve soon, Teri and Tony would be sleeping in the car and going without meals, a fate she did not want her daughter to suffer.

Answering a classified advertisement for an assistant manager position at a large Beverly Hills apartment complex, Teri interviewed for the job and ten days later was hired. The salary was minimal. The major benefit was that they got a free apartment to live in. When they began moving in and the manager saw Tony for the first time, Teri lost her job. The manager explained that the owner of the building did not allow blacks in his building. The lady seemed truly sorry and suggested that they contact Harold Smith. He was a track promoter, the manager explained, and he had once put up some athletes in the complex for a short time. The owner was not pleased at the time about having blacks in residence but had kept quiet when he found out Muhammad Ali was their sponsor. "Mr. Smith is a nice man," the manager said. "Maybe he can help you folks get settled."

By then, Teri and Tony had no money and little choice but to look up this Smith fellow. They drove to the Santa Monica address the manager had given them. While Teri waited in the car, Tony went in and talked to Harold. Nothing was forthcoming that day—Harold told Tony to be back in touch in a day or two—so Teri and Tony called the county welfare agency, seeking a place to stay and a hot meal. They were put up in a fleabag downtown hotel that had no hot water. The next day, Tony went down the block to a bar and sipped a glass of beer for a couple of hours so he could watch the Super Bowl on television. Teri tried to sleep but couldn't for counting all the cockroaches climbing the walls. It was the most horrible place she had ever been. Lying on a smelly mattress, she feared they had made a bad mistake moving West. Later in the evening, Tony called Harold, who said for them to come right over to his office. Luckily there was just enough gas left in the car for the drive.

As they walked in the door, the first thing Teri noticed was the aroma of a good meal. On top of a nearby desk was an incredible spread. Barbecued chicken and ribs, corn on the cob with melted butter, french fries, several kinds of hot and cold salads. To her eyes and growling stomach, it was a feast to behold. She wanted nothing more than to dive into the food. Yet when Harold came over and invited them to partake, her pride would not let her so easily admit to hunger. "Not right now, thank you," she said, trying to appear nonchalant.

Several people were sitting around the office eating off paper plates. Casual introductions took place. A portly Sammie Marshall. A business-like Gene Kawakami. A tall Ed Franklin. Lee Smith and her cute little boy, John. Teri was delighted to see that Harold had a white wife. Only another interracial couple could fully appreciate everything they had been going through the past few weeks. Harold told Teri and Tony to sit down at a desk in the back of the room and wait for him.

Harold returned with a plate full of food and a glass of champagne. "So tell me about what's been going on with you," he said to Teri.

"Well," Tony began, "as I—"

"Be quiet," Harold said a little harshly. "I want to hear her version. Go ahead, honey."

The thought occurred to Teri that Harold would be comparing their two stories. The one Tony told him the other day as she waited in the car and the one she was about to tell him. She only hoped Tony had told the truth because that was what she was going to do. She had never been able to lie and wasn't about to start now. She told Harold everything in detail, right up to and including the cockroaches.

"What kind of skills do you have?" he asked when she was finished.

"I've been a receptionist," Teri said.

"Would you be interested in helping out in the office here?"

"Sure, I'd be happy to."

"Okay. I'm not forgetting you, Tony. As soon as we get you settled, I'll see what I can do to help your music career. I know lots of people in this town."

"Great," Tony said, grinning. "I'd sure like that."

Harold reached into his pocket and took out a folded greenback. He handed it to Teri. She didn't dare look at the denomination. Five or ten dollars would be fine. They could buy coffee, milk, a couple of hamburgers.

"Now, we've got to get you out of that welfare dump," Harold said. "I'm going to have someone drive you over to a nice place near the beach. You'll stay there as my guests. In two or three days I'll help you find an apartment. Don't worry about working right away, Teri. Get plenty of food and rest. I'll be in touch and let you know when I want you to start."

Teri was about ready to cry. This man's generosity seemed to have no bounds. She managed a feeble "thank you" and added, "You—just don't know how much this means."

"I know," Harold said, his voice solemn. "I been down on my luck a few times myself. Don't worry. Everything's gonna be fine now."

Outside, Teri looked at the bill. It was a fifty. She had the idea right then that her fortunes were about to change.

From her first day at work at MAAS, Teri was treated nicely by everyone in the office except Sammie Marshall. She found him irritable and difficult to get along with most of the time. One day Harold told her that Marshall had complained about her not showing him enough respect. "I only show people respect who deserve it," she had replied unflinchingly. Harold warned her to "watch out" for Sammie because "he wants me to fire you." Teri guessed that Sammie resented her for doing some of the work he had previously done. Maybe she was even doing it better. She knew only one way to work: always do her best. If that meant showing Marshall up at times, then that was his problem. Her loyalty to Harold was unquestioned and her willingness to work long hours unmatched by anyone else in the office.

She started out answering the phones and helping around the office. "Is there anyone you don't want to talk to?" she asked her first day. "I'll just tell them you're in a meeting."

Harold said there were two people he was trying to avoid at the moment: Gene Kawakami with Wells Fargo and a guy from Telstar Travel. At the time, Harold had been planning the Australia trip. One day he asked Teri if she would like to go. She said sure. He said he needed her marriage license for a passport. On this point, he pushed hard. "Are you sure you're married?" he asked more than once. It was the only lie she ever told Harold. And actually it was only half a lie. She considered Tony her common-law husband—she had even taken his name. It was nobody's business whether or not they had ever stood up for an official marriage ceremony. She had a feeling, though, that it was important to her employer-employee relationship with Harold for him to keep thinking that she was legally unavailable. Teri kept putting him off on the marriage license that she could never produce until Harold, who she guessed might have been intending for her to stay home all along, said she was more valuable manning the office in his absence.

From the beginning, Teri got along well with Lee. Harold's wife began confiding in her the details of marriage that usually only intimate friends hear. She complained when Harold didn't make love to her and even about the intensity of his passion when he did. Lee voiced her suspicions that Harold was playing around with other women. At the time, Teri had seen no evidence of it and told Lee so. Sure, there were lots of pretty young women hanging around Harold all the time, but he always made a point of telling Teri there was "nothing between" him and any of them. "I'm just doing what I can to help these girls out," he would say. At the time, Teri had no reason to disbelieve him. After all, he had helped her with no strings attached.

Of all the other people working in Smith's operation, Teri liked Ben Lewis the best. If Tony wasn't in the picture, Ben would have been the only man at MAAS she would have been interested in dating. He was so nice, a real gentleman, and always looked sharp. He came into the office almost every evening, and he was there on most of the Saturdays that she had to work. He seemed so conscientious.

By the time Harold returned from the Australia tour, Teri had assumed many of the logistical and record-keeping functions of the business, and he was relying more on her every week. She picked up an early warning that things had not gone right on the "Down Under" tour when Harold came home griping about the "lousy job" Lee had done handling the advertising for the tour. Teri had already recognized a troublesome tendency in Harold. When things went wrong, Lee got blamed. When things went right, he took the credit. But it had been Teri's experience that such an imbalance was not uncommon in a marriage. Men often blamed their wives. That was just one little mark against a man who otherwise treated everybody generously and with apparent concern for their well-being.

As always, there was another side to the "Down Under" story. Lee blamed the problems in Australia on Marshall. She told Teri that Sammie had spent his days there touring the countryside in a rented limo, acting like a visiting dignitary, and his nights shacked up at the hotel with his girlfriend. Much of the legwork critical to a major promotion simply did not get done.

Within a few days of Harold's return, Teri answered the phone and it was a man who said he was calling from Australia. The line crackled with static. She put the faraway voice on hold and buzzed Harold, who picked it up in his office. Later, Harold came out and told her angrily that the man—an Australian boxing promoter—had taken off with their money. For a moment it puzzled her. Why would someone call and announce that he had embezzled money? But there were some other things about the boxing business that were equally strange, so she did not question it. She had never even been to a live boxing match and wasn't too anxious to do so. The only boxing she had even watched on TV was Ali-Spinks II and some of the 1976 Olympic competition from Montreal. The sport struck her as brutal.

Teri had worked in office settings before, and this one was much different. Harold would accept someone's call in the morning and refuse to take it in the afternoon. He would put off virtually all decisions until the last possible moment, causing his staff fits of nervousness and bouts of pressure-cooker work. Everything was rushed through with no apparent organization. There were many hangers-on—people who didn't really *do* anything other than stand around and get in the way or run an occasional errand for Harold. It seemed Harold gave these people jobs and money simply because he wanted a lot of people around him. What shocked Teri the most was the amount of cash that was around all the time. She knew that most businesses paid their bills by check and most businessmen used credit cards for expenses. Not Harold. It was not uncommon for him to get stuck at the track on a Friday and call Teri for her to cash a $30,000 or $40,000 check at the bank. This was money he needed for the weekend, he would explain, to close a fight deal or go to Vegas or show a visiting fight manager and his boxer a good time. After cashing the check Teri would not infrequently receive a call from Harold instructing her to give Houston McTear or some other athlete a few thousand bucks. She always kept detailed records—how much went out to whom. When she finally placed the money in Harold's hands, she never once saw him count it. Either he trusted her implicitly or he was careless with money.

One of the few things she knew about sports in general was the prohibition against amateur athletes receiving money. Like most Americans, she had heard the sad story of Jim Thorpe, the splendid Indian runner who, because he'd played semipro baseball, had all his Olympic medals taken away. The Amateur Athletic Union was firm: athletes who received payment for their athletic services were not amateurs. What was going on at MAAS clearly was in direct violation of that credo. Payoffs were flagrant. Harold supplied apartments, cars, clothes, travel and a regular allowance to his amateur boxers. If a boxer wanted to go home for a holiday, his round-trip ticket was paid. If a young man wanted his East Coast girlfriend flown out for a visit, she would come at MAAS's expense. Harold gave them almost anything they asked for. He wanted to keep them happy. He wanted their loyalty. They would make him famous when they swept to victory in the Olympics against the tough Cuban and Soviet boxers. Then they would all turn professional at the same time and hit it big.

The first time Teri met Ali was when he came in just before leaving for the Australia tour. By then she had already spoken to him a few times over the phone on behalf of Harold. The second time she saw Ali was a couple of months later when he came in to discuss an intriguing proposal by Texas oilman Kyle McAllister, who wanted to employ Ali as a representative to deal with oil-rich Muslim countries. The theory was that the most famous Muslim in the world would be able to get concessions out of the nationalistic leaders that no other Westerner could obtain.

Teri couldn't help but notice that Harold was just as nervous this time around as he had been before Ali's last visit. He flitted around the office making sure everything was spick-and-span, moving chairs around until he was finally satisfied with the seating arrangement. He warned Teri that there could be no smoking around the Champ. She could not even light up in the office but would have to do all her smoking outside.

Ali walked in with Veronica. After introductions, Veronica left to do some shopping. Harold led Ali and McAllister back to his desk. Ali asked for a Coke, so Teri got drinks for everyone. It was a strange discussion. Ali acted dumb on the subject of oil. "What do you need all this oil for?" and questions like that. Teri had a feeling he was either toying with the oilman or simply trying to figure out where the Texan was coming from. In either case, nothing was resolved. McAllister invited Ali and Smith to visit his ranch and left the office. (Neither ever visited the ranch. Despite gifts of cowboy hats and boots for both Ali and Smith, which kept arriving for the next several weeks, the business arrangement was never finalized. Smith, however, bragged to several people about his pending "big oil deal.")

Ali spotted a pack of cigarettes on Teri's desk and came over to her.

"Teri, light me a cigarette," he whispered.

She looked at him in surprise. "Champ, you don't smoke."

"Just light it and hand it to me behind my back."

Teri did as she was told, surreptitiously passing the cigarette to Ali sitting at an adjacent desk. He sneaked a puff and had the expression of a little kid who had tasted a forbidden treat just before dinner.

Harold walked by and spotted the smoke. He looked crestfallen. "Did you give him that cigarette, Teri?"

"Well, he asked me for it. I wasn't going to tell him no."

"That's okay, Harold," Ali said. "You know I don't do this very often."

Nancy Carter, an attractive black woman, arrived at the office. Teri realized from comments made by Smith and others that Nancy and the Champ were previously acquainted. She plopped down in Ali's lap, and they smooched openly.

Teri chuckled at Ali's childish innocence. This famous man was flesh and blood like anyone else. He had his strengths and weaknesses. Right now he was focusing all his powerful persuasion on a single object of desire, and he seemed to be trying to talk the lady on his lap into something. Finally he must have convinced her because they left together in the limo that had been waiting outside.

If there had been a mirror on her desk Teri might have looked in it now and marveled. The new "her" was doing well. She had a hard time believing how much her luck had changed in such a short time. It hadn't been that long since she didn't know where her next meal was going to come from. Now she was making more money—$200 clear a week, not including the extra cash bonuses Harold periodically gave her—and having more fun than ever before in her life. There was always something exciting happening around Harold Smith. Big trips and events being planned. Famous athletes and entertainers coming through the door. She was in the company of money and success, and she liked it.

California was turning out to be the promised land after all.

CHAPTER EIGHTEEN

Muhammad Ali sat at stage center behind a long table littered with microphones. Harold Smith sat next to him, looking smug. This was the official opening of the rented Santa Monica gymnasium, where many of Smith's fighters had been training for months.

The gym had been in rough shape when they first moved in. During workout lulls, everyone lent a hand cleaning, sanding, painting and polishing. There was a communal pride exhibited by all. This was their home, and they were proud of it. Few outsiders were made to feel welcome here. Ben Lewis was an exception. In turn, he rolled up his sleeves and helped every chance he got. When the clean-up project was completed, shiny new workout equipment was installed and the press and public were invited to the ceremonial grand opening.

In all, there were a few dozen media representatives, from television and radio stations, newspapers and magazines, together with another forty or fifty interested persons. The fighters were the young ones with bulging arm muscles and thin waists. The trainers were the older ones with thinning hair, leathery faces and bulbous noses. The rest of the ever-growing entourage came in all sizes and types. Ben was there, sitting with the boxers and proud to be a part of this classy operation that had such lofty goals.

Before giving Ali the floor, Smith explained to the press that all of the amateur boxers were required to attend college and most had enrolled at Santa Monica College. This was an important part of the MAAS program, he said, so the young men would be prepared for life outside the ring when their careers were over. It was a laudable goal, and the reporters, duly impressed, scribbled in their notepads or cued their camera crews.

The gymnasium had the look of money. It was a first-class training facility. Most in attendance assumed the backing had come from Ali. And why shouldn't they? The place had his name on it. He certainly had the money to spend. He had made more money in his career than any professional fighter—arguably any professional athlete—in history. And he had always been known for helping less fortunate people. It would not be uncharacteristic for him to have taken these young boxers under his wing. Only three people in the room actually knew the source of the money. But they were keeping quiet. They didn't tell anyone that Ali was himself getting paid for services rendered. The Champ was never asked to provide money to the operation, and he never volunteered. Quite the contrary, he often *asked* for money. But just having Ali at a function—like this press conference—was worth untold money in advertisement and promotion. It gave the entire operation an aura of credibility.

Hunched over the mikes, Ali did an unexpected turnabout. He directed his comments not to the press but to the young men whose pugilistic careers were just beginning. "Don't be bashful," he said gravely, as if that were a fatal flaw. "These reporters need you, remember that. Look at 'em all. No other reason why they're here. You got to learn to speak up. Be outspoken. Don't be shy just because you get surrounded by microphones and lights and lots of people. Without you these guys wouldn't have jobs. So stand up and be a man. Every chance you get. That's what I did. I didn't let nobody intimidate me."

This was the longest Ben had ever heard Ali talk. It was tantamount to a state of the union address. Ben could see the young fighters hanging on every word from their hero. They didn't see a pudgy, aged boxer in the twilight of his career. They saw the all-time heavyweight champion of the world. They saw a man who could demolish Larry Holmes. Who would have licked Joe Louis. Outfoxed Marciano. Flattened Dempsey. This was the man who hardly worked up a sweat against the fearsome Sonny Liston. Why, he had even told the draft board to go to hell and whipped the U.S. Government at its own game.

"Any time you need me," Ali said, opening his powerful arms in a paternal gesture, "or want to talk to me, maybe show me your stuff, just ask. I'll be here."

He received a rousing hand. The talk had been enough to stir powerful emotions in Ben. This went to the heart of what he wanted to see accomplished with the boxing program. It was the reason he had started financing Harold Smith. It was a dream, yes, and they were fighting against the odds. But that was nothing new to Ben and most of the other black people in the gym that day. How many of these young amateurs would have the stuff to win a gold medal? How many would be good enough to turn pro? How many would be world champions? Probably only be a handful. And in order to accomplish that they would have to be dedicated, work extremely hard and be more than a little lucky. But their successes would be enough to allow others to keep believing in their own dreams. They would show that some dreams come true and some underdogs *do* win. What a great and good man, this Muhammad Ali. What an inspiration. What a noble cause.

Being there and listening to Ali made Ben feel better about everything he was doing—which was plenty. After the hole Smith had found himself in following the debacle of the "Down Under" tour, Ben had started making direct deposits into the Bodak Promotions account. Harold kept asking for more money, saying that they were going to have to spend money to make money. But it was difficult to make money with amateurs, he explained. He kept trying—he had organized a ballyhooed match between MAAS and the Joe Frazier Boxing Club in Philadelphia, but it had bombed at the gate. In April 1979 alone, Ben had deposited $72,700 to the account. The money tap was flowing heavily. There was no way for Ben to turn it off even if he wanted to.

Muhammad Ali Professional Sports (MAPS) was incorporated in May 1979. The new company was to serve as Harold Smith's professional boxing arm. Smith wanted MAPS to be in place for his big move after the Olympics. In the meantime, though, he planned to promote a few pro fights. He selected Sammie Marshall to serve as president and promoter of record—he would have to be finger-printed by the California State Athletic Commission, checked for a criminal record and bonded. Ben Lewis, who opened an account in the name of MAPS at Beverly Drive, was appointed to the board of directors. In case anyone doubted who was actually going to be running MAPS, Smith installed himself as chairman of the board. He moved slowly at first, keeping his best boxers who had a chance for Olympic gold medals in the amateur program.

As expected, the first professional fight lost money. The inaugural MAPS fight was held on May 25, 1979, at the Santa Monica Civic Auditorium, featuring two mediocre lightweights. A few hundred people showed up at the gate, and there was no television coverage. Smith paid $11,650 in purses to the two fighters, and the gate income was only $4,239, resulting in a net loss of $7,411. (Losses and profits given for MAPS fights are based only on purses paid out and total gate revenues—adding TV and closed-circuit rights if applicable—that were collected. The figures do not reflect other monies spent on additional and sizable expenses such as advertisement, transportation and staff salaries. In other words, the true loss for this first fight—and others to follow—was even greater.)

Among the early MAPS expenses were "Ali's Angels." They were attractive, shapely and usually available young women hired as "card girls" by Smith. Their job was to squirm across the ring in skimpy outfits between rounds carrying a card that announced the number of the upcoming round. The women had answered newspaper classified ads for "models" and were "personally interviewed" by Smith. When he found what he wanted, he put them on full-time salaries. Some were given rent-free apartments, and a couple of lucky ones even received cars. There were blondes, brunettes, redheads and a stunning Hawaiian woman called Tweetie. The entourage was getting downright glamorous now.

And even more expensive.

***

"Listen, goddamn it, if you don't like it you can go to hell," Lewis yelled in anger. He slammed down a stack of paperwork on the counter and stomped away.

The customer who was the target of the verbal assault looked shocked, as did several bank employees, at the outburst.

Returning to his desk, Ben sat down and closed his eyes. He ignored Harold, who was conducting a routine transaction at a nearby teller's cage. Massaging his temples, he could feel his elevated blood pressure. He was upset at the customer, but he was also worried about himself. He was usually able to control himself with customers. An employee who made a stupid mistake was another matter; he would jump on him. But Ben believed in treating customers, even those who had fouled up, with patience and deference. That was the golden rule of banking as far as he was concerned. Unfortunately, nowadays he was sinning more than ever. He was feeling out of sorts on the job and had been for some time. It wasn't just one thing that was bothering him. There were two.

The first was his marriage. He and Gladys had separated. He loved her and his stepdaughter and hoped for a reconciliation. At the same time, he understood why they were having problems. They were opposites in so many ways. They wanted different things from life. She was happy with less than he ever would be. Her church activities were her paramount interest. She didn't like the fight crowd and didn't approve of his being drawn further into the business. She knew nothing about what he was doing at the bank to help Harold Smith. She would not have approved of that either.

The second worry was the rising debt at the bank. Already he had passed two high-water marks. One came when he realized the total was higher than he could repay out of his personal funds. Then came the realization that he was involved in a criminal embezzlement. That happened the day he walked into the bank, cut a cashier's check for more than two hundred grand and went out into the parking lot and gave it to Harold and Sammie. Though it was broad daylight and he was an employee of the bank, it was no different than a gang of thieves breaking into the vault during the night and cleaning out the safe. He had robbed the bank. There could be no sniffling excuses. It was no longer a "work out" situation with a customer. It was breaking the law. And his crime kept worsening. On June 19, Harold had asked him to make a $250,000 deposit to the Bodak account to cover expenses necessary for MAPS's biggest fight yet: a bout featuring heavyweights Ken Norton and Scott Le-Doux. He did. That same day, Norton received a $100,000 purse advance and LeDoux $15,000.

During all this Ben was having both the best and worst of times. Not having a wife at home meant he could put more time in at MAPS, like evenings and weekends. It also meant he could have a fling or two with a card girl without suffering pangs of guilt. Such adventures helped him feel younger. And although the ever-rising embezzlement ate at his innards all the time—particularly when he lay in bed at night bathed in sweat—he understood instinctively that he was gambling. A gambler has to increase the stakes in order to win big, and that's what he was doing every time he increased the debt at the bank. He was doubling his bet on what looked like a winning hand. It was too late to fold.

"You really blew up at that customer today," Harold said when Ben arrived at the MAPS offices later that night.

"I know."

"You can't get upset like that, man." Harold looked genuinely worried. "We have too many things to do. When we get upset, we make mistakes."

Ben nodded solemnly. He got Harold's meaning. They could afford no mistakes at the bank these days. Too much was riding on it. One slip and everything could be exposed. But Harold didn't have to go to work at Wells Fargo every day and sit on pins and needles, waiting for something to happen. It was a lot easier for Harold. All he had to do was spend the money.

"It's just—we owe all this money," Ben said. He produced a stack of branch settlement credit tickets, each representing the latest tally of a different chain. He had the grand total on another slip of paper. "As of today, the total is one point eight million."

Smith didn't blink an eye. "I figured it was about that. This pro operation is going to be a long haul, Ben. We're going to lose money at first. We have to establish credibility with the fighters and managers. That's the only way we can make a profit later on."

For Lewis, the bad news kept piling up. *We lost money on that fight. No profit yet. The expenses were greater than we thought. The gate was weak.* It was all having a cumulative effect on him. He agonized over his past actions, worried about the ones that would be required of him later and began to fear that he was throwing the bank's money—and himself—into a bottomless pit, from which there would be no escape. No wonder he couldn't sleep at night. No wonder Gladys had left him. No wonder he was starting to lose his cool with the customers. Things *had* to start getting better soon or he was going to have a breakdown.

"I know this business," Smith said, leaning back in the chair and putting his boots on the desktop like a man who had not a care in the world. "In three years, we'll all be millionaires. And we'll get the money back to the bank, don't worry."

***

The second MAPS fight featured Andy Price against Jose Figueroa on August 3. An early indication of the generous spending that would mark Smith's career as a boxing promoter was the fact that he nearly doubled the purses despite the earlier setback. Though only a few people knew it, this fight was an even bigger financial failure, losing nearly $10,000. Price, who was managed by singer Marvin Gaye, was awarded the decision in an unpopular call that even spectator Ben Lewis questioned. The angry crowd threw chairs in the direction of the ring and booed incessantly. The attendance at this fight was no larger than the first one. Ben knew, without even asking, that the fight had not made any money.

Sixteen days later MAPS presented its first big-time pro fight more than halfway across the country, when Ken Norton fought Scott LeDoux in Bloomington, Minnesota. The local boy, LeDoux, always drew well in his home state, and this fight was no exception. Even better, this was the first nationally televised bout for MAPS. Smith had first contacted LeDoux's manager, Joe Daszkiewicz, who had been in the fight game for more than thirty years, shortly after LeDoux had gained national recognition in a fight against Ron Lyle. Smith promised to double LeDoux's $25,000 purse for the Lyle fight if he would fight Ken Norton. Smith explained that he had been running track shows in Santa Monica in conjunction with Muhammad Ali and now wanted to expand into pro boxing. LeDoux wanted to jump at the opportunity to make bigger money, so Daszkiewicz exercised a clause in their contract with Don King which freed them to accept the MAPS proposal. Twice, Daszkiewicz and LeDoux visited Los Angeles at MAPS's expense. Both times they were picked up in a limo at the airport and taken to the MAPS gym and then to Ali's mansion, where the Champ blessed the fight, saying the Norton-LeDoux fight should be a good match and he was glad to see that it was getting put together. Ali told Daszkiewicz that Smith and the others involved with MAPS were "good men." That was a powerful endorsement, and when combined with the big money Smith was doling out, it made MAPS's offer impossible to turn down. To Daszkiewicz, Smith seemed extremely cool and soft spoken; he never seemed to get rattled. Daszkiewicz and LeDoux were duly impressed. Obviously they were dealing with substantial people here.

On the MAPS books the Norton-LeDoux fight showed a slim profit of $4,700—though certainly the fight still lost money if transportation and hotel bills were included. The total purse was $265,500, with Norton receiving the bulk of it. At ringside, Ben Lewis thought that if the final round had gone another thirty seconds LeDoux might have won by a knockout. Instead Norton won in a decision. For those most closely associated with MAPS, this was a time to rejoice. The fight made for good TV, what with the dramatic turnaround late in the fight. A few more donnybrooks like this and MAPS would have credibility with the TV people as an important promoter. Also, with this promotion they had moved into the heavyweight ranks, where the big money and big names resided. Of course, only the insiders knew the financial truth.

The prime importance of live gates is gone forever, along with the days of a Doc Kearns anxiously counting the gate as 104,000 people streamed into Chicago's Soldier Field to see his boy Dempsey do battle with Tunney. Back in 1927, that *was* how money was made in boxing. But by the 1980s, TV was king. Big matches were being held in arenas that only seated a few thousand spectators. Even with ticket prices of up to several hundred dollars, today's live gates come nowhere close to paying the multimillion-dollar purses that the champions and contenders demand. The big bucks come from the TV revenue, both network and closed-circuit cable. Sometimes TV money is paid in a flat fee as in most of the MAPS contracts; other times it is based on a sliding scale that goes up or down with the ratings on the boob tube. Ratings are the key. As promoter Bob Arum told an interviewer, they represent the "marquee value" of a particular boxer or bout. In fact, if the networks don't think a particular fight will draw a crowd—read "pull good *ratings*"—then that fight in all likelihood will not take place. And on the flip side, if TV people like the ratings prospect of two fighters, they will suggest to a promoter that he make the match. In a real sense TV has become the hidden promoter, the all-powerful behind-the-scenes match-maker no one can disregard.

The missing element as far as MAPS was concerned—the reason it continued to lose money—was not a lack of support from TV. On the contrary, Smith was shrewdly listening to the network sports people, and he understood the importance of putting on bouts they were interested in. Rather, the problem was Smith's extravagance. Day in and day out the organization was spending much more money than it was making. This was not so much careless budgeting—though there was certainly some of that, like booking last-minute flight reservations to attend bouts when those reservations could have been made weeks before on discount fares—as it was a premeditated spending spree designed to impress boxers, managers and everyone who dealt with MAPS and Harold Smith. The anger that Arum and King publicly and privately displayed toward Smith was at least partial proof that the strategy might work, as long as the money held out. Harold Smith was being taken seriously in the boxing world. Any man who spent so much money had to be.

Smith continued his successful wooing of big-name fighters, combining money with the appeal of Ali's name. On September 22, 1979, highly regarded prospect Tommy "The Hit Man" Hearns fought Jose Figueroa at the Los Angeles Sports Arena in MAPS's fourth fight. Another fight on the card was scheduled to feature lightweight contender Hilmer Kenty, but he failed to pass the California Boxing Commission's strict eye test when doctors reportedly discovered cataracts. The Kenty fight was scratched, though the reason was kept secret. (Kenty won the lightweight championship seven months later in Detroit.) Lewis would always remember the Hearns-Figueroa fight for another reason. Hearing about the plight of Joe Louis, Harold had turned it into a benefit for the former great now confined to a wheelchair following a stroke and other physical ailments. Seeing "The Brown Bomber" sitting at ringside slumped over in his wheelchair, drooling and unable to walk or talk, had a profound impact on Ben. He couldn't help but wonder about all the strong young men they were sending out into the arena to do battle. Looking at Louis, he wondered if Ali might have a similar end. Boxing was a mean, unforgiving sport. It looked for human weaknesses and then capitalized on them. It made no difference if a man had trained every day for a year—he could be cut down ten seconds into the first round, demoralized, humiliated, ruined.

The following month former Olympic star Leo Randolph beat Oscar Muniz in a junior featherweight bout before another modest crowd at the L.A. Sports Arena, which resulted in an income of only $9,656. Smith paid the fighters a total of $41,250. A likeable young man who admitted to Teri that he never wanted to be a boxer but only a truck driver, Randolph had been wooed by Smith and signed to an exclusive contract. Trained by Joe Clough, Randolph was to play a key role in the maturation of MAPS as a power to be reckoned with in the world of professional boxing.

There was a constant procession of boxers and their managers in the MAPS offices that fall. Heavyweight Marty Monroe, who always looked like he walked out of *Gentlemen's Quarterly* and, Teri thought, was more interested in clothes and cars than in getting his face messed up, came aboard on an exclusive contract. Interestingly, Monroe was managed by his beautiful wife, Jean, who looked like a high-fashion model from the pages of *Vogue*. Aaron Pryor and his manager were around. Though Pryor was a human dynamo in the ring, Lewis saw him as almost low-key out of it. Teri Key, though, thought Pryor was a little too cocky for his own good. Heavyweight contender Mike Weaver's manager spent time at the office and ended up signing for MAPS's next card, a November twenty-fourth fight with Scott LeDoux.

Daszkiewicz again flew to Los Angeles to get Ali's blessing for the Weaver fight. If Ali did not approve, Daszkiewicz was prepared to return home and look for another fight. But once again Ali supported Smith's plans. This was to be LeDoux's biggest payday yet: he was contracted to receive $150,000. As if that wasn't enough, there was even a sizable under-the-table bonus payment.

It was in connection with this clandestine payment that Lewis got a surprise call at the bank one day from Smith, who wanted him to person-ally deliver $50,000 in cash to Daszkiewicz and LeDoux in Minnesota. Ben asked why him. "Because you're the only person I can trust with that much money," Smith said.

Teri booked Lewis on an afternoon flight, and he left the bank early that day with the money stacked in neat piles—twenties, fifties and hundreds—in a shoulder bag. Never in his life had he carried such a large amount of cash. He had learned that the fight game was funny this way. Fighters always asked for a portion of their fee—maybe 10 or 20 percent— in advance and in cash, as "training expenses." He knew the chances that this money was ever declared on income tax forms were slim. Although it might be business as usual in the boxing world, it made him downright nervous to deal in cash. Cashier's checks, wire transfers, money orders— with those kinds of banking procedures he felt comfortable. Clutching onto the briefcase as if his life depended on it, he saw a would-be stickup man around every corner. He was nervous throughout the entire flight, even worrying that if the plane crashed the money would be destroyed. At the airport, Daszkiewicz and his son met Lewis. They went to a nearby hotel. There, on a table in a rented room, Ben said he had a "gift" from Smith. He took the money out of the bag and counted it. They shook hands, and three hours later Lewis caught a return flight home, feeling much relieved now that he had less than a hundred dollars on him. About the same time, Daszkiewicz was meeting with LeDoux and splitting up the money. As was their normal arrangement, Daszkiewicz received 25 percent, or $12,500, and LeDoux pocketed the rest, $37,500. (When questioned by the FBI in June 1981, LeDoux would have no recollection of this "gift.") Daszkiewicz was happy to be doing business with Smith. All the MAPS productions were extravagant, and a lot of money was being spent, much of it ending up in the bank accounts of boxers and managers. He recognized that Smith was willing to spend big money in order to attract attention to MAPS and draw other fighters into his fold so he could become the top boxing promoter in the country, or world, for that matter. And Daszkiewicz thought Smith had a good chance of accomplishing just that, as long as the money held out.

A few days later, Smith asked Lewis for a $150,000 cashier's check made out to LeDoux's company, The French Connection. Before stepping in the ring against Weaver, LeDoux had agreed to meet Ron Lyle in another MAPS promotion. LeDoux demanded his money for the Lyle fight up front. Daszkiewicz knew that his fighter was afraid the money for the second fight might be held up if he couldn't first get past Weaver. After an argument in the Registry Hotel cafeteria, Smith handed LeDoux a $100,000 check as an advance payment for the second fight. LeDoux's concern that he might lose to Weaver proved warranted, as Weaver overwhelmed him before another good Bloomington crowd and TV cameras.

Next came three fights for gentleman boxer Marty Monroe at the L.A. Sports Arena. On November 27 he beat unknown Henry Lumpkins. The purses were appropriately small for this one, totaling only $41,250. But the revenue was a minuscule $5,821, resulting in a sizable loss. Worse yet for the MAPS bottom line was Monroe's win on January 26, 1980, against journeyman Grady Daniels. With an almost identical purse total of $41,600, the entire proceeds from the fight came to a *minus* $276. Two months later, Monroe next stepped in against Scott LeDoux. It was Monroe's first national TV exposure, and he did well. Although Monroe lost, LeDoux had had to change styles in order to win. In fact, Lewis had never seen LeDoux look sharper. Later, Lewis—who had brought several cashier's checks and $20,000 in cash on orders from Smith—consoled a disappointed Monroe in the dressing room. "You lost nothing, Marty. You were fighting a veteran, and it took Scott's best fight ever to stay with you. Hold your head up high."

A few days later, Smith called Lewis at the bank and said he needed a $250,000 cashier's check made out to Larry Holmes. They had a chance to sign the heavyweight champion. Ben didn't hesitate a moment. If they could get Holmes away from Don King, it would be an unbelievable coup. Any promoter who had the heavyweight champion in his stable was a power to reckon with. It was gospel that whoever controls the heavyweight champion controls boxing. Smith took the check to Vegas, where Holmes was in town to see the Sugar Ray Leonard–Wilfred Benitez welterweight title fight. Smith, along with Daszkiewicz, LeDoux and Sammie Marshall, went to Holmes's suite. Smith claimed he had already gotten the approval of Holmes's manager to set up a Holmes-LeDoux fight. Smith proposed to pay Holmes $1.5 million for the bout. But when he stepped into the champion's room, Smith's way was blocked by an angry Don King. Smith would later tell people that King was brandishing a pistol. Daszkiewicz, still standing in the hallway, heard the loud commotion before he saw King. Then Smith came running out of the room, with King chasing him. Holmes, obviously unwilling to intervene, stayed in his room.

"You no good nigger!" King yelled. "You tell me you need help and then you double-cross me, you son of a bitch. If it's the last thing I do, I'll get you out of boxing."

"Look, I talked to your man and his manager," Smith said, stopping by the elevator. "I didn't do anything any other promoter wouldn't do."

"I'm gonna walk you down," King said.

"You're not gonna walk on anyone," Smith said defiantly.

When it was over, Smith went back to Los Angeles and turned the cashier's check over to Lewis, and Holmes stayed with Don King Productions.

But Holmes and Don King had not heard the last of Harold Smith.

***

Despite fight losses totaling well into six figures for the seven MAPS bouts in 1979, Harold Smith was flying high, *literally.* By the turn of the new decade, he was the proud owner of a private airplane and had his own full-time pilot on salary. What with the limos to and from the airport and a Cadillac and two Mercedes at home, Smith was traveling more like an Arab sheik with a harem these days than a boxing promoter who was losing money on each fight.

Pilot Pat Milstead was hired by MAPS in early 1979 for a charter flight to La Paz, Bolivia, where he picked up several Latin American amateur fighters and brought them to the U.S. for a bout. Bob Campbell, president of MAAS and the man who ran the amateur program on a day-to-day basis for Smith, went along on the trip. Milstead owned a twin-engine Cessna and leased it through his charter operation based at Long Beach Airport. Milstead first met Smith several months later, when he was hired to fly a group to Big Bear, a ski resort in the mountains east of Los Angeles. Muhammad Ali came along on the flight with two bodyguards. Other passengers were Sammie Marshall and bankers Gene Kawakami and Lewis. Later that month, they made a similar trip to Paso Robles. Following that flight, Smith told Milstead that he was interested in buying his own aircraft and asked the pilot to keep his eyes open for a good airplane at a reasonable price.

The following month, Milstead found a Beechcraft C18 for sale for $22,000, and Smith bought it. Milstead was hired to fly it several times during December and January. Smith soon complained it was too slow and didn't carry enough people. What he really meant was that the vintage aircraft was not his style. By now Milstead knew he could count on two or three young women accompanying Smith almost everywhere he went. Add to that a couple of boxers, their managers, Marshall, maybe Campbell and Lewis, and the plane was full. Smith told Milstead to look for a bigger plane. The pilot found one for sale in Florida, and on New Year's Eve day 1979, Smith hired Milstead as the full-time MAPS pilot and paid for him and his wife to fly to Fort Lauderdale and pick up a used Lockheed Lodestar. The price was $95,000. Smith paid for it with two Wells Fargo cashier's checks for $25,000 and $35,000 plus the trade-in of the Beechcraft.

In February 1980, on a trip out of Las Vegas, Milstead had several people on board the Lodestar and was returning them to Los Angeles after a fight. Shortly after takeoff, a fire indicator light went on in the cockpit. They returned to McCarran International Airport and landed safely. Smith, who was not on the flight, met Milstead at the executive terminal in the airport. When told about the scare, Smith told him to sell the plane. Milstead knew that Smith had a fear of flying in small airplanes, and though he obviously trusted Milstead to fly him, just hearing about the bad experience was enough to convince Smith that the plane had to be replaced. Later, Smith asked Milstead if he could pick up an executive jet for a reasonable amount. Milstead asked how much money he was willing to pay. "No more than two hundred thousand plus our plane," Smith answered. Milstead said he thought it could be done.

A few days later, the promoter cornered Lewis when the banker came to visit the gym. They went into an upstairs office and closed the door.

"We got to get another plane," Smith said.

"Yeah, I don't like riding in that trap."

"It's too slow anyway. The way our schedule is going, I think we should get a jet."

"How much is a jet?"

"Pat says maybe three hundred grand. We can trade in the Lodestar."

"I guess a jet does make more sense," Lewis said. "Fuel costs would probably be lower too."

"We'll keep our eyes open for one."

"Okay. I just ran a new tape on what we owe the bank."

"Give it to me."

Lewis rattled off the figures.

"Sounds right," Smith said.

A few days before the Monroe-LeDoux fight, Smith asked Lewis to go out to Hollywood Burbank Airport after work. He had something to show him. Outside a private terminal, Ben saw pilot Pat Milstead standing next to a sleek private jet, discussing its speed, durability and safety features with another man. When Smith arrived almost two hours late, with a voluptuous young woman in tow, he and Ben walked around the plane. Lewis had to admit the thought of flying in their own private jet did have a certain appeal to it. The next day, at Smith's request, he cut a $210,000 cashier's check and gave it to Milstead, who managed to get $90,000 for the Lodestar.

MAPS was moving up in the world on all fronts—except when it came to turning a profit. But then, Harold Smith was not under a great deal of pressure to make money, unlike King and Arum, both of whom had to justify expenses against revenues. To listen to his big talk, Smith must have believed he would eventually make money, but in the meantime there was never any problem when he needed an infusion of capital. He had Ben Lewis, hook, line and sinker now. Ben had to go along with the program and hope for the best. Smith went into 1980 brimming with confidence. The money tap at Wells Fargo was continuing to flow free and unobstructed, and his boxing empire was expanding daily. His dream was to *own* professional boxing. Don King, Bob Arum, Caesar's Palace, ABC and NBC and CBS—*anyone* who wanted to make a fight would have to come to him because he would have all the boxers in his corner. At that point, he would be writing his own ticket.

CHAPTER NINETEEN

Teri Key was enjoying the hard work. MAPS was averaging one event a month. The MAAS amateur program was busier, with more fighters, managers and logistics to keep her occupied. Though her duties had been expanded to include check writing and bookkeeping, she had no idea how much money the company was making. She naturally assumed that MAPS was *making* and not losing money. There was never any suggestion of belt tightening. On the contrary, there was unabated spending, purchases and additions to the staff. With her and the rest of the staff, Harold always emphasized how everything was going according to his master plan. She didn't even know where much of the money that appeared in the Bodak and MAPS checking accounts came from. Harold would say simply "TV money" or "personal loan" whenever she queried him about it in order to log the source in the check registers. A lot of money was coming in and a lot was going out. Though the accounts were sometimes overdrawn, the negative balances didn't exist for long. All she had to do was tell Harold, and he took care of it. More money would soon appear, sometimes in a matter of hours. The cash flow gave all appearances of being healthy.

By now Teri knew that Harold Smith was not the easiest man to work for. He ran on his own inner clock, which had nothing to do with the rising or setting sun or other people's eating and sleeping habits. Harold might waltz into the office at eleven o'clock in the morning only to leave at noon and spend the afternoon at the track. Then he might have meetings in and out of the office until past midnight. Despite such a busy schedule, he had plenty of time for regular dalliances.

Teri was not blind. It didn't take her long to realize that, despite his protestations to the contrary, Smith was intimately involved with several young women at any one time. Like a good secretary, she protected her boss and never let on to his wife. After Harold bought a yacht—a thirty-four-foot Tolly Craft purchased in July 1980 with a $72,336 Wells Fargo cashier's check—he began spending several nights a week there. As far as Teri knew, the boat rarely left its Marina Del Rey mooring. Harold told everyone he slept better on water. But Teri knew there were a few other reasons he wanted to be away from home, and they had nothing to do with sleep.

Smith had naturally found lovers among the card girls. Teri saw the women as pretty girls with nice figures and ambitious dreams. Most wanted to be models or actresses. Smith pampered them by paying to have their hair and nails done, buying them clothes and cars and renting beach apartments for them. He made them even bigger promises, regularly talking about putting them in movies or introducing them to people who could. His money was obviously real; so were the limos he rode around in and his connections to stars in entertainment and sports. Harold Smith seemed to know *everybody.*

The card girls would have done anything for him, and some did. Teri noticed sadly that each card girl romanced by Harold thought she was the only lucky one. He often had Teri call the various girls and set up dates for him. It would not be uncommon for him to have a 5 p.m. rendezvous with one, an 8 p.m. date with another and plans to pick up a third one at 11 p.m. to take out to the yacht for the night. While being warned by Harold not to let the women know that he was seeing others, Teri marveled at his apparent stamina. Typical was one afternoon at five-thirty when Harold asked her to call one of his current favorites. Her name was Pam—she and her friend Tracy had met Harold in Hawaii. He had invited both of them to return with him to the mainland and go on the payroll as card girls. They accepted his offer, and he booked them on his flight to Los Angeles. Smith had put them up in a Santa Monica apartment—at his expense, of course. When Teri got Pam on the telephone that afternoon, she recited Harold's orders. "He'll be there in an hour. He wants a steak, baked potato with sour cream, salad and Asti Spumante. Make sure the champagne is chilled." Pam, a tall redhead, said, "But I don't have all that stuff." Teri suggested she hurry out and buy it, and Pam did. Typically, Harold didn't even show up that night. He had been delayed at an earlier—uh, stop.

Despite such distractions, Teri felt more comfortable in her job all the time. She had become an important cog in the day-to-day operations. It gave her a secure feeling to be needed and wanted. Her life had literally been given back to her by Harold. He was a good man, she was sure, though he had some rough edges. But most men did. At times he could make her so mad that she wanted to walk out. It was difficult to stay mad at him for long, though. He would go from being as angry as a nest of hornets one moment to smiling sweetly, flattering her and acting adorable the next. He was like a puzzle, and the pieces were scattered around town. Just as she was ready to put the last piece in place, she discovered it didn't fit and she would have to start all over. His manipulation of the card girls was not a one-way street. They were all ambitious women trying to make it to the top in a big city where people played by unforgiving rules. She had seen Harold angry nearly to the point of violence at times, loving with children at other times, kind and generous with his athletes always and genuinely joyous in their victories. When they lost, he was supportive and gracious. "You can do it next time," he would say. "I know you're going to win." He almost always called them "Champ." It was part of the mental preparation for a match, which he obviously considered as important as the physical conditioning.

She also knew that Harold was big at making promises, whether he intended to keep them or not. He could keep people hanging on, feeding them a little bit at a time—just enough to give them hope. Like what he was doing with her Tony, who kept waiting for Harold to get his music career going. Teri lectured Tony about not waiting for Harold or anyone else to hand him success on a silver platter. He couldn't expect instant stardom, even though they were both running in a fast circle at MAPS. Meeting the likes of Marvin Gaye, Tony Orlando and Muhammad Ali could make a person's head spin, especially if you were from rural North Carolina. But Teri instinctively knew the importance of paying one's dues. Still, it was a giddy time. Once backstage at Vegas, she had her picture taken with Orlando and proudly sent it home to her daughter. All of this was made possible by Harold Smith, the great benefactor.

His largess kept him in good stead in the boxing business. Boxers, Teri had noticed, were often like children. They had the cockiness, immaturity and feelings of immortality of the young. They took a liking to anyone who gave them nice things. There were exceptions of course. Tommy Hearns and his manager, Emmanuel Steward, for example, were real gentlemen in Teri's book. But most fighters and trainers needed— no, *demanded*—constant attention, favors and flattery. Money was all-important to them, and Smith was good at giving it away. Of course, one could hardly blame fighters for being money-conscious, considering what they had to do to earn their living. Looking at Harold, they saw a big dollar sign, which was just the way he wanted it. They saw the paid luxury hotel bills, the airline tickets, the slinky women he always had around, the nice cars, the drugs, the partying, the briefcase he always carried stuffed with greenbacks. They were like little kids in a neighborhood candy store, and Harold Smith owned the store. Teri would sometimes get angry at him for giving away too much. But he could not be deterred. He seemed to find it impossible to say no. Teri had overheard comments from the professional boxers and managers. It was obvious that they were getting much more money from MAPS than they could get from any other promoter. Harold was clearly out-spending the other promoters in a battle for the loyalties of the top fighters and control of professional boxing. Without regard for cost, Harold would pay for boxers to fly relatives and friends to town for a fight. The "backstage" list for complimentary tickets at a fight was some-times two and three typewritten pages long. At one fight more than half the crowd had not paid for tickets.

Some days, Harold's exuberance would suddenly evaporate. Teri could spot it. Anyone could. He would sit silently at his desk, brooding with his hands folded in front of him. Clearly in no mood to be bothered, he would stare off into space, ignoring phone calls, staffers and visitors. Teri would try to insulate him during these spells by keeping his door closed and people at a distance. Then, in the evening when she was finished with her work, she would say good night and quietly slip out. She felt sad for him at such times. He seemed to have the weight of the world on his shoulders. And she guessed he did.

Yet she couldn't overcome the nagging feeling that there was a secret compartment in his life that she knew nothing about. She doubted that anybody—not Lee, not Ben Lewis or Sammie Marshall, and certainly not

Ali—knew the true Harold Smith. She wondered if her boss would ever trust her enough to reveal himself.

***

The announcement in the spring of 1980 by President Jimmy Carter that the United States would not compete in the Moscow Olympics as a protest against the Russian invasion of Afghanistan cast a pall over the MAAS-MAPS offices. Everything they had been working toward and planning for in the amateur program seemed lost. Everyone was bitterly disappointed by the turn of international events. It seemed cruel and unfair. President Carter was cursed for throwing sports into the political arena. But soon after Ali announced his support of the boycott, Smith jumped on the pro-Carter, anti-Soviet bandwagon.

An international track meet was scheduled for the Los Angeles Coliseum in a few days. When Smith heard that the Russian team would be competing, he decided they would all picket the event. Ordering new Ali warm-ups in patriotic red, white and blue for everyone, Smith had the entire MAAS staff and a horde of athletes ride in rented limos down to the Coliseum. In the best tradition of oppressed workers, they got out of the Cadillacs and Lincoln Continentals and paced in front of the stadium carrying hand-printed signs that read "Commie Go Home." It was all good fun. Teri Key wondered what the Russians would think about the bizarre scene of the picketers who arrived and departed in limos. *Crazy Americans.* It would sure be something to tell their friends back in the motherland.

Smith's depression over his derailed Olympic plans didn't last long. He moved swiftly to expand his presence in the professional boxing world. He was hopeful, even exuberant once again, and tried to convince everyone that it was no setback at all. They would be making big money sooner than they had planned. With the solid base he already had in the sport, including the loyalty of the fighters and MAPS's name recognition, he was on his way. He already had a following in the pro ranks. He had promoted a good televised heavy-weight bout. He had lots of other exciting pro fights lined up. It would not take him long to control pro boxing. He would be bigger than King and Arum put together.

Smith immediately began signing some of his talented "amateur" boxers to professional contracts. Heavyweight Tony Tubbs and light-weight
Davey Armstrong were among the first to come aboard. The inducements
were substantial. Smith bought a house in Cincinnati for Tubbs's parents
and gave the young man a $50,000 signing bonus. For Armstrong he pro-
vided money for home remodeling and new furniture in addition to a
$25,000 signing bonus. Others signed to MAPS contracts included Jeff
McCracken, an excellent middle-weight; middleweight J. B. Williamson,
a former Marine fighter; featherweight Daniel Avery; flyweight Sonny
Long; junior middle-weight Roosevelt Green. For their services, the
MAPS fighters would be compensated more than what most beginning
pros made. The exclusive arrangements called for Smith to serve as their
manager and Ali as a figurehead trainer. The actual day-to-day training of
the MAPS fighters would be done by people already on the pay-roll. Some
of the finest coaches available, like Chuck Bodak and former top heavyweight Jimmy Ellis, were hired. Those who worked with the amateurs—
like Smith's old friend Bob Campbell—saw the handwriting on the wall:
for all of Smith's earlier talk about helping kids and disadvantaged ghetto
youth and fighting for America's national pride, the MAAS program was
going to be playing second fiddle to the pro operation from here on.

Now was a particularly appropriate time for Leo Randolph to come
into his own. In light of the Olympics derailment, Smith and MAPS
needed a champion fast. Randolph had the first crack at it. A kind, religious man who always blessed a table before a meal, Randolph had quit
boxing after winning the gold medal in the 1976 Olympics. He worked a
couple of years as a laborer in the Seattle area before deciding to go back
into the gym and see how he could do as a pro. He tuned up on March 28,
1980, with a victory over Tony Rocha. Then on May 4, 1980, Randolph
met WBA Junior Featherweight Champion Ricardo Cardona in Seattle,
Washington.

Sitting near ringside, Ben Lewis, who had become a fan of Leo's, was
shocked when the no-nonsense Cardona came out in the first round and
floored Randolph. Ben held his breath. No, it wasn't fair. Leo had to get
up. He had to win the championship. He had worked too hard to be so
easily cut down. Gamely, the wobbly legged and bloodied Randolph got

up and went after the champion. He fought a gallant and emotional fight, and in the end Cardona was unable to answer the bell for the fifteenth round. The referee raised Randolph's hand in victory, and MAPS had its first champion.

The Randolph title victory was a joyous time for the MAPS entourage. Smith was delirious with pride and confidence. "No one is going to stop us now! Leo is only the first of many champions to come!" Though the fight lost nearly $20,000, this was hardly a time to worry. In fact, warned weeks earlier by a local promoter that May 4 was not a good date to have the fight because it was opening day of the boating season in Seattle and also the starting weekend for the popular Longacres Racetrack, Sammie Marshall had shrugged off the concern. Marshall explained that they didn't need a good gate because they were getting paid $100,000 for TV rights (less, it should be pointed out, than the purses). Marshall also said that it wasn't important for MAPS to make money on these early fights because they were attempting to develop champions in local fighters and the financial rewards would come in the future. Everything that MAPS had been working for was symbolized by Randolph's victory. They were on their way now.

Now that MAPS was in the big time, the company needed larger and fancier offices. Moving day arrived a couple of weeks after everyone returned triumphantly from the Randolph fight. The operation took over the entire second floor of a fashionable wood-shingled office building on Ocean Park Boulevard in Santa Monica, a vast improvement over the one-room space they had been renting. Everyone in the company—eight full-time employees now—had his or her own office in the new digs. They even had a separate office for Ali to use on the few occasions he dropped by. The new space was huge—at least three thousand square feet. The rent was in the neighborhood of $5,000 a month. By the time the interior decorator Smith hired had completed his task, Teri knew it had cost many thousands of dollars more. Lee had worked closely with the designer to make sure everything was done right. No expense was spared. Instead of hard-to-maintain real plants, the place was dotted with delicate (and expensive) potted silk plants. There was lush wall-to-wall carpeting. All new furniture. Art on the wall. One long hallway was dubbed the "Hall of

Champions," where they planned to hang pictures of all the MAPS title-holders. Randolph's picture went up right away, near a blowup of Ali, leaving plenty of room on the wall for future heroes. Every detail, right down to the matching ashtrays, was done tastefully.

Teri settled in with delight. Never did she dream she'd have her own well-appointed office. The operation was getting downright classy, and she was grateful to be an integral part of it as Harold's right hand. It was like being on a huge rollercoaster, and just when she thought she was at the top and they could go no higher, she suddenly saw another rise on the horizon. She didn't want the ride to end. She was having too much fun.

Among the first visitors to the new office were Emmanuel Steward and his fighter, Tommy Hearns. They were duly impressed with the surroundings. They were even more impressed when Smith ushered them into his corner office and started throwing numbers around. Figures like $500,000 for Hearns to fight WBA Welter-weight Champion Pipino Cuevas. Amazingly, Smith was ready to give them $100,000 cash that morning to sign a contract. Steward and Hearns didn't have to talk to their lawyer. They signed on the spot, and Smith sent someone over to Wells Fargo to get a cashier's check. Tommy's biggest payday as a professional fighter up to then had been $85,000. Steward and Hearns walked out of Smith's office that morning with more than that in their pockets and another four hundred grand to come, plus an additional $25,000 for training expenses. Smith called for his limo, and all three of them went out to the airport and climbed aboard the MAPS jet. Soon they were airborne for Mexico City, where they met with Pipino Cuevas later that day. He too signed on the dotted line. How could he refuse a paycheck that for him meant somewhere between one and two million dollars? That same day there was a news conference announcing the latest MAPS fight scheduled for later that summer. Smith kept himself in the background though, allowing the fighters and managers to share the spotlight. People thought it was a humble gesture.

Steward and Hearns were whisked back to Detroit that night in the MAPS jet, flown by Pat Milstead. What an incredible twenty-four hours it had been. Smith had put together a dream fight for them. Hopefully, Tommy would win the title and they could do some more business with

Harold Smith. The "Detroit Hit Man" and his manager left town as big fans of Harold Smith.

Everybody loves a big spender.

***

In May 1980, Smith made another move on the pride of Don King Productions: WBC Heavyweight Champ Larry Holmes. Flying on the MAPS plane to Easton, Pennsylvania, Holmes's hometown, Smith met with the fighter in the office of his attorney, Charles Spaziani. Along with Smith on the trip was MAPS's attorney Ed Franklin.

As usual, Smith had ambitious plans. He proposed to make and promote two fights for Holmes. He still wanted a Holmes-LeDoux fight. For this he was prepared to give Holmes a $250,000 advance. Then they would follow that fight with a Holmes-Ali bout. If Holmes was surprised that Smith was now attempting to put together a fight for Ali for the first time, he didn't show it. (If he had known what Smith was doing, Ali may have been surprised though, since he was still being promoted by Herbert Muhammad and Don King.) It's a good guess that Smith was trying to back his way into an Ali bout. If he had Holmes signed for such a fight, then Ali's people would have to let him promote the inevitable confrontation everyone knew would take place.

"I'll give you a $500,000 advance against the Ali purse," said Smith, "and $150,000 for training expenses."

Holmes sat impassively.

"I've got cash with me," Smith said, putting two cashier's checks on the table that totaled $900,000. He then reached into what looked like a pillowcase he was carrying and began pulling out fifties and hundreds. "I can have someone fly in with the rest in cash."

The fighter went over to the window and opened it wide. "It's gettin' real warm in here," Holmes said. "I can't agree to nothing until I see the contract."

Smith showed Holmes the contract but, once again, left without Holmes's signature. Holmes had simply made too much money through the years fighting for Don King to bust up that business association. Smith wasn't about to give up though. He kept the cash and returned the cashier's checks to Lewis. The following month, Smith telephoned Holmes at his home and made him another offer: a million dollars just for the right to promote two fights.

"A million bucks?" Holmes asked.

"Yeah, in addition to the purses."

"I already got a million."

"I'll make it two million."

But once again Holmes declined the offer.

It was getting to be downright frustrating. While MAPS was collecting champions in other weight classes—and would continue to do so in a big way during the next six months—the biggest prize of all, Larry Holmes, kept eluding Smith's best efforts.

***

Earnie Shavers was another big boxing name that Smith went after. Signing him in addition to Ken Norton, Scott LeDoux and Marty Monroe would give MAPS tremendous leverage in the heavy-weight ranks. Though Shavers had failed the test against Larry Holmes in September 1979—the referee stopped their fight in the eleventh round—the man dubbed "Acorn" for his shaved head was still a viable, top-ten contender. He had more fights in him, and there was money to be made on them. Most important for Smith and MAPS was that Shavers had a recognizable name. He had "marquee value." The TV people liked him, and he might end up attracting other fighters to MAPS.

Once again, the banker got the call.

"We need three hundred thousand cash," Smith said.

"What the hell for?" Lewis asked, lowering his voice as if someone had heard Smith.

"Got a chance to sign Shavers. His contract with that other guy is up in two or three weeks."

"Is Shavers worth that kind of money?"

"Yeah, he's got a name. I can make a good match for him. The TV guys like him."

"I don't know."

"Listen, without Holmes all we can do is sign the top contenders and hope for the best. Hey, man, I know what I'm doing. Get the cash together and come to Vegas with me. We'll play some craps."

"Keno."

Smith laughed. "You play your game, I'll play mine."

Lewis did not consider Smith a heavy gambler. At least whenever Lewis was around, Harold seemed to be more of a showman than gambler. He liked drawing attention to himself at the end of the craps table as he blew on the dice and threw them into the hole with a flourish. Ben only went to the craps table in the company of Harold, who liked setting up several people in the entourage at his end of the table, giving them money and directing their betting. He also enjoyed slipping someone unnoticed to the far end of the table. The kick for him was putting one over on the casino people. If the pit bosses saw someone winning big, they would come over and do anything they could to disrupt the action at the table. Smith's theory was that with all the commotion he was causing, his buddy at the other end could win big and no one would notice. Sometimes it actually happened. A MAPS associate sidled up to the table on the far end one night when Harold was causing a scene and walked away with $18,000. Personally, Lewis preferred keno because there was no hanky-panky or split-second decisions that had to be made. You just picked your numbers and either won or lost. He once won $1,500 and felt lucky.

"Okay," Ben finally agreed. "It'll take me a few hours to get the cash together."

They went to the airport to catch a commercial flight, accompanied by another MAPS employee who was anxious to see the black elephant bag stuffed with $300,000 go through the X-ray machine. In fact, the gofer made such a big deal of looking over the security agent's shoulder that the agent got suspicious and wanted to look inside the bag. He was distracted just long enough for Smith to switch bags, as he was carrying an identical one stuffed with fight contracts. After clearing security, Smith and Lewis both were relieved. Though it wasn't illegal to carry large amounts of cash, they probably would have had to identify themselves, and it would not have looked good for a banker to be associated with a bag full of money.

When Smith and Lewis arrived in Vegas, they went directly to the hotel and met Shavers in his room. The boxer's handshake was like steel, Lewis thought. Smith dumped the contents of the bag on a coffee table in front of Shavers and his manager, Frank Luca. The two men sat down on a couch and looked at the money before them.

"I wanna count it," Shavers announced in his high-pitched Willie Mays voice.

"Each pack has a hundred bills," Lewis explained. "That means the packs of twenties are $2,000, the fifties $5,000, the hundreds $10,000."

Shavers picked up one pack of twenties, studied it and then broke open the seal. "One." Then another bill, "Two."

Lewis looked at Smith in disbelief. The man was going to count every bill? Shavers might be a craftsman of sorts in the ring, but out of it he acted stone dumb. Shavers was known as one of boxing's biggest spenders. He had a swimming pool shaped like a boxing glove in his backyard. Next to his house was a private nine-hole golf course and airstrip. Shavers neither swam, played golf nor flew. Now, he said, he was wanting to buy a new house for his "babies"—his two little daughters, whom he adored.

"Three," the fighter said slowly. "Four."

"Listen," Luca said to Smith, "we're going to deny any of this until our existing contract expires." He explained that they were under contract to someone else but would be free to accept the MAPS offer in a couple of weeks.

"No problem," Smith said.

"Thirteen," Shavers droned on in the background. "Fourteen."

Lewis couldn't take it. He left the room and went down to the coffee shop.

A long hour later, Shavers was finished counting. Thankfully, Lewis had put in a lot of stacks of hundreds. Smith placed an exclusive MAPS contract before Shavers and the fighter signed it. Then Shavers put the money in a large briefcase he had brought with him. (Interviewed by FBI agents in May 1981, Shavers would deny receiving the $300,000 payment.) On May 30, Shavers received more money from Smith: a $30,000 "loan" on the terms that he would not have to repay it if he defeated his first opponent, Leroy Boone, which he did on June 14 in Cincinnati. The

$300,000 didn't show up on the MAPS books either; MAPS "officially" paid a total purse of $90,000 to the two fighters. Total revenue in the non-TV bout was a disastrous $2,270.

Five days later, MAPS paid out purses of $36,950 against revenues of only $3,667 for a nontitle heavyweight fight in Tacoma, Washington. This bout meant little to MAPS. The plan now called for concentrating on promoting championship fights. Such action would be easier to sell to television. Though he didn't even tell Ben Lewis the complete extent of his plans, Smith wanted to do something special for his next promotion. Something no promoter had done in the history of boxing.

* * *

What Lewis did know about from the outset was the Hearns-Cuevas fight set for August 2. Once again, Smith presented him with a list of cashier's checks that had to be cut for the fight. Ben looked at the list and said solemnly, "You don't have any money." If it had been possible for Harold to turn white, he would have then. Ben then broke up laughing, and a relieved Harold joined him. Lewis cut the checks, and Smith left without uttering a word about repayment.

Lately Lewis had begun to feel that he should get something out of all the money that was passing through his hands. He had told Harold about a house he wanted to buy, and Smith told him to go ahead and make the purchase. The $145,000 could be added to the total that he, Smith, owed the bank. Lewis bought the house. Ben would take a similar tack regarding a used Cadillac Seville he bought for himself. He also took $15,000 to pay off a new Buick for Gladys and bought his son, Tony, a Honda Civic for $10,000. Landscaping, remodeling and furnishing the home would come to another $150,000. Of the many millions he stole for Smith, Lewis converted approximately $320,000 to his own use.

The Hearns-Cuevas fight was a battle for the WBA welterweight championship held by Cuevas since 1976. Cuevas had been a good champion, with an international reputation for ferocity. His fight with Hearns would be his twelfth title defense. Also on the card: Earnie Shavers against Randy "Tex" Cobb. The TV people had liked the program and bought the rights. The fight was to be held in Detroit, Hearns's hometown, where he usually drew well. Unfortunately, even if it did *very* well, there was no way Wells Fargo was going to get paid back. When Lewis sat down with Smith and penciled in the latest cashier's checks and other estimated expenses for the bout, the new total owed the bank was *twelve million dollars* and some change. Smith gave his stock answer—"That's just what I thought"— then quickly changed the subject and started rambling on about all the closed-circuit TV locations in choice areas they had set up.

Only at the last minute did Lewis find out about the *other* MAPS fight scheduled to be held in Cincinnati on the same day. Smith may have been afraid to tell him for fear the banker would criticize his business judgment. Finally the promoter had to tell Lewis because he needed the usual financial assistance. He went to Lewis on July 31, three days before the fight, with a list of names for cashier's checks. Lewis complained about the late notice but went ahead and issued the checks. This second fight would also be a championship fight, featuring WBA Junior Welterweight-Champion Antonio Cervantes against Aaron Pryor. The TV people liked this one too; CBS picked up the rights to air the bout. No promoter had ever held two championship bouts in two different cities on the same day and that was one of the reasons why Smith wanted to do it. He would prove to any doubters in the boxing world that he was for real.

The thirty-four-year-old Cervantes was also a longtime champion. He first won the title in 1972 and had held it since then except for a one-year period when Wilfredo Benitez ruled the 140-pound limit. Since 1977 Cervantes had defended it six times when he signed for the Pryor fight. Not a "big money" champion like Cuevas, Cervantes agreed to a purse in the range of $100,000; Pryor was happy to get $50,000 for the fight.

Smith spent another $25,000 buying out Pryor's contract with Madison Square Garden after Pryor flew to Los Angeles on the MAPS jet and met Smith. The two men liked each other immediately. Smith saw a potential champion in Pryor. In Smith, Pryor saw a man who "gave fighters breaks." And Pryor was a fighter looking for a break. Translation: he wanted a title fight badly. He was a good contender, maybe too good, because both the WBA and WBC champions had been avoiding him. Now Smith had made a title fight possible, and Pryor was so grateful that he joined the MAPS stable and signed for three fights.

In Hearns and Pryor, Smith had two hungry contenders. If they both did what he expected and won their titles, MAPS would have three world champions. Each, of course, would have to defend his title, and all were committed to doing so under the MAPS banner.

The Cervantes-Pryor fight came first, around noon Cincinnati time. Smith flew into town on the MAPS jet with several card girls. It didn't last long. Though the unbeaten Pryor was knocked to one knee in the first round, he got up and remained the aggressor throughout the bout. Cervantes was knocked out in the fourth round. During those four rounds, Pryor threw more punches than most fighters would deliver in ten rounds. Enough of them landed on Cervantes to end his reign. Smith quickly congratulated his latest champion and then headed out to the airport with his entourage. The day was only half finished. About the time Smith was viewing Cincinnati from the air, Pryor was sitting before network TV cameras and microphones. "I just want to thank Harold Smith and Muhammad Ali Professional Sports for giving me this opportunity to fight for the title," said the newest pro boxing champion.

In Detroit later that day, Smith told Lewis all the details of the Pryor victory just before Cuevas and Hearns came out of their dressing rooms. Earnie Shavers had already lost in a preliminary bout to Randy Tex Cobb. In fact, at that moment Shavers was en route to the hospital with a broken jaw. Lewis began to feel that he had been right about Shavers: he was one big investment that wasn't paying off.

Then Hearns came into the ring, looking lean and mean. Both his nicknames—"Detroit Hit Man" and "Motor City Cobra"—were appropriate. A bean-stalk fighter who stood six foot two, Hearns had a seventy-eight-inch reach, longer than Joe Louis's. His glaring stare was chilling. In the ring, this man who Teri Key thought was such a gentleman was dangerous. Fighting him was a good way to get hurt. Cuevas came out trying to look like a suitable champion, but he couldn't hide the fear in his eyes. At the bell, Cuevas moved around cautiously as if he would just as soon not hit his opponent for fear of making him mad. Hearns struck quickly, hitting the champion again and again with devastating power. Cuevas was unable to muster any kind of defense and was knocked out in the second round. Lewis jumped from his seat and hugged Smith. They had done the impossible. In just six hours, MAPS had added two new champions. Their dream was coming true. Ben was particularly pleased because both his father and son had attended the fight and he had been able to introduce them to some famous people. It was all quite impressive.

That night there was a victory party in Sammie Marshall's suite at the Ponchartrain Hotel in downtown Detroit. There was a huge spread of food, hors d'oeuvres and, of course, chilled champagne. In the bedroom, a framed picture had been taken off the wall and its glass was filled with lines of cocaine supplied by Smith's mysterious coke connection, a black man named Conrad, who frequently accompanied him to the racetrack and was increasingly showing up at boxing matches around the country. Smith and Conrad disappeared often behind the bedroom's closed doors that night.

Several boxing luminaries showed up in the suite for the victory party. TV's Dick Stockton, who had worked the fight. Gil Clancy. Angelo Dundee, Sugar Ray Leonard's manager. A sky-high Smith, just emerging from the bedroom, goaded Dundee about when he was going to let WBC Welterweight Champ Sugar Ray Leonard go into the ring against WBA Welterweight Champ Hearns. "Doesn't make any difference to me," Dundee deadpanned. "I'm gonna be outside the ropes anyway."

Despite the victories, August was to end on a low note. Six days after the double championship day, Leo Randolph met Sergio Palma of Argentina in his first title defense. It was no contest. Palma floored the MAPS champ twice in the first round. Either Randolph was badly outclassed or he had trained too hard and was left with no energy or mobility. Mercifully, it did not last long. Randolph lost his crown in a sixth-round knockout.

After the fight, Lewis went back into Randolph's dressing room and was shocked to find the fighter all alone, crying. Shell-shocked by the loss, Leo was unable to stop sobbing. Ben patted his shoulder and told him everything would be okay. He'd come back. He'd show the world. Ben didn't leave until Leo's sister came in and took her sweaty brother in her arms. Lewis was saddened by the scene. How could they send such a fine young man into the ring and then, when he lost, desert him so? Despite the best intentions of some, boxing could be an unforgiving sport. The next day, the crestfallen Randolph announced his retirement from boxing, saying he wanted to "settle down with [his] family and have a normal life." He was twenty-two years old. His pro record was seventeen and two.

The Randolph-Palma bout was the fourth and final MAPS fight in the state of Washington. They were leaving behind at least one fan. It was the job of Dale Ashley, chief investigator for the Washington Athletic Commission, to collect the 5 percent state tax on the television revenues from prizefights. The total TV money generated by the four fights was in the neighborhood of $180,000—resulting in about a $10,000 tax for the state. Ashley never had any trouble collecting the money from MAPS. But more, for the state, was all the good publicity which had resulted from the televised fights—two of them title bouts. That kind of thing was good for business. Ashley was "damned pleased to deal with somebody who had some money to be able to fund the fights properly." In Smith, Marshall and Lewis, Ashley saw "very professional, real straight businessmen." He did know as a fact, though, that every one of the MAPS fights had lost money. Yet they were impressive shows, all of them. There was no skimping, no broken deals. There were never any complaints from the fighters or managers about not getting paid, as so often happened in the fight game. To Ashley, Harold Smith and MAPS seemed like a whiff of fresh air in the boxing game.

CHAPTER TWENTY

Gene Kawakami sat at his kitchen table, leafing through the morning paper over a final cup of coffee before leaving for work. As usual, the business section came first, then the front page. The entertainment section generally had a low priority, right down there with the sports page. The statistics Kawakami liked best had dollar signs in front of them.

Business at Miracle Mile was going well. The year 1979 had been a good one for Kawakami. He had been made a full vice president—at age thirty, one of the youngest in Wells Fargo's history. A medium-size man with black hair and a round moonish face, Kawakami's rise through the ranks had been rapid. Two years after graduating from the bank's management training program, he had been named assistant manager at Miracle Mile. Then, two years later (1976), he became branch manager. When he had taken over the branch, it had $14 million in total deposits. By midsummer 1980, under his stewardship, the branch's desposits were edging near the $30 million range. Miracle Mile was the third largest in what Wells Fargo called its Beverly Hills Region. Kawakami understood perfectly that his main function at the bank was to sell services such as data processing and bank credit cards while maintaining a positive funds flow by renting out (read "lending") lots of money. He was quite capable in all those areas, but in the latter he was particularly adept. There was no doubt in Kawakami's mind that his commercial loan skills were what had elevated him to the top so fast.

In Wells Fargo's overall strategy for penetrating the Southern California market, Kawakami was an important player. The bank controlled 15 percent of the financial marketplace in Northern California, where it got its start many years earlier. But in Southern California, where

Wells Fargo had gotten a late start by not opening its first branch until 1968, the bank had only 3 percent of the business. The bank hierarchy wanted a big push in the Los Angeles region during the 1980s. In order to accomplish that, it was looking for a different type of person to manage the branches in the southern half of the state than those in control in the north. The San Francisco-based bank knew it couldn't send what Kawakami and others called the "three-piece suiters" from that city into Los Angeles and expect them to do well. Bank officials figured, correctly, that a more aggressive and less conservative kind of person would show better results in Tinseltown and its environs.

Kawakami was the kind of wheeler-dealer supersalesman the bank needed. A native of Los Angeles, he was Southern Californian all the way. His promotion to manager came a couple of years sooner than even he had hoped might be possible. Usually the advancement would have required him to transfer to a smaller branch for the first managerial assignment. By leaving him in place at the important Miracle Mile office as the top man, one supervisor admitted to Kawakami, "We're taking a chance on you to see if you can handle it." He could and did. Wells Fargo now unabashedly considered him a rising star in the region, just the kind of person they needed more of in order to slice a bigger piece of the banking pie in Southern California.

But Kawakami had a problem. A severe problem that no one else—not even his wife—knew about. The loans he had made to Harold Smith were still outstanding. And he was still carrying several loans in phony names, loans he had made so that the proceeds could be used to roll over—or pay off—Smith's past-due notes. The problem worsened when none of the new roll-over loans were paid back. It had become quite a mess. If he blew the whistle on Smith, he would lose his job and be charged with embezzlement. That was not a viable option. The only thing he could do was to keep Smith on a short string so that when the promoter made some money he would be able to secure repayment to the bank. When he made the first phony loan in the name Ken Kato, Kawakami knew it was a coin flip that could go either way. Smith was going to be successful and they were all going to get rich, or Smith was going to fail.

Whichever way the coin came up, Kawakami knew the moment he moved the money into the Kato account that his banking days were numbered. He had crossed the line between legal and illegal. It was the kiss of death. His only hope was to get the money paid back and leave the bank with a good name. He had never intended to stay at Wells Fargo the rest of his life anyway. There were too many exciting prospects out there for making big money.

After the fiasco of the "Down Under" tour, when he realized that repayment was not going to be forthcoming from Smith, Kawakami had decided to consolidate all the outstanding loans into one superloan. Since it would exceed his lending limit, he would have to prepare a package to be submitted to Wells Fargo's regional loan committee. But that wouldn't pose much of a problem. Kawakami knew a good loan application when he saw one—and could make one up himself just as easily. He would tailor the application to his own liking.

First, he invented an entity known as Western Sales Limited. Then, he found just the right financial statement in his files. Hansch Brothers Insurance Company was a customer at the branch. Though Hansch did not have any borrowing at the bank, the firm did keep its accounts there and had a complete financial statement on file. Hansch was nicely diversified in the insurance business. A loan application by Hansch to start a new company named Western Sales would not look suspicious. He filled out the application asking for several hundred thousand dollars and submitted it to the loan committee, where it was quickly approved. This was just the kind of loan Wells Fargo wanted to make: big money to a solid customer. It looked good to the loan committee. This was the sort of loan activity they expected from Kawakami.

When the loan was funded, Kawakami opened a business checking account for Western Sales so that he could distribute the proceeds. He used the name Larry Fine as the authorized signatory on the account and signed it himself. Then he began writing Western Sales checks to pay off all the old loans to Smith.

About a month after Australia—back in April 1979—Smith had come in and told Kawakami of his plans to start another business, known as Muhammad Ali Professional Sports, and to sign the best pro boxers in the world and promote their fights. With his connections to Ali and the name he already had in boxing, Smith once again looked like a good bet to Kawakami.

The first time Kawakami had bet on Smith was right after traveling to New Orleans for the Ali-Spinks fight as Smith's guest. The day before the fight, Smith had taken him up to meet Ali. Kawakami was impressed because Smith had the power to walk right into Ali's room, interrupt a meeting and make an introduction. The man could get an audience with the most famous man in boxing. That had been good enough for Kawakami. Though Kawakami thought the expansion into pro boxing sounded lucrative, he would *not* provide Smith with any more funds. However, he could provide other help and guidance to ensure Smith's success. Kawakami had a personal interest to guard. The banker reminded Smith that when he started making money, he would have to immediately pay back all the "investors" Kawakami had brought to MAAS. He showed some loan documents that contained various names—Ken Kato was one of them—and said these people wanted their money back. Smith heartily agreed that they would all be repaid in full, plus interest. While he had Smith in such an obliging mood, Kawakami had him sign several blank promissory notes, saying they were necessary for renewal purposes. Actually Kawakami wanted some protection. If Smith's businesses folded, he wanted to make sure the books reflected that Smith—and not Kato or Western Sales or Gene Kawakami—was responsible for all the bank's lost dollars. It might work and it might not, but at least it was something. In September 1979, the Western Sales loan had to be renewed, since it was a six-month loan. The loan committee approved renewal. In April 1980, Kawakami had realized that it was not going to look good to go for another renewal. So he initiated still more phony loans to repay the Western Sales note. Kawakami was running out of tricks.

Now, sitting in his kitchen three months later, Kawakami noticed an article on the front page of the sports section. It was all about the Tommy Hearns versus Pipino Cuevas championship fight coming up in a few days. According to the sportswriter, there was considerable national interest in the match and ticket sales at closed-circuit sights were going well. The estimate was that more than a million dollars was going to be made on the fight. The paper said it was a MAPS show, which Kawakami knew because Smith had told him. Kawakami had regularly been going to the MAPS office to demand repayment. Sometimes Smith refused to see him, or his secretary, Teri Key, would say he had just left the office. Kawakami was sure Smith was hiding or slipping out a back door. Once when he did manage to corner Smith, the promoter alluded to a big fight coming up—the Hearns-Cuevas title fight—that was going to make "about $1.5 million." At the time, Kawakami didn't know whether to believe still another Smith story about making money down the road. By now he didn't trust Smith at all. Kawakami was getting the distinct impression that the promoter was rather comfortable with the idea of him and the "investors" getting stuck holding the bag.

But now the newspaper validated Smith's claims that the fight was going to be successful. Kawakami hurried out of the house. He would pay Harold Smith a visit this morning. They were going to have to work out something firm regarding repayment now that all this money was coming in. Kawakami was not about to take a dive for anyone.

A few hours later, Kawakami was sitting in Smith's office. Once again he showed Smith a sheaf of loan papers in various names.

"You've got a big deal here," the banker said. "By the time you sell cable and TV rights, you're going to make big dollars. I want my money. So do these people"—he held up the loan papers—"who invested their money in you."

Smith eyed Kawakami suspiciously. There was no hint of friendship. "Okay, when the money comes in, you'll get it," the promoter said slowly. "But then you're out, Gene. Out for good."

"Fine with me. All I want is my money." Kawakami couldn't care less about being out of Smith's future business deals. He had given up any hope of showing a profit. Maybe Smith would strike it rich in the boxing business. Kawakami no longer cared. The man was too flaky to deal with.

A few days after the Hearns-Cuevas fight, Kawakami called Smith several times before he finally got through. Smith claimed the money from closed-circuit outlets had still not come in. The banker found that hard to believe.

"When it comes in I can take the money out, right?" Kawakami asked.

"Yeah," Smith said, sounding distracted.

After putting the phone down, Kawakami decided to check for himself. A couple of months earlier, one of the MAPS boxers had come in to cash a check Smith had given him written off a MAPS account at Beverly Drive. That was the first time Kawakami knew that Smith was banking at that branch. Kawakami had written down the account number and put it aside. Now he ran the MAPS account number on the bank's computer terminal and saw a balance of $1.7 million. The money *was* in. What was Smith trying to pull now? He quickly filled out a transfer of funds notice, wrote "verbal authority" on the ticket and withdrew $357,000—the exact total amount of all the loans and accrued interest. He used the funds to buy cashier's checks and funneled that money into the individual loan accounts, closing each one in turn.

Within the hour, Kawakami had wiped the slate clean at Miracle Mile. He began to think that maybe he had saved his skin. All he needed now was a little luck. Maybe no one at Wells Fargo would ever discover what he had done.

* * *

Ben Lewis finally found the problem: a $357,000 bank-originated debit. Smith had called all upset because the MAPS checking account seemed to have several hundred thousand dollars less than it was supposed to. Lewis was used to such panicky calls. Harold never knew how much money was in his accounts. Sammie Marshall was the same way. It fell usually to Ben and Teri Key to make sense of all the account balances.

By now Smith and Lewis had developed an efficient message system for moving embezzled money into the MAPS accounts and verifying the deposits. When Smith needed more money, he would call or have Teri call Ben to see "if that wire for $200,000 from the network" had come in yet. After Ben had passed additional branch settlement entries in order to put more money into an account, he would call the office and if he couldn't reach Smith, leave a message: "That $200,000 wire Harold was expecting came in."

They were moving lots of money these days—always one direction: from Wells Fargo to MAPS—but this $357,000 transaction was a mystery to him. Someone at the bank had taken the money out of the account. Lewis called Difference Research and asked a clerk there to check the debit's offset, or justification. That afternoon the clerk called back. There were numerous offsets, she said. All of them were cashier's checks issued at Miracle Mile.

Lewis asked the clerk to send him copies of the checks, and then he telephoned Smith to explain the situation.

"They can't do that, can they?" Smith asked, implying that he had not given permission for the transactions.

"They're not supposed to," Lewis said.

"I'm going to find out what happened."

Not more than an hour later, Smith called back. He was angry and upset. "Gene put it through himself. Can he get fired for that?"

"Well yes." Lewis hesitated. This was not a good battle to fight. Regardless of whether the debit was justifiable or not, they could not afford to pursue a complaint. "Harold, with the position we're in here, you can't make a stink about it."

"I'm going over there and take this up with Kawakami personally," Smith said, hanging up.

Later in the day, when Smith showed up at Beverly Drive, he asked to speak to Lewis in private. They went into a small office at the back of the bank and closed the door.

Smith seemed not to know where to start.

"So what happened with Gene?" Lewis asked.

"He was crying all over himself."

Lewis raised his eyebrows in surprise. He couldn't imagine Kawakami, who always acted so cool, breaking down in front of a customer.

"He's got all these gambling debts," Smith continued. "Some people were holding his child and were going to cut the kid's toes off if they didn't get their money. So he took the money from my account and paid them off. He used the rest to pay off some loans we had at the bank."

Smith pulled out a folded piece of yellow legal paper. "I got him to give me an IOU."

He flashed it in front of Ben, who saw a signature below a promise to repay some money. He didn't notice the exact amount.

Smith looked at the IOU, then refolded it and put it back in his pocket. "It might not be worth much, but at least it's got his signature on it."

Lewis found the whole scenario difficult to believe. It just didn't ring true. *Holding his child? Cut the kid's toes off?* Farfetched would be the way to describe it. But the debit was real, that he was sure of. So were the cashier's checks, which, according to the clerk, bore Kawakami's signature. And Harold was holding this piece of paper with Gene's signature on it. So *something* was going on. Knowing Smith as he did, Lewis figured that Harold and Gene must have some arrangement of their own. Kawakami had been around the fringe of the MAPS operation enough to get pulled into something by Harold. Maybe something went sour, and Gene or the bank was really owed this money—it certainly wouldn't be anything new for Smith to owe the bank money. There might even have been a trace of envy in Lewis. If Kawakami had managed to get repayment from Smith, that was more than he had ever been able to do.

"What do you think we should do about it?" Smith asked.

"Forget it."

"Yeah, I guess you're right."

The next day, the copies of the Miracle Mile cashier's checks arrived at Beverly Drive. Lewis opened the package and looked at each one. The amounts varied and so did the name of the payees—one of them was Ken Kato. None of them rang a bell with Lewis. Considering the matter closed, he threw away the copies. This was Harold's problem from now on. He had plenty of his own problems at the bank to worry about.

* * *

Kawakami was quite pleased with himself. And he had reason to be. In one swift move he had cleaned up the MAPS mess at his branch. No longer was he quite as vulnerable to the actions or inactions of Harold Smith.

First he had heard from Smith by phone.

"You took too much money out of my account," he charged.

"The dollar figure is exactly what you owe with interest," Kawakami said.

"I'm coming right over." Smith's voice had a threatening tone to it.

It had been a pretty weird scene when Smith arrived. At first he was aggressive and belligerent. He threatened to report Kawakami to his superiors for making an illegal debit of his account.

"I'm not alone in this," Kawakami warned. "You're on the other end. You turn me in and you turn yourself in."

"I don't care," Smith said.

"I don't care either. It doesn't matter either way."

Kawakami felt reborn. It was as if he had taken control of his own destiny again after relinquishing it to someone else for the past year or so. Honestly, though, he wasn't ready to go down the tubes. He figured both of them were bluffing when they said they didn't care if the other reported the matter. He knew Smith didn't want his role in the bad loans to be exposed. And Kawakami certainly didn't want his part in the loans revealed either.

Smith took out some paperwork that had the original loan amounts. "I don't owe no $357,000."

Kawakami pulled out the latest loan documents that showed what each one had escalated to.

Smith seemed surprised, then became more reasonable. The promoter explained that he had it in mind that he owed around $140,000. And that's what he thought Kawakami would be taking out of his account.

Kawakami remained firm. He had only done what they had agreed he could do when the Hearns-Cuevas money came in. And he had only taken money that was long overdue. "I'm not going to reverse the debit," he said with an air of finality.

Confronted with this display of firmness by Kawakami, an amazing change came over Smith. He sat down, lowered his head and began to cry. Not in little snivels but in racking sobs. "Now I can't—go home to Lee."

Kawakami was stunned. Real tears rolled down Smith's cheeks. If this was an act, the man could win an Academy Award.

"She counts on me—to support her and our little boy. I told her I owed you some money, but not *this* much. What am I going to do?"

Kawakami was now embarrassed and uneasy. He wanted Smith out of his office as quickly as possible. The man was making an awkward scene. Kawakami was sorry he had ever gotten involved with him. Ali or no Ali, it had been a big mistake. It had cost him too much time and peace of mind. It might still cost him his job and reputation.

"I just—don't know what I can do," Smith said plaintively.

"I'm not going to reverse it."

"I know. Gene, you my friend—you always been my friend." Smith's tear-stained face came out from behind his hands. "Do me a favor, Gene. One small favor. Give me a piece of paper just to show Lee."

"An IOU?"

"Yeah, for the extra $217,000."

"But Harold, I don't owe you those dollars."

"Oh, I know. It's just for Lee. Then she'll know I didn't spend it. Here, I'll write something out."

Smith took a page of yellow legal paper from a pad on Kawakami's desk and penned a short note. He handed it to the banker.

Kawakami read the IOU. There was no provision for interest or any repayment date. It was, as far as the banker could determine, an unenforceable and therefore worthless promissory note. He knew if he signed it Smith would leave his office and he could get on with his business and his life. It was tempting. Too tempting.

"I'll sign it, but I'm not going to pay it," Kawakami said. He reached for a pen and signed his name.

Smith left his office a few minutes later.

The two men never spoke again.

CHAPTER TWENTY-ONE

To Ben Lewis, Harold's room at the Caribe Hilton seemed about the size of an aircraft carrier's flight deck. This was the premier hotel room in all of San Juan, Puerto Rico. Boxing's Pepe Cordero—Puerto Rico was his native country—had made sure it was available for Smith. Nothing was too good for the head of Muhammad Ali Professional Sports. Particularly as long as Cordero kept getting his due. For this trip and on orders from Smith, Lewis had stuffed $26,000 cash in his shoulder bag and personally turned it over to Cordero. Lewis noticed when he put the cash on a table in front of Cordero that the Puerto Rican lawyer didn't count the bills in front of him. No doubt there would be an accounting later. For his part, Ben didn't question the payments. It was small potatoes compared to the favors Cordero could do for MAPS and its boxers. Cordero was known as a man who delivered for his friends. Such things as making sure that important fighters he personally managed—like Ernesto Espana—would be available to fight. More important, it was generally believed that he could assure that favored fighters received special consideration in the WBA rankings. He helped in other ways, too, like arriving at the MAPS office off a flight from South America with a huge container of cocaine. In front of an amazed Teri Key, Smith divided it up and filled manila envelopes which he gave away as gifts. No doubt about it, Pepe Cordero was a good man to have in your corner.

The locals told Lewis that if the President of the United States were to visit the island this would be his suite. Such hyperbole was easy to believe. The suite was fabulous. Complete with sunken living room and a baby grand piano, it featured a formal dining room, a large den with fireplace and three bedrooms, each with its own bath. Most striking was the wide outside deck that encircled the room on three sides. The view was not of any dilapidated streets or ragged residents but rather of the majestic Caribbean Sea crashing against the rocks below, sending up fountains of spray and filling the suite with the rhythmic booming sound of the surf.

Everyone important in boxing circles was at this seaside location the third week in September 1980 for the latest MAPS championship fight: the Hilmer Kenty-Ernesto Espana rematch. Kenty, in only his seventeenth pro fight, had scored a big upset and taken the WBA lightweight title away from Espana on March 2, 1980, in Detroit. It was only the second defeat in thirty bouts for Espana, a native of Venezuela. After becoming champion, Kenty met with Smith and, "advised" by Pepe Cordero, decided to fight on a MAPS card. As usual, Smith agreed to pay the fighter handsomely. In a wise promotional decision, the rematch was being held in a part of the world where masses of people would turn out to root for a fellow Latin against an American.

Boxing has long been one of the most popular sports in Latin America. Panama, Puerto Rico, Mexico and, to a lesser extent, Argentina have developed large pools of ring talent through active amateur and professional programs at the grass-roots level. Recognizing both the large number of Hispanic competitors—champions as well as contenders—and fans who resided on the continent, Smith had started the Latin American Division of MAPS in June 1980. Based in Miami, it was run by Felix "Tuto" Zabala, an experienced Latin fight promoter who had good connections in the Southern Hemisphere. Working for a modest salary of some $1,000 a month and promised a percentage of the profits of any fights he promoted, Zabala soon became concerned with the large amounts of money MAPS was paying its Latin fighters. He told Smith they did not have to pay that much because these fellows just weren't used to that kind of money. Smith told him not to worry. The big paydays were okay—MAPS did it all the time. One of Zabala's early successes was delivering WBA Junior Welterweight Champion Antonio Cervantes for the MAPS card with Aaron Pryor. The other Latin champion to fight on that double championship day for MAPS, Pipino Cuevas, had been signed for the fight only after Lewis cut a $75,000 cashier's check destined for Cordero. Zabala had picked up the check from Lewis at the Beverly Drive branch, saying he was going to deliver it to Cordero as a "finder's fee." Lewis figured that the payment would insure that the Cuevas-Hearns fight would receive WBA sanction as a championship bout, an event that Lewis considered worth the extra expense.

Though the Kenty-Espana fight was not a Latin American Division show, the MAPS people were hopeful that they could take advantage of the interest in boxing in that part of the world and bring in a whopping gate in San Juan. An added bonus was the network TV money to be paid for rights to televise the bout back in the United States. The only problem with the location was Kenty's worry: he was a black man from Detroit fighting in the Latin boxer's backyard. Kenty's supporters felt that if it was a close decision, their man would probably lose.

The Detroit boxer went after the ex-champ with a vengeance, assaulting him with a barrage of rights and lefts that left Espana dazed, weakened and wobbly before his stunned fans. The fight was finally stopped in the ninth round, and Kenty's gloved hand was raised in victory. MAPS too was victorious. For once, the income ($281,640) of a fight far exceeded the purses ($82,950). On paper, at least, MAPS had turned a handsome profit for the fight. Of course, there were a lot of expenses not logged in the books. Like those that went for partying.

At the usual postfight bash—held in Smith's impressive presidential quarters—only the lack of dancing music left something to be desired. Light-heavyweight champ Matthew Saad Muhammad, one of Smith's dozens of guests flown in for the fight, volunteered to go to his room and bring back his tape recorder with various cassettes. Lewis went with him, anxious to have a moment to talk to the champ. It was the second time that the two men had met. Ben wondered if the fighter would remember the first.

"Saad, you remember the first time we met?"

"Yeah, I remember."

"Where was it?" A smile creased Ben's face. Considering how many people the fighter had come in contact with since winning his division crown in early 1979, Lewis would have wagered that Saad Muhammad wouldn't remember.

"On Bourbon Street," Saad Muhammad said matter-of-factly. "In New Orleans."

Lewis was surprised. He decided to take the test a step further. "Do you remember what you told me?"

Saad Muhammad nodded and spoke without hesitation. "I told you I was going to be champion."

Lewis couldn't believe it. Saad had actually recalled the details of their chance encounter on the street at the Ali-Spinks rematch, when he was walking with his son down the well-lit boulevard. Somehow it had been an important enough encounter for the boxer to remember. Lewis felt honored.

"Did I lie?" a grinning Saad Muhammad asked.

"No, you didn't," Ben said, laughing and slapping the fighter on the back. The kind of determination Saad had shown in making his dream come true was what made boxing great. "You sure didn't." In a real sense, this was Ben's dream coming true too, being on the inside of a sport he loved and chumming around with its champions.

Later, Ben was in the elevator headed back for the penthouse from making a phone call when it made a stop. He was surprised to see Harold coaxing a young Puerto Rican woman to come with him. He had last seen Smith wooing several other attentive women around a mirror full of cocaine in his suite. The promoter moved fast and had an enormous appetite for the opposite sex. But his latest find was spurning him.

"But I love you, baby," Smith pleaded. "I do."

The woman shook her head, unenchanted by his antics.

Empty-handed, Smith shrugged and boarded the elevator.

If Ben believed Harold on the subject of sex and love (he didn't), this rejection would have been one of the few times in Harold Smith's life that he didn't get his way with a woman. He was always bragging about his sexual conquests, saying things like "She finally had to ask me to stop" or "I was too much for her." He told Ben how the combination of marijuana and cocaine worked wonders for his sexual performance, bragging "It makes me into a Superman." When Ben tried the mix, hoping for the same results, he suffered from bouts of impotency, insomnia, depression, headaches and stomach cramps. Some of his miseries undoubtedly were related to stress and lack of rest, but the drugs sure didn't help any. He gave them up for the most part. It was not an easy time, and he needed to keep his wits.

Among the many things bothering Ben was the lack of attention the artistic promotions of Lewis and Smith Enterprises were getting from Smith. Their first event had been a four-day show in August at the Dorothy Chandler Pavilion featuring singer Shirley Bassey. She had been paid with two Wells Fargo cashier's checks totaling $100,000. Naturally the checks were generated by fictitious charges to the branch settlement system. The event had netted a profit of $11,000, made possible only because the $100,000 was not repaid to the bank. Lewis and Bruce Barrett, whom he and Harold had hired to produce events for their entertainment business, had some big plans for other shows, but Smith never seemed to have time to listen to them. He was too busy with the boxing business.

Another matter bothering Lewis was the way he was now being treated by Sammie Marshall. Marshall had long ceased to be the close friend he once was. Sammie treated most MAPS employees with an obvious lack of respect and often displayed a hot temper and surly impatience in dealing with them. Not many people around the office liked him. The two men spent virtually no time together anymore. Marshall seemed envious of Ben's friendship with Harold. Every time Ben went into Harold's office, Sammie seemed to find an excuse to come in and find out what was going on.

In some ways, Marshall didn't fit into the MAPS organization. He was not an outgoing type and didn't do well in party situations. He wasn't particularly close to the boxers either. He wasn't efficient, and it was often difficult to get a definite answer out of him. He waffled a lot. He was best in his role as the MAPS matchmaker. He studied boxers' records and knew who should meet whom and what matchup would make for an exciting bout. But as an advance man he had problems with logistics. Often when the MAPS entourage went into a town for a fight, much of the crucial work that was supposed to have been done by Marshall had been overlooked. Simple things weren't done, like arranging to have portable steps in order for the boxers to climb into the ring. Such carelessness irked Ben. Sometimes Sammie hadn't even reserved a hotel room for him. That really angered Lewis. After all, *he* was paying all the bills. By comparison, the amateur fights handled by Marshall's counterpart at MAAS, Bob Campbell, were well planned and staged. Campbell was good at what he did and was well liked by his colleagues at the MAPS-MAAS offices.

Though Lewis never discussed the growing embezzlements with Marshall, it was inconceivable to him that Sammie didn't know what was going on. After all, Marshall was keeping all the books on the fights. He knew the unbelievable amounts the boxers were being paid. He was renting the arenas and paying the vendors. Though, amazingly, he always had a hard time balancing a checkbook, Sammie clearly knew the fights were losing money and MAPS was losing big too. And Sammie had been there at the beginning, when the two of them had started doing favors for Smith at the bank's expense. Where else could Sammie think all the dollars were coming from?

Back upstairs, enjoying the picturesque view from the deck, Ben was reminded of all the changes that had taken place in his life. Who would have thought a few short years ago that he would end up in a luxurious San Juan hotel, having flown there on a private jet, rubbing elbows and joking with some of the biggest names in professional boxing? His life had taken quite a few surprising turns.

"I want you to meet someone," Smith said, approaching him with another man in tow. "This is Bilal Muhammad. Bilal, this is my partner Ben Lewis."

Lewis shook hands with the black man. Ben was pleased at the way Harold had introduced him as his *partner*. It was about time he started getting some credit around here.

"Bilal is Saad Muhammad's manager," Smith explained.

Here was another one of life's turns. He had run into this kid on the streets of New Orleans by accident and now that kid was a world champion, and he, Lloyd Benjamin Lewis, was helping to finance his future. MAPS and Saad and Bilal Muhammad had just agreed to a three-fight deal. Lewis had heard about it from Smith and heartily approved.

"I'm sure glad to hear about us signing Saad," Lewis said. "He's a great fighter and a wonderful young man."

Bilal smiled and said they were happy with the deal too.

They had every reason to be happy. The contract Saad Muhammad had signed with MAPS was extraordinary. The first fight set for November would pit Saad against top light heavyweight contender Lotti Mwale. For that Saad was to receive a purse of $650,000, plus $35,000 in training expenses. For the second fight—Saad's opponent was to be decided later—he would get $500,000, plus $50,000 training money. Then, for a unification of the two light heavyweight titles—WBC Champ Saad Muhammad against WBA Champ Eddie Mustafa Muhammad—Saad was to receive $1.5 million and an additional $150,000 for expenses. In all, the MAPS deal was worth nearly $3 million to Saad. Despite the impressive numbers, Bilal Muhammad had not inked the contract while in the MAPS offices in Los Angeles. He had taken it back home to Newark, New Jersey, along with Smith's good faith cashier's check for $25,000 and showed it to his attorney. The lawyer approved the deal, of course—the dollar amounts were bigger than any other promoter in the world would pay Saad Muhammad. But the attorney said he strongly advised that an advance payment clause be added to the contract. With Smith the attorney wanted no postfight payments, which were actually quite common in the business. He explained to his client that there was something about Harold Smith and all his big dollars that he did not trust. When Bilal informed Smith of the need for this added clause, the promoter readily agreed. Smith flew to New York, where they met and signed the revised contracts.

Despite his attorney's reservations, Bilal Muhammad was impressed with the MAPS people. The private jet, the parties, the fancy hotel suites, the millions of dollars being spent on fighters—hell, three million bucks for his own guy—all very persuasive. Hanging around these guys was a good way to get rich quick.

* * *

Two weeks later, but on a different continent, another wild MAPS party was being held in Harold Smith's hotel suite following a fight. The location was Las Vegas. It was October 2, 1980, a date that would go down in boxing history.

The MAPS entourage had taken over most of the swanky Carriage House and its fifty-odd rooms—all of them nicely decorated suites with living rooms, bedrooms, kitchens and dining rooms. At last count, Teri Key figured that MAPS was footing the bill for about seventy-five people, who had flown in from all parts of the country. Pilot Pat Milstead made several trips from L.A. with the jet loaded to capacity. Others came in on commercial flights booked by Teri and paid for by MAPS. The guests were fighters, managers, trainers, wives, girlfriends, brothers, sisters, buddies and other assorted hangers-on. Some of the people Harold knew well, others he barely recognized. Some he was doing business with, others he wanted to do business with. Ken Norton was there, so were Hearns, Kenty and Gerry Cooney with his people. In addition to transportation, the tab included hotel, food, fight tickets, even gambling money for some.

Once again the champagne was chilled and flowing and the cocaine plentiful. The mirror above the bathroom sink had been unbolted from the wall and placed on a coffee table in the middle of the living room. There was a mound of snow in the center of the mirror from which lines were cut. Communal straws were close at hand. Teri was encouraged by several partygoers to do a line, something she had never done before. She decided to go for it. Why not? Everyone else was partaking. She fumbled with the straw to the amusement of Harold and the others. The rush was nice and easy. Soon she didn't care if the party ever ended.

The party was not a victory celebration this time around. It was more like a wake. A few hours earlier Muhammad Ali had lost to Larry Holmes in the ring at Caesar's Palace, and most of the people in this crowd hoped that Ali's fighting days were over. He had taken more abuse in the ring than any one person should be asked to endure. Everyone in the MAPS office—including Smith—felt that Ali should not have fought again even before he went into the ring with Holmes. To his worried friends and associates, Ali claimed he had to take this fight because he needed the money. Teri found that difficult to believe. Considering all the money he had made over the years, he had to be a millionaire many times over. Undoubtedly his need to fight went deep and involved his lifelong desire to prove to the world that he was "the greatest."

The bout had the typical circus atmosphere that surrounded most Ali fights. There were the usual die-hard fans who bet on him even though they knew that he didn't have a chance. (Teri was sure Smith bet on Holmes, though her boss would never admit such a defection.) In the ring Ali seemed strangely determined to prove that he could take a punch. Time and again he waited for Holmes to measure him and then stood flat-footed as the WBC champ delivered his best shots to the head and body. (Ali, ending a two-year retirement, was now a contender instead of a champion. He had retired after regaining the title from Spinks in New Orleans. This fight was an attempt, however feeble, for Ali to win a title for an unprecedented fourth time.) Within a few rounds, Ali's face was puffy and reddened, his legs rubbery. It was an unbearable sight for his fans.

Teri and Tony Key sat in choice fifth-row seats that cost MAPS $500 apiece. They were surrounded by famous actors. Jon Voight was behind them, Sylvester Stallone and Jack Nicholson on either side. Nearby were Jayne and Leon Kennedy, who had recently used the MAPS gym to film their boxing movie, *Body and Soul*. Teri winced every time Holmes unloaded on Ali. How much punishment could the man take?

Ben Lewis wasn't that far away, sitting in his own $500 seat near basketball star Julius "Dr. J" Erving. Former football star O. J. Simpson walked by with a beautiful woman on each arm. Ben had watched the blows come raining down on his hero. He had been afraid this might happen. Several times the previous week he had called Harold to check on Ali's condition—Smith had arrived earlier to meet with various fight people. Smith had told him all along that everything was going great, that Ali's weight was down and that he'd be stepping into the ring lighter than he had been in years. On that score, Harold was right. When he went into training for Holmes, Ali weighed an enormous 254 pounds. By the time he weighed in the day before the fight, he had dropped to 217. He looked trim, with a flat stomach and hardened leg muscles. What Ben didn't know—and Harold only admitted to him after the lopsided fight—was that Ali had gotten dangerously weak during training. "Those last few days, he could barely run a mile," Smith claimed. Even when Ali suspended his training and simply rested and ate, he kept losing weight—dropping from 223 to 217 in the last few days.

In a way Lewis felt sorry even for Holmes. Here was a fine fighter who all his career had competed in the shadow of Ali. Now, finally, they were in the same ring. But the fight wouldn't prove anything. Holmes couldn't possibly come out a clear winner. If the incredible happened and he lost to Ali, Holmes would still be thought of as a second-rate champion. If he beat Ali as expected, people would say that he fought a washed-up hero. Worse yet, if he hurt Muhammad Ali, the public would never forgive him.

Sadly, Ali seemed to lack even the strength necessary to protect himself, let alone fight back. By the end of the tenth round, some ringsiders insisted they had counted only fifteen punches thrown by Ali. When he sat down on his bench, glassy-eyed and exhausted, trainer Angelo Dundee shook his head and decided that was enough. Ali didn't even attempt to rise at the bell. Dundee went to throw a white towel into the ring, and cornerman Bundini Brown tried to stop him. Dundee wouldn't be deterred, though. "That's it," he yelled to the referee, finally whipping the towel into ring center. Seeing that Ali had given up, the crowd alternated between cheering and booing.

Ben stayed in his room during the postfight partying, angry, tired and disgusted. Ali's feeble showing had hurt and upset him. No one likes watching his idol be dismantled. But actually his morose mood had started the previous day, when he had gotten off work at the bank. Ben sometimes felt as though he was the only one of the MAPS group who had to work for a living. He talked often with Smith these days of wanting to leave the bank and work full-time for Lewis and Smith Enterprises. All he wanted was the freedom and independence to work for himself and live comfortably in the process. Harold would usually acknowledge him with some vague assurance like "We'll get you out soon, don't worry." But Ben knew he could never leave the bank until the embezzled money had been repaid.

By the time Ben had gotten off work, all the MAPS people were already in Vegas with the exception of Teri Key, who had stayed behind to man the office phones. He expected to be flown to Vegas by Pat Milstead in the MAPS plane. But a message came in from Milstead just before Lewis left for the airport: the MAPS plane was on the ground in Vegas and would make no more flights that day. Ben and Teri would have to come on a commercial flight. As if that wasn't bad enough, they had to fight a crowd at the airport trying to get into Vegas for the fight. It was not a pleasant trip. Ben steamed the whole way and let Teri know that he felt more than a little jilted. Of all the people who flew to Vegas in the comfort of the private plane, he certainly should have been among those accommodated.

When they got to the Carriage House and walked into the lobby, Lewis couldn't believe all the women hanging around. Harold had brought along his former and current girlfriends and future prospects as well. It looked like an Atlantic City hotel during the Miss America contest. The usual MAPS contingent was in attendance, but there were a lot of extra people sponging off MAPS whom Lewis didn't even recognize. Meanwhile, the last MAPS fight, a heavy-weight bout between Marty Monroe and Eddie "The Animal" Lopez held at the Inglewood Forum on September 27, had been a real bomb. Only $7,560 was collected at the gate, and the purses amounted to more than $200,000. This kind of bad business *had* to stop. Not trusting his frayed emotions, Ben stayed in his room that night. After the fight the next day, he went back to his room and took a nap.

Later there was a knock on his door. Ben opened it to find Smith standing there with a glass of champagne in his hand.

"Why aren't you at the party?" Harold asked thickly. He was higher than a kite.

"Being as how you have half of L.A. here, I didn't think you'd notice."

"Come on, we're partying."

"You're *always* partying. You rented this whole fuckin' hotel. You had the plane make six or seven round-trips to pick up your friends, but *I* had to fly commercial. Get away from me, man. I'm fed up with you and your parties."

Smith left, pouting like a child.

Lewis picked up the phone and reached Milstead in his room. "Pat, this is Benjamin. I want that plane fired up at six o'clock tomorrow morning," he said sternly. "I'm leaving then. And Pat, there are to be *no* other flights. You got that?"

"Sure," Milstead said. "Harold said you're the only other person who can give orders on where the plane goes."

"You got that right."

Lewis returned to Los Angeles the next morning aboard the MAPS plane but not before he had to give Milstead money for fuel out of his own pocket.

Later that day, his phone rang at home.

"Ben, you know you're my best friend. Why'd you leave?" It was Smith. His voice sounded subdued. He was crying or at least trying to sound like it. "You hurt my feelings. Lee is all upset."

"I don't give a damn," Lewis said, still seething. The crying on the other end of the line sounded fake to him. But even if it was real, it didn't matter. "None of this is making any sense. You're spending money like water. You're not paying back the bank. We might as well go on top of a high roof somewhere and throw the money away. That's how you're wasting it."

"But I promised all those people," Smith sobbed, "that if Ali fought again I'd make sure they were there to see him. I'll take care of the money owed to the bank. We've got some big shows coming up—"

Ben hung up. He was disgusted. He had heard it all before many times. He was tired of Harold and his excuses. He had seen how the man used people. He would tell one person one thing and another person something else. Whatever suited his needs at the moment. Ben was fed up with all of it.

He avoided Smith for weeks. It took him that long to cool down. Nevertheless, he kept depositing money for MAPS. Now, instead of putting it into the Harold J. Smith Productions account and then having Smith move it to the appropriate MAPS account—a charade Smith had insisted on that seemed unimportant to Lewis—he started putting money directly into the overdraft account that needed it.

* * *

Smith sat back in a passenger seat of the Aero Commander. He took off his dark glasses and rubbed his eyes. It had been a busy month since the Ali-Holmes fight. He had crisscrossed the country several times making deals and signing fighters.

"Signing [Michael] Spinks was important to our plans," he explained to a small audience that included Lewis, Bruce Barrett and card girl Arlene "Tweetie" Alexander.

"The only champions we don't have yet are Ray Leonard, Duran, Hagler and Larry Holmes," Smith said. "But with all the other fighters we got, Holmes and the rest will have to come to us to fight *anyone*."

The plane was headed to San Antonio, Texas, for a MAPS card that included heavyweight Ken Norton going against local hero Randy "Tex"

Cobb. Smith had signed both heavyweights to promotional contracts but had especially big plans for Norton. The fight he really wanted to set up was Norton against Gerry Cooney. In the meantime, he was moving in the other weight divisions too. This was the first of six fights scheduled for November. The other five would be championship bouts. The titles at stake would include the WBA lightweight, WBA bantamweight, WBA junior welterweight, WBA light heavyweight and WBC light heavyweight. It was a classy lineup. There was no doubt about it, MAPS was now at the top of the boxing world. In terms of signing fighters and wielding influence, Harold Smith was on the verge of controlling an entire sport.

Aboard the jet, the topic turned to Lewis and Smith Enterprises. Smith had invited Barrett along because he wanted to discuss the entertainment business. Occasional attention to this topic was Smith's way of throwing Ben a bone when he needed it. Discouraged more than ever by the branch settlement treadmill he was on at Wells Fargo, Ben had recently threatened to cut back to part-time at the bank. Harold had gotten very agitated. "We can't afford that," he had said. "We need you there. We have lots of things to do. Maybe later." Lewis was no fool. He knew what Smith meant. *We can't afford to pay the money back, and we'll need more money down the road.* If Ben wasn't at the bank, all the financing would disappear overnight. MAPS would have to compete on an equal basis with the other promoters. The way MAPS was dropping money, it wouldn't last long.

"Lewis and Smith Enterprises could buy theaters in black neighborhoods," Smith said, eyeing Lewis for his reaction. "We'd own the projectors and screens and use the theaters as closed-circuit outlets for showing live concerts we're putting on in another city. Like Teddy Pendergrass and Diana Ross. They'd be big draws. We could make a lot of bread. What do you think, Ben?"

Lewis agreed it sounded like a good idea. He was sick of the boxing business.

"We can make a killing," Barrett said excitedly, "plus manage the entertainers."

"Management is the way to go," Smith said.

"Hey, I know what you want to do," Barrett said, as if a light had suddenly gone off. "By linking these operations up, you want to *control* the whole industry! Just what you're doing with boxing."

Smith smiled and offered his open palms for Barrett's give-me-ten slap. *Control.* That was just the kind of talk Harold Smith liked to hear.

At the fight, they all sat ringside. They had been joined by Sammie Marshall, who flew in from Detroit with a girlfriend. Norton looked over at them every time he hit Cobb, as if to say, "I told you I could beat him." And Norton did just that. Most of the cheers, however, were directed at the full complement of card girls working the fight. Tweetie and the gang took turns bending down and climbing between the ropes during rounds with their placards and their chests held high. While the entertainment was exciting, the money was disappointing, as usual. Cobb had received $100,000 and Norton slightly more. The total income was $57,514. Just like that, MAPS had dropped another two hundred grand.

After the fight, Lewis was in his room taking a nap when the phone awakened him.

"Mr. Lewis, this is Gerry Cooney. Where's the party?"

"I don't have parties in my room," Lewis said groggily.

"Gee, I'm sorry to disturb you, Mr. Lewis."

Cooney was always so polite it was impossible not to like him. He also had a warm, boyish sense of humor.

"That's okay, Gerry. The party is in Harold's room. It always is. Have fun."

Smith had flown Cooney and his manager, Dennis Rappaport, in from New York to look over Norton. Apparently they liked what they saw because they agreed to fight him after the first of the year. As usual, the money was hard to turn down. The MAPS deal was potentially worth millions of dollars to Cooney.

Cooney was quite an attraction at the party. Darlene, Smith's favorite card girl at the time, slipped him her phone number and address in Los Angeles. Later, when Smith winked and asked him if he had found anyone at the party that he liked, Cooney said he did.

"Her name is Darlene," the big fighter said.

Smith frowned. "No, not her. She's mine."

"I'm sorry," Cooney said, smiling like a teenager. "She gave me her phone number. I thought it was all right."

These days Lewis often found himself lecturing Smith on the number of women he had on a string. "You've got to settle down," he said. "There's no respect being shown for them or yourself." Smith kept promising he would pick one or two girlfriends and leave the rest alone.

At breakfast the morning after the fight, Smith and Lewis sat with Rappaport and Cooney, discussing the need to improve the fighter's rankings.

"I can do it," Smith said.

"What?" Rappaport asked.

"Get Gerry's ranking moved up."

"I'll believe it when I see it," Rappaport said.

Lewis cleared his throat. He knew how close Smith was to Pepe Cordero. He knew because he had cut all those cashier's checks that helped Harold get close to Cordero.

"I think you can believe Harold," Lewis said. "He can do it."

November was a big month for cashier's checks as the financial picture got much worse by the end of the month. The five championship fights lost a total of a half million dollars. Typical was the bout between Saad Muhammad and Lotti Mwale. Smith had matched a Philadelphia fighter and a Nigerian fighter in San Diego, a notoriously weak fight town, and lost $216,000. It was plainly a bad promotion, but then, a lot of people in boxing considered Harold Smith a bad promoter. He was overpaying fighters, attracting small gates and not selling TV rights for enough to cover his losses. Many times he failed to ask for an option on a boxer's next fight when he signed the fighter, a standard technique in the business. Most of his competitors had originally felt that he couldn't last long in the business. But he had gotten downright dangerous now that he had so many champions under contract. Obviously he had one heck of a thick checkbook.

The biggest MAPS loser of the month, weighing in at a negative $328,900, was the Mustafa Muhammad-Rudi Koopmans fight at the Olympic Auditorium in Los Angeles. But Smith didn't mind. He had big plans for both of the Muhammads and didn't mind spending—or losing—money on them. Right after Saad signed with MAPS, he had ordered Teri to count out $35,000 in cash for the boxer and make no receipt. As for Mustafa, when he came to Los Angeles to train for his fight, Smith rented a Mercedes for him, a Cadillac and condo for his manager and gave them a $300,000 cashier's check for training expenses.

Smith considered all this as mere seed money. Both these fighters were part of his plans for the biggest fight card in boxing history. MAPS was moving into position right where he had wanted it to be all along: in *control* of the fight game.

* * *

"Okay, here's the plan," Smith said. "Norton beat Cobb, so all we gotta do is get Cooney ranked in the top ten. A Norton-Cooney fight will highlight the card. Two big heavyweight names and a black-white matchup. It's a dream fight for us."

"That would be a good fight for New York," Lewis said. "Madison Square Garden or maybe Yankee Stadium."

"New York is a good idea. I like the Garden."

"What would we have to pay them?"

"Cooney would need three million, Norton a million."

"That's awfully high," Lewis said.

"We'll get it all back and more when Cooney fights for the title. He's a 'Great White Hope,' you know," Smith said, showing an ironic grin.

The two men were sitting in Harold's corner office at the MAPS office with the door closed. Each, for different reasons, wanted to make a killing on a big MAPS show. Lewis to pay back the bank so he could leave a job he now hated. Smith to make every major promoter in boxing have to come to him to arrange a fight. All that money flowing in would take the heat off from Ali's advisors, who were being so persistent about checking the MAPS books. After throwing the Champ a cool million or two, there would be less worry about the financial picture at MAPS. Smith wanted to be nothing less than the Godfather of boxing. *Pay me and you get your fight.* It would be that simple.

"We've got both Muhammads now," Smith continued, "so when we unify the title we own the champion no matter who wins, Saad or Mustafa. They'll need a million to a million and a half each. We got Pryor, we put him in with Arguello or Mamby. And don't forget Hearns-Benitez. Everyone is waiting for that one, and we got both of 'em."

The list went on. There were eight or nine fights. All of them major confrontations involving at least one reigning champion. If eight of them were put on one championship card, it would truly be the biggest boxing event in history. The closed-circuit and cable TV potential throughout the world would be enormous. But so would the expense. And Ben was worried about that.

"How much you think this is going to cost to put on?" Lewis asked.

"I'd say seven or eight million." Smith said the numbers as easily as if he were telling someone his height.

Lewis remained silent.

Finally Smith spoke. "Hey, man, this thing gonna make at least forty, fifty million dollars—maybe as much as a hundred million. This gonna be the greatest boxing show of all time," he said, mimicking a line of Ali's. "We gonna be able to retire to the Caribbean and live like millionaires."

"I want every penny paid back to the bank," Lewis said. "And I mean it." Ben's voice had taken on an edge. "You haven't paid back one penny yet. You've made no effort at all. I'm tired. I've had it."

"No problem. We'll get it paid back."

"No, I *mean* it this time, Harold. We take the money out for this fight and that's it, buddy. It's over. I'm definitely leaving the bank after this fight."

"Hey, I thought of a great name for the fight—'This Is It.' What do you think?"

"Yeah, that's good. Because this *is* it."

CHAPTER TWENTY-TWO

en Lewis could not remember ever being so sick. He had caught a cold toward the end of October, and within a couple of weeks it had gone into his chest. The busy traveling schedule—working all week and sleeping on the plane Friday and Saturday nights en route from one fight to another—had taken its toll. The morning after the Norton-Cobb fight in Texas, they had flown from San Antonio to Detroit for the Kenty-Fernandez bout, and he had been so tired when they arrived that he went to his room and slept right through the fight. It was the same almost every week. Each Sunday night he returned from the weekend trip exhausted, and then his alarm would go off at 5:30 a.m. on Monday morning for the start of another nerve-wracking week at the bank.

Finally, he started running a temperature in the low hundreds and went to the doctor, who told him he was "burning the candle at both ends." The doctor ordered bed rest, but Ben told him that was impossible. He *had* to go to work. The doctor had heard that before; a lot of his patients were workaholics. Then Ben developed pneumonia. That *did* put him in bed, flat on his back. There he got little rest for worrying. He knew that somehow he had to get to the bank in time to pass the necessary branch settlement entries to keep the embezzlement going. And he was the only one who could do it.

More money than ever before was being siphoned from Wells Fargo in order to fatten the MAPS accounts for the show at Madison Square Garden. Harold was giving Lewis regular updates on the fighters who had agreed to sign and how much money he needed to conclude each deal. Sometimes he required cash—once, when Beverly Drive was short, Smith had sent a limo around to various Wells Fargo branches to collect sacks full of greenbacks. The deposits to the various accounts had been nonstop, as had the expenses. Just the other day, for example, Lewis had sent the required deposit to the Waldorf-Astoria to rent a ballroom for the Lewis and Smith Enterprises dinner show featuring Tony Orlando that was to precede the big fight. The new money for the upcoming card already totaled in the millions. Ben saw the "This Is It" card as his big chance—maybe the last—to clear the books and become legit again. Sick or not, there could be no stopping now.

After missing an entire week of work, he had no choice but to drag himself down to the bank Friday evening. His timing had to be perfect. He couldn't be seen by Brian Feeley or anyone else in operations. It would look suspicious. They usually went home between 6:15 and 6:30 p.m. on Fridays. He had to show up after that but before the 7 p.m. armored car pickup, which took interbranch mail as well as cash and other negotiables. That left him precious few minutes to encode the latest batch of branch settlement tickets and stuff them into the outgoing-mail bag.

It went off without a hitch that first week. When he put the key in the door at 6:34 p.m. and walked into the bank, he found himself alone in operations. He was so intent on carrying out his mission that he didn't notice a female clerk sitting at her desk on the opposite side of the bank.

Ben did what he had to do and then dragged himself back home.

He was feeling even worse the following week. Again on Friday he climbed out of bed, bundled himself up, got into his car and headed for the bank. On busy Wilshire Boulevard he found himself stuck in heavy commuter traffic. Checking his watch constantly—it was already after 6:30 p.m. and he had ten or twelve blocks to go—Ben was shocked to see the Loomis armored car nearby, stuck in the same traffic. It was obviously on its way to Beverly Drive. He had to beat it there or—If he missed the pickup everything would be over.

Driving like the possessed man he was, Ben swung his car in and out of the traffic, running red lights, turning against the signs. He skidded the car to a stop in the bank parking lot at 6:50 p.m.—just ahead of the armored car that was being driven more sanely—and raced inside. He was in the middle of his work when the uniformed guard entered the bank. At that point, Ben had no choice but to take a chance. He asked the guard to wait until he was finished. Thankfully, the guard did not call him on the unusual request and waited patiently. Ten minutes later, Ben was finished and had all the necessary branch settlement tickets in the mail pouch.

It had been such a frighteningly close call, and yet he had gotten away with it.

As he headed back home to bed, Lewis wondered how much longer his luck could hold out.

* * *

It was the biggest party in boxing history, sponsored by MAPS—the same people who in two months' time would be putting on the biggest boxing show in history. The gala event was held at the Beverly Wilshire Hotel on November 29, 1980. The guest list read like a Who's Who of the boxing world. Muhammad and Veronica All were there, of course. Also on hand were two heavyweights Smith had big plans for: Ken Norton and Gerry Cooney, who had good reason to be in a celebrating mood. The WBA had just released its latest rankings: Cooney had suddenly moved up well into the top ten. It was an amazing rise, considering that many observers thought he had not fought anyone important. But then again, Harold did have a *very* good relationship with Pepe Cordero.

Teri Key estimated that the black-tie affair for two hundred and fifty guests cost MAPS more than $20,000. The open bar alone probably ran well into four figures. Everything was catered by the hotel, from the caviar to the flowers. Harold had even hired some high-class hookers to mingle as window dressing among the party guests, who included celebrities like Tony Orlando, Sylvester Stallone, former welterweight champion Carlos Palomino and Jayne Kennedy.

There was another party after the one at the Beverly Wilshire which cost some money too. Smith rented several suites at another hotel, and only certain men were invited. The women for this after-hours affair were provided by the generous people at MAPS. Some boxers who had not been real sure about Harold Smith went away thinking he was all right. The man obviously thought of everything.

More fighters were being signed all the time to promotional contracts. Plans for "This Is It" were rapidly coming together. Smith used all the goodwill he had built up with the boxers over the past two years—and the usual outlandish payments—to attract the fighters he wanted. The history-making card was scheduled for February 3, 1981, at Madison Square Garden.

In the meantime, Teri was working twelve hours a day in the MAPS office. Because she handled the checkbooks, she knew about the growing expenses. But the business was bringing in lots of money too. She did everything she was told to do, whether it was writing a rent check for the newest card girl, packaging a bundle of cash for a just-signed fighter or setting up a hot date for Harold. She did it all with no resentment, protecting her boss every step of the way.

Once, a local promoter who was handling some Texas outlets for MAPS let it slip to Teri that he had been in prison and was on probation. She immediately told Smith, who expressed surprise. Not long after that, Harold claimed $30,000 in cash had been stolen from a briefcase in his hotel room. He figured out that the card girl and this Texas promoter had been in his room. He immediately suspected the ex-con and made him take a polygraph test, which he passed. Smith then asked Teri if she thought it was possible the card girl might have stolen the money.

Teri had to answer yes. "She is young, Harold."

Smith seemed disappointed that someone he had given a car and mink coat—in addition to a beach apartment and regular pay—would rip him off. He asked that the card girl take a polygraph, but she refused. A screaming fight ensued.

"You're lucky you're not in jail for stealing," he yelled.

"You're lucky I just turned eighteen and you're not in jail for statutory rape," she yelled back.

She had a point. And actually, whether the card girl had taken the money or not, Smith was a particularly good person from whom to steal. He was always loaded with cash, and there was no way he was going to call the police with a theft complaint. Besides, what was a measly thirty grand?

There was plenty more where that came from.

***

Bay Meadows Racetrack is located across the bay from San Francisco. In this picturesque setting on a Saturday in December 1980, the thoroughbreds were running before a good-sized crowd.

One of them was a gray colt called Johnlee'n Harold. Named after the members of the Smith clan, its registered owner was listed as one Michael Blake. Actually, Blake was just a front man. The real owner was Harold Smith. This wasn't the only horse Smith owned. There were several others listed under the banner of Three Time Champ Stables, named in honor of Muhammad Ali. Several other horses were kept under the name B Team Stable, whose listed owner was MAPS hanger-on Johnny Poag. All of it was an interlocking web that led to the MAPS founder. But just as he had arranged for Sammie Marshall to be the individual who held MAPS's state boxing promoter's license, Smith had demurred when it came to being officially registered as the record owner of his horses with the California Racing Board. Again he used stand-ins for this purpose, though he was quick to tell friends and guests sitting in style with him in his private box at the track that the horses and stables were his. No one ever noticed that the common requirements for both boxing and horse-owning licensing were being fingerprinted and photographed.

Journeying to the track for Johnlee'n Harold's debut had been unscheduled. The MAPS entourage had been in Sacramento the night before for a fight. When fog socked in the airport and grounded the MAPS plane on Saturday morning, Smith got the idea of renting a bus and bringing everyone down to the Bay Area for the race. Lewis was along for the ride; so were all the card girls, Harold's wife Lee, various other MAPS employees, fighters and trainers. In all, the entourage numbered almost forty.

As Johnlee'n Harold headed to the starting gate with the rest of the allowance field—all were maidens, having never won a race—the track tote board showed that the experts and crowd didn't think much of his chances of winning. The morning odds had been in the ten-to-one range; a few minutes to post they were hovering around seven to one. There was really no reason to think that the colt would do much. According to his official records, this horse had been purchased at the Hollywood Park auction just nine months earlier for $2,500. His name then was Cow Buyer, foaled by Lord Stapleton out of Our Share by Fightin' Indian. It was an undistinguished bloodline; none of the colt's family had ever won a horse race. Put into training by his owners, Cow Buyer soon came up lame with a calcium deposit in one of his legs. That would have ended most racing careers. But in this case his owner called Harold Smith, an obvious high roller whom he had met in the clubhouse at the auction. They struck a deal. Cow Buyer's first owner would later claim that Smith bought the horse for $32,000, an unusually good price for a lame horse with low-rent heritage. Others would later wonder if the deal involved a "switch" of horses.

There was nothing lame about Johnlee'n Harold as he broke quickly from the gate. He wasn't difficult to spot, wearing black and gray colors with the outline of a boxing glove on his flank. He went to the front easily before the first turn and stayed there the entire way despite what appeared to be an inept ride by the jockey. It was a big upset, but no great surprise to Smith. He had bet heavily on his horse and encouraged everyone else to do likewise. He had even advanced betting money to those who were low on funds. The MAPS entourage crowded into the winner's circle, everyone whooping it up. An ecstatic Aaron Pryor was dancing around. Emmanuel Steward was smiling broadly. It was in the winner's circle that they learned for the first time that Johnlee'n Harold had broken a saddle strap as he bolted from the gate, and the jockey had done nothing more than hang on for dear life the entire route. With an added handicap like that, the colt's victory seemed even more amazing. Lewis walked away from the cashier's window with $6,000 in winnings, Smith with much more.

The MAPS plane caught up with them in San Francisco. However, the plane wasn't big enough to take the entire group back to Los Angeles on one trip. Harold made a big show of apparent concern in designating those who would go on the first trip while the others stayed behind. Everyone—especially Lee—thought it was so considerate the way he made sure to save a seat for her and put her on board last so she wouldn't have to sit in the plane waiting for the others. It wasn't until the door closed and the plane began taxiing, without her husband on it, that Lee realized what he'd done. The others standing outside with Smith as the plane pulled away—including Ben and a couple of Harold's favorite card girls—knew what he had in mind when he suggested that, instead of returning to L.A., they climb on the bus and go on to Las Vegas and continue the celebration.

Johnlee'n Harold soon went south too. On December 27 he won the $75,000 Breeders Stakes at Santa Anita in Los Angeles. Smith reportedly bet $6,000 on his horse to win and received $15 back for every $2.00—or about $45,000.

The day after that second victory, Teri Key overheard Smith's telephone conversation with a New York *Post* reporter who was inquiring about the source of all the MAPS money. "My wife's family is wealthy," Smith explained.

That's funny, Teri thought, *I've never heard Harold mention that*

"And I'm into horses," he continued. "In fact, I have a horse that's going to win the next Kentucky Derby."

After the reporter's article on Smith's finances was published, Lee came in and was making copies of it to pass around. "My family was wealthy," she whispered to Teri. "But I never got any of it."

Where *did* that extra money come from that kept getting transferred into the MAPS accounts? Teri was not going to let it worry her though. The fights seemed to be getting bigger, and there were those "transfers" from the TV networks that always seemed to come in when they needed them.

Teri was just glad the money was available. So she never stopped to think about it.

$$* * *$$

The New York *Post* reporter wasn't alone in wondering where Harold Smith and MAPS got all the money they were tossing around the boxing industry. The source of the funds that were being used to buy off the majority of the champions and top contenders was the subject of widespread speculation throughout the sports community.

Ferdie Pacheco of NBC Sports was suspicious about all of Smith's money and asked him on a couple of occasions where it came from. Smith told him that his wife had inherited a lot of money and that he also had a couple of millionaires backing him. Having money was one thing, but throwing it away like Smith did was quite another. Smith always presented himself as a big spender who was willing to overpay for everything. The effect was that he drew attention to himself. Pacheco would not have been surprised if someone had told him that Smith was in trouble with the IRS.

In Pacheco's mind, Smith was an amateur when it came to promoting pro boxing matches. Obviously he was spending much more money than he was making. The only reason he had risen to the top was because his money had not yet run out. As to Smith's announced intention to "control the boxing world," Pacheco found it hard to believe. Smith was an unnatural element in the sport that Pacheco loved. He had seen a lot of people come and go—though of course no one quite like Harold Smith.

Jack Fiske, a sports reporter for the San Francisco *Examiner* for more than thirty years, had caught up with Smith in Sacramento after a fight. Fiske put the question directly to the promoter.

"Where are you getting the money from?"

"My wife and I have put up four million dollars," Smith answered. "My wife comes from a very wealthy family. I got four million dollars more from one friend in Los Angeles and two million dollars from another. And two million dollars from friends in Mississippi."

People in the fight business were also curious about all the money being thrown into the ring by MAPS. Mickey Duff, an English fight promoter who managed WBC Lightweight Champion James Watt of Scotland and European Heavyweight Champion John Gardner, walked into the MAPS offices on January 2, 1981, and left with $350,000 in cash. The money was a downpayment for two fights. The first, Watt versus WBA Lightweight Champion Alexis Arguello, was tabbed for the "This Is It" card. Duff received a $150,000 advance payment for Watt, with his total purse set at $1 million. Duff received the remaining $200,000 as an advance payment for a proposed Ali-Gardner bout that Smith was trying to put together. Smith now told Duff he was sure he could put the fight together in Honolulu or Puerto Rico. It would take time, though. This two hundred grand was just a good faith payment to keep Gardner available for the fight. Gardner's purse would be another $300,000.

Duly impressed with all the cash floating around MAPS, Duff asked Smith about the source of his funds. The promoter said he had just received $5 million in cash from gambling winnings on the Leonard-Duran fight and from betting on his racehorse. Smith bragged that he had been banned from several casinos in Vegas because he was so successful there and prophesied that Johnlee 'n Harold would win the Kentucky Derby. Before leaving the MAPS office, Duff called a friend to come over and escort him back to the hotel. The next day, he flew to New York and placed the money in a safety deposit box.

Donald "Buddy" La Rosa, manager of junior welterweight champion Aaron Pryor, lost a similar big payday when his fighter was shot by his girlfriend just before New Year. When La Rosa visited the MAPS office a few days later, it was still questionable whether or not Pryor could take part in the "This Is It" card. Though not seriously wounded, Pryor was quite sore. Smith, nevertheless, gave La Rosa $35,000, then took it back a few minutes later when Pryor called to say he would not be able to fight. While La Rosa was at his office, Smith had bragged that he could raise $4 million or $5 million in cash in forty-five minutes.

Other fighters were luckier than Pryor. Those already signed for the "This Is It" card included Gerry Cooney, $1,250,000; Ken Norton, $1,100,000; Tommy Hearns, $1,500,000; Wilfredo Benitez, $1,000,000; Matthew Saad Muhammad, $2,100,000; Eddie Mustafa Muhammad, $1,500,000.

Sammie Marshall also found himself fielding queries regarding the MAPS money. At a press conference in New York announcing the big card, Marshall responded to the familiar question by trying to laugh it off, saying "We make our money the old-fashioned way. We *earn* it."

***

By mid January the running total of the undetected embezzlement was $20 million.

According to Smith, advance ticket sales at the Garden had been strong, despite the steep seat prices. Cable TV arrangements were all but concluded, promising to rake in millions more for MAPS. And serious negotiations were underway to syndicate the fight card in Europe and worldwide by satellite broadcast. Smith even predicted MAPS's total take might run as high as $100 million. All agreed it would be the richest fight in history. Ben Lewis figured there would be more than enough to pay back what had been taken from Wells Fargo and still have millions left over.

Ben had already figured out how to replace the money. He told Smith he didn't want one large check for the total amount. Rather, he wanted twenty-four individual checks, one for each branch settlement chain. He would then use a debit and a check to clear the last branch settlement in each chain he was holding. This would consign the dozens of prior tickets in each chain to microfilm storage forever, where no one would have occasion to look at them. Fed the paper it wanted, the bank's computer system would never utter a peep.

No one would ever know.

PART THREE

CHAPTER TWENTY-THREE

The television flickered in the dark room. Suddenly the screen was filled with his own image. It was a black and white photo someone had managed to dig up. His face, spread in a wide smile, dominated the screen. There was a flower in his lapel. The shot had been taken on a happier day when they still had the world on a string.

Ben Lewis had never before seen himself on TV. To do so now under these circumstances was disturbing. The likeness was fine. He had always taken a good picture. It was the announcer's words that chilled him. The TV newsman was talking about a story reported that day in a Long Beach newspaper. *Wells Fargo Operations officer. A prime suspect. Disappeared. Largest embezzlement in history. FBI investigating.* For Ben, the words formed a tapestry of fear.

Since that fateful day of Friday, January 23, 1981, his life had been a series of indistinguishable hotel rooms. He was now in his third or fourth—he had lost count. He couldn't spend the rest of his life like this.

Vivid in his mind was his last conversation with Harold. He had read off all the branch settlement amounts, one digit at a time, even halting to tell Harold where to put the commas. He still couldn't believe how incapable Harold was of getting the numbers down right. Had Harold been high? Or had he been that bad with figures all along? What about all those fight contracts he had negotiated? Is that why MAPS never showed a profit?

Since then, Ben had heard nothing from Smith. It was a one-way street. Harold knew where he was and could get in touch with him if he wanted, but Ben didn't know Harold's whereabouts. He felt he had been deserted.

He could think of no one to turn to. He drew the blackout curtains and didn't know whether it was night or day, nor did it matter. Since shaving off his beard for the passport photo, he hadn't touched a razor. Brushing his teeth and showering seemed unnecessary distractions. He was in a trance. He had to look at an ashtray to remember he was in San Diego. He didn't have the stomach to eat. Liquor had no effect. The cocaine kept him awake but a nervous wreck. To try to cheer him up, Tony had brought a couple of hookers up to their hotel the other night. Left alone with the woman, Ben felt no sexual desire. Instead, he paid her to stay all night and listen to him talk about his dreams and disappointments.

As he remained sealed in his latest hotel room, he wasn't even sure he was sorry the end had finally come. He had gotten so tired of it all. It had been inevitable that their luck would run out one day. The only true frustration he felt was knowing how close they had come to pulling it off. Just a few more weeks and they could have put all the money back in the bank. They would have been home free.

He wasn't sure if his life was over. Maybe it was—he could think of no way to redeem himself. He was a crook and he was guilty. The best choice might be to end his misery and embarrassment. There were all kinds of things around that he could use. He could draw a hot bath, cut his wrists and lie down in the soothing water. He would just go to sleep and it would all be over. He would get the rest and peace he so badly needed. It would be so easy.

Somewhere deep inside his burned-out psyche remained a spark of life. There was one person he could call. He found the number and reached for the phone. If there was someone home, maybe he would get out of these depressing surroundings. He didn't want to call anyone at MAPS. He had had enough of Harold. If there was no answer, well—he wasn't going to think that far into the future. As the phone began ringing, he didn't particularly care one way or the other. He was at the end of his rope—emotionally, physically, mentally.

"Hello," answered a woman's voice on the third ring.

Ben Lewis had a future after all. For the time being, anyway.

CHAPTER TWENTY-FOUR

ssistant U.S. Attorney Dean Allison was busy fielding queries from the press. He made a regular practice of answering his own office phone in order to free his secretary to work uninterrupted on typing his written work. Normally, this arrangement worked well. But now he was getting so many calls from the press—fifty to sixty daily—that he found it difficult to get anything else done. One fact was undeniable: the Wells Fargo scandal had become a major story overnight.

The New York *Times* went with the headline BANK ALLEGES A $21.3 MILLION FRAUD BY SPORTS GROUP and reported "The Wells Fargo National Bank charged today that it had been defrauded of $21.3 million by a group of sports promoters and companies that used the name of former heavyweight boxing champion Muhammad Ali. Sources in the Federal Bureau of Investigation said they believed that if the allegation is true, the fraud is one of the largest in the history of American banking."

An in-depth article appeared in the Los Angeles *Herald-Examiner* which began with this quote from boxing promoter Don Fraser: "This is a story that ought to be made into a movie." The story captured the essence of Harold Smith. "There was plenty of cash. Rolls of bills—$10,000, $15,000 worth—stuffed in [Harold Smith's] pockets as he strolled around Santa Anita racetrack. He had limousines to ride in, a private jet to fly in and a yacht to sail the seas. Harold James Smith had it made, and two years was all it took." The story also quoted Bruce Barrett, who claimed his reputation as a concert promoter had been "damaged beyond repair" by the bank scandal. "I don't understand it," Barrett said. "Lewis was one of the most honorable, trustworthy men I've ever met." And Smith? "Generous. The man was well loved and well respected."

Sports Illustrated rushed into print with a story titled "Boxing Gets a Sudden Case of the Shorts." The article began "Four years ago Harold J. Smith didn't have the price of airfare from Los Angeles to New York. Two years later, on May 25, 1979, he promoted his first boxing show at a small club in Santa Monica, Calif., through a corporation named Muhammad Ali Professional Sports (MAPS). Within another year Smith, who suddenly seemed to have a limitless supply of cash, was threatening to take over the sport ..."

Since the story had broken, a fire storm of media interest had come down upon the U.S. Attorney's office and the FBI. The main characters in the story—Ben Lewis and Harold Smith—weren't available to the press. Neither were the FBI agents. As a matter of official policy, the Bureau routinely refused comment on any open investigation. And few "unofficial" sources at the Bureau were cooperating with reporters at this stage of the game because with Lewis still at large and Smith among the missing, saying the wrong thing could threaten the investigation. So the frustrated reporters called the one person they could reach.

Their questions to Allison were always the same. Were the feds investigating Muhammad Ali? Was it possible that the Champ might be involved? Did the government have plans to indict anyone? Where did the money go? Did they have a line on the whereabouts of Lewis and Smith? Could arrests be expected soon? Was the MAPS-promoted Madison Square fight card going to be held as scheduled? To all of these queries Allison's response was the same: a firm "no comment." He wasn't about to talk to the media and allow everyone who read the papers or watched TV—including Smith and Lewis—to know what the government knew, or more importantly, what it didn't know.

Over the weekend, around the same time Ali had met with the press, a Wells Fargo spokesman in San Francisco was doing the same thing. "The total amount of missing funds is $21,305,000," the spokesman declared. "This was accomplished through an internal manipulation of funds involving some thirteen accounts." The bank followed through on Monday, February 2, by filing a civil suit in Los Angeles Superior Court naming MAPS, Smith, Lewis and some of their MAPS associates as defendants, seeking recovery of the lost millions.

Allison did not agree with the bank's public relations assault. He considered it premature and dangerous. Experience had taught him that such fast-breaking situations required patience. The facts and figures were still changing. Things might look different a few weeks from now. With the kind of intense media attention that the scandal had caused—virtually every recent development was being reported on page one in newspapers across the country—the bank would find itself having to live with every utterance and having to publicly eat crow in the event it had to back away from a previous declaration. But Allison had not been asked by the bank for his opinion. The bank's position was its business. The prosecution was Allison's, and he was already protecting himself and his case from encroachment from both public and private sectors.

The prosecutor was not going to be pushed before he was ready to move.

***

Although Harold Smith was gone—he had dropped out of sight on Friday, January 23, the day Brian Feeley confronted Lewis at the Beverly Drive branch—he was certainly not quiet. He launched an aggressive media campaign the day after the bank filed suit against him. His intentions were obvious: to put forward a plausible cover story, embarrass the bank and enflame the press.

He was succeeding on all counts.

Flushing Smith out—at least verbally—was one ironic result of the bank's early offensive. The day after the bank's civil suit was filed, Smith called sports newsman Bud Furillo at KABC, L.A.'s top-rated talk radio station. For his first public statement since disappearing, Smith used the information released by the bank and twisted it to fit his story. It was a clever ploy, shifting the focus of public attention from a scenario in which Smith was a fugitive rip-off artist to one in which he was a victim of racist persecution by the white establishment and a Watergate-style conspiracy by shadowy power brokers of the business world. He hadn't run away because he was guilty, Smith claimed, but only to ensure that he would live long enough to prove his innocence. Smith promised the listeners that he possessed evidence which would prove him innocent and that the bank was involved in a far bigger scandal than was being reported. Often crying or sobbing in the course of a fifteen-minute conversation, Smith said, "I may not be alive in two days."

Smith's claims about a sinister conspiracy inside the bank involving hundreds of millions of dollars wreaked havoc on the bank's image and business. The bank's immediate response to this—"preposterous," an indignant bank spokesman told the press—was reported with less weight than Smith's allegations because the denial was not nearly as sensational as the charge. There was concern for the bank's stock on Wall Street. Depositors were flocking to their local branches and withdrawing their savings. A chill ran through the institution right up to the board of directors and its chairman.

The bankers would have felt even worse if they had known that Smith had only just begun.

***

Teri Key bent low over the oval mirror. She put one end of a thin straw in a nostril and aimed the other end at a long line of cocaine. She inhaled with a rush, deftly moving the straw down the line. The tiny white crystals that packed such a wallop disappeared under it like so much dust under a Hoover. She switched nostrils and inhaled another line. The rush came almost immediately. Liz Walczer had brought some mighty fine snow.

The two of them were sitting on the floor in the darkened living room of Key's small apartment. Teri passed the mirror back to Liz and reached over to turn up the volume on the stereo. The sounds of jazz filled the room. The flickering of two candles, the only light, heightened the sense of peacefulness in the small apartment.

It was Saturday night, early February. As they had all that week, they were once again waiting for a call from Harold Smith, while Teri's common-law husband, Tony, was out running an errand. Their waiting would have been made more difficult—or at least more boring—without the coke. In two nights the two women had gone through five hundred dollars' worth of cocaine. It went down quite easily. Neither of them could

sleep anyway, and food held little interest. Their lives had gotten so confusing. They had things to talk and reminisce about and new scenarios to
speculate and worry about all the time, as apparent threats from all sides.
From the FBI. The bank. The press.

"I sure wish Harold would call," Liz said again.

"He will," Teri said.

"I love that man so much," Liz said wistfully. "I want to help him so
bad. We got a special thing going, Harold and me. We really do. No shit."

Teri knew of several other young women who felt the same way about
Harold. He had a way with them all right. Liz was another blonde. Not
that Harold had a particular weakness for blondes. He liked brunettes and
redheads too. He just had two requirements for his women: they had to
be white and willing. Teri wondered how much of his preference had to
do with the old status game. She had learned that some successful black
men—especially, it seemed, athletes and entertainers—went out nearly
exclusively with white women. She was convinced that they often did it
for status. Other than that prejudice, Harold was open-minded when it
came to women. He'd take them short or tall, thin or robust, smart or
dumb. He loved them all—literally.

Liz was talking about Harold dreamily. "One day I was driving
along—this is no lie—and I heard Harold's voice. It just came flying out of
nowhere, from up above. I forget what he said, but he was talking to me.
The next day when I saw Harold, he said, 'Did you hear me talking to you
yesterday?' "

"Come on," Teri said disbelievingly.

"Yeah. It really happened. It blew my mind. That man has powers that
are out of this world. He doesn't even know his own strength. Our bound-
aries together are limitless. Together, we can go anywhere. Harold says
I'm going to be replacing Lee. He wants me by his side, helping him run
the business."

"I don't see him dumping Lee," Teri said. "They've been together too
long. And what about all the other girls? Don't you think he may have told
a few of them the same thing?" Teri had long ago accepted women as her
boss's main weakness in life. She didn't particularly approve of the way
he treated them and used them. But if they were willing to go along for

the ride, who was the victim? He could show them a good time. But Liz sounded as if she was getting too serious.

"The other girls don't bother me," Liz said. "He only uses them to try to make me jealous. But it doesn't work. He can do anything he wants with his body. I want his mind and spirit. Lee doesn't understand him like I do."

Liz was about Teri's height, five foot five, and they both had fairly easygoing personalities, which was why they got along. But that was where the similarities ended. Teri saw Liz as a typical California surfer-girl type. In her early twenties, she had long sandy blond hair, blue eyes, no makeup, scrubbed-clean looks, and was a tad too heavy in the hips. Teri cut a trimmer figure, had dark hair and liked to wear nice clothes. Liz was more gullible—though Teri, no cynic herself, tended to believe the best about everybody.

When the phone rang, it sounded far away. They both jumped up, and Teri reached it first.

"Hello," she said cautiously. Some of the reporters had gotten her home number and had been pestering her.

"Hi, Teri."

It was Harold.

"Go to the Marriott at the airport. You'll hear from me there."

He immediately hung up. That was the way Harold wanted it. No conversations on home or office phones. They might be bugged. He would always tell Teri where to go and then call her at a prearranged pay phone or page her on a hotel phone.

"Did he ask about me?" Liz asked anxiously.

"No, Liz. He's too rushed."

"Can I come? *Please.*"

"Okay."

While they drove to the hotel near the airport, Liz kept talking. Teri was thinking about something else. She had visited a Century City lawyer two days ago. His name was Rick Rosenfield, and he was a former Assistant U.S. Attorney. His specialty these days was criminal defense. Rosenfield had been blunt with her. She had made some stupid mistakes, the main one being the removal of records from the MAPS office. But at least this took place before a subpoena had been issued. That transgression could be overcome, he thought. Teri spoke anxiously about Harold. She repeated what he had told her about a line of credit at the bank and his fears for his life. Her belief in his innocence was overpowering. Teri had told Rosenfield the truth about everything, and his reaction was that she hadn't done anything criminal. The attorney said he thought there were some ways he could help Smith too.

All this was on her mind as she drove to the Marriott. She intended to tell Harold about Rosenfield. And she also wanted to tell him that she thought he was making a mistake by launching a campaign in the media. Rosenfield had agreed. If Smith had documents that could prove the existence of a line of credit and his innocence in the mounting case, he should turn them over to an attorney to handle.

But would Harold listen to her?

* * *

The next day, Teri found herself following new directions from Smith. In his phone call to her at the Marriott the night before, he asked her if it was possible for her to type something secret for him at the MAPS office. She said it wasn't because there was an L.A. county marshal on duty around the clock as a result of the restraining order Wells Fargo had obtained when it filed suit against Smith and MAPS. The marshal was supposed to check everyone who left the office to make sure no business records of any kind were being removed. He was a little casual about the search, and Teri had found the courage to smuggle out a few checks which had come in for Smith. But she didn't want to push her luck. She said she would do the work for Harold if he could find her another office to work in. Smith said he had an idea.

Tom Bole, the travel agent who had made so much money booking trips for MAPS, agreed that Teri could use his office on Sunday morning. She went there and was met by Bill Shaeffer, a MAPS gofer who had several pages of handwritten notes. Teri recognized the scrawl as Harold's.

It was a prepared statement for the media. As she typed it, she kept thinking that this was silly. Why was Harold doing this? He had not paid any attention to her last night when she suggested he drop the media campaign and come with her to see the defense attorney. "I haven't done anything wrong. You just don't know everything that's going on," he had said, using a tone that he might have used in talking to a child. The message she typed was typical Harold. Verbose and dramatic.

February 7, 1981

To Whom It May Concern:

I am in good health, mentally and physically. I am not afraid and I'm not alone because I know that God is with me. And I believe that more so now than ever before in my life; for only with God could my family and I have survived the ordeal of the past two weeks. I am determined to come out of the situation victorious.

I refuse to show up and present certain documents to Muhammad Ali because upon returning to this country, I learned that Muhammad Ali had removed his name from our companies. That convinced me that outside influence (consisting of leaches, hangers-ons and bad advisors whom Ali and I have spent thousands of dollars supporting) have caused him to take a less than total stand in my behalf. Removing his name also indicates that pre-judgment of me has been made.

Muhammad Ali has always had my total support.

I have also been waiting the past few days for word as to the whereabouts and condition of Ben Lewis, a fine man. I am convinced that Ben Lewis is dead or being contained against his will.

I appeal to the media to go to the Miracle Mile branch of the Wells Fargo Bank and question the manager, Gene Kawakami. It is there you will find the beginning of what I guarantee is one of the biggest cases of fraud, embezzlement, illegal loans and kick-backs involving numerous branches and personnel within the Wells Fargo Bank system.

A thorough investigation at the Miracle Mile branch will unravel, reveal and prove that Ben Lewis and Harold Smith unknowingly became what amounts to being two minnows in a sea of sharks, reaching from Wilshire Boulevard to San Francisco Wells Fargo branches and involves officers and bank personnel in a $200—$300 million rip-off of the bank, that has gone on for a period of nine years or more.

I appeal to the media; ask Mr. Kawakami the following questions, which are just a few of many to be asked and answered.

1. Why did you, Mr. Kawakami, during the first 15 days of August, 1980, make an *unauthorized debit* of the Muhammad Ali Professional Sports account of over $300,000—all of which went for your personal use.

2. What was your reason for signing a statement (which I alone have) that reads: August 1980—I owe $217,000 to Harold J. Smith or to his son, John Alexander Smith—to be paid back at my convenience. Signed Gene Kawakami.

Ask Mr. Kawakami what that was all about. For it was during the month of August 1980, that I learned what the media will learn once these questions are asked and pursued. I learned the magnitude of the situation I had unknowingly became involved in, appeal to the media to understand that the following information is but a small portion of what is involved—but it is the first step to the unraveling and it is the road to the big ones—once pursued.

People with no credit, no signs or means of income obtained personal and business loans as well as auto loans from Wells Fargo.

For example, Marty Monroe got financing on a Mercedes costing over $20,000. He was turned down everywhere else, but not turned down at Wells Fargo.

Perscell Davis got financing on a $15,000 Cadillac, was turned down everywhere else.

J. B. Williamson got financing on a car costing more than $10,000, was turned down everywhere else.

And the list goes on and on and though these are little ones as the big ones surface the amounts involved increase to proportions that will boggle the mind and shake the entire banking system.

At this time, I would like to point out that I have not sought or given anyone authorization to seek legal assistance on my behalf. Other than speaking to Muhammad Ali Professional Sports' ex-attorney Ed Franklin, who advised me to seek a criminal attorney (and who I then advised to go to hell) because I haven't done anything criminally wrong.

On Monday, I will seek an attorney to file suit against Wells Fargo Bank.

Signed, Harold J. Smith.

Much of this was news to Teri Key.

She knew Gene Kawakami, of course. He had been in the picture for a couple of years, providing banking services to MAPS. Kawakami had even gone on some trips with the MAPS entourage. She knew this because she had booked flight and hotel reservations for him. But she had never heard Harold say anything about fraud, embezzlement or illegal kickbacks involving the banker. Why hadn't Harold told her? After all, she was handling all the company bank accounts. She remembered a surprise debit in the neighborhood of $300,000. She recalled that, at the time, Smith had indicated to her that it had gone to pay for an overdraft in a MAPS account and some promissory notes.

She did know that Ali had ordered his name off the company title. Instead of "Muhammad Ali Professional Sports," she was now answering the phone "Professional Sports." She was sure that the distance the Champ was putting between himself and Smith was the work of Ali's lawyers and advisors. After all, Smith had originally promised to show Ali certain documents that would prove the bank conspiracy against Smith, but Harold was now publicly saying that the Champ was no longer in his corner.

She had not heard about Harold's split with Ed Franklin. That was too bad. Franklin seemed to be a nice guy. *Wait a minute,* she thought. *Sammie Marshall had turned over the MAPS records to Franklin a few days after the subpoena had been served. Had Franklin given them to the authorities before being fired by Harold? What had happened to the MAPS records?* She hoped they had been properly handled because that was such a sore point in her own mind.

After she finished typing the statement, she made two dozen copies and waited for another call from Harold. When it came, he gave her a list of media representatives he wanted to receive the statement. They included all the local newspapers and radio and TV stations. Bud Furillo of KABC radio was on the list. So were TV sportscasters Jim Hill of KNXT (CBS) and Ted Dawson of KABC. "But don't do anything until I tell you," Smith told Teri.

Late Sunday afternoon Smith called Teri at her home and asked her to deliver the statement along with copies of a tape of Smith reading his own words to the people on the list. It was raining, and she didn't look forward to the prospect of driving around town delivering the statement. She suggested that Tony could make the media rounds. Smith agreed. That evening, the tall black man went out into the rain on his mission.

A few hours later, Teri received a call from a newspaper reporter. He had received a package that purportedly contained a tape from Smith. He wanted to play it for her over the telephone so she could determine whether or not it sounded like her boss. The request caught her off guard, but she pretended not to know anything about the tape. After the reporter played a minute or so of the message, she told him it sounded like Smith but that the tape recorder seemed to be playing it a little too fast. She also received a call from a TV newsman who wanted the same verification.

When the evening news came on at 6 p.m., Teri and Liz were glued to the set, watching the CBS affiliate. About fifteen minutes into the coverage, Jim Hill came on with an excited announcement about Harold Smith dropping off a tape at the station's front gate.

"Oh no," Teri moaned. "They think that Tony was Harold."

Before they could figure out what if any confusion the faulty identity was going to cause, the voice of Smith came from the television set.

Teri and Liz jumped up and down, clapping. It was like rooting for their team. To see something that she had typed being read on television gave Teri a feeling of accomplishment.

Maybe Harold's media blitz was the right move after all.

CHAPTER TWENTY-FIVE

Three days after Harold Smith's taped message to the world, Wells Fargo was back on the defensive. A bank spokesman announced that a second bank officer was no longer on the job. The official bank version had it that Miracle Mile manager Gene Kawakami was being sent home on "paid leave to avoid unnecessary publicity." Within a week or so, Kawakami would be fired.

Actually, Kawakami's troubles had nothing to do with Smith's public accusations or the media attention surrounding it. Unbeknownst to the press and public, Kawakami's fate was in the process of being sealed. Bank investigators were subjecting his lending activities to intense scrutiny. The auditors had begun the investigation immediately when the Lewis embezzlements were first documented by the bank's Lloyd Gasway. They had quickly realized that Kawakami, like Lewis, went back several years with Smith. That alone made him a candidate for investigation. Of primary concern was the series of loans Kawakami had made over the years to Smith and some of his buddies, the ones Smith had referred to in his public statements. Ironically, they would ultimately find no real problems there. It was the other transactions—as yet unknown to the bank investigators, the government or Harold Smith—that would prove Kawakami's undoing.

Kawakami's actions did not hold up long to the scrutiny. The announcement of his "leave" sent the press into a tizzy and heightened speculation that, as Smith had charged, Wells Fargo was attempting to hide a much larger financial loss. It was not difficult to understand the reaction of the media to Kawakami's departure from Miracle Mile. The bank's unexpected move gave credence to Smith's recent charges of a "$200—$300 million rip-off" involving Kawakami and many other Wells

Fargo branches and officers. Why else was Kawakami being removed from his job?

At the *Herald-Examiner*, reporter Dave Palermo was inclined to believe the bank's explanation of the embezzlement. He was fairly certain that Lewis had been in a position to carry out the embezzlement alone at the bank and that he had done so, as the bank had charged. He doubted the theft involved other employees at the bank. Palermo's own background investigation of Harold Smith led the reporter to believe that the promoter had undoubtedly benefited from the missing money. In fact, his spendings in the boxing world, at the track and on personal luxuries were so out of proportion with the financial success—or, more accurately, the lack of it—achieved by MAPS that there should have been earlier suspicions about Smith.

Although his interest was piqued by Smith's public allegations—why was Kawakami singled out unless Smith had something on him?—Palermo tended to doubt that Kawakami was the kingpin of any sinister conspiracy inside the bank or that he was linked to organized crime, whether the "Japanese Mafia" or anyone else. Palermo's discreet "off the record" inquiries about the Miracle Mile manager indicated that Kawakami just wasn't that close to Lewis and apparently had not been involved in MAPS's activities for some time. Still, despite the improbability of Smith's wild accusations, Palermo was nagged by the feeling that there might be some real dirt there. Obviously, Kawakami had somehow become an embarrassment to the bank, which necessitated his sudden leave of absence. Palermo had no idea why. If he wasn't involved in the Lewis embezzlement, then what *was* Kawakami involved in? The reporter refrained from making any speculations in print. He worried that he might end up sorry for not being more skeptical of the bank's story. But he kept such insecurities a secret in the city room, where not everyone agreed with his assessment.

The *Herald-Examiner* sent a reporter to stake out Kawakami's Rancho Palos Verdes home. After two days of surveillance, the staffer reported that Kawakami was nowhere to be seen.

Kawakami had moved his family and slipped into hiding.

"The big story here is the cover-up by the bank," an assistant city editor told him. "The loss is a lot bigger than they are now admitting. They're just trying to save face."

"I'm not so sure," said Palermo. "I don't want to jump to conclusions."
Palermo was the first to admit that he had developed a healthy dose
of cynicism during his reporting career. Even so, he wasn't ready to hop
aboard the bandwagon which found Wells Fargo guilty of something that
some headline writers were dying to call "Bank-gate."

***

The FBI had reached Kawakami a week earlier, before he left the bank.
Special Agents Larry Cross and Anne Ralston, who had joined a slew of
agents assisting Joe Woodall and Chuck Jones in handling preliminary
witness interviews and gathering basic background information, talked
to Kawakami at the Miracle Mile office.

To the agents' trained eyes, Kawakami had initially seemed professional and collected as he answered their questions, like a man with nothing to hide. He told them about his background at Wells Fargo Bank and
his rise to his present position. He freely explained the circumstances surrounding the branch settlement tracer being received at Miracle Mile for
the mysterious $250,000 transaction. He spoke in detail about his discus-
sions with MacLardie and his advice for her to call Brian Feeley at Beverly
Drive as soon as it became apparent that Feeley's branch was somehow
involved in a suspicious transaction.

The agents asked Kawakami about Sammie Marshall, his former
Wells Fargo colleague. Kawakami explained that he had met Harold
Smith through Marshall but had not seen Smith for a year. Kawakami
said that Marshall had left banking on his recommendation, when he
gave Marshall poor ratings on an evaluation as potential bank managerial
material. No, he said, it had not surprised him that Marshall had gone to
work for Smith after leaving the bank because the two men had obviously
been close to each other for some time.

Since Smith had made his first public statement the night before in a
telephone call to Bud Furillo at KABC radio and talked of a "$200-million
embezzlement … look to Miracle Mile … Gene Kawakami is involved
with the Japanese Mafia," the agents asked Kawakami about the charges
which had been broadcast to millions of listeners. Kawakami emphatically

denied Smith's claims. He said Miracle Mile was not involved in the bank's loss. He denied any such wrongdoing. It was only at the end of the interview, as the agents were leaving, that one of them noticed a slight change in his demeanor.

Back at the FBI office in Westwood, the agents went over their notes before turning them in to be transcribed. Then Anne Ralston called Dean Allison and told him the results of the interview, which overall had to be categorized as routine.

"There *was* something that struck me as strange," she said finally.

Allison's radar went off. He knew that casual observations by field agents could be invaluable. "What was that?"

"He was very uptight about something. There was a moment as we were about to leave when I thought I saw tears in his eyes."

Allison thanked her and hung up. He wondered what Kawakami had done wrong. How did the nisei banker fit into the overall picture?

Allison was only mildly surprised when Kawakami was placed on leave the following week. He had mixed thoughts about the bank's action. On the one hand, he would have preferred for Kawakami to be left in place. The public perception of his departure would be that there must be some truth to Smith's widely publicized charges. On the other hand, Allison could understand the bank's position, and at least the bank had come up with a halfway decent public relations explanation for Kawakami's leave.

Like the rest of the press and public, Allison did not know whether Kawakami was blameless in the $21 million embezzlement. Moreover, while not nearly as ready to assume the worst about Kawakami as many in the media, Allison was troubled by doubts. He too realized that Smith must have had a reason for singling Kawakami out. Likewise, he noted that other bank officers whose names had come up in connection with the embezzlement story—Judy MacLardie and Brian Feeley, for example— had not been relieved from their duties. Could there be some scintilla of truth to Smith's charges? Just what *was* the relationship between Kawakami and Smith? Would those dealings, whether illegal or not, create enough smoke for Smith to con his way out of what sure looked like criminal involvement in the embezzlement? After all, even if he were culpable, it was clear that Smith himself had not been the one who actually embezzled the money; his was the more passive role of a recipient. Proving his guilt would depend upon showing an unquestionably "dirty"—in law enforcement jargon—state of mind.

If Smith's relationships with people at the bank were complicated and confused enough, or if Smith and a smart defense attorney could make them appear to be, there was a good chance that a jury might give Smith the benefit of the doubt. Then the man who had clearly received and benefited from $21 million in stolen money would walk away scot-free. And even from the little he had seen of Smith's style so far, Allison knew that it would not stop there. Smith would delight in self-righteously thumbing his nose at his critics and pursuers, claiming vindication of his innocence and painting the bank, the FBI, the U.S. Attorney's office and his detractors in the press as racists who had conspired to frame him.

In Harold Smith, Allison knew he had a worthy foe.

CHAPTER TWENTY-SIX

It was sunny the day Lloyd Benjamin Lewis walked into FBI head-quarters to admit the horrible truth that he had been living with for the past two years. Much later he would come to remember the date—Monday, February 2, 1981—as the beginning of the rest of his life.

Turning himself in to the FBI had not been a difficult decision once he started thinking straight again. He was an embezzler, yes, but he was not an experienced criminal. Even if he had been able to count on a few million dollars hidden away in a Swiss bank account, he would have had a difficult time living with the guilt. But he didn't have any secret cache, and he *did* have the guilt. It was the worst of both worlds.

The woman he had called from his hotel room was Carol Alexander, a casual friend from way back who was a good listener. He told her he was in trouble and needed to see her. She and her mother drove down to San Diego, arriving around three o'clock in the morning. He checked out of the hotel, leaving no messages of any kind, simply disappearing. They went to the mother's apartment in Los Angeles. He talked frankly to Carol about his problems, then got his first sleep in days. It felt good being in a home instead of a hotel. It also was a relief not being on a leash pulled by other people. Harold would have to find a way to live with what they had done, just like he was trying to live with it.

Over the weekend he repeatedly tried reaching his old friend, attorney Virgil Roberts, but there was no answer. Ben ate, slept, talked and generally tried to regain his equilibrium. He was still depressed about the sudden downward spiral his life had taken. It would require a great deal of strength, physical and mental, for him to face the authorities and admit everything.

Lewis called his wife, Gladys, and learned for the first time that the FBI had interviewed her. He could imagine how much the entire situation was upsetting Gladys.

"Ben, I think you should go talk to the FBI," she said.

"I've already decided to do that."

Before hanging up, he told her that he was going to be all right. But he wasn't so sure himself. Facing up to the problems at the bank would be the hard way to go. It would have been easier to slip away and become a nonperson, avoiding everyone he knew and giving up on his life. But if he thought there was something worth saving, then it would take a struggle of epic proportions. He had never had an easy time admitting mistakes. Now he would have to admit that his life over the past two years had been based on one theft after another. He had stolen more money in one day than Bonnie and Clyde had in their entire lifetimes.

After spending the weekend in his sanctuary, he felt ready. Early Monday morning, he finally reached Virgil Roberts. After their conversation, the attorney agreed to accompany Ben to the federal building in Westwood, where the FBI's Los Angeles division was located.

As they rode the elevator to the seventeenth floor, the two men were quiet. Ben kept going over in his mind how and why he had gotten into this mess. In the beginning, he had done it a step at a time, overcoming minute doses of conscience with each bad check of Harold's. It hadn't taken long for the embezzled amount to escalate far beyond his—or Harold's—foreseeable ability to repay. He blamed Harold for much of his predicament, but he did not forgive himself; he was fully responsible for his own actions. Without Harold and his connections, he would have had a very different life the last couple of years. The question now in Ben's mind was whether he was going to have any life left worth living.

***

The five men sat around a standard government-issue gray metal table. Other than the matching chairs, it was the only furniture in the small interview room. There were two ashtrays on the table, but nobody was smoking. The atmosphere was cold, sterile, just-the-facts-sir.

The three agents sat around the end and one side of the table with pads and ballpoint pens. Ben and Virgil sat next to each other on the opposite side of the table. They had already been introduced to Special Agents Woodall, Jones and Dale Taulbee. Taulbee was handling the identification and location aspects of the investigation, putting addresses, occupations, vehicle descriptions and prior criminal record information together with the corresponding names and hoping for leads to the whereabouts of the elusive Smith.

Lewis was read his constitutional rights and signed an Advice of Rights form stating that he understood and was willing to waive his privilege against self-incrimination and be interviewed. Lewis and Roberts then recited their addresses and phone numbers. Lewis gave his position at the bank.

"Just tell us what happened, in your own words," Jones said in his easygoing style.

Ben sat back and took a deep breath. He was here to tell the truth. He had already made that decision. There had been too many lies already. But where should he start?

"I've always been interested in sports and young people." *Yes*, that was the beginning. He had almost forgotten. It had been so long, so much had happened, that he had never really focused on why it had all begun. His intentions had been honest in the beginning. He had just wanted to help the kids. "Muhammad Ali was an idol to me. When my friend at the bank, Sammie Marshall, told me he was working on weekends with the Ali Track Club, trying to get it off the ground, it sounded like a good idea. Sammie had met Ali personally and had opened an account for the Club at our branch. I volunteered my time. I wanted to help out."

He talked on. It was a purging process. He talked for an hour, then another hour. There was an added benefit Ben never expected: he began to feel a sense of relief wash over him.

It felt good to tell the truth again.

* * *

The next day, Ben Lewis showed up at the FBI office with two lawyers. In addition to Virgil Roberts, a civil attorney, Ben was accompanied by

Cornell Price. Another former Assistant U.S. Attorney, Price was now a criminal defense attorney.

Knowing federal prosecutors and the FBI as he did, Price had decided that the prudent thing to do was to cut a deal for his client before he allowed him to continue the interviews. In fact, Price was not pleased that Lewis had already confessed. If he had been on the defense team yesterday, that would not have happened. Of course, Price would never advise his client to withhold the truth. He was too ethical a lawyer to engage in such tactics. It was more a practical matter as far as he was concerned. Having a client spill the beans before he had worked out an arrangement with the prosecutor would cut down the number of cards Price was holding when he sat down to negotiate.

Not that he had much of a hand with Ben Lewis anyway. But after listening to Lewis tell his story until late the night before in his office, Price decided that the remorseful banker deserved some credit for helping the government make its case against Harold Smith, who, according to Ben, had started the scheme rolling that produced more than twenty million embezzled dollars.

After all, Lewis was setting himself up to be the star witness for the prosecution. And, considering the cast of characters, that might prove to be risky business.

CHAPTER TWENTY-SEVEN

Dean Allison was struggling with a classic prosecutorial puzzle. A crime had obviously been committed, but he wasn't sure exactly how it had happened. He did know the amount of money missing and the documented chains of branch settlement tickets which had quickly been amassed against Ben Lewis—thanks to bank investigator Lloyd Gasway. But Allison still knew precious few facts, especially about Harold Smith's role in the embezzlement. Certainly not enough evidence had yet been collected to seek arrest warrants in the case. There were far too many gaps in the government's information—vital gaps which had to be filled with accurate information.

To prosecute a major financial crime, a prosecutor needs three important things. First and foremost, the documentary records to show where the money went and who benefited from it. Second, an insider to explain the way the scheme worked, to show how the business in question operated and to fasten responsibility for the fraud on the right person or persons—those who would end up as defendants. Third, corroboration of the insider's testimony, something that could be accomplished through documents, other witnesses or miscellaneous bits and pieces of evidence such as telephone records, charge slips, virtually anything. What could never be counted on in a financial fraud prosecution was the type of physical evidence present in so many other criminal cases—fingerprints, surveillance pictures, blood types, carpet threads under the fingernails and the like.

On all three fronts, Allison had problems. The vital MAPS records had still not been turned over, despite a subpoena and earlier assurances from MAPS attorney Ed Franklin that they would be forthcoming. Franklin had finally called Allison to tell him he had given them back to

Sammie Marshall. That could be trouble. Almost nothing could make a prosecutor as uneasy as having the critical documentary evidence in the hands of a possible suspect who might have a motive to alter or destroy it. Second, the government had yet to find an insider to describe what had happened at MAPS. And without the necessary insider witness, or an accurate overall picture of the embezzlement scheme, the government did not even know *what* to corroborate, much less where to look for the supporting evidence.

There was another complicating factor too, and a big one: many of the potential witnesses were unlikely to cooperate. From the little he had seen and heard already, it was plain to Allison that the MAPS employees and the fight people associated with Smith were strongly loyal to him personally. Moreover, their natural instinct to rally around a friend and close business associate had been heavily reinforced by green cement—all the cash Smith had been throwing their way. "These people have been feeding at the MAPS money trough for years," Allison told Woodall and Jones. "They're not about to kill the golden goose by saying anything that might incriminate Smith."

Last, as much as he disliked thinking in these terms, Allison knew there was the racial factor to consider. Allison was not about to treat anyone—even Harold Smith—better or worse because they were black, but the realist in him knew the racial factor could not be ignored. And in terms of getting his job as a prosecutor done, it clearly spelled trouble. The agents—the majority of them clean-shaven white males in business suits—would be perceived by Smith's black entourage as "The Man" personified. He and the agents would be asking these people, in effect, to cooperate with the white establishment to put another black man in jail. And Smith himself was playing the role of unjustly oppressed black martyr to the hilt, claiming that the accusations against him were trumped-up charges of a white power structure that couldn't stand to see a black man succeed.

Apart from the racial overtones, Allison was also troubled by the fact that the media had jumped with such glee on Smith's claim of innocence—that he had possessed a line of credit and that the bank was now setting him up as a dupe to hide crimes by bank employees. If someone knew only what was in the newspapers, Smith's defense had a superficial plausibility to it. In the hands of a sharp defense lawyer, it could be made to sound convincing.

Allison played with the courtroom scenario in his mind. What about the fact that Smith's and MAPS's spending was public? About as public as you could get, with money being thrown around to boxers and their managers for main events that were televised by the major networks. He could hear the defense lawyer say *Will the government kindly answer how an "embezzlement" could have gone undetected for so long?* And for two long years Smith traveled openly with Ben Lewis. The two men even went into the entertainment promotions business together. Explain your way out of that, Mr. Prosecutor. *If the bank didn't approve of Mr. Lewis's relationship with Mr. Smith, why did they allow this contact to go on so long? And why hadn't the bank's computer missed all that money long before January 23? Why, why, why?* Allison had an abundance of questions and a shortage of answers.

Several times daily, Allison heard from FBI Special Agents Woodall and Jones. They had been joined by two dozen other agents in beating the bushes looking for witnesses who knew Smith and Lewis and could provide further information concerning their whereabouts and activities during the past few years. Allison considered speed the biggest advantage the government had at the beginning of any investigation. The idea was to get to people while they still had their memory and before they had been "influenced" by anyone. Information collected by the agents was turned over to FBI clerk-typists back at headquarters and transcribed onto Forms FD-302. The official "Bureau-ese" writing style was terse and factual, with no room for observations or opinions of the agents. Usually, Allison wouldn't receive the typed 302 reports until ten days or so after the interview. So he had asked all the agents to be sure and call him with any important information they had developed at any time of the day or night, giving them his home phone number. And he always made a point to ask for the personal observations and opinions of the agents, the sort that Special Agent Anne Ralston had given him about Kawakami. Although the Bureau taught its agents to keep those reflections to themselves in writing their reports, experienced prosecutors sought them anyway.

Various addresses were checked out by the FBI. Several of them turned out to be apartments rented by Smith for women friends. At one, Special Agent Taulbee, a tall handsome type who looked every bit the TV image of a federal agent, found himself interviewing a voluptuous young woman dressed in tight, sexy attire. He noticed a photograph of a topless woman looking like a Playboy Playmate hanging above the fireplace.

"Do you like the picture?" the woman asked. "It's me."

"Oh, yeah, it's real good," Taulbee stammered. "Now—you were an employee of MAPS?"

"Yes."

"How much did you make?"

"Two hundred a week. Plus a car and this apartment."

Taulbee guessed the rent was in the range of $600 a month. "And what did you do at MAPS?" he asked.

"I was a card girl."

"A what?"

"A card girl. You know, hold up a card with the round number on it?"

"That's all you did?"

"Yes. That and accompany Harold when he wanted us to."

Checking out a Santa Monica address, Taulbee and another agent, who happened to be the best runner in the FBI's Los Angeles office, knocked on a door and heard suspicious sounds. Taulbee told his partner to go around back. As he did, a young black man ran out the back door. The agent tore off after him. A few minutes later, the agent came back out of breath and empty-handed.

"I don't know who that guy is," huffed the agent, "but he can *move*. I didn't have a chance."

Interviewing the next-door neighbor, Taulbee asked who lived at the address.

"Why, Houston McTear lives there. The world's fastest human."

Meanwhile Woodall and Jones interviewed Ali a few days after his press conference. They met Ali and his lawyer, Mike Phenner, at the Beverly Wilshire Hotel. While Ali said that he had been suspicious for sometime of the source of MAPS's money, he claimed that the furthest thing from his mind was the possibility that Smith had stolen the money.

Ali promised the agents that if Smith should contact him, he would advise him to get a lawyer and turn himself in to the FBI. Before the agents left, Ali reached into an attaché case and took out a black and white photograph of himself in the ring. He happily autographed it—"From Your Friend Muhammad Ali."

After the interview, Allison asked the agents to repeat the Champ's statements regarding his dealings with Smith. Allison agreed with the agents' impression: Ali was *not* involved in any crime. Though his name and immense influence had been used for promotional purposes by Smith, the Champ had obviously not participated in any of the illegalities. In fact, Phenner had explained to the agents during the interview that his law firm and Ali's accountants had been badgering Smith for weeks before the scandal broke for a detailed accounting of MAPS's finances and a look at its books. They had been among the first to suspect problems with Smith's finances. Ali's advisors—who were understandably protective of the Champ's image as well as his business affairs—had wanted to be sure there wasn't any hanky-panky going on at a company that carried their client's name.

As bits and pieces of information came trickling in, Allison grew more certain that his suspicion that Smith was culpable would turn out to be right. From an objective standpoint, however, he knew the government still had virtually no hard evidence against Smith. His sudden flight could be explained away based upon a claimed apprehension of being harmed by others with something to hide or by jealous Muslims around Ali or upon a black man's fear of being accused just because he was black. Similar excuses could be found for the delay in responding to the Ali camp's requests for an audit. And the government did not know how company documents might describe the source of the funds. What if the MAPS books described the monies as "bank loans" or "draws against line of credit"? Even a truly guilty con artist could write himself a nice insurance policy for trial by structuring his records to reflect a supposedly innocent state of mind. At this point, the government was about as far away as it could be from proof beyond a reasonable doubt.

Then, late on February 2, one of the FBI agents called to say that Ben Lewis had just come in and confessed to the embezzlement. Allison was ecstatic. This was the break he had hoped for. Lewis could help put all the pieces together, particularly as to how the embezzlement had actually been accomplished. The government's immediate goal now was twofold: to keep Lewis talking and to make his cooperation a closely guarded secret. Smith must not find out that his former crime partner was talking. Allison preferred that Smith be allowed to dig himself a deeper hole with all his public statements. The government's time would come.

Though he was still giving official "no comments" to the press, Allison began to give "off the record" guidance to certain reporters in order to lead them away from Muhammad Ali. The prosecutor saw no reason to besmirch the Champ's name when he was clearly not involved in the embezzlement. Ali's noninvolvement had already been verified by Ben Lewis. Allison also set out to warn inquiring reporters—totally off the record—not to swallow Smith's stories about a line of credit, a $200 million embezzlement at Wells Fargo, the involvement of the Japanese Mafia and the role of Gene Kawakami.

Now more than ever, Wells Fargo was putting not-too-subtle pressure on Allison for the government to make arrests and issue indictments. The bank's lawyer, George Link, started calling regularly to ask the same question: "How long do you expect it will be?" Wells Fargo wanted public vindication in order to clear its name and restore public confidence. But Allison could not help the bank right now. And in any case, that was not his role. As far as Smith was concerned, even if the FBI knew his whereabouts—which it did not—Allison was not yet prepared to seek his arrest. There was no way the prosecutor could go before the federal grand jury with the limited information he now possessed. A good prosecutor knew better than to go for an indictment before his case was fully developed. Once an indictment is handed down, the Speedy Trial Act requires that a defendant be tried within about two months—not enough time to put together a solid case in a complex fraud matter like this if much work remained to be done, as it did here. Since the burden of proof is always on the government to prove its accusations beyond a reasonable doubt, Allison could not afford to commit himself while the government's case was only half-baked. After all, everyone is innocent until proven guilty. Even Harold Smith.

✳✳✳

Allison was not surprised when Cornell Price telephoned for an appointment. The agents had told him that Price was now representing Ben Lewis in criminal matters and that he would be calling to try to work out a deal. Though they possessed totally different styles—Price was laid-back, a term that certainly did *not* describe Allison—the two men had become good friends when Allison had first started in the U.S. Attorney's office, where Price had already served a few years. Some time later, Price left the government to go into private practice. This was their first meeting as adversaries. Privately, Allison was pleased that Price had not come on the scene a day earlier. He knew that Cornell would never have allowed a peep out of Ben Lewis until he had his deal. Now, because Lewis's confession was a matter of record, Allison held all the cards.

As usual, the affable Price sidled around to the real issue in an unhurried manner. Allison waited, a fixed smile on his face, exchanging abbreviated pleasantries and knowing what to expect.

Finally Price got to the point. "I was thinking, Dean, considering what Ben can do for you, he deserves a break. He got taken in by Harold too, you know. I think under the circumstances he shouldn't get more than three years and the government should agree to stand silent at the time of sentencing."

Allison's smile disappeared. "Get serious, Cornell."

Both knew how the game was usually played. The defense attorney's first request would be unreasonable. Then the prosecutor would come back with his own offer. Depending upon which side had the bargaining leverage, a compromise would be struck somewhere between the two. But Allison wasn't going to play that game today.

"Look, Cornell, we don't have to bullshit each other. You know the lay of the land around here. Your guy's name is the only one on all the branch settlement tickets that were used to embezzle the money. He's already given a full confession. He's got no defense. We can convict him on everything at this point with no deal whatsoever. If what he told the agents is true, it's important he testifies and makes clear that he's not the most culpable of the conspirators and that his personal benefit from the scheme was limited. That's what will determine the amount of time he gets. He'll get brownie points from the court for having walked in and fessed up. I'm prepared to be reasonable. I'm not going to crucify him just for kicks. But when you get down to it, he's got no chips to bargain with. And let's face it, he's no angel. This guy stole twenty-one million dollars. So he's going to have to do some serious time in any event."

"What did you have in mind, man?" Price had not stiffened at all. He had expected to hear this, and if he had been in Allison's position he would be using some variation on the same theme.

"For starters, he's going to have to plead guilty to multiple felony counts," Allison said. "You know in a case like this with a huge dollar amount that there is no way a one-count plea would be appropriate. Second, of course, he will have to comply with the usual condition of complete cooperation and candor. My thinking as to what is fair is for him to plead guilty to three counts, one of which will be the conspiracy count, since he's telling us it was a conspiracy." Allison left unspoken—because they both knew it—that each count would carry a five-year maximum jail sentence.

"What about sentencing?"

"We'll *recommend* concurrent." That meant that *if* the court followed the Government's recommendation, the sentences on each count would run concurrently—as opposed to consecutively—and he would not spend more than five years behind bars. "But he'll have no guarantees. As you know, the court will be free to give him the full fifteen. It will be up to him to convince the judge through his cooperation and truthful testimony that the government's recommendation is appropriate." And, Allison knew, it would give Lewis one hell of an incentive to be as cooperative and scrupulously accurate in his testimony as possible. Lewis would know that if he were exposed in a misstatement or half-truth under cross-examination that it would be his ass, not just the government's case, on the line.

Price showed his patented little-boy smile. "Well, that's not bad for a first offer."

"That's the *only* offer," Allison said. "That's the way it's going to be. We're prepared to do some other minor things to accommodate him, like issuing a summons instead of a warrant for him and allowing him to be on a personal recognizance bond pending sentencing. But in terms of the major elements of any agreement, that's it, Cornell."

"Okay, man, I'll talk to my client and let you know. Say, does the name Sammie Marshall mean anything to you?"

"He used to work for Wells Fargo before joining MAPS."

"Yeah. You know, he's the one who suggested this branch settlement stuff to Ben. He got Ben into it in the beginning." Price stood up and winked. "I may be back to you with a counter offer."

"Let's sign off on it and start doing both our clients some good."

The next day, Price called and said Lewis had accepted the government's deal. They would sign an agreement and then the interviewing by the FBI could resume. It would only be a matter of a few days.

"Listen," Price added, "I told Joe Woodall and Chuck Jones that I'm sure they weren't the only people looking for Ben Lewis, and I didn't think it would be safe for him to stay in his house. So they're putting him up in a hotel."

Allison concurred with the action.

In Ben Lewis, the government now had a star witness to protect.

CHAPTER TWENTY-EIGHT

The next attorneys on the scene were two of the best white-collar criminal defense lawyers in Los Angeles. Doug Dalton and George Buehler were old adversaries of Dean Allison's. They had crossed swords before in a huge corporate bribery case involving a subsidiary of one of Japan's largest firms, Marubeni America Corporation. Dalton and Buehler had represented the Marubeni executive who coordinated the exchange of money for inside bidding information with an Anchorage, Alaska, public official. The government had come out on top in that battle—Marubeni was convicted on sixty-three counts and the executive on fifty-nine counts of racketeering, conspiracy, wire fraud, mail fraud and interstate travel to commit bribery. Allison came away from the Marubeni case with great respect for the way Dalton and Buehler handled themselves, in court and out. The three men got along well too, particularly Allison and Buehler, both of whom were single and approximately the same age. They would beat the heck out of each other in court and then go out in the hallway during a recess and share cigarettes.

Dalton and Buehler came aboard as counsel for Sammie Marshall, which in itself was interesting to Allison. The fact that Marshall would turn to such a high-powered defense team could not be construed as a definitive indication of his guilt, but it was an important development in the prosecutor's effort to identify all the players in the case. From what he was hearing and surmising—based primarily on the interviews the FBI was conducting with Ben Lewis, who was now ensconced in a Culver City hotel room—Marshall was well on his way to becoming a target of the government investigation. That being the case, the former banker had made a wise move in turning to Dalton and Buehler.

Though the two defense attorneys would never volunteer information that would hurt their client, they did help solve a major frustration for Allison. The long-missing MAPS records, which had been passed around like a collection of hot potatoes, finally ended up in Dalton's possession. Unlike other defense attorneys Allison knew, Dalton could be trusted to obey a lawful subpoena and hand the records over promptly with no funny business. That was just what Dalton did. Once the FBI finally received the boxed records, it didn't take long to determine that many of the most crucial documents were not in this group and were still missing. Of particular interest were the ledgers and journals for MAPS' receipts and disbursements. Allison was sure they hadn't disappeared while in Dalton's hands. So where were they?

In Allison's mind, there was no doubt about it now: Harold Smith was a first-class con man and guilty as hell. Still, the government would have to prove that in court. Ben Lewis's testimony alone would not make an airtight case. After all, he was the banker who stole all the money. If it came down to his word against Smith's, the jury would start from the proposition that Lewis was trying to save his own skin. His testimony would have to be corroborated by other witnesses as well as documentation. Without the records, it would be tough going. If the records were never going to surface—Allison now considered that a definite possibility—then he was going to need an insider who had worked at MAPS and possessed a near photographic memory to testify about how all the millions of bank money were spent.

As of now, the government knew of no such person.

* * *

Though Harold Smith was still in hiding, claiming to fear for his life, his lawyers arrived at the federal courthouse on February 24 for a meeting with Allison. In all, there were five of them, but the two that counted were Jennifer King and Al Sheppard.

King was representing Smith in a $275 million countersuit just filed against Wells Fargo Bank. She *looked* like the former TV weathergirl she was, Allison thought, as she sashayed into his office. Tall and leggy, wearing a silk blouse, flashy jewelry and a touch too much makeup and flashing a cocktail party smile, she cut a striking figure. Sheppard was an older, conservatively dressed man with salt-and-pepper hair and a walking cane. All Allison had been able to learn about him was that he was a criminal defense lawyer with a good reputation, whose experience seemed to have been primarily in state court.

Also present at the meeting were FBI Special Agents Woodall, Jones and Taulbee. Before the outsiders arrived, the government men all agreed that their posture at the meeting would be to listen rather than talk. "They're coming here to pump us and find out how much we know," Allison had warned. "We're not going to tell them anything. We're not going to give them any free discovery. And let's make sure no one makes a slip about Ben Lewis. We can't let them know he is talking."

They sat around a large conference table, with Allison at one end, flanked on his left by the agents. King was to his immediate right, and Sheppard was at the far end of the table.

Sheppard was obviously the nominal head of the Smith legal team. "I'm so glad we could get together face-to-face," he said. "I don't believe in trying my cases in the newspaper. Never have."

Allison had the feeling the remark by the older attorney was meant to distance him from King, who had already given several press conferences on the matter of Harold Smith's purported innocence.

When the roundtable discussion started, everyone agreed—even Jennifer King—that it would be best to proceed in an orderly, professional manner and not resort to press releases.

"Tell me, Dean," King said, placing her hand on his arm, "has a warrant been issued for our client yet?"

The pumping had begun.

"No."

"Is he a target?"

"At this point, the facts have not been sufficiently developed. I'm not making any representations either way. But if you want to play it safe, consider him a target."

King asked several more questions. A couple of them made it embarrassingly clear to Allison and the agents that she was not particularly knowledgeable about federal criminal procedure. Then she offered a rehash of the statements Smith was making in the press about being afraid for his life and how he had been chased in Northern California by gun-wielding men.

"We think they were FBI agents," King said.

"I don't know if he was chased by anyone," Allison said, "but if he was, I can assure you it wasn't by FBI agents."

Two things were happening. First, she was trying to take the lead role away from Sheppard. And second, she was throwing off more sexual vibes than a guy might find in a weekend at singles bars. The touchy-feely stuff and patronizing smiles were just part of the act. Her blouse was unbuttoned to the top of her cleavage, and she made a point of bending forward toward whichever government man she was talking to. Allison and the agents exchanged sideways glances and tried not to smile at each other.

"We're convinced there's organized crime involvement here," she said, leaning toward Allison.

The prosecutor wanted to make clear that this sort of behavior was not welcome. He pushed his chair back from the table and said, "Frankly, we haven't seen anything to indicate that, but we'd be happy to listen to anything your client has to say."

Subtly, the nature of the dialogue had changed. Now it was the defense lawyers giving information to the government about their client's position. The pump had reversed direction. Allison and the agents tried to keep things going this way by being passive listeners, not volunteering comments of their own and acting genuinely interested in what King had to say. The last part was easy. They *were* interested, if only to learn more details of Smith's apparently far-fetched story.

"He's really afraid for his life," she said earnestly.

"Shut up, Jennifer." The stern approach had come from the far end of the table. Sheppard obviously could take no more. "Would it be possible to arrange for Harold to come in and talk to you?" he asked, directing his question to Allison. "Perhaps to testify before the grand jury?"

Allison had two simultaneous thoughts: *Boy, would I love that* and *fat chance.* "We'd be happy to give him an opportunity to tell his side of the story. A grand jury appearance might not be appropriate at this point because the grand jury has not really begun hearing evidence, although an investigation technically commenced with the issuance of certain subpoenas. But when the time comes, we will present to them any evidence you want to give us, and that would include letting Mr. Smith testify on his own behalf if he so chooses."

"Would you agree not to arrest him?" Sheppard asked.

"We would be willing to give you that assurance provided the other conditions for such an interview were satisfactory. To begin with, he'd have to agree to answer our questions too, not to just walk in, tell us his version of events and then walk out and have a press conference." There was no way Allison was going to allow Smith to make it look as if he were cooperating and the government believed his story. "Secondly, we'd want some assurance that he really has no fear of a full and fair investigation of the facts. We would want him to surrender his passport, either to us or to a mutually acceptable third party."

"Oh, I think he would do that," Sheppard said.

"You guys wouldn't tell the press if Harold came in?" King said, speaking for the first time since Sheppard's rebuff. "It could be a secret?"

"No problem," Allison said. "*We* aren't talking to the press."

"There are major organized crime connections here," King repeated. "We can help you blow this case open."

"We're interested in any hard information you have to back up his claims," Allison said. "Do you have any specific facts you would like to share with us now?"

That *did* shut King up.

But not for long.

Immediately after the meeting, as the government men were talking among themselves upstairs, King stepped in front of a TV camera crew on the steps of the courthouse. She had called ahead to a friendly reporter—KNBC's Warren Wilson, who had been consistently emphasizing Smith's side of the story in his televised reports—and told him about the meeting.

"We're here making arrangements for Harold Smith to come in and cooperate with the government in its investigation," she announced. "He wants to tell them about the threats on his life and Gene Kawakami's organized crime connections."

So much for keeping the meeting a secret or for the defense attorneys' protestations that the case should be kept out of the press.

When Allison heard about King being on TV that night, he was not surprised by the double cross. It simply confirmed his gut feeling from the meeting: Jennifer King was not someone to turn your back on.

***

Another attorney had an encounter with Jennifer King a couple of days later. Virgil Roberts, representing Ben Lewis in the civil suit filed by Wells Fargo, was at a deposition in the case. Roberts, who had never before met King, was pulled aside by the woman lawyer.

"We have to coordinate our defense," she whispered. "We want you to tell your client that if he will testify he did this because of the Japanese Mafia, we will support him. We need to get together and discuss this."

Roberts said nothing but two days later agreed to a meeting with King in her office. He knew her associate, Robert Michaels. The two men had attended UCLA together in the late 1960s. Michaels had been a big man on campus then, serving as president of the student body.

"We want Ben to give us a sworn declaration saying Harold was innocent and that he had a $21-million line of credit that Ben had given to him," she explained. "Then you get Ben to say the Japanese Mafia made him do it. He'd have a duress defense. We have witnesses who will support him."

The problem, as far as Roberts was concerned, was that this scenario simply wasn't true. There was no line of credit, and Lewis did not embezzle the money because of the Japanese Mafia. It was all hogwash, and he told King that they couldn't go along with the suggestion.

"Then I have a message for Ben from Harold," King said somberly. "Tell him Harold is tired of protecting him and won't do it any longer."

Roberts left King's office shocked and insulted. Of course he had not mentioned a word about Ben cooperating with the government. What King had proposed, in essence, was that his client—whom she assumed to be still in hiding—lie to federal investigators. Such conduct was unethical and improper. When he got back to his office, he told his colleague Cornell Price about the incident.

The next day, Price repeated the story to Allison. Price felt that Allison ought to know what kind of person he was dealing with in Jennifer King.

* * *

Teri Key was in the company of her own lawyer, and he was angry with her. Rick Rosenfield felt that his client was an innocent bystander to the embezzlement he was reading about in the newspaper. Except perhaps for her part in helping the MAPS records disappear. But at the time, as Rosenfield saw it, Teri had no idea that there was any legal trouble, nor did she comprehend that Smith might be trying to hide incriminating evidence. Her motives were those of a loyal employee: do what the boss asks. Now, however, Teri was telling him something that caused him great distress.

"But why did you go see him last weekend?"

"Harold called and asked me to come," Teri said softly. "He was crying. He said the whole family missed me."

Rosenfield was in the process of working out a deal with the government. He didn't want anything screwing it up. He wanted his client to stay away from Smith and his entourage. Teri would just get pulled deeper into the mess.

The next day, Rosenfield accompanied Key to the federal court-house. Today would be an important day for her. Allison had agreed to give her immunity from prosecution in exchange for her candid disclosure of all the information she had about MAPS and Smith. In his earlier telephone discussions with the prosecutor, Rosenfield had been forthright about his client helping move the MAPS records on orders from Smith. The prosecutor said her limited role in that effort so early in the game didn't sound like a problem as long as that was all, and if she would be completely cooperative and truthful on all matters.

Teri was scared to death. She had been frightened of the government ever since the FBI agents had served the subpoena on the MAPS office and had threatened everyone with obstruction of justice charges. Too, she had heard tales from Harold's group about supposed "grillings" of the card girls and other MAPS employees. When Rosenfield had suggested she talk to the government, she had not been keen on the idea. But, he asked, wasn't she willing to tell the truth? Of course, she said. Then tell the truth and let the chips fall where they may, the attorney said. Pushing her over the line was Key's conviction that if she told the truth the government would realize that Harold had been a good man and honest businessman.

Shown into Allison's office, she was introduced to the prosecutor and FBI Special Agents Joe Woodall and Jannell Salveson. Salveson had been brought in because Woodall had heard that Key was nervous; he thought it might be easier for her to talk to a sympathetic female agent.

Allison and the agents had decided to play it cool. They did not want to interrogate Teri closely at the outset but to win her confidence. It became immediately apparent that she was still loyal to Smith. It would take time, but Allison wanted her to realize that he and the agents, not Smith and his followers, were the good guys, and that they were not out to oppress or railroad anyone.

After discussing and signing the letter of agreement regarding her immunity, Key volunteered a few details of life at MAPS. She told of her responsibility for keeping the checkbooks. That caused a light to go on for Allison: the company checkbooks and ledgers were still missing. Allison was impressed with Key's memory for details. She could be the key insider witness. At a minimum, it looked like she could corroborate Ben Lewis.

As to Smith's obvious culpability in the case based on the government's widening investigation, Allison did not push that on Key. He and Woodall had decided to allow her to reach that conclusion on her own. They would simply lay the information out in front of her and see what she could remember. It stood to reason that eventually she would realize how Smith had been manipulating everyone, including her. If she made that discovery herself, instead of being pressed to take the government's word for it, she would be a better witness for the prosecution.

Out of the blue, Rosenfield said at one point, "I'd like to have a word in the hallway with Teri."

They returned in a couple of minutes.

"There is something I think Teri needs to get out in the open," her lawyer said. "I have advised her to do so now."

All eyes turned to Key.

"Well," she said hesitantly, "I spent last weekend at a condominium in Lake Tahoe with Harold and Lee and some other people." She looked nervously at Rosenfield, who nodded his assurance. "There was a whole box of MAPS records there. Ledgers and stuff., Some of the same records he had me take out of the office."

"Oh really?" Allison said, trying to appear more nonchalant than he felt. "That's interesting. *Very* interesting."

***

The interview sessions began in earnest for Teri Key the day after her visit to Allison's office. She and Rick Rosenfield arrived at the FBI office and were shown into an interview room by Special Agents Woodall and Salveson.

For hours Key talked about her job at MAPS, how money ended up in various accounts, her writing of checks to pay bills, gathering cash for boxers and the business of the company. Her attitude was that this had been a successful and legitimate operation and whatever was going on with the bank had nothing to do with Harold or Ben. She liked both men, she explained, and could not see either of them involved in anything illegal.

To Woodall, two things were obvious: Teri was telling the truth and she was naive. During the lengthy interview, she began relaxing with the agents. The mild-mannered Woodall even got her to laugh when he joked about keeping pins in a nearby drawer to stick under her fingernails if she didn't cooperate.

Toward the end of the marathon session, Teri told the agents about meeting Jennifer King during the Lake Tahoe weekend. "She said if I was questioned by the FBI or grand jury I should say that Harold had a line of credit at Wells Fargo," Teri explained. "I said I didn't know anything about a line of credit. Jennifer told me it was all right to tell a little lie. She said no one would know the difference. But I told her *I* would know the difference. You see, I was raised to believe that lying was the worst thing a person could do."

The door to the interview room opened at one point, and another agent stuck his head inside. "Say, Joe, there's a call for you. Some guy named Lewis."

Woodall tried not to look horror-stricken at the agent's slip. But he didn't hide it well. He thought the remark might have passed over Teri's head, but he was sure there was recognition in Rosenfield's eyes. Woodall and Salveson left the room.

"That confirms what I thought all along," Rosenfield said to his client. "I knew they had to have Lewis."

"I guess so," Teri said. She was relieved to not be the only one talking to the government.

"You could see from Joe's reaction that he's worried," Rosenfield said. "I think it would be good for our working relationship with him if we assured him that we aren't going to tell anyone."

When Woodall returned to the room, Rosenfield said, "We know you're talking to Ben Lewis, but we're not going to tell anyone."

"I won't tell a soul," Teri said.

Woodall didn't immediately respond. He feared doing so might confirm that the FBI had Lewis. He couldn't do that.

"Honest, Joe, it won't leave this room," Rosenfield said.

"Thanks," Woodall finally said uncomfortably.

CHAPTER TWENTY-NINE

Dean Allison had seen and heard enough of Jennifer King's questionable practices. Her condescending nature, her manipulative use of the media, the unethical proposals she was apparently making to various individuals—all this struck Allison as a desperate effort on her part to fabricate a defense for Harold Smith. She seemed to Allison to be the kind of lawyer to whom truth and honesty meant little, who believed in winning at any cost. The tales he was hearing about her—even from her fellow defense lawyers—made his skin crawl. The report from Teri Key that King had told her to lie about the missing MAPS records simply confirmed his impressions.

As much as he detested lawyers who operated this way, Allison was not inclined to go after King at this point. Allison did not want to get sidetracked. He did not want to be accused of tampering with Smith's legal defense. Everyone was entitled to representation. But he *did* want those missing MAPS financial records. If Jennifer King was somehow involved in their disappearance, well, that was going to be her problem.

Allison wrote out grand jury subpoenas ordering Jennifer King and her law partner, Robert Michaels, to appear before the grand jury with any MAPS record in their possession. In that official setting, Allison intended to question them thoroughly. Even a lawyer who advised people to lie to federal investigators in private conversations might think twice about lying to a federal grand jury. King and her partner might be persuaded to cough up the records after all.

After being served with the subpoenas, King and Michaels called Allison. They spoke to the prosecutor on a speaker phone and began by asking whether personal appearances were really necessary.

"Yes, an appearance is necessary," Allison said. "We want you to appear and describe the records. But both of you don't have to come. I'll accept a representation from the one who comes that the other has no documents." Frankly, Allison didn't particularly care who came to testify. He was more interested in the records than in personalities.

"To the extent you're going to ask us to describe records," Michaels said, "you're talking about records in our possession?"

"I will probably also inquire what you've had in your possession within the last thirty days," Allison said. You *bet* he was going to ask about that.

"I don't know if that's relevant," Michaels said.

"One of the purposes of the grand jury is to find out where evidence is," Allison said. "The government is entitled to know if you had them, say, twenty-four days ago and gave them to someone else, so that we can find out where they are now."

Jennifer King appeared before the grand jury on March 11. The foreperson of the jury swore King in. "Do you solemnly swear that the testimony and evidence you shall give in the proceedings now before this federal grand jury shall be the truth, the whole truth and nothing but the truth, so help you God?"

"I do," King said, then sat down in the witness chair.

Allison began by taking her through all the records she had brought. Some of them, curiously, were loose, as if they had been selected and removed from a larger collection. She had brought a check register for Bodak Promotions and a substantial number of individual bank documents concerning other Harold Smith entities, such as check stubs, deposit slips and monthly account statements. With the exception of one folder—marked "Television Agreements"—all of it fit a suspicious pattern. Allison recognized it immediately: the government could get copies of the same things, or at least get the same information, from Wells Fargo. In effect King was giving up only what was already available. The most important records—the ones that could *not* be reconstructed by the government from other sources—were still missing. He intended to find out whether this was only a coincidence or whether King was hiding something.

"Are these the only records that you have within your possession today within the scope of this subpoena?" Allison asked.

"Yes, they are."

"To your knowledge, does any other member or employee of your firm have any other records called for by this subpoena?"

"No."

"Tell us where you got [these records] and when, approximately, to the best of your recollection."

"I can't recall when any particular documents were given to me." King's evasiveness was painfully obvious to Allison and, he hoped, to the grand jurors. "They came from various sources, and [at] various times."

What's the matter, Jennifer, Allison thought, *don't you want to talk about the weekend at Lake Tahoe? Let's see if I can refresh your memory.*

"Where in terms of geographical location were those records delivered to you? The grand jury is interested where other records within the scope of the subpoena might be stored or kept."

"I was out of the state."

"Where?" *You don't get away that easily, lady.*

"I was in Tahoe."

"Can you tell us where in Tahoe?" he asked.

"I have no idea."

At that point, Allison sensed King had moved from cat-and-mouse evasion to deliberate perjury. "You do not remember where in Tahoe you were?" he asked, his tone obviously incredulous.

"I was driven so I didn't really pay any attention to the location."

Bullshit, Allison thought. But it didn't seem worth pursuing. He was more interested in finding out if there were other witnesses.

"Besides your client, who else was present at the time?" he asked.

"I don't recall. I'm not sure anybody was." *Another clear evasion.*

Now Allison was fed up. Teri Key had said she saw King with the ledgers and journals that weekend in Tahoe and, in fact, they had reviewed them together at King's request. Yet Jennifer King had not brought them with her today and was pretending she knew nothing of any other records. She had claimed, under oath, that the only documents delivered to her in Lake Tahoe were the check register for Bodak Promotions and a folder containing various loose documents. Now was the time to make the questions as specific as possible, so that if King was committing perjury she could be held accountable for it.

"At that time ... were any *other* records delivered or shown to you which would fall within the scope of this subpoena?"

"No."

One more chance.

"In other words," Allison said, "those [two records] were the *only* records shown or delivered to you at that time?"

"That is correct."

Either Jennifer King had just flat out committed perjury or Teri Key was terribly mistaken. Which was it?

Before the session was over, Allison threw King a curve. He suspected that the Smith defense team was dying to know whether or not the government had Ben Lewis. He was just as determined to make sure Lewis's cooperation remained a secret.

"Between the time you received [the records] and today, have any of these records been handled by L. Ben Lewis?"

He saw a glint in King's eyes. Why would the prosecutor ask a question like that if the government already had Lewis? They must not have him.

"No," she answered.

For Jennifer King, it was obviously a sweet thought that Ben Lewis might still be keeping his mouth shut. Just as the rest of those MAPS records could hurt Harold Smith's defense, there was much Lewis could say that would be damaging.

As the truth often is.

* * *

Gene Kawakami had hired his own criminal defense lawyer. Richard Trattner, a former IRS special agent for ten years, contacted Dean Allison in early March about making a deal for his client. The first conversation did not go well. Trattner claimed his client was completely innocent, yet said that Kawakami would only talk to the government if he was given complete immunity from prosecution. Allison had told him that was impossible under the circumstances. A few days later, Trattner called back to make another appointment.

"Are you coming alone or with your client?" Allison asked.

"Alone," Trattner said. "I've done my homework. I know what the facts are—I've talked to my client in detail. I see where Smith's attorneys had another press conference and laid out the same scenario blaming Gene for the missing money."

Allison knew already, from information supplied by Ben Lewis and Teri Key, together with the branch settlement records corroborating Lewis, that Kawakami was not a participant in the embezzlement, much less its mastermind. Kawakami had already admitted to the FBI agents to having written several phony loans while at Miracle Mile, but Allison was not going to agree to any blanket immunity until he had more facts. "What Smith's people are saying doesn't trouble me," Allison said. "By the way, I don't want to waste your time, so don't bother coming down here if you're just going to repeat what you told me the other day about your client being innocent and wanting immunity. Because that's not going to happen."

"Well, I have the answers to the questions you asked and some facts to present. Then you can tell me what you're going to do."

"Okay."

They met in Allison's office.

Trattner was forthcoming about his client's indiscretions. He told about how Kawakami had made loans to Smith that were never repaid and that in order to protect himself Kawakami had taken loans out in various phony names—Western Sales and Ken Kato, to name two of them.

"You need Gene Kawakami," Trattner said. "Smith is telling the world he got a line of credit, and Kawakami is the only one who can say he didn't."

That was not quite right—Ben Lewis could sure say Harold's money didn't come from a line of credit—but Trattner was doing a good job representing his client. He was trying to sell a deal to the prosecutor that would keep his client out of jail, which was exactly Trattner's job. Allison had to admit—though he did not verbalize the thought—that it would be nice to have Kawakami testifying for the government.

Allison proposed that Kawakami plead guilty to one count of Title 18, United States Code, Section 1005, which prohibits making a false entry in any bank book, report or statement with intent to deceive. Trattner said Kawakami sought no assurances with respect to what sentence he might receive and promised to testify fully and completely before the FBI, the federal grand jury and in U.S. District Court. In exchange, Trattner wanted the government to make clear that Kawakami had no involvement in the $21 million embezzlement of Wells Fargo, that Kawakami had no idea the $357,000 debit he caused in the MAPS account was embezzled money and that none of the phony loans written by Kawakami benefited him personally; at the time of sentencing, the government would make known the extent of Kawakami's cooperation and take "no position" at his sentencing.

Allison was certainly not going to sign the proposal drafted by Trattner. He would write his own agreement, one much more favorable to the government. For instance, there was nothing in Trattner's version about the truthfulness of Kawakami's information. Allison wanted the government to be protected if the facts turned out to be different than Kawakami claimed—if, for example, there were other transgressions by Kawakami that he had not told his lawyer about. Allison always prepared his "cooperation" agreements with disclaimers that allowed the government to cancel the deal if the facts changed later. Another standard term he used was one that effected a waiver of the witness' self-incrimination privilege and allowed all the statements he'd made in the course of "cooperating" to be used against him if the agreement were later rescinded. That gave the witness an incentive to come completely clean the first time around.

Allison knew that Trattner and Kawakami would agree to his version of the deal. They had little choice. Otherwise the former Miracle Mile manager would stand trial and undoubtedly go to prison on numerous felony counts arising from the phony loan transactions.

Like Ben Lewis, Gene Kawakami was about to come in out of the cold.

CHAPTER THIRTY

FBI Special Agent Dale Taulbee had been in this line of work long enough to know when something was not right. And there was something very wrong about the identity of Harold James Smith.

Taulbee had attempted to do a complete background check, searching all the records—some public and others confidential, available only to law enforcement. But he could find nothing on Smith earlier than about 1974. The agent had seen this sort of thing before. Usually it meant problems with the law or an ex-wife. It was really not that difficult to acquire a new identity these days. Taulbee had a drawer full of phony birth certificates sold through the mail. Blank driver's licenses could be found for the right price; the same with Social Security cards.

Smith had claimed, on several documents, that he was born in North Carolina. Taulbee telephoned the local courthouse in Charlotte and had a clerk there hand check all the birth certificates for the appropriate year. There was no record of a Harold Smith ever being born.

It was at this stage of his investigation, on March 16, that Taulbee took a long-distance phone call from a man who introduced himself as Dewey Hughes. The man claimed to be calling from Washington, D.C.

"I might have some information on the Harold Smith case," he said.

The Bureau gets lots of calls like this, and most are a waste of time. People say they have important information about a wanted fugitive, but really they are just sharing a pet theory that they picked up over the fence from their neighbor. Big help.

"What kind of information?" Taulbee asked routinely.

"Let me explain my situation first."

Here goes, Taulbee thought.

"I have a radio station here in Washington, and I'm an on-the-air disc jockey. There's a chance that what I know about Harold Smith is very important. I want to give you that information, but I want something in return."

They always do. Didn't they know the FBI makes no deals?

"I can't discuss that with you until I know what you're talking about," Taulbee said. "Give me an idea of what kind of information you have."

"Well"—the man was obviously trying to decide how much to tell before he had his deal—"if he's who I think he is, he's not Harold Smith."

Bingo. Taulbee sat bolt upright in his chair and reached for a pencil. This was right in line with his own suspicions about Smith. "What do you want?" the agent said.

"I want exclusive rights to any story on his arrest," Hughes said. "I don't want to get scooped on my own story."

Taulbee was quiet for a moment. Actually, the Bureau *had* been known to accommodate sources now and then. Especially if the information was unusually valuable. This DJ wasn't asking for a whole lot. If he did know Harold Smith's real identity, it would blow the investigation wide open.

"I can't make that kind of commitment to you," Taulbee said. "I'll have to take it up with my superiors. But I'll give you my word I'll do everything possible to get the exclusive for you. Will you give me your information on the promise that I'll do my best?"

"Talk to your supervisors and call me," Hughes said, giving the agent his phone number.

It didn't take Taulbee long to get back to Hughes with the FBI's proposal. "If your information checks out, the very first phone call we make after his arrest will be to you. You might get two or three hours on the rest of the press."

Hughes seemed to be hesitant.

Taulbee decided it was time for a strong patriotic pitch. "You know something that may help a federal investigation," he said. "We need all the help we can get from concerned citizens."

"Okay," Hughes said. "Your man's real name is Ross Fields. He used to have a nightclub here in Washington. It was called the Sammy Davis Jr. Nightclub. He also did some small-time concert promotions and put on a couple of boxing cards. Fields was always writing bad checks. You couldn't trust him with money. He left town owing everyone, including me."

"You've seen a picture of Harold Smith?"

"Yeah, in the papers and on TV."

Taulbee had heard about Smith's appearances on television. The MAPS head had claimed that one FBI agent in particular was going around roughing up his friends and employees, some of them women. Smith was pointing a finger at him, Taulbee was sure. Taulbee had handled most of the interviewing with the card girls. The charges were, of course, ludicrous. Sure, he had been stern with them when they became evasive. But Taulbee didn't go around beating up on people. That's not the way the FBI works. An agent who did that in today's Bureau wouldn't last. On TV, Smith also had asked rhetorically why he wasn't yet under arrest if he had stolen all that money. Taulbee could do nothing at the time to rectify that, but the agent sure was looking forward to the day that he could.

"It's him, I'm sure," Hughes said. "A couple of years ago, I went to the Super Bowl in New Orleans. When I was walking in I saw Fields. I called out to him. He said, 'No, that's not my name anymore. I'm Harold Smith now.'"

Taulbee went to work as soon as he was off the phone. He found an FBI file on Ross Eugene Fields. It was a fairly thick one, containing a wanted poster that had hung in post offices around the country a few years back. The poster pictured a younger Fields and his white common-law wife, who matched the description Taulbee had heard of Barbara Lee Smith. Her real name was Alice Vicki Darrow.

The agent had to be sure. He asked FBI headquarters to facsimile a complete set of Fields's fingerprints to him. They soon arrived. As luck would have it, Harold Smith had allowed his thumb print—an optional form of identification in California—to be taken for his driver's license. Next, Taulbee called in an agent who had previously worked in the FBI's fingerprint division. Comparing thumb prints, the agent got a hit on ten points, or characteristics. There was no doubt about it. Harold Smith was Ross Eugene Fields.

Taulbee was pumped up by the recent turn of events. The Harold Smith mystery had been solved. There were no old identification records for Smith because he didn't exist before 1974.

Now there was just one thing Taulbee wanted to do: slap the cuffs on the man who called himself Smith.

***

Wells Fargo Bank wanted the cuffs on *both* Harold Smith and Ben Lewis. Having them behind bars would show the world that these two men were responsible for the embezzlement—as the bank claimed—and that it was not a theft involving hundreds of millions of dollars and several other branch offices and employees—as asserted by Smith and his lawyers.

Bank attorney George Link called Dean Allison regularly, inquiring as to the government's latest plans for apprehending Smith. Allison could not tell Link what the bank lawyer wanted to hear. The government was still conducting its investigation and was not ready to arrest Smith. Allison couldn't say anything about Smith's real identity or even about the government having Lewis in its fold. There was also a limit to how much he could sympathize with the bank's desperation. As he had feared, Wells Fargo had gotten itself in a jam with its public statements.

A month after news of the embezzlement broke, bank chairman Richard Cooley had told the press that the $21 million fraud was accomplished with a "simple mechanical manipulation of accounts" rather than through a sophisticated computer scheme. He had gone on to explain that this was managed by filling out tickets for crediting and debiting funds from the bank's branch settlement system, a "river of funds" with a daily volume as high as $300 million. If these transactions did not clear within *five days*, Cooley said, the bank's computer would detect it and send out a tracer.

Shortly after that, Harold Smith and Jennifer King gave various news organizations copies of Ben Lewis's airplane ticket to Australia for the "Down Under" tour. Sure enough, Lewis had been out of the bank more than five working days—more like eight or nine days. So, Smith's people claimed—and the press speculated—that Lewis could not have single-handedly carried out the embezzlement at the bank. The documentation suggested the existence of more perpetrators and yet a bigger scandal at the bank. In a follow-up announcement, the bank soon backed away from

Cooley's mistaken explanation, stating correctly that the computer didn't detect any problem or send out a tracer until *ten working days* had passed.

"I wish you could keep your people from making any further statements," Allison told Link.

"So do I," Link admitted. "But there's a tremendous amount of pressure on them to respond to Smith."

Allison knew all about pressure. The FBI was getting antsy about arresting Smith too. Here they were putting enormous manpower into a well-publicized investigation while their target, Smith, was running around giving press interviews and making them look like fools for not apprehending him.

The Bureau talked to Allison about arresting Smith on the basis of some of the old warrants uncovered by Taulbee. Sure, there were state warrants out for Ross Fields for forgery and bad checks, but they had been issued in places like North Carolina. This meant that if the feds arrested him in Los Angeles on a fugitive warrant—unlawful flight to avoid prosecution would be the technical charge—Smith would be sent back to the state in which the charges were pending and would pass out of the U.S. Attorney's office jurisdiction. Allison didn't want to lose control of the situation. So he was cool to the arrest idea at first.

The prosecutor was also afraid that, at the first sign the government had the goods on him, Smith might flee the country. Getting arrested on old warrants might just be the last straw. No one knew for sure whether Smith had any money left. Even Ben Lewis couldn't say for sure. But so many millions of dollars had gone through Smith's hands it seemed unlikely that he didn't have a sizable stash somewhere. One scenario Allison could well imagine had Smith standing before a local judge in a distant state, posting the low bail he would get on the old bad check charges, then walking out of the courthouse and catching the next plane to South America or the Caribbean. That kind of thing had certainly happened before. The government officials had to be careful. They couldn't flush Smith out into the open before they were ready with a charge that would stick and keep him around.

And, try as they might, they were not ready yet. The absence of the most important MAPS records wasn't helping any. Allison and FBI Special

Agents Joe Woodall and Chuck Jones were burning the midnight oil. The agents were still trying to piece together the complex movement of money through the various MAPS accounts. Allison was reviewing stacks of FBI 302s. Of special interest were the results of the interviews with Ben Lewis and Teri Key. These were proving invaluable. But he would need other witnesses to document the entire MAPS operation. Putting the case together was going to take still more time.

In the meantime, Smith was having a heyday in the media. Even entertainers like Johnny Carson were getting a ride out of the splashy crime. "There's good news and bad news on the economic front today," Carson deadpanned one night during his monologue. "The good news is that the country is going back on the gold standard, which ought to help ease inflation. The bad news is that the gold is being kept in the Wells Fargo vault."

Allison tried not to let the hoopla bother him. He kept reminding himself that the government's day in court would eventually come.

* * *

ABC network news producer Peter Shaplen had caught wind of Jennifer King's efforts to stage an "exclusive" interview for Harold Smith with the two TV newscasters who seemed most sympathetic to his side of the story: KNBC's Warren Wilson and KNXT's Jim Hill. When Shaplen called King to make arrangements for an ABC crew and correspondent to attend Smith's first public appearance since the scandal broke, King demurred. The network couldn't come, she said, because she didn't want too many TV trucks leaving in a caravan to the secret location where Smith was hiding out. She was afraid that the FBI might be watching her in an effort to find Smith.

Shaplen was desperate to get some tape of Smith. In TV, pictures were crucial. So far they had been running their stories of the Wells Fargo embezzlement on "World News Tonight" without Smith's likeness. At ABC there was special interest in the story. It came all the way from ABC President Roone Arledge's office in New York. Arledge, formerly long-time head of ABC Sports, had even assigned his right-hand man to help research the story from the East Coast. Some staffers thought it was just because of Arledge's interest in sports; others were more cynical. There was no love lost between Smith and ABC—they had sued and counter-sued each other concerning the TV rights to a Leo Randolph fight. With Smith signing up so many champions and contenders, ABC had been finding it difficult to obtain top-quality fights to televise.

Shaplen told his superiors of King's turndown, and one of them called her. Finally, after forty-five minutes of negotiations, they came up with a solution: ABC could come if it rented a school bus to transport *all* the reporters and crews from King's Century City law office to Smith's hideout.

"Get me a big yellow school bus," bureau chief Don Dunkel growled to a subordinate. "Preferably one that has 'Kindergarten' on the side of it." That was just about what the big, gruff bureau chief thought of this dog and pony show. A bus was soon located. Unfortunately, it came without Dunkel's editorial comment on the side.

When Shaplen and correspondent Tom Schell arrived at the Avenue of the Stars address, Wilson and Hill were already waiting with their crews and vans. Wilson was shocked to see the ABC crew.

"What are you doing here?" Wilson demanded.

"We're going along for the bus ride," Schell said.

"No you're not," Wilson snapped.

"The hell we're not. This is ABC's bus."

"This is my story," Wilson said defiantly.

While Wilson ran upstairs to complain to King and Shaplen followed after him to protect ABC's interest, Schell stayed down on the street with his crew. The veteran correspondent wasn't worried about being excluded now. Spending a couple of hundred bucks for a bus and driver had been a smooth move. But there was something that concerned Schell. He was regularly checking with researchers at the ABC bureau in Hollywood to see if Harold Smith's real identity had been uncovered yet. ABC had gotten a tip from some radio guy in Washington, D.C., that Harold Smith was not Harold Smith. It made perfect sense to them because Shaplen, a dogged researcher, had been unable to find anything on Harold Smith predating about 1976. It was like the guy came from another planet. But the radio man wouldn't tell them Smith's real name, so there was no way

Schell could go on the air with a scoop. Meanwhile, Schell had interviewed Wells Fargo Chairman Richard Cooley and had come away with a better understanding of how the money had been stolen by Ben Lewis and diverted to Harold Smith's accounts. Cooley had even showed him some of the actual branch settlement tickets filled out by Lewis. Even before finding out that Harold Smith was a possible alias, Schell believed the bank official's sober explanation and gave little weight to Smith's wild accusations. Now Schell was hoping that they could find out Smith's real name before he sat down with the elusive promoter. Schell dearly loved the thought of springing the on-camera surprise. In fact, that was the only reason he had come along on this trip. Though he knew that some of his colleagues from other stations were here to report the gospel according to Harold Smith, Schell had already had it in mind that whatever the boxing promoter was going to say would probably be of little value. So far, Smith's public statements to the media had defied verification, though they had usually made for colorful copy.

Wilson and Shaplen returned with King. She ordered all the reporters to climb aboard the bus. Just like Schell figured, she told an unhappy Wilson that ABC had to come along because they had rented the bus. But King did complain that ABC had too many people—in addition to Schell and the crew, there was KABC's sports reporter Ted Dawson, who had been brought along because King had insisted on local sports coverage. So Shaplen was told he couldn't go on the bus. That was all right with the producer because, with Schell and the crew along for the ride, ABC was well covered. Shaplen went off to have lunch.

The TV reporters and crews on the bus were leaving behind their TV microwave trucks and vans. These vehicles were equipped with transmitting devices which could feed the images on a videotape directly to their respective studios. All they had to do was remove the three-quarter-inch tape from the camera, slip it into the transmitter and beam it by microwave signal off a receiving dish on a nearby hill and down to the station, where it could be shown directly on the air or edited if time allowed. The reporters worried aloud about how and when they would be able to rendezvous with their vehicles. King promised them that she would call all of their newsrooms no later than

4 p.m. with word on where the vans could rendezvous with the reporters after the interview.

On the bus, King sternly told all the reporters to turn their beepers off. "We don't want your stations monitoring you," she said knowingly.

Schell had to smile. The beepers were transmitters, not receivers. Didn't she know that? This wasn't the first time that King had failed to impress him with her intellect. A couple of weeks ago, he had attended a press conference at her office after she promised "major new developments" in the case. When he got there, it had been nothing more than a staged event, with King exhorting the press to "do your own investigations … you'll see that what Harold says is the truth." Schell's first inkling that that was not going to be a legitimate press conference came when he entered the fancy law office digs and saw that the affair was catered—triangular-shaped finger sandwiches, for Christ's sake. People didn't feed the press like that unless they wanted something. When Schell asked King a tough question—as a result of information he had gotten in his Wells Fargo briefing—King angered visibly and accused him of being a "racist." Disgusted, he had grabbed Shaplen and the crew and departed.

Schell sat back for the ride, trying to figure out exactly where they were going. It wasn't easy. The driver was following a confusing route dictated by King, apparently in an attempt to shake any potential tail. Finally they got onto the San Diego Freeway north and went through the Sepulveda Pass. They headed west on the Ventura Freeway. Past Woodland Hills—into Ventura County—they pulled into a parking lot of the Vagabond Motor Inn and stopped next to a motor home. There was a momentary hesitation, then both vehicles pulled away. Soon they were back on the highway, heading back toward Los Angeles. Eventually they pulled into a roadside Holiday Inn and ended up in a far corner of the parking lot. At King's directions, the newsmen got out of the bus and climbed into the motor home, where Schell got his first look at Harold Smith. A big man, he was sitting slumped over, wearing a cowboy hat. A small boy was next to him.

King suggested that the interviewing get started, but the TV people vetoed the idea. It was too dark and too cramped to do any shooting. The reporters huddled and decided to rent a room in the hotel. Jim Hill went off to pay for a room, where soon they all converged. While the others waited on the opposite side of the room, the reporters and their crews took turns with Smith. Schell declined to interview Smith. The ABC correspondent had heard enough already. If he couldn't drop the bombshell, then he wouldn't take part in a charade. He pushed Dawson—who did not know about the tip on Smith's phony identity—out to ask a few questions for the benefit of the ABC crew.

"Did you steal twenty-one million dollars from Wells Fargo Bank?" Dawson asked.

"I couldn't have stole twenty-one million dollars from them, I don't even work in their bank," Smith said, with his son sitting on his lap and a smiling Jennifer King sitting next to him. "I don't understand. How can I be an embezzler when I don't even work in the bank?"

"Do you know that someone stole the money?"

"From what I have learned since all this happened, sure, somebody stole money from Wells Fargo Bank. But it wasn't just Ben Lewis."

Smith made more than one reference to a fear that his life might be in danger as a result of the growing bank scandal.

"What makes you think your life might be in danger?" Dawson asked.

"Well, we were shot after. We had to run through the rain, through the woods, through the snow—"

"Where was this?"

"Up in Sacramento. My son was scared, hollering 'Dad, I'm scared.' Even now when he sees people dressed in suits, he call them 'bad people.'" Smith furrowed his brow. "Even now."

The interviews concluded, the reporters boarded the bus and drove toward Los Angeles. Soon they stopped in a muddy parking lot where the microwave vans were already waiting. In a hurry to get his tape on the air, Warren Wilson stumbled and almost fell flat on his face. As far as some of his press colleagues were concerned, Wilson was falling on his face journalistically too. Wilson had swallowed Smith's version hook, line and sinker. Wilson was avidly portraying Harold Smith as a black man who was being victimized by the racist Establishment. From what Schell had seen, the truth was the exact opposite. He didn't like to see this happening because he had known Wilson for a long time and had always liked him.

Schell was tempted now to tell Wilson "Smith isn't even who you think he is, Warren," but of course he couldn't. He had to save that important information.

That night the Western edition of ABC News carried a story about the day's activities. "This is Tom Schell in Los Angeles. Harold Smith, the boxing promoter accused of cheating the Wells Fargo Bank out of twenty-one million dollars, temporarily interrupted weeks of hiding today to deny the charges. Smith, who heads Muhammad Ali Professional Sports, had reporters take a long ride on a bus to a secret location where he told his side of the story ... Smith explained why he had been in hiding."

A clip of Smith showed him sitting with his son. "I'm here to stay. I mean, I'm gonna hide, but I'm not hiding in the sense of hiding. I'm hiding for my son's life, for my life."

Schell continued, "Other boxing promoters have raised questions about extravagant purses Smith paid his boxers. Smith admits that his Muhammad Ali Professional Sports lost six million dollars."

"Yeah," Smith said, "I was paying fighters more than I was bringing in. But my plan was a long-range plan, which was to take place this year. I predicted we would do over eighty million dollars this year. So, if I'm going to make eighty million, then it should be no problem for me to pay back twelve, twenty or twenty-five million."

Schell: "In what may well be just wishful thinking, Harold Smith said he hopes the entire matter is cleared up in a couple of weeks."

"All I want to do," Smith said, "is to be able to continue my business and pay back whatever I may owe to Wells Fargo Bank."

Schell: "Smith said his attorney, Jennifer King, tried to set up a meeting with Wells Fargo Board Chairman Richard Cooley, but bank attorneys turned it down."

For Schell, the aired story was frustrating. There was so much more to tell and, yet, they had only begun to scratch the surface. He wondered when the full story could be told.

CHAPTER THIRTY-ONE

An FBI agent who took part in one too many toasts at a retirement party bragged to a friend that Ben Lewis was cooperating with the government. Unfortunately, that friend happened to be a correspondent for *Time*. In the magazine's next article on the Wells Fargo case—toward the end of March—there was an explosive line, buried partway down a column of text, which told of Lewis's defection to the government.

Allison and the agents held their collective breath. Their ongoing worry was that Smith would figure out that Ben Lewis was talking. Eventually it was bound to happen. But they had hoped to get further down the road with their investigation before it did. In fact, they hoped it could be after Smith's arrest. With the *Time* story, they thought the cat surely was out of the bag. But incredibly none of the local press picked up on it. Neither, apparently, did Smith or his lawyers.

Toward the end of March the pressure was increasing on Allison to authorize the arrest of Harold Smith. This time, Dale Taulbee came up with an intriguing idea. Allison found himself giving the proposal serious consideration.

"Fields got a passport in the name of Harold Smith," Taulbee explained. The agent had continued his work on the case and put together quite a file on Ross Fields/Harold Smith. "Let's pop him for making false statements in a passport application."

Ideally, Allison would have preferred not to touch Smith until after the grand jury had issued an indictment in the Wells Fargo case, but Taulbee's suggestion seemed like a prudent compromise. In all likelihood, the grand jury hearings would last for many weeks. An indictment might not be handed down until summer. Leaving Smith unfettered that long was unconscionable, especially with the possibility that he might use a secret cash hoard to flee the country at any time. Arresting Smith would go a long way toward preventing that. And Allison could keep control of the situation by prosecuting the passport violation himself.

"This guy is going around bragging that we haven't arrested him," Taulbee said, his frustration evident in his voice. "He's affecting the investigation. He's getting to people, telling them to get out of town and not talk to us. I think we should go out and get him and urge the magistrate to set a high bail. Maybe Smith will pick up some [jail] time on the charge. That will give us the time we need to put the embezzlement case together."

Though Smith undoubtedly would eventually make bail on the passport rap, the government could ask for a high bail and hope for the best. Allison doubted Smith would leave the country in the face of such a relatively minor offense. Going with the passport charge could even work as an effective feint; Smith might hope this was all the government had on him. They could go to trial quickly, probably in a month or two. The verdict would almost certainly be guilty, as there appeared to be no defense. If Smith ended up getting time, it would all but guarantee his presence at the embezzlement trial. In the meanwhile, Woodall and Jones could keep sorting out the financial records while Allison kept the grand jury on course. It wasn't a bad idea.

"Okay," Allison finally said. "Draft up a complaint as soon as you can and I'll review it. Then if you can find him, you can arrest him."

Those were the words Taulbee had been waiting a long time to hear. "We'll find him," the agent promised.

***

Ironically, Wells Fargo Bank attorney George Link played an important role in the effort to arrest Harold Smith. Quite innocently, Link had called Allison to get an update on the case and mentioned that they were taking Smith's deposition that coming Saturday in the bank's civil suit.

Link explained to Allison that Jennifer King had initially refused to produce her client for a deposition, but when the bank moved for a judgment in its favor due to Smith's failure to appear, she changed her mind and agreed to make him available to the Wells Fargo lawyers. She insisted, though, that the meeting take place on her terms.

"They're going to pick me up on a street corner downtown and drive me to some location where Smith will be," Link said, chuckling at the cloak-and-dagger tactics of Smith's defense team.

"Listen, we're now in a position to arrest Smith," Allison said. "Would you be agreeable to helping us out?"

The bank attorney was happy to oblige.

"Please call the FBI right away," Allison said.

***

Dale Taulbee lowered the binoculars. "I see a black guy with a beard," he said over the shortwave radio. "I think he's wearing a cowboy hat. It could be our man." He signed off, reminding the two dozen agents in the area to hold their positions until they received word from him.

It was Saturday, April 4, 1981. They were in Elysian Park, near Dodger Stadium and not far from the Los Angeles Police Academy. This was where George Link had been taken after being picked up by Bob Michaels in a canary yellow Cadillac. It hadn't taken Taulbee long to realize that Michaels was nervous, as the lawyer tried to "clean" himself of any possible tails by driving his big car into alleys, hanging sudden U-turns and pulling over to the curb. That might have been the way it was done in movies. But in real life, agents in cars back off and stay out of the way, allowing the FBI plane overhead to keep contact. Just as Taulbee and his crew had done.

The Cadillac had pulled up next to a camper in an empty parking lot. Only after the two attorneys had disappeared through a rear door in the van did the agents take up their positions. Some of them, like Taulbee, who was in charge of the operation, remained in cars nearby but out of sight. Other agents—and this *was* like the movies—were dressed as joggers, lovers and winos and faded into the surroundings.

Taulbee had arranged matters carefully with the bank attorney. The agents would not arrest Smith until after Link was finished with his deposition. To do so, they needed to receive a signal from Link when he was through with his questioning. Taulbee gave him what looked like an ordinary pen. Actually it housed a tiny radio transmitter. When the top was taken off, a signal was sent out which was picked up by an FBI radio receiver as a beeping sound. Link was only to make the signal if Smith was at the meeting. The last thing the FBI men wanted to do was tip off Smith's people that they were after him with an arrest warrant. The agents wanted to close in only if their prey was inside the net. They waited for the signal.

An hour or so later, it came. The staccato beep-beep sent Taulbee into action. He picked up his car's dashboard mike and said, "We've got the signal. Let's move in and take him." Taulbee started the car and hit the accelerator, sending the four-door sedan leaping forward from its outpost on a nearby hill. Other agents, he knew, would be closing in and sealing off all possible escape routes. The idea now was to get down there and make the arrest as fast as possible. Taulbee wanted no trouble. He was worried about the rumor that a couple of the guys around Smith carried weapons. He hoped that wasn't true. He didn't want a gun battle, especially with the bank attorney in the middle of it.

Taulbee arrived at the motor home first, braking the car to a screeching halt near where two men stood outside. The agent recognized one of them as attorney Bob Michaels. The other, a black man, turned away from the advancing agent and dove into the cab of the van. It wasn't Harold, Taulbee could now see. It was Hilton Nicholson, an old friend of Smith's and employee of MAPS. What was he doing jumping into the vehicle? Was he going for a gun?

Taulbee drew his 357 magnum from under his suit coat and yelled, "FBI, freeze!" He grabbed Nicholson by one arm and yanked him out from behind the wheel as he was trying to start the engine. Taulbee handed him off to another agent and went around to the rear of the van. He opened the door and said sternly, "This is the FBI. Everyone freeze." There were a lot of people inside, but no furtive movement that Taulbee could detect. At that point Taulbee ordered them to come out one at a time "with your hands up." George Link, looking decidedly uncomfortable, was one of the first out. Several other people came out, but no Harold Smith. Taulbee didn't want to think about the consequences of this little show if their man wasn't even here. Not with all these lawyers around. Had Link's transmitter gone off accidentally?

The last person out was a black man wearing chinos, a cotton shirt, prescription dark glasses and a sheepish grin.

"Hello, Harold," the agent said.

"Hello, Dale," Smith answered.

It was a strangely casual greeting for two men who had never met before. Each had obviously heard a lot about the other.

Taulbee had Smith place his hands against the van. He carefully patted him down for weapons. Smith was clean. Of course he would be—guns were not his modus operandi. Taulbee explained to Smith that he was under arrest and cuffed him. He was reading him his rights when a red-faced Bob Michaels came forward and flailed his arms at Taulbee.

"I'll kill you!" Michaels screamed.

Taulbee couldn't believe what he had just heard. A federal agent—*any* law enforcement official—took such a threat seriously. Taulbee handed Smith to another agent and went for Michaels. "What the hell are you saying?" Taulbee stuck his face directly into the lawyer's face, making no attempt to hide his anger. "Come on, let's see you do it now!" He pressed toward Michaels, who gave ground and began backing up. "Take your best shot, you sonova-bitch!" Michaels kept walking backward, ten feet, twenty feet, thirty. "Come on, go for it!" Only a cement wall stopped them, halfway across the parking lot. Taulbee pinned Michaels against the wall with his pure physical presence. Adrenaline was pumping through Taulbee's system; he got a rush every time he made an arrest. He was waiting for Michaels to make one threatening move—he *wanted* Michaels to try something.

With everyone in the lot watching them, Michaels turned beet red. "No," he said hoarsely. "No, that's not what I meant. I didn't mean I would kill you for real. I meant—" he coughed nervously—"I would kill you in—*court*."

"In that case," Taulbee said, "I don't have to take you in. Now get back over there and stop interfering with this arrest or I'll change my mind."

Taulbee had calmed down and was beginning to feel a sense of elation. They had their man. He went to a nearby pay phone and called Allison, who was waiting in his office, to give him the good news.

Several hours later, at the Los Angeles County Jail, the agents were booking Smith when the promoter noticed a North Carolina "hold" on him. That meant that even when he made bail on the federal charges he would have to deal with the East Coast state charges before he could get out. It was an added complication to his life, just what the government intended it to be.

"North Carolina?" Smith said worried. "What's this?"

FBI agent Joe Woodall looked up from the paperwork. "An old outstanding warrant for you, Harold."

"What name's that in?"

"Ross Fields," Woodall said matter-of-factly.

"Oh," Smith said softly, dropping his head.

Harold Smith knew for the first time that the government knew his real name. All in all, it was turning out to be a real bummer of a weekend for the promoter.

***

The arraignment was held Monday, April 6, before U.S. Magistrate Venetta S. Tassopulos. The arrest had been announced by an FBI press officer on Saturday, and the courtroom was packed with reporters. Also present, as Allison walked in with the agents, were a dozen or so people who were obviously Harold Smith supporters. Allison spotted Warren Wilson in the crowd. *Is he going to be surprised when he learns the truth about Smith,* Allison thought.

Smith came in with the other prisoners from the lockup downstairs, escorted by a federal marshal. "Hi, everybody," he said to the spectators.

Magistrate Tassopulos took the bench, and the clerk called the calendar. Smith's case was first.

Allison stood up. "Who is this man?" he asked rhetorically. "We have established without question that Ross Fields, also known as Harold Smith, is a long-time fugitive, a bad check and bunco artist who is currently wanted in at least three different jurisdictions. He has a record that goes back to 1967. Between 1967 and 1973 he had six arrests for fraud and false pretenses. In the 1970s he joined forces with his purported wife in bad check and bunco schemes. She is not Barbara Lee Smith, but Alice Vicki Darrow, wanted in Alabama for interstate transportation of fraudulent securities. In 1973 and 1974 they cashed over one hundred bad checks from Massachusetts to California. That was how they worked their way out here. Over the years Ross Fields used five different aliases, and Ms. Darrow used approximately twenty."

Allison had two purposes in detailing Smith's background so extensively. The first was to paint Smith as a professional con man with a history of flight, a bad bail risk. The second was to expose Smith as a charlatan to all the media representatives who had listened seriously to his stories so far, thereby putting an end once and for all to Smith's ability to manipulate the press. The last half of his presentation was addressed exclusively to the bail issue. Smith had no roots in the community, Allison argued, no family and no property. His lack of community ties was evident from his readiness to abandon Los Angeles when the Wells Fargo scandal broke. Furthermore, he had no visible means of support; his business had folded when the embezzlement was discovered. The probability of conviction on the passport charge was high, and there were several other charges waiting to be answered back East. Given his lifelong and recently demonstrated history of flight, Allison summarized, Smith presented an unusually poor bail risk. The prosecutor recommended that bail on the passport charge be set at $500,000, knowing he would never get it but hoping for a six-figure amount.

The defense team of Bob Michaels and Jennifer King had its say after a short recess. Allison suspected that his bombshell about Smith's true identity and extensive criminal past had caught them by surprise. Glossing over Smith's prior record and fugitive status, Michaels and King claimed that their client's most recent flight was caused by his fear that his life was in danger. They suggested that FBI agents had been harassing and chasing him. As Allison knew they would, they stressed the fairly minor nature of the present passport offense, pointing out that no charges had been filed against Smith on account of the Wells Fargo embezzlement and noting that it would be unfair to consider this in setting bail. Then they asked permission for Smith—or Fields—to address the court himself.

Speaking on his own behalf, Smith said he was glad that his years of running were now over, saying he was now a "free man." He pictured himself in his former identity as a good-hearted, struggling young black man, asserting that he came from a home so poor that he had learned "the difference between Alpo and bologna" the hard way. He claimed to have been responsible for a series of charitable acts during his life as Ross Fields, including discovering singer Roberta Flack and setting up a scholarship fund for disadvantaged youth in the name of Sammy Davis, Jr. "I'm a man of God," he proclaimed with evangelistic fervor. "I been to the mountaintop. I walked with Martin Luther King in Alabama. Ross Fields is a good man, you'd like him, your honor. I wrote a few checks, paid my dues, but I'm comin' back." He reiterated his claim of innocence in the Wells Fargo scandal, ostensibly weeping and throwing himself on the mercy of the court. "Your honor, I could have been long gone, especially if I had twenty million dollars," he said, sobbing.

Magistrate Tassopulos heard it all, then set bail at $200,000.

Allison was pleased with the amount. It was asking a lot to get bail that high on charges that carried a maximum sentence of five years and a $2,000 fine. Obviously, the magistrate had taken into account Smith's past record and his tendency to flee when things began to heat up.

Things got even hotter for Smith the next day when L.A. County Municipal Court Judge Patty Jo McKay set bail on the North Carolina State charges at $200,000. "This is a lot of money to raise," Michaels told a reporter. He admitted it was unlikely that his client could make the combined $400,000 bail anytime in the near future.

How ironic it must have seemed for Smith sitting behind bars. There was a time, not that long ago, when $400,000 was but a paltry sum. It easily fit into a briefcase. It was bonus money for a boxer and his manager. It was spent on airplanes, horses, drugs. It was always there when he needed it.

But Harold Smith no longer could pick up the phone and call Ben Lewis, his personal banker.

Those days were gone.

CHAPTER THIRTY-TWO

Since Teri Key had kept the MAPS checkbooks, she knew how most of the money had been spent. But where much of this money came from still remained a mystery to her. At the time, she had believed Harold's explanations. She had known all along that there were a lot of things Harold had bought—like the boat, the plane, the horses—which did not show up in the checkbooks. She just assumed that he had used money from his personal accounts or cash from gambling winnings. That was what he had led her to believe, and she had taken him at his word.

At one of their interview sessions, Joe Woodall put before her a list of cashier's checks issued by Ben Lewis. Poker-faced, he asked her to show him from the MAPS bank account records the checks that had been written to purchase the cashier's checks. Actually, Woodall knew that these cashier's checks had not been purchased at all but were offset by branch settlement tickets and were part of the free money Smith had received from Wells Fargo thanks to Lewis. There was no investigative reason for Key to be shown this list. There was nothing she could prove or disprove. The agent simply wanted Teri to start drawing her own conclusions about Smith.

She carefully reviewed the list. One cashier's check for $75,000 had gone for Smith's boat. Another was in the amount of $100,000. Still another was for $200,000 and had gone for his private jet. She looked over the entire list. It totaled one million dollars. She looked up at Woodall and sadly shook her head.

"I never wrote checks for any of these," she said.

"You didn't?" Woodall pretended to be surprised.

"No. I thought he paid cash for these things. Maybe he paid for them out of a personal account?"

"Actually, these cashier's checks were offset by phony entries in the bank's computer."

"Phony? You mean, he just *got* them—without paying for them?"

Woodall nodded his head, showing no joy in the confirmation. It was as if his own best friend had been caught embezzling.

At that moment Teri was on the verge of crying. The accumulation of incriminating details had finally had its desired effect. Additionally, Harold had stopped calling her regularly and reassuring her that everything would work out all right. When he was doing that during the early days she had still felt a part of the MAPS team. She had still felt needed by Harold. Now she was beginning to feel shipwrecked. She had sensed that Harold was beginning to turn his people against her—people with whom she had worked at the office in the old days. People like Bobby Campbell, the head of the amateur program, and even Liz Walczer, with whom she had shared so many confidences. Teri could tell in the lukewarm greetings she got and the phone calls she didn't get. That only made her feel more isolated. Harold's arrest and exposure as Ross Fields had also come as a shock—and a major blow to her belief in him.

The list of cashier's checks was the end. These large dollar amounts staring up at her in black and white convinced her, once and for all, that Harold had fooled them all. He had lied to her. He had manipulated Ben into giving him the money. He had used them all. He was a thief, and he had made Ben a thief too. They had all been tainted by association. She felt ill and turned pale. The session was over for that day. She went home and broke down for the first time since the troubles at MAPS had begun.

It wasn't too many days later when Woodall made his next move. He noticed Teri had seemed to have found a new resolve. At Dean Allison's suggestion, he showed her a deposition given by Bob Michaels in the civil suit by Wells Fargo. Like the list of checks, it too was designed to have an impact.

Teri took the transcript from the agent. She lit a cigarette and began reading.

Because she felt a growing trust in Woodall, Teri had filled him in completely on her discussions with Jennifer King. Woodall had said it was unethical and illegal for King to be advising her to lie to a grand jury.

Woodall had suggested several times that she wear a body recorder to her next meeting with King in order to document King's prior improper suggestions, but Teri had resisted. It was a long step from no longer believing in Harold's innocence to helping get one of his attorneys indicted. "I'll tell you what I know," she had said, "but I won't be a snitch."

Woodall explained it would be Teri's word against King's, and, since King was a lawyer, that would not be enough without a tape to back Teri up. But Teri remained firm, and Woodall knew better than to push her too hard.

Now, as she worked her way through the transcript, Teri felt her anger rising. Michaels had sworn under oath that she, Teri, knew all about the "line of credit" at the bank. That was untrue, and both Michaels and King knew it. Before the last week of January, 1981, Teri had never heard of any line of credit. Even then, she had only heard it from Harold, as he tried to explain the problems with the bank. These people were obviously going to start ganging up on her—pointing the finger at her. They were making it clear that if she didn't join the "line of credit" defense, she would look like the liar when she was actually the one telling the truth.

"I can't believe they're doing this," she said. "Harold must know."

"See what kind of people we're dealing with here?" Woodall asked.

By the time she had finished the transcript, she had undergone a complete change of heart. She would wear the body recorder, she told Woodall. Harold Smith was a cheat and a liar, and his lawyers were obviously not much better. She was fighting for her own reputation. It was her against them.

The turning of Teri Key was now complete.

* * *

Teri felt a mixture of fright and excitement as she entered Jennifer King's office. Wearing a blouse and skirt a size too big to allow for the recording equipment, she felt like a character out of a James Bond movie. She had been briefed by the FBI on technical things, like not suddenly changing positions, crossing her legs or rustling her blouse because it would cause static on the tape. She had also been briefed on legal concerns, especially the danger of entrapment. She was also told to try to avoid the topic of Smith's legal defense. The government didn't want to be accused of prying into a defendant's protected conversations with his lawyer. Jennifer King had to be allowed to hang herself. All Teri could do was give her the rope.

A part of Teri hoped that King would *not* repeat her prior suggestion to lie to the authorities. Teri really didn't like to prove anyone a liar. She didn't like hurting anyone, even though people apparently were willing to hurt her. Throughout her life she had always attempted to avoid such confrontations.

They sat in King's office, the attractive lawyer behind her glass-topped desk and Teri sitting in a chair opposite her. Teri almost crossed her legs but stopped herself.

"You look tired," Teri said.

"On my God, I've been working around-the-clock and on the weekends."

Teri could well imagine that, as Harold had been arrested just days earlier. King and Bob Michaels had been working frantically since then to bail him out of jail.

The week before, Teri had called Jennifer and told her of the subpoena she had received from the grand jury. As Teri and Joe Woodall had expected, King suggested they get together *to* "discuss" Teri's upcoming appearance. They guessed that King would want a coaching session designed to get Teri's story straight as far as King and her client were concerned.

"I don't think I'm going to take my lawyer, Rick Rosenfield, with me on this thing," Teri said now, referring to the grand jury appearance.

"You mentioned that." Most lawyers, knowing that someone like Teri had her own counsel, would at least have called the other lawyer to confirm that it was all right to meet with that lawyer's client. Many would not meet the client without getting advance permission from the other attorney. King had done neither.

"Are they going to ask me about that passport thing?"

"No, I doubt it," King said. "I think they're going to try to get *me* on perjury on Ta——up in Tahoe about those records."

Teri knew from the agents that King had herself been before the grand jury, but she had no idea what King had testified about. The fact that King brought up her own concern about a perjury rap showed that she was not worried so much about Smith's overall defensive posture as she was whether Teri would back up her own testimony.

"Why?" Teri asked innocently. Let Jennifer do the explaining.

"That's a new trend. Get the attorneys. You don't know these grand juries, you don't know the U.S. Attorney, you don't know the FBI, they'll go to any length … Did you say anything about documents when you were in there with the FBI?"

"Just what they have from the bank and the ones we turned over initially," Teri said. She certainly had been asked about the records that never showed up and had told them she saw them in Tahoe, but she wasn't going to volunteer this information until King asked her.

"Okay, could you testify that … you kept the records and … you were a damn good little bookkeeper … and nothing seemed awry and after it all came down in January the records were gone, period." The suggestion was made as if it were to be accepted automatically.

But Teri wouldn't play. She realized that King was getting awfully close to telling her to lie. Teri kept thinking about the tape that was running.

"You mean that they just disappeared?" Teri said.

"Urn, hum."

"I'm the one who took 'em out of the office."

"Oh, you were the one … Oh shit." King seemed to be measuring her.

"What do you think they're gonna ask me, and what do I do?"

"Okay, all right, I think they're going to ask you 'When was the last time you saw the documents?' See, if you say you gave 'em to Harold, then Harold is gonna be slapped with a subpoena in two minutes."

"And if they say 'When is the last time you saw the documents?' … I have to say 'Lake Tahoe,' " Teri said.

"Did you really see them?" King asked. "*I* didn't …"

Of course King had seen the ledgers in Tahoe. She had asked Teri to sit down and go over them with her. King had said she was trying to find out where the notes payable had been put in the ledgers.

"We went through the Harold J. Smith Productions book and the ledgers," Teri said.

King looked worried for the first time. *"I* didn't see that ledger," she said firmly. "And you gotta cover me on that babe. They're gonna fuck me out of my bar card if you—"

"How are we gonna do that if you say you didn't see the ledgers and we went over 'em? I mean, how am I gonna get out of that?"

"Just lie," King said, coolly.

There it was, with no subtleties of emphasis or tone about it. Teri was careful not to move a muscle. She wanted all this to be perfectly audible on the tape.

"So, I've got to just come right out and lie about it?" Teri asked. "Jennifer, how can I? Oh God, I wish there was a way of getting around that."

"This is what you call loyalty," King said.

"So it comes down that I'm the one who has to lie about the whole thing, right?"

"Let me tell you something," King said. "You took the records when all that shit was hitting the fan. You were an aider and abettor." Now King was trying to scare her, to make Teri think she had to lie to save her own skin too.

"But I didn't know at the time. Harold just said to take them because he felt that people connected with Ali were gonna break in and try to take the records ... I'd rather not do [this], I'd rather not have to go to the grand jury."

"I don't blame you ... You just want to tell the truth all the way down the line?" King sounded almost incredulous that someone would be this honest.

"That's the way I feel, yeah."

King looked disappointed. "I'll tell you right now the bank's lying. Everybody lies. I hate to tell you about life and about the court system. It's really sad."

"It is?"

"The first six months I practiced I got ulcers when I saw what was coming down. And unfortunately I found out if you're honest, you lose. It's really sad. That's life. And that's what the judge is there for, to find out who is lying the least."

"Really?" Teri said, genuinely appalled. "I wish I was back in North Carolina."

"With a black husband you wish you were back in North Carolina?"

"Yeah. At least I wouldn't have to play the games that go on out here."

"That's the legal system for you. It stinks."

"See, Jennifer, I had a very religious, moral upbringing. My daddy would rather have me steal than tell a lie."

"That's the way I was brought up," King said. "That's why I got ulcers ... They'll say 'Did you see any other documents?'"

"You want me to say no?" Teri asked. Both women knew that the only truthful answer was yes.

"Just say 'Not that I can recall.' Then you're safe. That's not really a lie, you forgot. 'Cause you can always go back and remedy it."

"Okay."

"Okay, so you removed the books and then you gave them to Harold that weekend. I guess we'll have to live with that. That's where you feel comfortable."

Teri nodded. "But, you know, I took the majority of 'em back. That's what was turned over to the FBI."

"You could forget the rest. Say 'I don't recall, I presume I took 'em [all] back to the office.' Would you be uncomfortable with that? See, Harold could say he went and took the rest of 'em ... But [on] Tahoe I would just as soon you didn't see anything. You didn't see any records. Can you live with that? You're going to fuck me up royally. See, I go on the line for people, especially when I know it's harmless, you know. It's not like [he] killed somebody. We're covering up for somebody."

"Let me go home and think about it."

"All right ... Don't talk about this meeting."

For good reason, Jennifer King wanted the contents of the meeting kept confidential. Since she was not Teri's lawyer, there could be no claim of attorney-client privilege. Moreover, conversations in furtherance of a crime—like obstruction of justice—are not privileged under any circumstances. But at that moment FBI agents in a car down on Avenue of the Stars already had a complete tape of the conversation. In addition they had been monitoring the meeting live over the body mike worn by Teri.

They did that whenever someone went into such a situation, just in case the recording equipment was discovered and the situation got dangerous. They didn't have to worry about that now, though.

Jennifer King was the one who had to worry.

***

Less than twenty-four hours after Teri Key left Jennifer King's office, a four-count indictment was handed down by the federal grand jury charging King with perjury and obstruction of justice in impeding the FBI's investigation of the Wells Fargo embezzlement. After playing the tape for the grand jurors, Allison left the room. They had been appalled, as he had, at the dishonest and unscrupulous attitude and utter contempt for the legal system that they heard reflected in King's voice on the tape. The deliberations lasted no more than five minutes, just long enough for the foreperson to fill out the ballot. The indictment was quite specific, accusing King of lying herself to the grand jury about the documents she had seen in Lake Tahoe and of telling Teri Key to "testify falsely" about documents King had examined and the MAPS records that were still missing.

When the news media reported the indictment the next day, Jennifer King for once had no comment.

CHAPTER THIRTY-THREE

Harold Smith was freed April 15, 1981, on $355,000 bail.

A few weeks later he was found guilty of making false statements in a passport application following a one-hour trial before U.S. District Judge Manuel Real. It was what lawyers call a "stipulated facts" case, meaning that the defense did not contest the evidence presented by the prosecution but went to trial merely in order to preserve certain pretrial issues for appeal. Bob Michaels's defense strategy had been to petition the Ninth Circuit U.S. Court of Appeals in an effort to block the trial on procedural grounds. After an emergency argument late the previous afternoon, the appellate court had denied his request. When Smith walked into the courtroom, he might as well have been waving a white flag.

Dean Allison handled the case for the government, but it certainly couldn't be considered a dress rehearsal for the courtroom show yet to unfold, as the charge was a relatively minor one and the verdict was predictable. Smith would certainly not roll over so easily on multiple embezzlement, interstate transportation of stolen property and conspiracy charges.

The incriminating facts in the passport case were clear and in-defensible: the defendant had falsely identified himself on his passport application as Harold J. Smith, born April 21, 1943, in Charlotte, North Carolina, to parents named Edward Smith and Nancy Taylor, when in fact his true name was Ross Eugene Fields and he had been born in Birmingham, Alabama, on the same date to Edward Fields and Nancy Taylor.

As expected, Judge Real made a quick ruling from the bench and scheduled a sentencing date. In randomly drawing his name from the wheel that contained the names of all the federal judges in the courthouse who were available for new assignments, the government had been fortunate. Formerly the United States Attorney for the Central District of California, Judge Real was a tough, no-nonsense jurist who would brook no shenanigans from anyone in his courtroom.

When Allison walked into the court for the sentencing hearing on the passport charge, he had a pretty good idea what was coming. A few days earlier he had listened to a radio tape of a phone call Smith had made to a sports commentator. Trying to explain away his passport offense, Smith related how before the "Down Under" tour the Australian amateur boxers had come to the U.S. to fight his amateur team and the small son of the Australian coach had asked him to bring Ali to visit Australia someday. "So I only got the temporary passport in order to keep my promise to a child," Smith said on the radio show, as if it were a perfectly rational excuse for his federal offense. In fact, it was pure malarkey. Even if the promise had been made, there was no reason why Smith had to falsify his identity on the passport application in order to keep his word—except, of course, to conceal his true identity as the fugitive bad check artist, Ross Fields. Nonetheless, Allison fully expected Smith to try the same story again on Judge Real at sentencing.

Actually it worked out somewhat differently. Speaking on Smith's behalf, Jennifer King was the one who told the judge a version of the promise-to-a-child story. Then Smith began his own show, flattering the judge for being a "man of compassion ... a man of God" and proclaiming himself a "man of God too." Smith repeated his now familiar story of having come from a family that knew "the difference between Alpo and bologna," then threw himself on the mercy of the court.

Groaning inwardly, Allison sat silent, not by choice but because Judge Real had a firm rule that the government was not permitted to speak at sentencing time. In Judge Real's view, sentencing was the court's prerogative alone.

Judge Real gave Smith a three-year prison sentence and five years' probation and ordered him to serve fifteen hundred hours of community service as a condition of probation. Then, the judge suspended all but eighty days of the prison sentence and ordered Smith to serve it on forty consecutive weekends beginning the following week. After the proceedings, Smith walked outside and told reporters the sentence was "very fair" and that he had "no problems" with serving it. He seemed to think that his impassioned pitch had worked and he had gotten off easy.

Allison was not disappointed. It seemed to him that the judge had guaranteed Smith's stay in town for some time. If he had given Smith a stiffer sentence, the defense undoubtedly would have appealed, and Smith probably would have been back on the streets on bail awaiting the outcome. This way, he had to turn himself in every weekend. The first weekend he didn't show, a warrant would be issued for him. Once caught, he probably would be packed off to serve the full sentence. Smith was tethered to what could only be called a short leash.

Forty weekends was plenty of time for what Allison had in mind.

***

Under Justice Department internal guidelines, issuing a grand jury subpoena to a target in a major investigation is done only under extraordinary circumstances. Allison consulted with U.S. Attorney Andrea Ordin about the grand jury's genuine interest in hearing Harold Smith's side of the story and the desirability of questioning Smith concerning the whereabouts of the ledgers and other missing documents. It was agreed that an exception could be made in Smith's case.

Though defense attorneys like to criticize federal grand juries for being tools of the prosecution, Allison disagreed. He had long ago discovered that when lay people were put together as jurors there was a wide spectrum of backgrounds, personalities and opinions. Although it was his job to forcefully present to the grand jury the evidence indicating a suspect's guilt, he knew the grand jurors could be valuable independent colleagues in conducting a thorough investigation of a suspected crime. The subpoena power of the grand jury was a powerful lever in assisting white-collar crime investigations. Moreover, an experienced prosecutor considered his presentation to the grand jury as an important first test in any case. If he couldn't convince the jurors of guilt in this setting, there was no way the case would survive at trial, where guilt is determined by the *reasonable doubt* standard instead of the lower *probable cause* test used at the grand jury stage.

After the subpoena was served on Smith, Bob Michaels called Allison to tell him that Smith would refuse to testify but would obey the subpoena and appear and produce the records in his possession. Taking the Fifth Amendment was of course any witness's prerogative.

Although he thought it a strong possibility, Allison was sorry to hear that Smith apparently had no plans to talk. From what he had heard and seen of Smith, he figured that the decision to clam up had been urged upon him by his lawyers. Given half a chance, Smith would talk a blue streak. Federal law did not allow Smith to bring his attorney into the grand jury room with him because of the secret nature of the proceedings. The only attorney present is an Assistant U.S. Attorney—in this case Allison—serving in the role of legal advisor to the grand jury. The closest a witness's attorney can get to a client's testimony is in the hallway. If the witness says he would like to consult with his attorney, he is allowed to step out of the room and converse. But then the witness must go back in and face the grand jury alone.

The morning of Smith's appearance, Allison was standing outside the grand jury room with Doreen Taylor, the foreperson of the grand jury that was looking into the Wells Fargo case. They were waiting for Smith, his lawyer and some of the grand jurors to show up so the proceedings could get started. Taylor was a trim, pleasant woman with brown hair and a quick smile who worked as an executive secretary for a large corporation. Enjoying her responsible role in the grand jury, she was excited at the prospect of seeing Harold Smith in person.

"It will be interesting to see what he has to say for himself," she said.

"I don't know that you are going to hear much from him today," Allison replied. "I hear he's going to take the Fifth."

"Oh, that's too bad."

"You know, I'm sure he has no great love for me by now. I mean, even if he were otherwise inclined, I doubt he'd want to talk to me. You're certainly free to try your luck with him if you want. After all, it's your grand jury."

"I'd like that," Taylor said. "What were you going to ask him?" She was obviously keen on the idea and had begun searching for a pen and paper in her purse.

"The same stuff we've been interested in all along," Allison said. "How his business worked, whether it made or lost money and how much, where the money came from and the facts about the line of credit he claims he had."

"Do you mind if I ask him questions about those things?" she asked.

"Not at all. Just let me give him the usual admonitions and advise him of his constitutional rights to begin with, and you can start it off, if you want."

"Okay."

The more he thought about Doreen Taylor asking Smith some questions, the better Allison liked it. Like most con men, Smith probably would think he could snow the grand jurors. Allison also suspected Smith would be somewhat disarmed by a woman doing the questioning. And this procedure would give Smith and his lawyers that much less room to claim that there had been prosecutorial misconduct before the grand jury, a standard argument that the defense raised nowadays in almost every complex case as an excuse to get its hands on the grand jury transcripts, which would otherwise be kept secret. The chief disadvantage, of course, was that Taylor's questions were unlikely to be as well focused as his own, since she had no legal training. But then again, *any* testimony by Smith was better than none, which is what they would probably get if he handled the questioning by himself.

Harold Smith stepped into the grand jury room at 2:10 p.m. on May 13, 1981. He took his cowboy hat off when he came in. He had brought along a cardboard box containing some thirty documents. Most of them were files pertaining to specific fighters; he also had files on his horse racing business and two that were marked "Yacht File" and "Airplane File." Allison made a mental note that the latter had been among the files Teri Key had removed from the MAPS offices back in January and had sent off to Smith in hiding.

After Smith was sworn in, Allison asked in a friendly manner, "What would you like me to call you when I am asking you questions?"

"Call me Harold. My mother said it was all right as long as I put the Ross Fields on it." The man with two names was now billing himself as Harold Rossfields Smith.

Allison was going to bend over backward to be nice to Smith for one reason: to get him talking. Just a few weeks earlier, Allison had stood in front of a federal magistrate and described Smith as a longtime criminal. Now he was asking for Smith's cooperation.

"Harold, before you answer any questions in here, I want to make sure that you understand the nature of these proceedings and your constitutional rights in connection with these proceedings." Allison went on to explain the charges being investigated by the grand jury. At that point, before he had even started on the constitutional rights, he was interrupted by Doreen Taylor, who was clearly anxious to get the show on the road.

"Could I say something?" she asked.

"Sure," Allison said. *Doreen, not yet.*

"The grand jury—" she began, then halted, obviously deciding on a different tack. "Hi," she said, smiling sweetly at Smith.

"Hi," he replied.

"We'd like to know a little bit more about you, if you don't mind," Taylor said. "I know you've been asked to bring some records here, but before you begin, we'd like to know for ourselves a little more about your company and yourself."

Allison thought Taylor had started on the right note, only it had come too early. He could not allow questioning of the witness yet. He had to protect the record.

"I have to finish giving him his rights," Allison said, "but I understand that you want to talk when I'm done." A few minutes later he was finished, and he said, "Now, Ms. Taylor, I understand that you wanted to speak."

"May I say something before she starts, please?" Smith asked.

"Sure."

"Have you made the nice people here aware of the fact that you have spoken to my attorney and that he has given me a statement to make? This will be [my answer] to all questions."

Nice try, Allison. "I have advised the grand jury that Mr. Michaels has advised me you were going to invoke your constitutional rights under the Fifth Amendment at least with respect to matters other than questions about the documents," Allison said, "and maybe as to those questions as well. But you can tell the grand jury anything you want to tell them." He threw the last line in just to reinforce that in this room a witness had to make his own decisions.

"Well," Smith said, looking down at the small piece of paper he had removed from a pocket, "what he advised me to do is to read this statement on every question that you ask me except my name, and I think you know the reason why that is."

"What you might want to do—" Allison had to be careful here. He didn't want to be accused of giving Smith legal advice. "Keep in mind the only person who can give you legal advice is Bob Michaels. I cannot and neither can the grand jury. Keep in mind that the Fifth Amendment privilege is only properly invoked if you really believe that your answer would tend to incriminate you. All right?" Subtly, he was challenging Smith—if you're as innocent as you claim, fella, what do you have to hide? "Now, you might, if you want to, talk to Mr. Michaels about this at any point including now. Go ahead. But I know that the grand jury has some questions."

Smith sat back and looked at Doreen Taylor. He smiled. "She just wants to know a little bit about me. I'll answer her question and then talk to him."

"Fine," Allison said.

"Can you describe MAPS and"—Taylor looked questioningly at Smith—"is it MAAS?"

"It's Muhammad Ali Amateur Sports," Smith said patiently. "That's MAAS."

"Okay."

"Do you want me to define it, what it meant?"

"Yes?"

"In order to answer that question, first I want to give you a little history of how the idea came about." Already, on his own and responding to Taylor's gentle prodding, Smith was off and running.

"I came from a very poor home myself. I came from a family that knows the difference between Alpo and bologna. That's because I've seen and tasted dog food and tasted bologna as well as filet mignon. I come from a home that when it rained, my mother used to put buckets in different parts of the room to catch the water. I climbed the fence every morning except Sunday—because I went to church every Sunday—to run. I trained very hard. In fact, I trained so hard that people in my town called me crazy, but I had a goal: to get out of Alabama. To answer your question, I was reading an article one day here in Los Angeles about a kid by the name of Houston McTear, and [he] came from a similar situation ... To make a long story short, my wife and I agreed not to turn our backs on this kid ... Ali was returning from Tokyo ... and I went over to see him ... There was a story out about Houston and his family, showed pictures of the home he was living in. Ali [looked] through the magazine ... And he said, 'They live in a house like this, and he's the fastest man alive and has the chance of winning three gold medals? This is just a shame.' He gave me a check for thirty-five thousand dollars. He said, 'I want you to go down there and get him out of that shack. Get him some clothes and some furniture.' I did. We put him in a four-bedroom brick house."

Smith was barely pausing for breath. He talked about putting on the First Muhammad Ali Invitational Track Meet and then beginning MAAS to help "talented kids [who] didn't have the finance[s] to get an education or have a place to live or a place to train for the purpose of winning gold medals for this country." Then, he talked about going into amateur boxing and finally into the professional arena. He proudly listed some of the fighters he had been associated with and outlined a few big deals he had negotiated.

Allison casually took over, keeping Smith on track as best he could, leading him through the business and banking arrangements of MAPS and MAAS, questioning and probing deeper for more details all the time. It was at this point that Smith told the grand jury a fantastic story about how Gene Kawakami offered him a line of credit at the bank for "whatever I needed," just for the privilege of being introduced to Muhammad Ali, so that Kawakami could pitch the Champ on an "oil deal" involving a rich Texan, Kyle McAllister. While the oil deal admittedly never went through, Smith said, he started receiving money from the bank by "just writing a check for it" whenever he needed money.

The line of credit was for $12 million, said Smith. "[But] you got to understand now what I'm saying," he said. "Twelve million was my figure. It could have been twenty million or thirty million." In other words, Kawakami was giving Smith carte blanche at Wells Fargo.

"So you had a line of credit with the bank?" Allison asked.

"That's just what we always felt."

"Did you sign a note like you had for the [other] loans?" Allison had earlier asked Smith about the prior unsecured personal loans he had obtained from Kawakami.

"No. [Kawakami] told me—he came in, and I signed some papers, blank papers … He said, 'This is to make sure you have all the money you need in your accounts.' I sign[ed] all the papers."

This oil deal business was news to Allison. He made a note to alert the agents to interview this McAllister fellow and also to discuss the subject with Kawakami. If this was going to be presented as Smith's defense, he needed to have it fully checked out.

"Did you ever get a copy back of any of the papers you signed?" Allison asked.

"No, I didn't. I trusted him."

"Did you ever make any payments to the bank to pay back for your draws on your line of credit?" Allison asked.

"All the money that we got had to come in. We turned it over to the bank. We deposited it into the account."

"Depositing to your account is not the same as paying it to the bank, though. Were any checks, for instance, paid to Wells Fargo in repayment of the line of credit?"

"No. Because I wasn't suppose to do it until '81. Gene asked me how long it would take, and I said, 'By '81 I should have it done.' "

"Is there anybody else from the bank besides Gene that you discussed the line of credit with?"

"Oh, Ben knew about it."

"How did he know?"

"Brian Feeley knew about it. Because he had to."

"You are just assuming?"

"That's who Gene sent me to. The same thing we did at the Miracle Mile branch, we did at the Beverly Drive branch. It was Kawakami's idea to move accounts."

"What do you mean, the same thing that was done at the Miracle Mile branch?"

"Well, if I was overdrawn or whatever, it was covered. I'm thinking it's from my line of credit. You see, let me say this to you nice people. I'm not a dumb person, and I'm not stupid. If I had twenty-one million dollars, we wouldn't be sitting here having a meeting."

"Why would you flee if you had done nothing wrong?"

"I didn't flee ... How can I be an embezzler? I don't even work in the bank. If someone was giving me money illegally, why would I take money that was coming in and put it back into their bank? Why wouldn't I just take that and stash it?"

It was clear to Allison that Smith was altering the facts to fit his story at any particular moment. He possessed the con man's ability to blend fiction with a few facts, making the result a relatively plausible story that had some verifiable details. Allison was afraid to press Smith too hard because at any moment he might get flustered and refuse to answer further questions. That would ruin his strategy of getting Smith pinned down to inaccuracies and inconsistencies in the grand jury room before they began trying the case in court, where Allison could bring out Smith's grand jury testimony and shoot holes in it. So in place of interrogating Smith and challenging him now, Allison had decided on the Socratic method of asking simple, well-directed questions and hoping that the jurors would see the absurdity of some of Smith's answers.

Smith was almost impossible to pin down. For instance, at one point he said that Brian Feeley was one of the people he talked to at the bank whenever he needed money withdrawn from his line of credit; then he went on to another thought.

Allison patiently backed him up. "Did you ever have a conversation yourself with Brian in which you made a reference to the existence of this line of credit?"

"I didn't. I figured he knew. He had to. He was one of the ones putting money in the account."

"I am just asking if there was ever a conversation in which you—"

"No, because—"

"Was there ever a conversation between you and Brian Feeley where there was an explicit reference made to the line of credit?"

"Let me tell you something. Brian Feeley—and this is why I can't understand why he's still at the bank. Whenever—see, you've got to understand the—there was a strong relationship between Brian and Ben. Their whole purpose when Ben first came to me and he wanted to borrow fifty-seven thousand dollars to start a promotional company—"

"When was this?"

And so it went, Smith talking in a rapid, jumbled fashion. He couldn't answer a question without opening a new Pandora's box of supposed wrongdoing by others. It was frustrating to question him—almost impossible to try to make sense of what he had to say.

More than an hour later, Smith began talking about Teri Key. He referred to all the money he had given her over the years. Obviously bitter at what he regarded as her betrayal, Smith could find nothing good to say about his former personal secretary, who, he knew by now, had turned her back on him and was cooperating fully with the government. "You've got a person—you've got a person that—anybody who sits around the house at night and looks at porno movies and makes a puppy part of their sex habits, that person ain't well. That has happened."

A puppy part of their sex habits? This was the most absurd attempt at character assassination Allison had ever heard. If one knew the unassuming, upstanding Key, it was even more ridiculous. He could barely keep a straight face, and several members of the grand jury shuffled uneasily.

"I am not sure we want to discuss anybody's sex habits in the grand jury," Allison said.

"I just think the grand jury should know a little bit about people that come up in front of them. I gave Teri Key ten thousand dollars about seven months ago."

"That is a lot of puppies." Allison had been unable to resist.

"That's right."

Late that afternoon, when Smith finally emerged from the grand jury room, Bob Michaels looked like a wreck. He had obviously paced the hallway all afternoon. His client had gone into the grand jury room with orders to take the Fifth on all questions. He should have been in and out in fifteen minutes. But it had been hours. A smiling Smith approached his lawyer, saying reassuringly "Don't worry, man. They love me in there."

Alone with the grand jury, Allison asked, "Well, ladies and gentlemen, what do you think?"

"Maybe it *is* plausible," said one woman from the front row. A couple of other jurors nodded their heads in agreement.

Allison was surprised by these initial reactions. He had to admit that Smith had put on a good show, alternating between seeming sincere, being emotional and appearing dedicated to helping young struggling fighters. All and all he had come across as a likeable guy. And Allison knew that juries often focused on the personal aspects of a case or a witness rather than the facts of his story. An impression—good or bad—was created more by demeanor than by what was said.

Allison's role was the exact opposite: gathering, storing and analyzing hard factual information for future use. Factually, of course, the prosecutor knew a lot more about Smith, MAPS and the Wells Fargo embezzlement than the grand jury did at that moment. He had not yet presented all the information regarding the details of the branch settlement manipulation and the routing of the money into Smith's pockets. The grand jury had only heard about Ben Lewis's first interview with the FBI, which lacked many of the details the government now knew about the crimes. Then too, most of the grand jury members were not very sophisticated when it came to business financial matters. They included a telephone repairman, a few housewives, several retired tradesmen, a schoolteacher. Probably none of them had ever opened a commercial line of credit at a bank. They didn't know how it was or wasn't done. While Allison was legally prevented from testifying personally before the grand jury, he was allowed to indicate his own opinion, provided he did not "inflame" the emotions of the grand jurors.

"I'd be less than candid if I didn't tell you that I find Mr. Smith's story to be highly implausible," he said. "Here's a guy who never got more than twenty-five thousand dollars to fifty thousand dollars from the bank—and each time he signed a promissory note—and he tells you that, just for introducing Gene Kawakami to Ali, he was going to get all the money he needed. He says it was twelve million, but it could just as easily have been twenty or thirty million. Ask yourself if that's reasonable. And he has no copies of the documents he says he signed to open that line of credit. Can you imagine indebting yourself for that much and not having copies of the papers?"

"But they kept putting money in his account and paying his checks," said a juror.

Foreperson Doreen Taylor spoke up in reaction to her fellow juror's remark. "You mean to tell me if all of a sudden you got a bank statement and saw that the bank had put an extra one hundred and fifty thousand dollars in your account, you'd feel as if you could spend it? As if it belonged to you?"

"Yeah, why not?" the juror answered. "If they put it in my account?"

Taylor rolled her eyes in disbelief.

Allison had two troubling thoughts. The first was his concern at the lousy citizenship displayed by this one juror. The second was that he couldn't believe that people could hear Harold Smith and think he was telling the truth. Allison knew from experience that an operator like Smith always came across best on the first go-around. After that, major holes began to appear in his story. But Smith was a good actor, no doubt about that. He had gotten teary-eyed more than once, attempting to come off as an underdog who had been mistreated by society. It was a role in which he had some experience, and he played it with gusto.

A grand jury could issue an indictment with the vote of a simple majority—twelve out of twenty-three members. But no prosecutor wanted such a narrow decision. In order to win a verdict in court, the vote had to be twelve out of twelve jurors. If a prosecutor couldn't get a unanimous vote in the grand jury, when all the government had to show was probable cause, how in the world could the government win in court when it had to prove guilt beyond a reasonable doubt? Allison had never gone to trial with less than a unanimous indictment by the grand jury. He considered it the only acceptable resolution if he was going to further pursue a prosecution.

Allison had a feeling that if he could get Smith back before the jury a second time, and start to pin him down, the man's story might start to crumble. Knowing what he did about the swindle at the bank from Ben Lewis and the operation of MAPS from Teri Key, Allison knew that Smith's testimony was full of exaggeration, innuendo and outright lies.

It would be interesting to see how long Harold "Rossfields" Smith could keep up the big act.

***

When Smith made his second appearance before the grand jury he brought another bundle of assorted documents with him. Eleven pages of telephone messages. Travel vouchers. Hotel bills. An overdraft slip from the bank. A bank statement. Three checks. All of it harmless stuff. Still missing—and Allison was beginning to believe they would stay missing—were the all-important general ledgers. The ledgers that Jennifer King had gone over with Teri Key. The ledgers that were probably the most incriminating records kept at MAPS.

"Good morning," Allison said. "This is a continuation of your appearance here last week, is that right?"

"Yes, but I would like to say that on the basis of my deep belief that this man is biased toward me," Smith said, pointing to Allison, "and it's [his] true intentions only to hurt me and my family and my friends, any questions that you ask me at this point I would invoke my Fifth Amendment right. I'll be happy to talk to you, my peers," he told the jurors. "I would be happy to do so as long as this man is not present."

"Well, that is going to create a problem for us," Allison said. "Because I am the Assistant U.S. Attorney supervising this grand jury investigation. And it's unlawful for a grand jury to meet without an Assistant U.S. Attorney present. May I remind you that the Fifth Amendment privilege is properly invoked only on the basis of a sincere belief that your answers will incriminate you and not, for example, on the basis of personal feelings about anyone … But if it is your intention not to say anything, then let's not say anything."

"Okay. That's my intentions."

Allison's intentions were to take him through a list of questions and, after Smith refused to answer them, haul him before a duty judge and ask that Smith be compelled to answer because he had waived his Fifth Amendment privilege by testifying the previous week. Allison had spent many hours poring over the transcript of Smith's first grand jury appearance. He intended to probe Smith's line of credit defense and get him on record in more detail.

Allison asked forty-one questions, and forty-one times Smith answered, "I refuse to answer on the ground that it might tend to incriminate me."

The forty-second question, "When did you first meet your wife?" received the same answer.

Then came Doreen Taylor's soft voice. "Mr. Allison, may I ask a couple questions?"

"Sure," Allison said. He doubted it would work this time.

"Well, this is just strictly from a woman's point of view. I don't know if the other grand jurors are curious, but I was curious. How did your wedding go?"

"Very nice," Smith said, beaming.

Over the weekend Smith and his common-law wife had tied the knot, and afterward they had thrown a big reception at their house. The event was attended by more than a few media people, and their picture had appeared on the society page of at least one local newspaper.

"Were you married in the courthouse or what?"

"No, we had a poolside wedding."

"Oh, a garden wedding? How nice. Did she have a special dress or anything?"

"She wore the dress that she got arrested in."

"Bless her heart. How did you meet your wife?"

"Well, I was going into this grocery store and—"

"Here in Los Angeles?"

"No, in Washington, D.C."

"Oh."

"And she—she was a model and she was, you know, sometimes they have models inside grocery stores, you know, demonstrating special foods."

"Foods?"

"Cheeses, stuff like that. And she overseed a lot of the girls that was in there. And I had gotten out of my friend's car and I was walking past a car, and it was a Volkswagen. And this dog [in the car] barked and bit me on the arm. Wasn't a bad bite. So I was going to stand there and wait until the owner of the car got back. And then this big, pretty woman came out and it was her car ... That was the best dog bite I ever had."

"Oh, my gosh," said Taylor. "You started dating then?"

"Right."

And Smith was talking once again.

As he had planned, Allison bore in on the oil deal/line of credit defense. Smith admitted he was never asked to put up any collateral and there were no restrictions as to how the money could be spent. It was sounding more fantastic all the time. Just as Allison had figured: given the opportunity, Smith would dig a deeper hole for himself. In several instances Allison read back from Smith's previous testimony to show an inconsistency, trying to get Smith to stick to one version or the other. Sometimes he would come up with a third version, making it even more difficult to pin him down.

Smith continued his character assassination of people he thought had lined up against him—like Teri Key. He now claimed that Teri had destroyed the missing MAPS records. Interestingly, Smith now added Ben Lewis to his list, though other than that one slip in *Time* there had been no indications that Lewis was talking to the FBI. Allison guessed that Smith had surmised it, given Ben's disappearance.

"There's no doubt in my mind," Smith declared, "that Ben Lewis was storing cocaine in the Beverly Hills branch bank."

Allison suggested, rather pointedly, that the subject of cocaine be dropped. Smith got the hint; he knew he was in deep enough trouble. He certainly wasn't interested in having drug charges added to the list.

Smith tried his best to convince the jurors that everyone at the bank knew about his line of credit and their failure to disclose it now was simply a cover-up of far greater problems at Wells Fargo. He also kept trying to illustrate Kawakami's involvement both in establishing the line of credit and in further widespread misdeeds. He brought up the $357,000 debit of the MAPS account by Kawakami—which had been used to pay off all of Smith's overdue loans—as an example.

"I [didn't] have no $357,000's worth of loans ... [Kawakami] said he had done that to cover loans ... I went down to the bank ... and I got to arguing with him and using a little bad language. That's when he said, 'Let's go back in the back room.' Then he started crying, actually crying, saying that he had made a bad investment in some condominiums and that he needed the money to pay off a—some gambling debts. He said, 'In fact, the guy's downstairs now.' He took me downstairs and showed me this Oriental guy in this black Corvette. Then he came back upstairs. He said they—'These people, they cut your head off. They threatened to cut my baby's fingers off.' He was crying so hard foam was coming out of his mouth ... It was heavy ... Snot coming out of his nose and he was shaking. I said, 'All right. Then keep the money.' "

One of the values of such a performance, from Allison's point of view, was that as Smith told his story he often revealed the identities of friends and loyalists who, he said, would be able to corroborate his version. Allison knew that these people could be expected to come out of the woodwork at the trial and testify—or, possibly, perjure themselves—on Smith's behalf. Allison made note of these names so that he could subpoena them to appear before the grand jury. The idea was not to be surprised in court by what they had to say and also to lock them into a story that they could not change at a later date to fit a new bend in Smith's defense.

At one point Smith dropped a bombshell. He said he had a film taken on a trip to Big Bear which showed Ben Lewis and Gene Kawakami conversing about financial support available to Smith from the bank. "I have on film, which you can see, and it has sound, [Kawakami] saying 'Don't worry about money, we [will] work everything out for you, the whole thing.' " Such filmed documentation might help illustrate Smith's claim that he thought he had a line of credit and that Kawakami was making available to him "all the money" he needed.

"Let me understand about this film," Allison said. "You have a film with sound that shows you and Gene Kawakami and Ben Lewis discussing how you are going to get all the money you ever need?"

"Yes. The whole trip was concerning this."

"Was there anything on the sound track of that film referring to your line of credit?"

"No. It was just a little short film, but it has pictures of Gene pointing out where his house is going to be and Ben pointing out where his house is going to be." Smith said he would try to find the film because he "definitely" wanted the grand jury to see it.

During a break Smith went out in the hallway and spoke to Bob Michaels, who soon asked Allison to join them. What Smith really wanted was for Allison to leave the grand jury room when he continued his testimony, but both attorneys explained to him that was not possible. A compromise was reached: Smith would go back in and testify if he would have the opportunity to come back *again*, prior to the grand jury issuing an indictment, and answer further questions regarding the evidence against him. For Allison, it was a deal struck in heaven.

Satisfied, Smith walked back in to talk to his "friends" on the grand jury, apparently serene in the belief that, given an opportunity, he could convince them of his innocence.

CHAPTER THIRTY-FOUR

Sammie Marshall was an enigma to the government. No one had yet been able to figure his exact role in the Wells Fargo embezzlement. Marshall's lawyer, George Buehler, in an attempt to convince federal officials of his client's innocence of the crimes they were investigating, brought him to the FBI offices in late May to meet with the prosecutor and case agents.

A couple of weeks earlier, a disgusted Buehler had called Dean Allison to tell him of the pressure being put on his client by Jennifer King to verify Harold Smith's story. "She kept asking Sammie if he was *sure* he didn't remember Harold's line of credit," Buehler reported. "Even after Sammie told her he knew nothing about it she kept repeating it and stressing how important it was for him to corroborate Harold. Sammie told her that he would like to help Harold but that he wasn't going to lie. She said, 'You might have to.'" By then, of course, Allison knew enough about King not to be shocked.

Allison and FBI Special Agent Joe Woodall questioned Sammie Marshall for an hour or so on his role as a loan officer at Wells Fargo and then on his later employment as president of MAPS. Marshall vigorously denied holding any NSF checks for Harold Smith while he worked at the bank. As to Ben Lewis's claim that he and Marshall had bounced numerous bad checks back and forth between Beverly Drive and Miracle Mile as a favor to Smith, Marshall said he hadn't understood at the time why *Ben* kept sending the checks back to *him*. According to his understanding of the proper procedure, Marshall explained, the branch that had cashed a bad check was supposed to take the responsibility for pursuing the customer to make good on it. That was why he had sent the checks back to

Lewis—it was the Beverly Drive branch's responsibility to collect on them, not his.

Finally, having saved what they considered the strongest evidence against Marshall for last, Woodall and Allison asked him to explain what they called the "Telstar cashier's check." This was a $19,000 cashier's check issued in October 1978 to Telstar Travel, the travel agency to which Smith was then in arrears. The check had not been paid for but had been off-set with the debit half of a branch settlement ticket, so that it had been "charged," in effect, to the bank. The credit half of the branch settlement form had been sent to the Beverly Drive branch, where it ended up being offset, along with the various checks that had been bounced back and forth, by the first falsely encoded branch settlement Ben Lewis had used to start the roll-over or "daisy chain" process a few weeks later. The cashier's check bore Marshall's signature as the issuing bank officer, and the debit ticket used to offset it was in his handwriting. In the space used to explain the reason for the transaction, the debit ticket read "Item posted incorrectly"—a statement which obviously did not fit the facts.

Marshall admitted issuing the cashier's check and debit ticket. The presence of his signature and handwriting on them left him little choice. His explanation was casual, delivered without apparent strain, as if the transaction were nothing out of the ordinary. "The travel agent, Peter Van Schoonhoven, came by the [Miracle Mile] office. He demanded payment of his bill and threatened not to book any more travel for Harold if it wasn't paid. I called Ben over at Beverly Drive, and he said to pay it and branch settle the charge over to him, and he'd take care of collecting from Harold."

"Why did you put 'Item posted incorrectly' on the branch settlement ticket?" Allison asked.

"Ben told me to put that on there," Marshall said evenly. "I know it looks bad now, but at the time I didn't think anything of it. Another bank officer who I knew had asked me to put the transaction through, so I did. That sort of thing happens all the time."

"In the interests of candor," Buehler interjected, "you should know, Dean, that we've talked to Van Schoonhoven, the travel agent, and he doesn't remember it the same way."

After Marshall and Buehler left, Allison and Woodall sat quietly for a moment, sorting out their thoughts and impressions. To Allison, Marshall's demeanor was not clearly that of a guilty man. He came across as sincere. His nervousness at the outset was to be expected; most people would be nervous when questioned as a suspect by the FBI. Marshall had freely admitted the damaging facts about the Telstar cashier's check, and stuck with an explanation that involved Lewis and the travel agent. Knowing of Lewis's cooperation with the government and the travel agent's different recollection of events before he came in for the interview, Marshall could have adjusted his story to avoid these discrepancies. But he didn't, suggesting at least some degree of honesty.

Still, the evidence against Marshall was pretty strong—issuing a large cashier's check for Smith without any payment, using an admittedly false explanation on a branch settlement to cover it and continuing to bounce Smith's bad checks back to Beverly Drive even after Lewis had sent them over to him at Miracle Mile several times. Moreover, although Marshall might have forgotten it, at least two of those checks showed on their face that returning them to Lewis for him to collect was useless. One check bore the stamp "Payment stopped." Another had already been put through for collection three times, the maximum permitted under bank rules. As an experienced bank officer, Marshall clearly knew that the only course left was to charge these checks back against Smith's Miracle Mile account, but he hadn't done so. Then too, the circumstances indicated that Marshall had an obvious motive to help Smith at the bank's expense at the time—he was on the verge of resigning from the bank to join Smith in business.

"Joe, what do you think?" Allison finally asked.

The agent sighed. "I don't know."

"I keep thinking we're missing something when it comes to this guy. He comes across as if he really doesn't believe he did anything wrong, but the evidence is pretty clear he did."

"C'mon," Woodall said. "I hear what you're saying, but he's just playing dumb."

"Yeah, or maybe he's just not that bright. But he still has no convincing explanation in the face of some of these incriminating documents. They back up Ben, and Ben says Sammie was involved. If we believe Ben, then

Sammie's culpable." And both Allison and Woodall certainly *did* believe Ben Lewis, who was baring his heart and soul in ongoing interviews with the FBI. Nothing Lewis had said to date had been proven untrue or exaggerated.

Later, Buehler called Allison to feel him out about what he thought of Marshall and his explanations.

"I wish I could believe him," Allison answered. "He seems like a nice guy. But his story is pretty lame. We've got him dead bang on a false entry charge based on the branch settlement ticket—he even admits to it. I'm thinking it might be appropriate for him to plead to one count of false entry in bank records."

Compared to the other possibilities, Allison was offering Marshall a reasonably good deal. Plead guilty to one count and avoid a trial on the entire $21 million. The false entry charge was a fairly technical one, creating a good possibility that Marshall would just get probation, even though the statute authorized up to five years in jail. Of course, Allison added, the government would require Marshall's complete and candid testimony against Smith. Allison didn't feel he was letting Marshall off too easily. The prosecutor had already figured—largely from the information gleaned from Lewis—that after he left the bank and went over to MAPS, Marshall had kept his nose pretty clean. With one notable exception, the business with the bank's money thereafter had been kept between Smith and Lewis. Still, Allison was pretty sure that the grand jury would indict Marshall on the overall scheme, which meant that Marshall had considerable incentive to make a deal.

Buehler now told Allison something new. Buehler said he had asked Marshall to take a polygraph test, which his client had done willingly. According to Buehler, Marshall had answered no to four critical questions: "Prior to 1981, did you know Lewis was making fictitious deposits to accounts of Harold J. Smith and his related entities?" "Did you know Harold Smith or MAPS were obtaining money from Wells Fargo by fraudulent means?" "Did you conspire with any person or persons to defraud Wells Fargo while employed with MAPS?" "Did you ever tell anyone that Harold Smith or his related entities had received a line of credit from Wells Fargo?" All of Marshall's "no" answers were judged truthful by the examiner, Buehler said.

Before Allison would credit any polygraph results, they would have to come from a test administered by the government. Contrary to popular belief, polygraph tests carry a critical subjective element; the way the questions are phrased, the background and expertise of the operator and the setting in which the operator asks the questions can make a big difference. Polygraph results are seldom admitted in evidence. Their biggest value is not in the courtroom but in assessing evidence gathered during an investigation. Allison hung up from talking with Buehler even more intrigued by Marshall. He probably would not volunteer for a polygraph unless he felt he could pass it. Just what was going on here? But if Marshall was willing to submit to an FBI polygraph, Allison was more than happy to oblige him.

Marshall took his second polygraph on June 4. This time he was answering questions framed by an expert FBI examiner. His "no" answer to "Did you know Ben Lewis was carrying checks for Harold Smith?" was judged inconclusive by the operator. He answered "no" to two more questions: "Are you lying when you say Ben Lewis authorized issuance of the Telestar cashier's check?" and "Did you have any conversations with Ben Lewis regarding improper use of branch settlements to Harold Smith's benefit?" Both those answers, Joe Woodall reported to Allison, were "clear flunks." In the opinion of the experienced operator, Sammie Marshall was lying.

In a conversation with Allison a few days later Buehler said, "Privately, I strongly counseled Sammie to accept your plea offer. But he's still adamant that he did nothing wrong. I have no alternative except to take him to trial. I can't have a guy plead to something he says he didn't do."

"I wouldn't want you to, George," Allison said. "That's what we have trials for—to decide guilt and innocence. See you in court."

* * *

Meanwhile, a slew of witnesses streamed through the grand jury room. Most were past and present employees of MAPS; some were associates Smith had mentioned during his own testimony, and others were simply hangers-on. With Allison directing the questioning, the jurors heard all of them out.

Travel agent Tom Bole, a short, heavyset Scot with a thick brogue, came across as Mr. Outraged Citizen at being torn away from his business and called before the grand jury. He failed to bring all the financial records listed on the subpoena, used a lot of I-don't-remembers and let everyone know that he felt the government had no business investigating Harold Smith. Allison knew from Teri Key that Bole and Smith were close. Bole had allowed the use of his office for Teri to type one of Smith's early messages to the media. The government also knew—from Lewis—that a $3,000 bad check payable to Smith and written by Bole was the first one "held" for Harold by Marshall and Lewis back in the late summer of 1978, when the scheme began. As it turned out, the bank never succeeded in collecting on the check. Asked specifically about this check, Bole claimed he remembered nothing.

Next came Frank Wheeler, a big, tall, black man who resembled Sammie Marshall. A part-time carpenter, he did handyman jobs around the MAPS gym and served as a gofer for Smith. In the witness chair Wheeler acted dumb and claimed to know nothing. Allison took him through a list of questions about MAPS's finances—like "Was it your job to handle MAPS's financial records?"—anyway. At least negative responses would keep Wheeler from turning up as a trial witness concerning Smith's supposed line of credit.

Chuck Bodak testified the same day as Bole but proved to be an entirely different sort of witness. A longtime and highly respected fight trainer, Bodak had worked for several years with Muhammad Ali, starting way back in the early Cassius Clay days. A middle-aged white man with a Vandyke beard, who usually wore a baseball cap tilted back on his head at a jaunty angle, Bodak obviously was not involved in the embezzlement, even though his name was on the Bodak Promotions checking account through which much of the stolen money had been funneled—an account that Bodak couldn't even write a check on since he wasn't an authorized signatory. Allison figured that the trainer would be another partisan advocate for Smith, but he turned out to be his own man. Bodak had slept many nights on the floor of the MAPS-MAAS gym and obviously had little regard for money. He dedicated himself to helping the young men in the boxing program. At one point, when Allison referred to him as a "trainer" for MAAS, Bodak corrected softly, "I'm not a trainer. You 'train' *animals*. I was a coach, a teacher and a friend to those kids."

Bill Shaeffer's appearance marked a return to partisanship and evasion. A lanky Caucasian in his late twenties or early thirties who favored cowboy boots and hats and was married to one of the MAPS card girls, Shaeffer was a complete Smith loyalist. Allison had a feeling that he would not hesitate to perjure himself in order to cover for Smith. Allison suspected that if any of the MAPS records had been destroyed, this urban cowboy might have been the one who had deep-sixed them. Also, the prosecutor was concerned that Shaeffer might try to provide false corroboration for Smith's line of credit story. Both Key and Lewis had told about how Shaeffer always carried Smith's briefcase full of money. When Allison asked him about it, Shaeffer answered, "I may have been asked to hold Mr. Smith's briefcase once or twice, but I never opened it or saw what was in it." Asked whether he had ever dealt with anyone from Wells Fargo, he said flippantly, "I have taken my paycheck down to the bank. I do go to the bank once in a while, you know." Shaeffer came across as a smart aleck. His behavior angered the grand jury. Allison remained low-key and persistent during the questioning, trying to hide his own rising animosity toward Shaeffer.

Bruce Barrett literally bounced into the grand jury room. He was so hyped-up that Allison wouldn't have been surprised if someone told him that Barrett had just eaten a bottle of amphetamines. He spoke in a reedy voice, had a machine-gun delivery and could hardly wait for the end of a question before he began answering it.

Allison knew Barrett was a close friend of Smith's and that he had just filed his own multimillion-dollar civil suit against Wells Fargo, claiming that the bank's failure to fulfill its promise of a line of credit to Smith had irreparably damaged Barrett's business prospects and reputation as a producer of shows for Lewis and Smith Enterprises. Since the civil complaint was verified (sworn to under oath), it effectively locked Barrett into saying that Smith had a line of credit from the bank. It was no coincidence that the name of the attorney appearing on Barrett's complaint was Bob Michaels, Jennifer King's law partner and Smith's co-counsel in his own civil suit. Allison strongly suspected, therefore, that Barrett's recollection had been influenced by one or more private chats with Smith and his attorneys.

After speaking with Barrett in the hallway outside the grand jury room, Allison was even surer. It turned out that Smith had invited Barrett over to his house for a little talk and then had taken him directly over to Michaels's law office, where the complaint was prepared on the spot. The prosecutor could just see Smith wheedling Barrett and subtly massaging his recollection when they were alone, saying things like: "Don't you remember that time when I told you about the bank givin' me that line of credit?" It probably hadn't taken too long.

Placed under oath, Barrett claimed to have heard Smith mention his credit line once or twice, but he couldn't remember when or under what circumstances. Barrett also volunteered that he had first learned of the embezzlement when Ben Lewis had called him and asked to meet him in a motel room on a Saturday night in late January. "Ben said all the money was *stolen*," he said. "I couldn't believe it." Despite being told to calm down and slow down, Barrett seemed to get even more nervous as he testified. Clearly, Barrett was not an effective witness, and Allison wasn't particularly worried about the prospect of his being called by the defense at trial.

And then there was Bob Campbell. He wore Ivy League clothing— creased wool slacks, loafers, a dress shirt and conservative tie. If this handsome black man was a class act at first sight, he was also obviously wary and more than a touch hostile. On the face of it, he had every reason to shade the truth in favor of Smith, as some of the other MAPS loyalists had done. Allison knew he was a longtime friend of Harold's, because the two men had run track together at American University when Smith was still going by his real name, Ross Fields. It did not bother Campbell that his old friend had changed his name. It was not unusual for blacks who got in trouble in the South to change their names as they moved on to more promising futures. What was in a name? Campbell fervently believed in his old friend and the boxing program they had developed. And Campbell was proud of his work as president of MAAS and head of its amateur operation. It soon became clear that Bob Campbell was nobody's dummy—and he was certainly not a liar. He was an intelligent man caught in the middle; he didn't want to tell the government anything that would sink his friend Harold Smith, but he was an honest man who would not compromise his integrity. His loyalty to his good friend and fellow black man notwithstanding, Campbell would tell the truth even if it hurt.

Within fifteen minutes it became clear to Allison and the grand jury that Campbell had been deeply committed to the kids. What had happened to those young amateur boxers since the scandal broke was one of the real human tragedies of the entire sordid affair. Most of them had packed their bags and returned home, in many cases to squalid conditions that they had worked so hard to escape. The money had run out, and there was no more Muhammad Ali Amateur Sports. The Champ was no longer behind them. The dream was over.

Campbell disclaimed any significant financial responsibility for the MAPS-MAAS empire except for budgeting his amateur operation and then turning the results over to Smith. He had nothing to do with anyone at Wells Fargo. Allison took him over the amateur program fight by fight, trying to get Campbell to recall how much money each one grossed, then comparing the revenues with expenses. Surprisingly, Campbell insisted that the MAAS program just about broke even overall. Considering how much money Smith's businesses had gone through, this was difficult for Allison to believe. But, indeed, Allison would later find out that Campbell had run a tight ship and that the amateur boxing program might even have made money but for all the outrageous side expenses for friends' travel, hotel bills, parties and the like that Smith had run up.

Then came the critical question. "Did you know anything about a line of credit?" Allison asked.

"I really do believe Harold had a line of credit, but I have no personal knowledge of that," Campbell said. "We always had all the money we needed. No secret was made of that."

"Did you ever see any document reflecting the existence of a line of credit?" Allison asked.

"Yes."

Oh no. Please don't tell me Bob Campbell is going to lie like the others, Allison thought. From the bank witnesses and record, the prosecutor knew for a fact that there had been no line of credit and certainly no documentation for one. "When was that?"

"I don't know exactly. But one time I was sitting at my desk when Harold came into the office with some papers in his hand and said, 'We got it made now. I just finished talking to Gene Kawakami. We're going to have all the money we need.'"

"Did you actually see the papers?"

"Well, no. But I believed them to be related to a line of credit," Campbell said stubbornly.

Allison mentally breathed a sigh of relief. Campbell was simply saying that *Smith* had told him there was a line of credit. The reliability of that source would not be difficult to impeach.

The grand jury heard a lot from FBI Special Agents Joe Woodall and Chuck Jones. Through them, the jurors also heard the words of Teri Key and Ben Lewis, spoken during their many hours of interviews at the FBI office. Allison had decided against bringing Key and Lewis before the grand jury in person. The primary reason was that he didn't want the defense lawyers to have extensive prior transcripts of the testimony of his two star witnesses to use for cross-examination purposes at trial. The investigation was not complete, and the facts were not all in yet. There were undoubtedly numerous matters that had not been covered with Lewis and Key in their interviews, as thorough as the agents had been. Testimony by Lewis and Key now on this incomplete basis could later be used unfairly to impeach them by making it look like they had selective recollections. Moreover, witnesses never told the same story twice in exactly the same words, no matter how honest and sincere they were. The defense was going to get the voluminous FBI interview reports on Lewis and Key anyway under the Jencks Act, which required the disclosure of prior statements by government witnesses. To create another sworn statement for each by questioning them in the grand jury was simply giving the defense lawyers free ammunition to nitpick the witnesses over purported discrepancies in their statements. There was no need to subject them to this, since hearsay presentation through the case agents was totally proper and quite common in grand jury proceedings. The jurors, after being fully advised of their right to require Lewis and

Key to make personal appearances, had agreed and decided not to call the government's star witnesses in person.

Woodall testified to the painstaking analysis of the MAPS financial records that he had undertaken. He laboriously went through the MAPS check stubs and pointed out the marginal notations made by the conscientious Teri, such as "wire transfer from NBC" appearing next to one day's $200,000 deposit. Then he pulled the bank records which showed an improper branch settlement transaction in the exact same amount and on the same day, clearly proving that the money did not come from NBC, as Smith had told Teri at the time, but was embezzled from Wells Fargo. Demonstrations like this were effective in order to prove Smith's criminal intent. If he really thought he had a line of credit, why did he lie to Teri and others about the source of the money?

Allison knew that proving Smith's criminal intent would win or lose the case for the government. To be acquitted or hang the trial jury, Smith did not have to prove he actually *had* a line of credit. He simply had to convince the jurors that he *thought* he had a line of credit, because fraudulent intent, in one form or another, was an element of every proposed charge against Smith that the government would have to prove beyond a reasonable doubt. This mental element is what con men almost always base their defense upon because it is the most elusive and the most difficult thing for the government to prove. Only the defendant himself knows and can testify directly to his true intent; the government must ask jurors to *infer* deceitful intentions from the defendant's actions and other surrounding circumstances. For this reason no fraud case—in the absence of a confession, which is rarely present—could ever really be considered airtight, no matter how strong the government's proof of the acts and transactions constituting the swindle.

Special Agent Jones was questioned about each and every MAPS fight and took the jurors along the path the embezzled money had taken from the time it left the bank in each instance until it wound up in the pockets of the recipients, like fighters and their managers, across the country. The instances of money being taken out of state for various MAPS purposes would form the basis for the interstate transportation of stolen property (ITSP) counts in the proposed indictment.

Presenting the evidence to the grand jury allowed Allison to begin shaping the case for trial. Since jurors were only human, it would be important at trial not to bore them with a dry, technical banking case. Rereading the FBI's 302 interview reports by himself, Allison knew he would want to show the fantastic extravagance of the racehorses, the automobiles, the airplanes, the yacht, the card girls and the parties and the incredible spending in connection with the MAPS and MAAS fight events. This would not only hold the trial jury's interest but enable the government to paint Smith as the high-living con man he really was. Proving this evidence would also help rebut any version of the expected line of credit defense: people don't spend like this when they are struggling to build a new business with borrowed money, and no reputable bank would lend out substantial sums—much less $21.3 million—without restrictions making this sort of extravagance impossible. Evidence of such "sudden unexplained affluence" was perfectly relevant and admissible in theft and embezzlement cases like this, and Allison hit the books for hours until he had a raft of precedents supporting the government's position on this point.

Allison realized that the government's case at trial would need to be half banking and half boxing. So much of the embezzled money had gone to fighters and their managers. Moreover, the ITSP charges were involved with the boxing business—moving huge payments across state lines to pay fighters and managers. This was a natural bridge from one half of the case to the other. One night as he was reviewing the evidence, Allison came to a chilling realization. *Harold Smith and his cohorts had almost stolen boxing.* Smith had been using the embezzled funds to outspend rival promoters, buy up all the top fighters in almost every weight class and corner the market in promising young amateurs, whom he would move from the amateur to pro ranks. With a claimed potential $100 million gross from the "This Is It" fight in New York, they had been within a couple of weeks of pulling it off when the embezzlement was detected. All the stolen money might have been put back in the bank with no one the wiser, and Smith would have controlled an entire sport.

Allison's anger at what had almost happened to his favorite sport fueled his prosecutor's desire to convict the guilty. He was determined not to let them get away with it. Once the case got to trial, not only the jury but the entire world would see that the high-rolling kingdom of Harold J. Smith, aka Ross Fields, had been an enormous con game.

But while the evidence against Smith seemed overwhelming, it was less strong against Sammie Marshall. Every scrap of evidence against Marshall would have to be presented at trial because his role in the scheme had been limited. If he left anything out, Allison feared, the jury might not find the weight of evidence enough to convict the ex-banker. Another worry was an inevitable motion for a separate trial that would be made by Marshall's lawyer, George Buehler. Buehler would have good reason to want his client tried separately from Smith. If he succeeded, the evidence that involved Smith alone could not be presented at Marshall's trial, which would greatly reduce the seriousness of the crime in the jurors' eyes. To ward off a severance, Allison would have to show that Marshall was a full participant in the conspiracy, just like Ben Lewis and Harold Smith. After all, Marshall had started it by showing Lewis how to manipulate the branch settlement system, and he was the first to start holding checks for Smith.

Technically there were literally hundreds—indeed, thousands—of potential counts against Smith. Obviously the government could not put all of them in the indictment. There were certain rules of thumb about how many counts to file. The more serious the crime, the more counts. An enormous crime and a highly culpable defendant deserved a substantial indictment. But there was a limit to what any judge would accept—most wanted representative counts, selected to show the scope of the alleged crimes but not so numerous as to be burdensome to the court and jury. After reviewing the incidents that would be required to illustrate the entire scandal, Allison began to choose the counts.

There was no doubt it would be a fat indictment.

***

Gene Kawakami was indicted on one count of misapplication of bank funds in connection with the preparation of the false and fraudulent Western Sales loan application and supporting documentation. He entered into a plea arrangement with the government, agreeing to plead guilty with the hope that when the government informed the court of his cooperation in the MAPS case that the judge would not impose a harsh prison sentence.

The FBI's Chuck Jones, who had extensively interviewed Kawakami and was running down pieces of information supplied by the former Miracle Mile manager, soon came to think that Kawakami was not being straightforward. Kawakami's style in the interview sessions was to wait until he was asked something and then give as little information as possible. Jones would check on what Kawakami had told him, only to uncover more damaging information. In the face of the new information, Kawakami would offer another narrow view of his actions, and once again Jones would be operating on incomplete facts. The agent felt he was getting the runaround, and he didn't like it. Jones told Allison of the difficulties with Kawakami.

The prosecutor said he would discuss the problem with Kawakami's attorney, Richard Trattner. Allison called the defense attorney and said it appeared Kawakami was not being "completely cooperative." Trattner suggested it might be a personality clash between his client and the agent.

"Chuck is one of the best agents around," Allison said. "I don't think he's ever had this sort of problem before. I don't want the government to have to withdraw from our agreement, but one of the conditions is complete candor. I suggest you talk to your client."

Jones went back to interviewing Kawakami. The agent was able to discredit the story Smith had told the grand jury about the big oil deal that he had supposedly helped Kawakami engineer, for which the banker had supposedly rewarded him with an unlimited line of credit. The facts showed that Kawakami had simply introduced oilman Kyle McAllister to Smith and had not attended the subsequent meeting between McAllister and Ali at the MAPS office. Jones also had McAllister interviewed in Texas and determined that there had never been an oil deal—nothing at all had come of the talks. McAllister added that, not long after the meeting, Smith called and asked him to buy some $50,000's worth of tickets to the amateur boxing match in Houston between the Ali and Frazier clubs. When he declined, McAllister said, Smith had asked for a "donation" anyway. Smith's behavior was strange, Jones thought, for someone who claimed that his meeting with McAllister had gained him an unlimited line of credit.

But on other matters—such as tracking down all of Kawakami's loans and complex financial deals—the agent had difficulties. Jones came to see Kawakami as a wheeler-dealer who played things fast and loose while falsifying loan documentation at the bank. Most worrisome: there appeared to be some additional losses to Wells Fargo, involving other customers, that Kawakami had not told the agent about. Overall, Kawakami's degree of cooperation continued to be questionable at best.

When Jones reported the latest developments, Allison didn't hesitate. There was no way the government could keep an agreement with a witness who was not being forthright. Not only was the bargain being unfulfilled, but keeping a deal with such a witness could prove highly damaging to the prosecution in court. Cross-examination could elicit all Kawakami's evasions and incomplete statements. Then the defense would argue that "this is the kind of witness the government must resort to in order to obtain evidence against Harold Smith." It would look bad.

"The agreement is off," Allison told Kawakami's attorney. "The indictment against Gene stands. If he wants to plead guilty, fine. Depending upon what turns up, there may be no other charges filed against him, but there are no longer any guarantees. I would still prefer to have Gene as a cooperative witness, and frankly I think it's still in his interest to proceed this way, but it's strictly up to him."

Trattner said he too would like to see Kawakami keep working with the government and would recommend that to his client.

Chuck Jones noticed the difference within a few days.

Gene Kawakami, obviously fearing prison time more than ever, got cooperative real fast.

* * *

For his third appearance before the grand jury, Harold Smith brought along the film he had said was so important for the jurors to see. It was set up and played, but there was no sound track. It showed several men getting out of a small plane and looking over some property. Smith pointed out Ben Lewis and Gene Kawakami and a few others. According to Smith, the film was supposed to prove that he had a line of credit, but it did nothing of the sort.

Smith's appearance brought defense attorney Howard Moore on the scene as his chief defense counsel. It was now Moore waiting in the hallway instead of Bob Michaels. A flamboyant black civil rights attorney, Moore reportedly had achieved his reputation in part by defending Muhammad Ali in his draft case and later black activist Angela Davis.

For the government, Smith's final grand jury appearance was icing on the cake. He had been asked back only because of the deal Allison had made with him, promising he would be allowed to return before the grand jury made the decision whether or not to indict him. And it was getting to be that time.

Under close questioning by Allison, Smith admitted to causing the interstate transportation of several embezzled checks, which Allison planned to use as the basis for ITSP counts in the indictment. Smith continued to dig a deeper hole for himself regarding his line of credit. He now had a ridiculous story that he could be pinned to in court.

Four weeks later, on July 30, 1981, the grand jury issued a thirty-two-count indictment against Harold Smith, aka Ross Fields. Lloyd Benjamin Lewis was also indicted. Sammie Marshall was named in four counts, including a count alleging conspiracy in the overall scheme to embezzle $21 million from Wells Fargo Bank.

CHAPTER THIRTY-FIVE

The Jennifer King trial was handled by a colleague of Dean Allison's in the Special Prosecutions Unit, Assistant U.S. Attorney Richard Drooyan. Allison figured that by the time the King trial began he would be fully occupied preparing the MAPS prosecution, and he did not want to divide his attention. There was another reason he had stepped aside: word was out that Jennifer King was going to charge that Allison had been "overzealous" in trying to "get" her. He didn't want personal issues like this to mar such an obviously strong case against King.

Allison was not even allowed in the courtroom as a spectator. King's defense team told the judge that it might call Allison as a defense witness and therefore wanted him barred from the proceedings. Though Allison knew quite well he would never be called (and he never was), there was nothing he could do but steer clear of the courtroom and check periodically with Drooyan to see how things were going.

Despite the apparent strength of the evidence against King, things did not go well for the government from the start. U.S. District Judge Mariana Pfaelzer made it clear she was offended that the government had taped an attorney. Though the judge clearly thought King's perjurious conduct distasteful, she seemed as upset with the government for the way it had made the case as with King for allegedly being involved in such unethical behavior.

Teri Key was the star witness for the prosecution. She testified about Jennifer King telling her to lie, and then the tape of the conversation in King's office was played for the jury. To lawyers in the U.S. Attorney's office—the tape had been played many times in that office—it seemed to be a dead-bang case. The consensus was that the recording of King admitting her own falsification before the grand jury and urging Key to commit perjury was worse than the most blatant of the Watergate tapes. The tape showed a lawyer admitting to illegalities herself and advising someone to lie. It was weighty and dramatic evidence that would undoubtedly lead to conviction. Or so the prosecutors thought.

On cross-examination, the defense attacked Key's character, trying to smear her by implying that she had been heavily involved in drugs and by questioning whether she had stolen money from Harold Smith. Impeaching a major witness who had given damaging testimony was an old legal stratagem. Although the defense insinuations were false, Teri became nervous and flustered. Though Drooyan thought she came across as believable despite the assault, he worried that in the eyes of the jurors a few cracks might have been chiseled in Teri's credibility.

Harold Smith testified at length, attempting to portray both Teri and Tony Key in a bad light. Smith claimed that in a phone call he had made to the Keys' home shortly after his arrest Tony tried to extort money from him. "'We can start with twenty-five thousand dollars ... and a contract with Tony Orlando to back my music career,'" he quoted Tony as saying. Unbeknownst to Smith, however, the government had another tape that was soon to be played for the jury: the conversation in question had been recorded by equipment the FBI had put on the Keys' home phone. It proved that Tony Key had made no such statement and asked for no money. To the contrary, it had been *Smith* who had suggested that he might be able to get some money for Tony if he and Teri were more helpful to him. (Though government lawyers briefly considered filing a perjury charge against Smith, the idea was abandoned due to the score of more serious charges he faced.)

When Drooyan began his cross-examination, Smith did a complete turnabout: he invoked the Fifth Amendment and declined to answer. For the record Drooyan asked a litany of questions, and Smith refused to answer them all. The government then asked the court either to rule that Smith had to answer cross-examination questions about points to which he had willingly testified or that his direct testimony should be stricken and the jurors admonished to disregard it. Judge Pfaelzer finally ordered Smith to answer the questions. He did, and once again inconsistencies filled the air.

However, despite the vivid evidence of King's lying and obstruction of justice, the jury returned acquittals on two of the three obstruction of justice counts and hung on the last two obstruction and perjury counts. On her own, Judge Pfaelzer acquitted King of the perjury charge because, the jurist held, the question that gave rise to the perjury wasn't specific enough. The government would have to retry King on the one remaining obstruction count.

The King legal victory was cause for celebration by Smith and his followers. Smith penned a poem, "The Promoter," which was handed out on the federal courthouse steps after one of his court appearances. In it he talked about a "snitch named Key" and a "railroad job" and how much he was looking forward to the "main attraction."

* * *

Allison was also looking forward to the main attraction, though he anticipated a far different outcome. The case against Harold Smith seemed especially strong. But then so had the case against Jennifer King. The legal system was made up of people and personalities as well as laws and precedents. There were no sure things in the business. The first hurdle was the assignment of a trial judge. Allison knew from experience that there were certain judges that would be better for the government than others. Not that he had any choice in the matter.

At Smith's arraignment, the duty magistrate spun the wheel a few times, then reached in and removed a sealed envelope. Allison suspected the feelings he was now suffering were not unlike those experienced by a nervous Academy Award nominee. He was standing next to several defense lawyers. George Buehler. Howard Moore and his associate Patricia Conwell. Cornell Price, Ben Lewis's attorney. Price's main concern—since Lewis was not going to be standing trial—was the sentence his client would receive. Obviously he and the other defense lawyers preferred one of the more liberal and lenient judges on the bench. Allison hoped for the exact opposite.

Inside the envelope was a small card with a name printed on it. The magistrate said in a monotone, "This case has been assigned to Judge David Williams. Report to his courtroom at eleven o'clock this morning."

Allison kept a poker face. He looked at Price, who was trying his best to suppress a grimace. The attorneys left the courtroom in a group. Allison and the agents separated from everyone else and stepped into the elevator. The prosecutor said softly between clenched teeth, "Terrific." But only when he reached his twelfth-floor office did he finally exclaim "This is great! Judge Williams won't put up with any of Harold's bullshit."

Allison had been before Williams a number of times and had tried his first case as an Assistant U.S. Attorney before him. Judge Williams was known as a strict judge when it came to following the rules and maintaining proper decorum in his courtroom. For a long time he had been the only black judge on the Los Angeles federal bench, but this would provide no comfort to the defendants. Williams didn't allow defense antics of any kind and generally permitted the government to put on its own case, while a few other judges occasionally took it upon themselves to decide what witnesses and evidence they thought the jury ought to hear, excluding some evidence even though it was legally admissible.

The phone rang on Allison's desk, and he answered it. His smile quickly disappeared. "We've got to go back down and draw another judge," he told the agents dejectedly when he hung up. "Judge Williams just got over an operation and doesn't feel up to handling a big case."

When the name of Judge Consuelo Marshall was drawn from the wheel, the emotional climate changed completely. This time it was Price and the others who were pleased. Allison wasn't displeased as much as he was concerned. Frankly, he didn't know much about Judge Marshall because she hadn't been on the bench long. Incredibly, for the second time in a row they had drawn a black judge—and there were only three on the seventeen-member Los Angeles federal bench.

Later that day before Judge Marshall, Harold Smith, as expected, pleaded not guilty. A hushed Sammie Marshall also pleaded not guilty. Then it was Ben Lewis's turn. He stood before the tall bench and pleaded guilty to three felony counts—the conspiracy charge and two embezzlement counts—as required by his plea agreement with the government. Rule 11 of the Federal Rules of Criminal Procedure requires that the court ensure there exists an adequate factual basis for the defendant's guilty plea. Lewis therefore described to Judge Marshall how he had embezzled the millions of dollars for Smith and how Sammie Marshall had gotten him involved in the scheme, first by asking him to hold Smith's bad checks and later by telling him how to roll over falsely encoded branch settlement tickets. In this respect, the government gained another benefit from having an insider plead guilty and cooperate: the first thing the trial judge heard about the case was one of the persons charged admitting that the defendants had done exactly what the indictment alleged they did. Lewis's sentencing was postponed until after the trial since he was to be a witness and his cooperation and truthfulness were to be taken into account for purposes of punishment.

As he left the courtroom, Ben could sense the icy stares of his former friends, but he wasn't going to be deterred. He had put the past behind him. He was willing to tell the world about what they had done.

***

Now that the clock was running under the Speedy Trial Act, Allison began working extra long days, sleeping only a few hours a night. His wrinkled suit usually came off well after midnight, and the freshly pressed one went on around daybreak. He was smoking more unfiltered Camels than he wished to admit and downing coffee by the quart. Warm food was a luxury he seldom found time to enjoy.

There were some sixty potential trial witnesses. Allison had to figure out what order they should be called in so as to present an interesting and informative picture of the crimes and the sports promotion empire built by Smith. First, all the dozens of witness interview reports had to be analyzed. When Allison decided someone would be needed as a trial witness, a subpoena had to be served and a pretrial interview arranged. Finally, each witness was given an approximate date when he or she would be required in court and was asked to stay in touch with the government by telephone.

As he plowed through the FBI 302s, Allison realized that before the scandal broke a number of statements by Smith concerning the source of his money had been reported in the media. He saw these statements as potentially powerful evidence against Smith. Juries could be specifically instructed that if a defendant were found to have given a false story then the jurors were permitted to consider this as evidence that the defendant was conscious of his own guilt. Evidence like this would knock the underpinnings from Smith's I-thought-I-had-a-line-of-credit story.

Taking a conciliatory approach—he did not want to start dropping subpoenas on news reporters—Allison contacted legal counsel for the various newspapers and TV stations involved and let them know he was *not* interested in any confidential source material, reporter's notes or outtakes. He explained that the government was simply looking for reporters to testify to the statements by Smith that they had actually published or aired. KABC radio, ABC and CBS television, the New York *Post,* the San Francisco *Examiner* and others saw no problem in complying with his request. In fact the media response was uniformly cooperative with a single exception: the New York *Times.*

An attorney for the *Times* responded to Allison's request by simply repeating over and over that the paper had a firm policy forbidding its reporters from appearing as government witnesses in court—"We never have and never will." He claimed that the *Times* feared future sources might be afraid to talk if they thought the reporters could end up testifying in court. Allison understood this position well, since both his parents had been journalists, and he would have accepted it if he had intended to delve into sensitive areas involving confidential sources or unpublished information, but all he wanted was testimony to the *published* accounts. There was nothing confidential about them, and no source who spoke for publication to millions of readers could legitimately complain about the same statements being repeated in court later. And if it was the *appearance* of compulsion that the *Times* was worried about, Allison said, he would not issue a subpoena and would accept the word of the *Times* that its sportswriter Dave Anderson would appear voluntarily. The clips alone would not suffice, he explained, because they were hearsay—Allison needed the reporter available in court for cross-examination in order to use any published statement against Smith. He even offered to accept an affidavit if the defense would too, but Howard Moore refused this proposal point-blank.

Left no choice, Allison had the *Times* reporter served with a subpoena, which the paper's attorneys promptly moved to quash. In a court hearing, Judge Marshall agreed with the government that the subpoena raised no problem under the First Amendment. Rather, she said, the issue was the burden for the New York-based reporter in having to travel to Los Angeles to appear, which had to be weighed against the importance of his appearance to the prosecution. Judge Marshall finally quashed the subpoena but ruled that if the government decided during trial that it absolutely needed the *Times* reporter, it could serve a new subpoena. (The government never had to issue a new subpoena for Anderson. Ironically, the willingness of other media representatives to do what the *Times* would not do ended up letting the *Times* off the hook.)

There was also a last-ditch effort to persuade Sammie Marshall to come clean. "I don't know why Sammie wants to go through with this," Allison told George Buehler. "I see no reason why he should go down in flames and get convicted as part of the conspiracy to steal the entire twenty-one million dollars. I'll concede his role was secondary. But he *was* involved. Has he put blinders on his conscience? Does Smith have something on him?"

Buehler said he too was at a loss to explain Marshall's stubborn attitude.

"George, let me suggest something neither of us would ordinarily do, but since we know and trust each other, it might be workable," Allison said. "Why don't you think about bringing Sammie in to let me tell him the facts of life face-to-face? You would be present, of course. It might help to avoid a result that neither of us thinks is in his best interest."

Buehler promised to think it over. A week later he brought Marshall into Allison's office for one final attempt at an agreement. Joe Woodall was also present.

"Before we get started," Marshall said, "there's something I want you to know, Mr. Allison. I appreciate the way you all"—he gestured to the agent to indicate that he meant the FBI too—"have treated me. I know there are things that don't look good for me. I've struggled with this decision and thought about what I should do. I couldn't look other people in the eye if I pleaded guilty to something I didn't do."

Allison realized at that moment that this meeting wasn't going to solve anything. But he was determined to try. "Joe and I don't consider you a master criminal or a professional embezzler," he said. "In a real sense, you may have been taken in by Smith too. But on the facts, it's inconceivable to us that you didn't know what was going on. For instance, you knew that he didn't have a line of credit?"

"That's right," Marshall said.

Buehler had already told Allison that Marshall wasn't going along with the line of credit story. But the prosecutor had to make sure Marshall hadn't changed his mind. That would be a strong point for the prosecution in court. *Ladies and gentlemen, even the president of MAPS didn't know anything about a line of credit.*

"You knew the company was losing money," Allison continued. "Where could you possibly think the money was coming from, Sammie? You knew how close Harold and Ben were. You knew back when you first became acquainted with Harold, and when you left the bank to join him, that he didn't have a dime to his name. So, if it wasn't coming from business income, bank financing or personal wealth, where the heck *was* it coming from? Plus there are specific documents incriminating you—the Telestar cashier's check and the phony branch settlement ticket you admit you filled out. The net effect was that the cashier's check wasn't paid for. That's a false entry in the bank records and probably a nineteen-thousand-dollar misappropriation of bank funds too. Those are the kinds of things that make it difficult for us to accept that you are completely innocent of any wrongdoing. But frankly, based on our overall view of the evidence, we don't think you were the mastermind—Harold was. We hate to see you force us to crucify you by going through a full-scale trial on the conspiracy charge. And let me tell you something—and George will tell you that I'm not just posturing—there is no doubt whatsoever in my mind that if we go to trial against you on the conspiracy charge you're going to be convicted and you're going to do some serious jail time. This meeting is a final effort on our part to avoid a result that is going to be bad for you. We only want you to admit what you did."

"I hear what you're saying and I appreciate it," Marshall said. "But I just don't feel I've done anything wrong. I couldn't live with myself if I plead guilty."

"Sammie, I can't tell you how sorry I am to hear that," Allison said. "I guess we're going to have to do this the hard way."

* * *

In presenting the picture of Harold Smith's empire to the jury, Allison knew the government would need someone to describe the MAAS amateur boxing program. He wanted the jury to get a feel for the spending that was required to keep the amateur program going. The obvious person to talk about MAAS in detail was its president, Bob Campbell. Allison thought—based on Campbell's grand jury appearance—that he could count on Campbell telling the truth on the witness stand.

The problem was that Campbell did not want to cooperate with the government. He refused to come in for a pretrial interview. He told the FBI that he was too busy trying to find a job so he could pay his mortgage payment. His obvious irritation left Joe Woodall, who had called Campbell, with the distinct impression that Campbell believed the government was responsible for his failure to find employment. Finally, Campbell even stopped returning the agent's phone calls.

By mid September it was getting too close to trial for comfort. Allison decided to try the direct approach himself. He called Campbell's home. A woman answered. She said Bobby wasn't home, but she would be happy to take a message.

"Is this Mrs. Campbell?" Allison asked.

"Yes it is."

"My name is Dean Allison. I'm an Assistant United States Attorney. The prosecutor in the Wells Fargo embezzlement case."

I see.

"If you've got two minutes, maybe I can explain the situation and see if there's some way you can help." Allison knew he was taking a chance. He was going to try to win the wife over in the hope she could convince her husband. He knew that the result might be to alienate Bob Campbell even more, but at this point Allison figured he had little to lose.

"Go ahead." Her voice sounded cool but not unfriendly.

"I know you're up against it financially and that Bobby hasn't worked since MAPS was closed. I know he's having a hard time finding a job. From what I've heard, Bobby seems to think the government has black-balled him with prospective employers. If he thinks that, I can see why he doesn't want to cooperate. One reason I'm calling is to let you know we are not doing that. In fact, he can refer prospective employers to us, have them call this office or the FBI agents, if he wants to. We'll tell them the truth—that he's been cooperative and that he's not suspected of any wrongdoing. We haven't seen one iota of evidence that he was involved in any criminal activities."

"I appreciate that," she said. "I'll talk to him about it."

"Thanks very much, Mrs. Campbell. I hope to hear from Bob."

Later in the week Campbell called and said he was willing to come in for his interview. Allison told Woodall, "There are some things I want to show him. I think they might change his mind about Smith."

Actually there were three things Allison wanted to show Campbell. The first two were excerpts from Smith's grand jury testimony. Since the transcripts had been released to Smith's counsel, they were no longer protected by grand jury secrecy requirements. The third item would be, Allison suspected, an emotional bombshell for Campbell.

"Bob, I appreciate your coming down," Allison said. "I hope by the time we're finished that you're going to consider it time well spent."

"I don't know what you said to my wife, but it made an impression on her," Campbell admitted. "She sat me down, and we had a long talk. I decided she was right, and I had better come down and talk to you. But I've got to tell you, up front, for me it's poison to be here talking to you. In my community, you just don't cooperate with The Man."

"You're under subpoena," Allison said. "Tell people it was compulsory. They don't know a subpoena doesn't cover pretrial witness interviews."

"Even so, it's going to hurt that I'm a witness for the government against a black man. Where I come from, you just don't do that. Now let's get it over with, since I'm here. What do you want?"

"The first thing I want to do is to let you see who's been playing straight with you and who hasn't," Allison said. "I know you've been a buddy of Harold's all the way back to college. But you and I have seen different sides of him. I think you owe it to yourself to expose yourself to some things we've got here. Let me show them to you, and then you draw your own conclusions."

"What are they?"

"Remember telling the grand jury about that day when Harold came into the office with some papers talking about how he'd just obtained all the money the business was ever going to need? You indicated he led you to believe that those papers were for a line of credit."

Campbell nodded.

"All right. I want you to read this." He pushed a thick black three-ring binder containing Smith's grand jury transcript in front of Campbell. The appropriate section was marked. In it Smith swore that he had *never received any papers* relating to his supposed line of credit.

When Campbell was finished, he pushed the binder away. To Allison's surprise, he seemed unimpressed.

"You're a sophisticated businessman, Bob," Allison said. "Forget this is Harold Smith for a minute. Would you believe, based on your business background, that someone would indebt himself for that amount of money and not have any paperwork reflecting it? Ask yourself if that makes any sense."

"Okay. Now what?"

Allison flipped the binder open to another section. "Read the next two pages. You'll see that Harold testified he got an unlimited line of credit—no fixed amount—from a bank that had never lent him more than fifty thousand dollars before, with no security, no collateral, while his business was losing money hand over fist, with no restriction on what he could do with the money, no fixed repayment date, and he can't even remember what *kind* of papers he signed."

Campbell read and then looked up with a smidgen of a smile. "Yeah, I have a little trouble accepting that."

Allison smiled too. "Obviously, I have a *great* deal of trouble accepting that. Finally, this last thing I suspect is going to be painful for you. I know you are close to Harold and have stayed loyal to him."

Campbell nodded. He was proud of his loyalty to his friend.

"I'm going to play a tape recording of a phone conversation between Smith and Tony Key. It was made in April of this year, within a few days of

Harold's arrest, around the same time he was calling you and other friends almost daily for help." *It'll show you,* Allison thought, *how two-faced your friend really is.*

Campbell looked unconcerned as Allison set a dictating machine in front of him and plugged it in.

"You're welcome to listen to the entire tape to satisfy yourself that it's genuine and that we haven't taken this out of context," Allison said. "There are some other things you might find interesting. But this is the portion I want you to hear." He hit the play button and sat back.

Smith's voice was loud and audible, answering a concern voiced by Key that Teri was being criticized by Campbell. "Fuck Bobby Campbell," Smith said with apparent disdain.

Campbell, sitting with his arms crossed, dropped his head.

Allison reached around and turned off the machine. Nearly a minute of silence ensued. He had no intention of interrupting Campbell's troubled thoughts.

Finally, Campbell took a deep breath and looked up. "All right, let's get down to business. What is it you expect me to testify to?"

***

It had been a difficult few months for Ben Lewis. In fact it had been the worst time of his life. To avoid public attention and the press hounds who staked out his house, he slipped out at midnight to grocery shop at a twenty-four-hour market. Though he had changed his phone number and had given the new one out to only a few people, he monitored his calls with a message machine, deciding which ones to pick up. Ben realized he was not famous as much as he was infamous. He had always felt he was going to make a mark in life. But he had had no intention of doing it this way.

In the two months or so before Harold Smith's arrest, Lewis had lost twenty-three pounds. He had been unable to eat or sleep, and he desperately needed to do both. His brother in St. Louis invited him to come back for a visit. Everyone—Allison and the FBI included—agreed that the break might do Ben good. When Ben had stepped off the plane, his brother had almost walked past him. He had not recognized the gaunt, defeated man who stood before him with no smile or sparkle. In the supportive environment of his brother's family, Ben had gained some weight and gotten some rest. He returned to Los Angeles just in time to hear of Harold's arrest on the television, which was a blessed relief. It was time Harold started paying for what he had done too. Since then, Lewis had been going over the past couple years of his life in painful detail with the FBI agents. In fact he had visited the FBI office so often that he knew all the receptionists by their first names. A weight had been lifted when he finally entered his guilty plea before Judge Marshall, but he still had to get through the trial. That, he knew, would not be easy. Harold and Sammie and their lawyers would all be out to get him.

Then, on September 13, Lewis arrived at the FBI offices for his first pretrial interview with the prosecutor. He couldn't believe that he had to repeat everything he had already told the agents. But Dean Allison said he had to hear it with his own ears. Compared to the easygoing personalities of Joe Woodall and Chuck Jones, Allison seemed intense. Ben found himself tightening slightly, trying to get used to the change in style. That first day it took them six hours just to get to the first check Ben had held for Smith. Allison was clearly a stickler for detail. Ben was feeling worn-out as they kept on going into the evening as if the sun had never set.

For his part, Allison could see Lewis needed to understand why they were doing this, why he was here and why he had to go over the entire story again. It was time for a pep talk. "Ben, at the trial all gun barrels are going to be aimed at you. I follow a theory like Vince Lombardi's: if you make practice as tough as possible, then the game is not nearly as difficult. By the time you walk into the courtroom, you'll feel comfortable. You'll know your stuff cold. You'll be telling the truth and will have nothing to hide. You're going to have to make these last two and a half years of your life into a movie that's running on a continuous strip in your head. You have to be able to stop it at any point and tell the viewers—in this case, the jurors—what happened, who was there, what they said and what they were wearing. You're going to have to memorize these years. You've got to know them in your gut and in your head."

That struck a responsive chord with the former competitive athlete in Lewis. They went on for several more hours that night. Allison was impressed with Ben's memory and demeanor. He came across as sincere and likeable, two crucial attributes for any witness. He didn't make things up, either. If he didn't know the answer to a question, he would say so. But with time to think, he could usually fill in the gaps. In each instance they would check his memory against the records the government had amassed from the bank and MAPS, and almost every time Lewis was accurate.

The two men had several more brutal marathon sessions before they had gone through the entire sequence of events. Allison had some other matters to attend to, and he gave Lewis a week off. "But every night I want you to sit down and replay a portion of that movie in your head," Allison said. "Do it in a hot bath, sit in your favorite chair with a glass of Scotch, wherever it's most comfortable for you. You've got to treat this as homework."

It hadn't taken Allison long to begin to feel sympathetic toward Lewis. Obviously he was no angel; he had stolen more than $21 million from his employer. If the prosecution won, he would have to go to jail for it; Allison would have to recommend that Ben Lewis spend time behind bars. Still, the two men on opposite sides of the criminal justice system's fence began to develop a friendship. They came to like and respect each other and look forward to their sessions. Both hoped the effort was going to help convict Harold Smith.

CHAPTER THIRTY-SIX

After two days of jury selection, the United States of America versus Ross Eugene Fields and Sammie Marshall began on October 5, 1981, at 8 a.m. sharp. The court clerk asked the four attorneys standing at the bar to announce their appearances for the record. Then Judge Consuelo Marshall addressed the jury. "This morning we are going to actually commence the trial by starting with opening statements. We will start with the government."

Allison's plan was to introduce the players, familiarize the jurors with the terminology involved and give them an overview of the embezzlement scheme. As he began, he was precise, calm and confident, a tone that would not change throughout the ten-week trial.

"This case involves a scheme by three men—Sammie Marshall and Harold Smith and a third man, codefendant Lloyd Benjamin Lewis, whom you will hear referred to throughout this trial as Ben Lewis. A scheme to steal over twenty-one million dollars from the Wells Fargo Bank right here in Los Angeles and to use these embezzled funds to create a boxing empire and to support a lavish life-style for themselves and their associates. Mr. Lewis will testify as a government witness. Right in front of you he will admit his own guilt, and he will describe the entire scheme to you from the inside out. From Mr. Lewis's testimony and from the dozens of other witnesses and hundreds of documents that the government will produce to corroborate him, you are going to learn how this money was stolen and how the scheme all began."

Because it was important for the jury to understand exactly how the money was stolen, Allison then gave an explanation of the branch settlement system, using a large chart with an overlay to illustrate the complex flow of debits and credits. The jurors had to appreciate how all that money was siphoned out of the bank without alerting anyone. "If you understand the Wells Fargo branch settlement system," he told them, "you will have no trouble understanding this case." He was pleased to see jurors nodding their heads throughout his explanation. In concluding an hour later, he said, "When all the evidence is in, I don't think there will be any doubt in your minds that these two defendants did exactly what the grand jury's indictment charged they did, and I expect that at that time you will find both of them guilty as charged."

Howard Moore went next, after George Buehler reserved his opening statement on Sammie Marshall's behalf. "You will see that over a two- or two-and-a-half-year period of time, the Muhammad Ali Track Club and Boxing Club won over twenty trophies and awards," Moore said. "That was the kind of program that Harold Smith had … Harold kept struggling and kept hustling, kept working hard, he and his wife and others who believed in him, until he ran into a fellow who worked at the Miracle Mile branch of Wells Fargo Bank. Now, he wasn't just a person who worked there. He was a manager of the Miracle Mile branch. His name is Gene Kawakami, who will probably be a witness in this case. Mr. Kawakami believed in Harold's program to the extent that he even took money from his own relatives to invest in the program but without telling Harold that he had done so. And Mr. Kawakami told Harold Smith whatever he needed from the bank, he had it … Wells Fargo is the nation's eleventh largest bank, with branches throughout California and in many foreign countries, with assets over twenty billion dollars—not million, but *billions* of dollars. It is certainly in a position to advance Harold Smith a line of credit. But in any event, Harold Smith believed that he had a line of credit from the bank, and he acted on it.

"Mr. Smith contends in this case that there was no criminal intent on his part to steal money from Wells Fargo Bank. He contends further that there was no knowledge on his behalf to take any money from Wells Fargo, that is, that he didn't know that there was stolen money from Wells Fargo that was coming into his bank account … We are going to ask you at the conclusion of this case, as reasonable, intelligent people, to return verdicts on thirty-two counts. I want thirty-two verdicts of not guilty as to each count. It is pure and simple: the evidence shows that Harold J. Smith was engaged in legitimate business which he conducted in a legitimate way."

* * *

Brian Feeley was one of the government's first witnesses. He explained the nature and duties of Ben Lewis's job at the bank and how much he had trusted Ben to do his job properly. It was straightforward and largely uneventful testimony. During cross-examination, Harold Smith handed Howard Moore a note with a question to ask the witness, something which would happen often throughout the trial.

"Mr. Feeley," Moore said, looking down at the slip of paper, "did you have occasion to borrow the sum of six thousand dollars from Harold Smith?"

"No, sir."

"You never borrowed any money from Harold Smith?"

"No, sir."

"In any amount?"

"No, sir."

Allison couldn't imagine where Moore was headed. Then the defense attorney dropped the line of questioning just as suddenly as he had begun it and went on to something else. Feeley was dismissed from the stand a few minutes later. To Allison it appeared that Moore had reached a dead end with the borrowed money query.

Feeley was only one of several bank employees who testified about the innermost financial operations of the bank—which Allison knew would be the most boring part of the case. But he had decided to put on the banking testimony first because these witnesses would be precorroborating what Lewis would later say about bank procedures generally and, specifically, about the impropriety of the procedures he had followed to carry out the embezzlement at Beverly Drive. Judy MacLardie, the persistent Miracle Mile assistant manager, testified about sensing trouble with the computer tracer and being disturbed by Lewis's behavior. Lloyd Gasway, the ex-cop turned bank auditor, told about uncovering the numerous progressions on microfilm during that long weekend in late January. Luna Einy, a tiny, shy Indian woman employed at Beverly Drive, told of seeing Mr. Lewis slip into the bank after hours, go to the branch settlement encoding machine and thereafter place slips of paper into the office mail pouch. All of this testimony was designed to set the stage for Lewis.

Allison had made an important decision regarding his two star witnesses: Ben would go on the stand early, after the first few banking witnesses, to lay out the embezzlement scheme in full and give the jury a sense of overall perspective on the conspiracy. This also had the advantage of allowing the prosecutor to surround Lewis with corroborating witnesses both before and after he testified. Teri Key would be saved for the midway point. She would provide a natural transition between the evidence showing where all Smith's money came from and the evidence showing where it all went. She would begin the boxing testimony with a bang and strongly corroborate Lewis as well. The last portion of the evidence would then prove the multiple charges of interstate transportation of the stolen money and also outline the motive for the entire scheme: to take over boxing.

Lewis seemed ready for his court appearance. He appeared strong physically and psychologically. He was jogging daily and going to church regularly with Gladys. He knew the facts of the case and was anxious to get on with his testimony, to tell the world about how he had been drawn into crime by the master manipulator, Harold Smith, and his former best friend, Sammie Marshall. Still, like any careful trial lawyer, Allison worried about his chief witness until the day he actually took the stand. Witnesses could seem fine right up until the night before and then fall apart, showing up for court zonked on tranquilizers or reeking of booze. It had happened before.

It was not going to happen with Ben Lewis. He strolled into court looking refreshed, relaxed and ready to go. No one would have guessed that he had just slipped into the men's room and doused cold water on his face, trying to calm himself. His turmoil was inward, where it had been stored for the past three years. As he passed the defense table before the jury came in, he waved an index finger at Smith as if to say "Now you're gonna get what you have coming."

Allison started off by taking Lewis through the checks he and Sammie Marshall had held for Smith at the bank at the beginning of the scheme. These were illuminated for the jury on an overhead projector. Ben also showed the jury on a blackboard how these checks had mounted up until he rolled them over with his first falsely encoded branch settlement ticket in early November 1978. He had rehearsed this with Allison, the two of them practicing long hours in an empty grand jury room upstairs in the courthouse. Ben started out sounding nervous and speaking too fast. But he soon settled down. All the work was paying off. He clearly knew his stuff—dates, amounts, who called him about specific checks, how the money was spent, who spent it, all the essential points. In relating the details, Lewis began to implicate both Smith and Marshall on the criminal charges. For example, Ben told of the February 13, 1979, meeting in the Beverly Drive parking lot—when Harold and Sammie had asked him to give them a cashier's check for $223,000 payable to Muhammad Ali so that the Champ would take part in the "Down Under" tour. He described many direct discussions with Smith concerning the embezzlement, but the parking lot meeting was one of the few incidents that tied Marshall directly to the overall conspiracy to steal $21 million from Wells Fargo.

Lewis was on the stand for the government for three days. At the end of one session Allison asked him, "Did Harold Smith have a line of credit at the bank?"

"No," Lewis said. "He had *me.*"

The defense lawyers objected vigorously. Judge Marshall carefully considered the objection—throughout the trial she was judicious at every turn, obviously wishing to avoid grounds for a retrial or reversal—and struck the last three words from the record, advising the jury to disregard them. But the fact was that the jury *had* heard the words—"he had me." It was a telling comment on Ben Lewis's role as Harold Smith's "personal banker" at Wells Fargo.

In the hallway, as they left the courtroom, Allison casually asked Lewis if he had noticed that they always seemed to end his testimony before a recess—morning, lunch, afternoon and at the end of the day—on a strong, dramatic point.

"Come to think of it, yeah," Ben said, beginning to grin. "It's almost like it was planned that way."

Allison just smiled.

Lewis had seen up close how hard Allison prepared for the trial. Despite the grueling preparation on the facts and substance of the case, the prosecutor still was not taking any chances. Appearances counted too, as Allison had explained to Lewis. For instance, Ben had shown up for court the first day wearing a silk pocket handkerchief. Allison didn't like the looks of it—"Too flashy"—and had Lewis take it off and put it in his briefcase. Also—and Allison was most insistent about this—Lewis was to leave his telephone-equipped black Cadillac Seville at home. "I don't want a juror ever seeing you get into it," Allison had explained. (In fact the car had been purchased with embezzled money, and Wells Fargo eventually seized it, along with Lewis's home.) For his court appearances, Lewis was driving a friend's beat-up car.

Of course the prosecutor wasn't alone in appreciating the importance of external appearance in court. Sammie Marshall had shown up his first day in court festooned with gold jewelry: neck chains, bracelets, rings. Allison couldn't believe it—here is a banker accused of embezzlement and he's wearing a ton of expensive gold jewelry. It must have had the same effect on Marshall's attorney because that was the last time the former banker appeared in court so adorned.

Howard Moore's cross-examination of Lewis did no harm to Ben's version of events. In fact, if anything it seemed to strengthen rather than weaken the case against Smith. Moore's questions related almost exclusively to minor incidents—the 1979 trip to Australia, ownership of the racehorses, that sort of thing. From the viewpoint of the prosecutor and the FBI agents—Woodall and Jones had observed many criminal trials—Lewis's most crucial testimony regarding the embezzlements and Smith's role in them had been left unchallenged. They just hoped the jurors saw it that way.

George Buehler's cross of Lewis was a different matter. He did just what Allison would have done in his place. Buehler took Lewis through his testimony against Sammie Marshall, trying to show that with respect to each critical incident it was simply a matter of Lewis's word against Marshall's. Then Buehler retraced Lewis's admitted crimes and dishonesty. In short, the defense attorney was doing what he should have—attacking the credibility of the government's star witness. Every experienced criminal trial lawyer is aware of a tendency on the part of juries to disbelieve people who are "singing for their supper." Witnesses who have made deals with the prosecution to save their own skins are inevitably held in less regard than those who are not guilty of any wrongdoing. But Lewis stood his ground throughout the ordeal, maintaining his cool even when Buehler finally asked about his friendship with Marshall and then concluded rhetorically, "How many other people are you willing to betray?"

Teri Key began her testimony in an extremely nervous state. After her experience in the Jennifer King trial—when the vicious personal attacks had caused her so much anguish—she could hardly be blamed. No one in the courtroom knew her secret weapon: a small gold cross she kept clutched in one hand throughout her appearance. It made her feel closer to her late grandfather, a minister with whom she had lived for much of her childhood. She prayed for strength and patience to get through this final test.

As Allison took her through the story step by step, she began to relax. She had spent almost a week preparing with him too. She described how Smith spent millions of dollars for women, cars, planes, partying and fighters, all in an effort to build his boxing empire. She knew this information firsthand from handling the company checkbooks. At Allison's direction, she used the check register to identify check by check the huge amounts of money spent on Smith's luxurious life-style. In addition Teri related how Smith had misled her by describing the embezzled monies Lewis was depositing into the accounts as "transfers" from the TV networks and withdrawals from a nonexistent personal savings account.

Key corroborated Lewis on a host of small details and incriminated Sammie Marshall by testifying that the cashier's checks Sammie gave to fighters and to the California State Athletic Commission had never been paid for out of the company checkbooks. Lewis had testified that these were "free"—meaning embezzled—cashier's checks he had issued on Smith's instructions, which Marshall would usually pick up at the bank.

Smith's story that he had been given a line of credit by Gene Kawakami looked weak at best in light of Key's testimony. As a MAPS insider for two years, she had never heard anything about a line of credit. Furthermore, she testified that while Kawakami had been around the office a lot in early 1979, when she first began her job at MAPS, the last year or so the two men had not been close at all. Smith, she said, regularly avoided Kawakami's phone calls and visits to the office. The significance of this was obvious: if Kawakami was giving Smith an unlimited credit line at the bank, why would Smith be avoiding him?

On cross-examination Moore challenged Key to name all the guests in attendance at one party she testified about. He hoped to impeach her credibility by showing that she couldn't back up her statement with specifics. The effect was just the opposite. Methodically counting them off on her fingers one after the other, she named all fifty guests. Teri came off sincere, believable and knowledgeable. Better yet, she was not singing for her supper. Here was a good-hearted woman who had believed in Harold Smith throughout the years and then, painfully and reluctantly, came to understand that she had been conned like so many others. Her testimony, delivered in her soft, Southern accent, gave no indication that she was out to get anyone or had a chip on her shoulder.

Then came the boxing witnesses. One who could do damage to Sammie Marshall's claim that he knew nothing about the embezzlement scheme was Dale Ashley, chief investigator for the Washington Athletic Commission. In his pretrial interview Ashley had told the prosecutor and the agents how he had met Marshall in connection with a Leo Randolph fight in Seattle. While Marshall and Ashley were talking in a hotel room before the fight, Sammie had mentioned that MAPS had a "line of credit at Wells Fargo," according to Ashley. That could be potentially explosive testimony, Allison thought: Marshall was going around talking about a line of credit that he knew full well did not exist. False statements like that about the source of MAPS's money tied him directly to the conspiracy.

Ashley wanted very much to be a good witness, but, on the stand, when Allison asked him what Marshall had said in the hotel room regarding MAPS's source of funds, Ashley responded, "I just said to Sammie, 'I hear that Mr. Smith's wife is a millionaire and that he was getting his money from a bank based on his wife being a millionaire,' and Sammie just passed it off and said, 'Yes,' and that is all he ever said."

Allison couldn't believe Ashley had neglected to mention the all-important remark by Marshall about a line of credit. But there was nothing the prosecutor could do about it except let it go.

A few minutes later, during a recess, Ashley came up to Allison in the corridor and asked how he had done.

"Fine, Dale, except what happened to the line of credit business?"

Ashley suddenly looked stricken. "Oh no!" he exclaimed. "I forgot to mention what Sammie said about the line of credit!"

"Don't worry about it," Allison said. But the prosecutor was in fact worried. He needed every bit of evidence that could be mustered against Marshall.

A highlight of the trial—at least for the boxing fans in the courtroom—was the day heavyweight champion Larry Holmes showed up to testify as a prosecution witness. Holmes was nattily dressed in gray wool slacks, dress shirt, maroon tie and tan tweed jacket. He walked through the hushed courtroom with the rolling stride of an athlete who cannot hide his raw physical power. When he sat at the witness stand, he folded his hands in front of him. Clearly visible was a large ruby ring—a blood-red stone set in gold and encircled with diamonds. It was the WBC heavyweight champion's ring, worn by only a handful of men in history.

As usual, after the witness identified himself and spelled his last name for the record, Allison asked the standard question: "What is your occupation?"

"Heavyweight champion of the world—the only champion."

"I beg your pardon?"

Holmes wagged his finger at the jury. "The *only* champion. And don't you forget it!"

Holmes told about the various times Smith had tried to sign him and all the money that the man from MAPS had brought with him each time. Describing an incident when Smith had come to his office in Easton, Pennsylvania, with $925,000 in cash and cashier's checks, Holmes explained, "He opened up a bag, and I never seen this kind of money before. It was a whole lot of money. And I says, 'Damn'—excuse me— and I says, 'It is getting hot in here,' or something like that, 'and I think I might open the window and cool off.' " When he asked Smith where all the money came from, Holmes said Smith answered that he had "some friends in Las Vegas."

Following Holmes to the stand was a host of other witnesses associated with boxing. They all described different stories from Smith regarding the source of his vast funds. Representing the media were two sportswriters:

Mike Marley of the New York *Post* and Jack Fiske of the San Francisco *Examiner*. From the boxing world came English fight manager Mickey Duff, who one day in early January 1981 had walked out of MAPS carrying $350,000 cash for two planned fights. Dr. Ferdie Pacheco of NBC Sports testified, "[Harold] said, 'My wife's relatives died and left her a lot of money and I have two millionaires behind me.'" New York fight promoter Sam Glass had the most bizarre tale to tell: "[Harold] told me that he had investors from the Middle East and that they were supplying some of the money ... He [said] he was walking down the street when he saw an older man in the process of being mugged, and he intervened. And that fellow introduced him to other people and they became friendly with him and they were interested in boxing ... and they put up part of the money." It all formed a clear picture of Smith deceiving the boxing world about the source of his seemingly unlimited funds.

Former MAPS card girl Arlene "Tweetie" Alexander appeared as a government witness. On a clothes rack the blue business suit worn by her might have been described as conservative. But Tweetie was no clothes rack. She filled and overfilled the suit in a stunning, sensual way, causing a couple of the male jurors to wink at the prosecutor as she approached the stand. She was fully made-up, with bright red lipstick and nail polish. Her almost waist-length black hair shimmered in the light, and her perfume wafted through the air as she settled in the witness chair. The voluptuous image cut by the ex-card girl helped illustrate the glamorous, high-flying nature of life at MAPS during the Wells Fargo embezzlement better than any documentary evidence ever could. Though in a pretrial interview Alexander volunteered that she had slept with Smith, Allison promised that the government would not go into such personal details at the trial.

Tweetie testified that she was employed as a cocktail waitress and that she had been hired by Smith in January 1980 as a card girl.

Allison kept the questioning at an easy pace, hoping the jury would think about the scenario of so many beautiful young women getting paid so much money for such little work.

"Did you ever receive any money from Harold Smith other than your regular salary as a card girl?"

"Sometimes we received money for going shopping in different cities or if we went to Las Vegas ... or if he won at the horse races, he would give us some money."

"To your knowledge, did any of the other card girls receive money from Mr. Smith under circumstances like the ones you have just described?"

"Yes."

"Did there come a time when you received a bonus from Mr. Smith?"

"At one time we received a check ... because we weren't working or doing any other jobs."

"How much was the check you received?"

"Three thousand dollars."

"And how many of the other card girls received three-thousand-dollar checks at that time?"

"All of them, which was probably about nine or ten of us that were working at that time."

Now for still another version of where Smith got all his money. "Let me direct your attention to late December of 1980. Did you have occasion to hear Mr. Smith make certain remarks concerning money at that time?"

"Yes."

"Where was it you heard him make those remarks?"

"In his home."

"Tell us what he said."

"He said that he was tired of the boxing business and after February he was going to take a vacation. Then he started going into a conversation about money, saying that he had some money saved in his wall. And if he decided to quit the business that he would still be okay. He took us outside and showed us the wall, and then he came back in and proceeded to tell us that his wife's father had died and she had inherited $20 million. She told Harold to take the money and do what he had to do with it."

"Do you recall Mr. Smith making a remark on the subject of fame at that time?"

"Well, Harold had a statement that he didn't care who got the fame, just so he was the one that went to the bank."

***

Though early in the investigation there was indeed fear that Harold Smith might have a multimillion-dollar stash, the government eventually stopped worrying about that. The reason was the meticulous accounting work done by FBI Special Agents Chuck Jones and Joe Woodall.

Chuck Jones took the stand and testified to every dollar that was received and spent in the MAPS and MAAS fight operations. Then Woodall testified to an accounting of the embezzled funds, using a chart that was uncovered and shown to the jury.

"Will you describe," Allison said, "line by line, how the chart illustrates the summary calculations that you prepared?"

Woodall used a pointer to help the jury follow along. "In going through the [branch settlement] progressions—the total of deposits to the Bodak Promotions account was $5,297,500. The deposits to Harold J. Smith Productions account was $7,680,500. Adding ... cashier's checks ($5,232,434.81), wire transfers ($79,633.88), and deposits to other accounts, the total amount of the progressions is $21,305,705.18. The difference [between this and Chuck Jones's total expenditures figure] is exactly 18 cents. We have accounted for 11 cents of that difference."

The FBI had accounted for all but *seven cents* of the embezzled money.

They also knew exactly how the money had been spent—with the exception of checks made out by Harold and Lee Smith to "cash." That totaled in excess of $1,600,000—clearly just pocket money for the high-rolling Smith and his entourage.

***

Sammie Marshall's attorney, George Buehler, put on a good defense for his client. Marshall testified in his own behalf and came across as sincere and sympathetic, just as he had when he had met with the prosecutor and the FBI agents prior to his indictment. While in Allison's judgment there was strong evidence against Marshall on the false entry and embezzlement charges—based upon Marshall's issuance of the Telstar cashier's check—there was not nearly as much evidence against him as against Smith on the conspiracy count. Allison knew that the case against Marshall was still up for grabs.

On the stand Marshall insisted upon his innocence. Buehler handled his client well—in legal slang, the defense attorney "drew the teeth" by asking Marshall directly about the most damaging evidence against him rather than letting the prosecutor do it on cross-examination. Buehler had his client give reasonable and apparently plausible explanations for each potentially damaging incident. As Buehler had expected, the thrust of the government's case against Marshall appeared to be coming down to Lewis's word against Marshall's—and Lewis's testimony would be presumptively suspect in the jurors' eyes because of his confessed involvement in the crime. Holding checks and approving overdrafts for Harold Smith had been Ben's idea, Marshall said. He had sent Smith's bad checks back to Beverly Drive because Lewis had cashed them there. It was Lewis, not he, who had done all the favors for Smith at the bank, according to Marshall. Lewis had called and asked him to issue the $19,000 Telstar cashier's check, telling him to branch settle the charge over to Beverly Drive and reflect the transaction as an incorrectly posted item. Bankers acted on instructions like these from their colleagues all the time, he testified. Marshall denied he had told Lewis how to manipulate the branch settlement system. He denied that he was in the parking lot with Smith that day Lewis handed over the cashier's check for Muhammad Ali. He also denied having any idea there was a massive embezzlement going on during the two years or so that he was president of MAPS.

Allison figured that the cross-examination of Marshall would make or break the case against him. He would have to be tough but at the same time not bully the likeable defendant. He didn't want to create a backlash of sympathy for Marshall among the jurors. Rather, he wanted to show— pointedly and irrefutably—that Sammie had been up to his neck in the scheme from the beginning.

The prosecutor began carefully. His first objective was to get Marshall to discredit Smith's story. *Here was the president of MAPS, and he never heard of the alleged line of credit.* Marshall also acknowledged that as a member of the MAPS board of directors he had never even voted upon any resolutions authorizing bank financing or loans. So much for external sources of funding.

As part of his early effort to put the blame on Gene Kawakami for "one of the biggest cases of fraud, embezzlement, illegal loans and kickbacks involving numerous branches and personnel within the Wells Fargo Bank system," Smith had pointed accusingly, in a letter released to the press, at the $357,000 debit to his account made by Kawakami. Allison had previously put a copy of the letter in evidence and now asked Marshall about these claims by Smith.

"Who was it who told you about the debit?"

"Harold told me first."

"He didn't say anything to you about a scandal involving numerous branches and personnel in the Wells Fargo system, did he?"

"No."

"Let me direct your attention to the latter portion of this letter, referring to a '$200-$300-million-dollar rip-off of the bank that has gone on for a period of nine years or more.' Do you see that?"

"Yes."

"Mr. Smith didn't say anything about that in August of 1980 either, did he?"

"No, he didn't."

Now that Marshall had been used as a weapon against Smith, it was time to change the focus. Marshall had claimed in his direct testimony that he had no idea MAPS and MAAS were funded by embezzled money. At this point he had already admitted knowing that the companies' millions had not come from a line of credit, bank loans or any other third-party financing. Now Allison took him through the losses on the fights. Yes, Marshall admitted, he knew quite well how much money MAPS was losing, as much as several hundred thousand dollars on each fight. Yes, he knew that MAPS's losses totaled in the millions. That left only one other possible source for all the money. Marshall was quickly boxed in by that one too. He acknowledged that from the time he had first gotten to know Smith until early 1979 (when the embezzlement scheme was well underway), both Smith and his wife Lee had been almost constantly broke. As far as he knew, Marshall conceded after a few minutes, MAPS's millions were not coming from the Smiths' personal or family fortune, because there wasn't one. Now the trap was closing, and Marshall's admissions had sealed off all possible avenues of escape. Yes, he knew of the phenomenal amounts being spent to pay fighters. Yes, he knew that enormous sums were going for fancy offices, racehorses, planes, women, travel, parties, new cars, etc. So where did he think all these millions were coming from if not from third-party financing, operating revenues or Smith's personal funds? Marshall had nowhere to turn.

The next subject was Marshall's claim that it had been Ben Lewis, not he, who had done all the banking favors for Smith. Continuing to use the misdirection technique so that Marshall would not see where they were headed until it was too late, Allison asked him about his early relationship with Smith, opening that first account for him and approving dozens of overdraft checks for him, first at Beverly Drive and then at Miracle Mile. Ben Lewis had no part in any of that, Marshall acknowledged. And then there were the loans. Not one or two, but a total of *nine* loans ranging from $3,000 to $35,000 in just a few months. Again, Ben Lewis had nothing to do with any of these transactions.

Moreover, Marshall's loans to Smith followed a distinct pattern, which emerged as the prosecutor relentlessly took him through them one by one. Each time, the loan had been short-term, disbursed in the form of a cashier's check. Each time, Smith's checking account had been overdrawn, and the loan was made to tide him over when his business was short of funds. It was no coincidence that the same pattern fit Marshall's issuance of the Telstar cashier's check in October 1978.

The series of questions about Marshall's approving overdraft checks and making loan after loan for Smith also showed that he had a lengthy history of doing financial favors for Smith at the bank's expense. The prosecutor's questions further established that Marshall had been dishonest and had falsified bank documentation several times in order to do banking favors for Smith. Marshall admitted that he had put someone else's name down as the borrower on three of the nine loan applications in order to conceal the fact that the money was really for Smith.

The last questions in this series were designed to show that besides this suspicious track record Marshall had plenty of motive for showing Lewis how to embezzle money for Smith by falsely encoding and then rolling over branch settlement tickets. In October of 1978, when it had all started, Marshall conceded, he had felt bitter about the bank telling him he had no future there and had already made plans to leave Wells Fargo and go to work for Smith. Given his track record of doing big favors for the promoter at the bank in previous years, it was only logical that Marshall would do another one as he prepared to throw in his lot with Harold Smith and his sports business.

Then came the coup de grace.

Allison handed Marshall a government exhibit that had been entered in evidence. "That is the credit half of the branch settlement you issued to offset the Telstar cashier's check?"

"Yes."

"It is in your handwriting?"

"Yes."

"The transaction description in your handwriting says 'Item Posted Incorrectly.'"

"That's correct."

"And the 'item' was the cashier's check, isn't that so?"

"No."

Allison acted surprised. "It was not?"

"No, it wasn't."

"Was there any other item offset by that branch settlement?"

"When Peter Van Schoonhoven [Telstar Travel's owner] came into the branch, he had an item in his hand. It was some type of invoice … when I called in, I told Ben what I had. Ben indicated for me to put that on it, send it to him, which I did."

"It is your testimony that the word 'item' on that branch settlement referred to nothing?"

"Didn't refer to an item that was to be posted. Correct."

"It didn't refer to *any* item that was to be posted?"

"It didn't refer to an item that had been posted."

"So you put 'Item Posted Incorrectly' referring to something that had never been posted, is that correct?"

"That's correct."

"So that was false entry on that document, wasn't it?"

"That's correct." *Bang—Marshall had just confessed to one count of the four against him.*

"And you told us earlier that a transaction description on a branch settlement is supposed to reflect the reason money is being transferred between branches?"

"That's correct."

"The statement you put on this branch settlement wasn't the reason that money was being transferred between branches, was it?"

"It was misstated. You are correct."

"Now, it is your testimony that your reason for offsetting that cashier's check with the branch settlement was that Mr. Lewis asked you to do it?"

"That's correct."

"And at the time you discussed it with Mr. Lewis, you had no funds in hand to pay for the cashier's check?"

"I did not."

"Mr. Smith's accounts at your branch were overdrawn?"

"That's correct."

"You knew Mr. Smith's account at Beverly Drive had been closed?"

"That's correct."

"And you told us yesterday that you did not ask Mr. Lewis at the time whether he had any funds to pay for the cashier's check, isn't that so?"

"I don't recall saying anything about that."

"So at the time he asked you to issue that cashier's check to pay Mr. Smith's travel bill, you had no knowledge whether or not there were funds available to pay for that check, isn't that true?"

"That's correct."

"So Mr. Lewis was asking you to disburse bank funds for Mr. Smith's benefit without any way of knowing that the money was available to pay for the cashier's check?"

"In theory, you will be correct."

"And it was at the same time when Mr. Lewis asked you to falsify a bank form in order to carry out that transaction, isn't that true?"

"That's correct."

"So as far as you understood it at the time, Mr. Lewis was asking you to disburse bank funds for Harold Smith's benefit without any identified source of payment and falsify a bank document to carry out the transaction, is that correct?"

"That's correct."

"And you agreed to do that, isn't that right?"

"I did." *That was the clincher. Marshall had admitted agreeing with a coconspirator to commit illegal acts.* Now to sew it up tight.

"Mr. Marshall, did you testify this morning that you never conspired with Ben Lewis to embezzle bank funds?"

"That's correct."

"And you never conspired with Ben Lewis to make false entries in bank records, is that correct?"

"That's correct."

"Do you know what the definition of 'conspiracy' is, Mr. Marshall?"

"Two people sit down and plan something, I believe, is a brief definition of 'conspiracy.' "

"When two people agree to do something unlawful, isn't that so?"

"When two people sit down and plan to do something that is unlawful."

"And then one of them goes ahead and does it?" *Like you,* the prosecutor meant, and everyone in the room knew it.

"That's correct."

Thank you, Sammie Marshall, Allison thought with satisfaction.

* * *

As the trial wore on, a key point of speculation was whether or not Harold Smith would testify. Allison figured there was some chance he would not. Thanks to Smith's three appearances before the grand jury—where he had concocted his untenable line of credit defense—the government had reams of damaging testimony to confront Smith with on cross-examination if he took the stand. Smith's lawyers certainly knew this. Also, they had seen their client heavily impeached on cross-examination at the Jennifer King trial, where Smith came across as a poor witness in his own behalf, especially when pressed about the details of his glib explanations. Finally, Smith's lawyers had seen what had happened to codefendant Sammie Marshall on cross-examination.

Then too, there was less need for Smith to testify than was usually the case for a defendant. The government had introduced lengthy portions of his grand jury testimony in evidence as part of its case, including virtually all of the testimony about his supposed unlimited line of credit and how he had obtained it. Shabby as it was, Smith's story was thus already before the jury so that Moore could argue it in summation without putting his client on the stand and subjecting him to grueling cross-examination.

But then again, Smith was a con artist. As a veteran of many fraud trials, Allison knew it was almost impossible for this sort of defendant to sit silent. Con men seemed congenitally incapable of resisting the urge to try and talk their way out of anything. They usually thought they'd be able to put one over on the trial jurors and convince them of their innocence just as they had convinced victims of their honesty and good intentions so many times before. Allison had never had a fraud defendant decline to take the stand. And Smith was not only a classic con man but had demonstrated a penchant for trying to talk his way out of things many times before. His phony stories to the press about death threats and the Japanese Mafia and his willingness to come in and lie repeatedly to the grand jury had demonstrated this beyond question. So, despite the logical reasons for him not to testify, Smith might find it psychologically impossible to stay off the stand.

The prosecutor would have liked nothing better than to get him on the stand, even though the conviction rate for defendants who fail to testify in their own behalf is extremely high. It would be a fitting climax to the prosecution to prove to the public and the press—out of Smith's own mouth—that this was one of the most dishonest men the banking and sports worlds had ever seen. Smith taunted him about the prospects for such a confrontation. One day when court was over, as the attorneys were packing their boxes of documents and a few reporters were milling about the gallery, an exuberant Smith jumped up onto the witness stand.

"You ready, Mr. DA?" Smith hollered, pounding on the rail. "Let's do it right now! Come on!"

"I'm ready if you are, Harold," Allison said coolly. "Go for it."

As the defense case wore on, Allison tried more than once to ascertain from Howard Moore whether or not Smith would take the stand, but the defense attorney kept hedging. Judge Marshall would order only that the defense and the government reveal their witnesses three names in advance. In Smith's case the notification was next to worthless. The Smith defense team had submitted an absurd initial witness list that included President Jimmy Carter, U.S. Senator Alan Cranston, actor Carl Weathers (who played Apollo Creed in *Rocky)* and other notables. None of them ended up being called. Instead there was a procession of MAPS loyalists who testified about what a fine boxing program Smith had run and how good he was to the young fighters. It was a limp defense, designed only to create sympathy for Smith and almost totally unresponsive to the government's massive evidence of Smith's central role in the embezzlement scheme. If things continued along these lines, Allison told the FBI agents, "Smith is dead and gone."

But nothing is a sure thing in a court of law.

Take the trial appearance of Michael Phenner, Ali's Chicago lawyer. He gave straightforward direct testimony about the money Ali had received for participating in the "Down Under" tour and about a telephone conversation he had had with Smith on February 13, 1979, the day of the "parking lot incident." The following day, Phenner said, Smith showed up in Chicago with the $223,000 cashier's check. Then, on cross-examination, things heated up when Howard Moore had a handwritten note marked for identification. When Moore tried to read the document to the jury, Allison strongly objected. The judge excused the jury so that she could hear from both attorneys and make a ruling.

This was a battle Allison had anticipated because he had turned the document over to the defense attorneys as potential exculpatory evidence. It was a slip of paper, dated January 30, torn from a yellow legal pad. Gene Kawakami's name was written in Phenner's handwriting at the top of the page. Harold Smith's name was also on the note. There were other words and phrases on the page: "February 12 leave Los Angeles"—obviously a reference to the date Ali was originally scheduled to leave for Australia. "Smith had borrowed money but had paid it back." "Jogging suit." And—most important— the phrase *"line of credit."*

The references to the names of Kawakami and Smith were critical to the admissibility of this evidence. If these were notes of a conversation

Phenner had had with Kawakami, then it would give credence to Smith's claim that Kawakami told him he had a line of credit. Here was Kawakami, the defense attorneys would surely argue, telling someone else about the line of credit, just like he'd told Harold about it. On the other hand, if the notes reflected a conversation between Phenner and Smith, then they would be admissible to show Smith's supposed *belief* that he had a line of credit, the heart of his defense. Worse yet, the date of the conversation—whether it was with Kawakami or Smith—was right around the time Smith claimed to have been promised his line of credit, according to his grand jury testimony.

In his pretrial interview with Phenner, Allison quizzed the lawyer extensively about whom he talked to that day. Phenner couldn't remember whether he had talked to Kawakami or not. At Allison's suggestion, Phenner reviewed his time sheets—records lawyers keep in order to bill their clients for their services—for the two-week period overlapping January 30, 1979. During that period Phenner had marked down a number of telephone conversations with Kawakami—but none on January 30. Since Phenner was scrupulous about writing down whom he spoke to, it stood to reason that he probably hadn't spoken to Kawakami on January 30. And Phenner had no recollection of talking to Smith about banking arrangements for the Australia tour either.

"Frankly," Phenner had said in the pretrial interview, "I don't remember whom I talked to that day. I just don't know where the line of credit business came from."

"Okay," Allison had said. "That's the truth then and that's what you should testify to."

At that point Allison had breathed a sigh of relief. In the prosecutor's judgment, Phenner's inability to recall a conversation with either Kawakami or Smith meant that note would be inadmissible as evidence in court. On the other hand, if the note had reflected or brought back Phenner's recall of a specific conversation, then the note or the conversation it reflected would have been admissible. That would have been quite dangerous for the prosecution. Allison saw this note—if its contents got into evidence—as possibly creating a reasonable doubt in the minds of some jurors as to whether Smith thought he had a line of credit.

After a tricky procedural tug-of-war, Judge Marshall ruled that the note could not be entered as evidence unless Phenner said it reflected a conversation that day with a specific individual, either Kawakami or Smith. On the witness stand, Howard Moore tried to squeeze such a recollection out of the Chicago lawyer, but Phenner coolly stuck to the truth and refused to be badgered.

Still, it had been a close call.

* * *

Allison was surprised to see Brian Feeley in the hallway before court one morning. Feeley had testified and been cross-examined by the defense weeks ago. He was standing next to a man in a business suit.

"Morning, Brian," Allison said, smiling. "How are you doing?"

"If you knew why I was here you wouldn't be so friendly," Feeley said. Close up, the banker looked pale and uneasy.

"What's the matter?"

"The defense subpoenaed me to come back and testify."

"So, what's the problem?" While Allison couldn't imagine why the defense would want to resume cross-examining Feeley, he certainly wasn't worried about it. The banker had been a solid government witness.

"We'd better step into a room where we can talk," the man in the suit said.

"This is my personal lawyer," Feeley said, introducing the two attorneys.

They found a small vacant witness room nearby, went inside and closed the door.

"Remember when they asked me if I ever borrowed money from Harold Smith," Feeley said weakly, "and I said no?"

"Yeah," Allison said. "You never did, did you?"

"Yeah, I did."

"How much?"

"Ten thousand dollars."

"Did you pay it back?"

"Oh yes. Within a couple of weeks. I wrote Harold a thank you note and sent him a bottle of champagne. You see, I was selling my house and buying another one. I had two escrows going, and I needed a bridge loan. I couldn't borrow from Wells Fargo, naturally, and Ben heard me talking about it and said he would ask Harold and see if he would lend me the money."

That Feeley had borrowed money from Smith was not nearly as important now as the fact that he had made a misstatement on the witness stand. Allison quickly figured that the information about the loan itself would not seriously harm the government's case. But he was concerned about the appearance of a government witness—and a Wells Fargo banker, since it was Smith's position that the bankers were the real culprits here—knowingly giving false testimony on the stand.

"Why did you testify differently?" Allison asked.

"I—forgot."

"You what?"

"I'm afraid I'm going to lose my job. It's against bank policy for an employee to borrow from a customer. What should I do?"

Feeley's lawyer spoke up for the first time. "I think he should say that he didn't recall the loan in his earlier testimony."

"He should tell the *whole* truth," Allison said. "Brian, tell the jury the truth, that you *did* make a misstatement. Act ashamed—you ought to be."

Feeley took the stand less than an hour later. Howard Moore handed him a document that had been marked for identification before and asked Feeley to describe it.

"It is a thank you note."

"By whom is it written?" Moore asked.

"By myself."

"To whom is it written?"

"To Harold Smith."

"To Harold Smith, the defendant in this case?" Moore was obviously enjoying this.

"Yes, sir."

"When was it written?"

"It was written over a year ago."

"Was that in August of 1980?"

"Around that time, I guess, yes."

"It is in your handwriting?"

"Yes, it is."

"Would you read it out loud to the jury, please?"

Feeley cleared his throat. " 'Harold, I want to thank you very much for helping me out in my time of need. I will have the rest by the end of August, plus interest. I hope that is okay with you. I hope I can reciprocate for you sometime.' "

"Is this acknowledgment of your repayment to Mr. Smith of a loan from him?" Moore asked.

"Yes, it is."

"How much had you repaid?"

"I paid the whole thing back within two weeks."

"Now, do you recall my having previously asked you if you had a loan from Mr. Smith?"

"Yes, I do."

"You stated you did not, is that correct?"

Feeley's face had begun to redden. "I had forgotten about it."

Allison was disappointed in Feeley but decided not to ask the banker any more questions on redirect. It would serve no purpose as far as the government's case was concerned but would simply attract more attention to what was actually a minor incident in terms of the merits of the case. The prosecutor stared stoically ahead as Feeley passed the government table on the way out of the courtroom.

What Brian Feeley had feared would happen a few weeks earlier happened a few hours after he stepped down from the witness stand that day: Wells Fargo Bank dismissed him.

***

During his pretrial preparation, the prosecutor agonized about what to do with Gene Kawakami. If he called him as a prosecution witness, Smith's attorney would score heavily on cross-examination, making much of the fact that the government had canceled a plea agreement with the former banker because he had not been forth-coming. Because Moore would be able to use leading questions—permissible in cross-examination—the defense would have a field day if Kawakami were put on by the government, which would appear to be sponsoring his testimony in the jury's eyes. *You say there was no line of credit and you never told Mr. Smith he had one? Tell us, Mr. Kawakami, aren't you lying now like you lied to the government?* On the other hand, if the government didn't call Kawakami, the defense might be forced to call him. Then the prosecution would be allowed to ask leading questions on cross. *Mr. Smith never repaid the small early loans you made him, did he? And by January 1979, you had closed out all his accounts at Miracle Mile, hadn't you? You never even talked about a line of credit, did you?* Kawakami, of course, would go wherever the government led him.

No matter which side called Kawakami, the substance of his testimony would be favorable to the government. He would deny Smith's ridiculous charges of a $200—$300 million scandal at the bank and his alleged involvement with the Japanese Mafia. The question was how to posture Kawakami so that those denials would be credible to the jury.

After a great deal of thought, Allison decided that he would *not* call Kawakami. Smith's attorneys would then have to put Kawakami on the stand cold, without an opportunity to interview him before trial, because Kawakami certainly would not voluntarily cooperate with them, given their objective to make him out as the real villain. Any good lawyer knew the dangers in asking witnesses questions he didn't know or couldn't force the answers to. On the stand Kawakami would simply deny, again and again, the innuendos and charges Smith had made against him. Kawakami did not *look* like the crook Smith claimed he was, either. Defense counsel would probably get little, if anything, out of him on direct examination.

The chance Allison was taking, of course, was that the defense wouldn't call Kawakami either, and so Kawakami's denials that Smith had a line of credit or that he had been promised one would not come out at all. The importance of that information was not to be underestimated. There was a risk, moreover, that doubt might arise in the jury's mind about what *really* happened if Kawakami never showed up in court. *Who is this mysterious Kawakami character? Do you think it's possible he might be behind all this?* It was a farfetched chance, one of the few the defense might turn in its favor.

As a prosecution witness, Kawakami would be a big bull's-eye, vulnerable to cross-examination. But as a defense witness he would be a powder keg, waiting for the prosecution to set him off. And Allison could light the fuse. That scenario sounded much better.

Howard Moore played into Allison's hands by calling Kawakami to the stand as a defense witness. In direct testimony, Moore got virtually nothing out of Kawakami. Moore asked the judge for a ruling declaring Kawakami a hostile witness, which would allow the defense to ask leading questions on direct. Allison had guessed that would become an issue and had researched the question. Since Kawakami was a defense witness and since he had no plea bargain arrangement with the government, he could not be considered hostile unless he actually showed hostility on the stand, Allison argued. Judge Marshall ruled in favor of the government.

Moore probed Kawakami's loans at the bank, the fact that he had pleaded guilty to a felony and his banking relationship with Smith. The banker also handled Moore's more difficult questions well, remaining calm and composed throughout. It was nonexplosive stuff.

"Mr. Kawakami, did you use embezzled funds to clear overdrafts which Mr. Smith had at the Miracle Mile branch?" Moore asked.

"Yes, I did, sir."

"When did you clear those overdrafts?"

"Approximately September, October, November and December of 78."

When Moore tried to lead Kawakami he got shut down fast.

"And is the reason that you debited the account in August of 1980 because you wanted to be certain that you didn't pay the loans with money advanced on Mr. Smith's line of credit?"

Allison was immediately on his feet. "Object to the leading, your honor."

"Objection sustained."

So went the direct examination.

Allison, as planned, got more latitude and better results on cross-examination.

"Did you have any discussion with Harold Smith about a line of credit on *any* occasion?"

"No, sir."

"Did you ever demand that you be put on the board of Muhammad Ali Amateur Sports as a condition to giving Mr. Smith a multimillion-dollar line of credit?"

"No, sir."

Kawakami was frank in admitting to his indiscretions in rolling over loans that Smith had failed to repay and preparing false loan documents to cover his tracks. But rather than being a fellow perpetrator of Smith's— or someone who had led the innocent Smith down the wrong path— Kawakami was coming across as still another victim of the manipulative and untrustworthy boxing promoter. It was a point Allison wanted to drive home with a vengeance.

"Mr. Kawakami, before you met Mr. Smith was your career at Wells Fargo Bank making progress?"

"Yes, sir."

"Did you expect to go further with the bank in the future?"

"Yes, sir."

"And then you made some loans to Mr. Smith?"

"That's correct."

"And you invested some personal funds with Mr. Smith?"

"That's correct."

"It wasn't repaid until you took matters [the $357,000 debit] into your own hands?"

"That's correct."

"And today you have been convicted of a felony as a result of those transactions?" *As a result of Harold Smith,* he really meant, and everyone in the courtroom knew it.

"That's correct."

"I have nothing further," Allison said, sitting down.

***

Much to Allison's disappointment, the defense rested its case without Harold Smith ever taking the stand. The trial then went into its final phase.

Allison still had a couple of surprises: two rebuttal witnesses (new witnesses are allowed in a trial at this stage to rebut earlier defense evidence). Their testimony was potentially explosive.

The witnesses had been a surprise to the prosecutor too. A couple of days earlier, they had called the U.S. Attorney's office after reading newspaper accounts of Sammie Marshall's denial that he was in the Beverly Drive parking lot on February 13, 1979, when Ben Lewis handed over the $223,000 cashier's check for Ali. Both of the new witnesses worked at the Beverly Drive branch. They were Dennis Ortiz and Robert Nix. Ortiz had worked in operations under Lewis. Nix was a security guard.

Both told Allison they clearly remembered seeing Smith, Lewis *and* *Marshall* together in the parking lot that day. Allison immediately had them come down to his office for an interview. "Why didn't you come forward sooner?" he asked. "Because we didn't know Marshall was denying being there until we read it in the paper," Ortiz answered.

After hearing their stories, Allison kept them under wraps until the end of the defense case. Under the federal criminal discovery rules, rebuttal witnesses are one of the few surprises left in a trial these days. Rebuttal evidence like this could leave the jury with a few parting thoughts before deliberations began. In this case, if the jury disbelieved Marshall's testimony that he wasn't in the parking lot, they almost had to find him guilty on the conspiracy charge. These witnesses, Allison thought, had the potential to achieve just that.

Nix went first. He testified that the bank had closed and he was letting the last few customers out the locked front door when he saw Smith, Marshall and Lewis standing outside the side door in the parking lot. They were there for "two or three minutes," according to Nix. He got busy but noticed them a few minutes later, standing next to a pay phone. Allison had him draw the parking lot, the bank's side door, the positions of the three men and the location of the pay phone on a blackboard. Nix did so in great detail.

On cross-examination, Buehler went after Nix on a personal level. He had to in order to create doubt as to Nix's reliability. Buehler knew that to believe his client was in the parking lot asking Lewis for a free cashier's check for Ali was to believe that he was guilty of the embezzlement conspiracy as charged.

"Have you ever had a problem with alcoholism?" Buehler asked.

"Yes."

"Is it correct that you have taken leaves of absence from Wells Fargo Bank because of that?"

"Took one."

"How long was that?"

"Twenty-one days."

Howard Moore also scored points on Nix, getting him to say that Smith had been wearing a cowboy hat with "a big feather in it" that day in the parking lot. The minute Allison heard Nix give this answer, he knew Nix probably wouldn't be believed. Feathers had never been Smith's style, and the whole courtroom knew it.

Then it was Ortiz's turn.

"Did there come a time in February of 1979 when you had occasion to see Mr. Marshall, Mr. Smith and Mr. Lewis in the vicinity of the Beverly Drive office?"

"Yes."

"When was that?"

"February the thirteenth, approximately three-fifteen. Mr. Marshall and Mr. Smith and Mr. Lewis were outside the Beverly Drive office."

"How is it that you are able to recall the date?"

"It was the day before Valentine's Day, and the staff had gone home early. We let them go home early."

Ortiz drew the relevant diagrams and figures on another blackboard. The positions he put the three men in were almost identical to the way Nix had drawn them.

"For how long did you observe them standing next to that wall?"

"Approximately ten to fifteen seconds."

"Now, after you saw them there, did you see Mr. Lewis do anything?"

"Mr. Lewis came back into the branch at that point in time and went to his desk and did a couple of things—he was there for a ten, fifteen-minute span, when at that point in time he said he was leaving, that he had to go give something to Harold and Sammie. He would be back ... He proceeded to leave the bank."

"Which way was he heading at that time?"

"Toward the side door."

"And did Mr. Lewis have anything with him at the time he said he had to give something to Harold and Sammie?"

"He had a white letterhead envelope with him at the time." "Did you see what was in the envelope?" Allison asked for effect.

Ortiz's answer, which had to be no, didn't matter. The prosecutor just wanted the jurors to think about it.

Inside that white envelope *had* to be the cashier's check for Ali.

* * *

It was now time to play a tape Allison had been saving. It was an interview of Harold Smith by TV sportscaster Jim Hill. Allison thought it would dispense with Smith's line of credit story once and for all.

The tape recorder was on the government's table, with two large speakers facing the jury. Agent Woodall pushed the play button. Smith was criticizing Gene Kawakami and, as usual, blaming him for everything. Then, these words: "That was in August 1980, and *that's when I found out that the line of credit I was supposed to have wasn't no line of credit at all.*"

While the words were fresh in the jurors' minds—Smith was admitting that he knew the monies he received from Wells Fargo after that date were *not* from a line of credit—Allison recalled FBI Special Agent Joe Woodall to the stand.

"From your accounting, how much embezzled money from Wells Fargo did MAPS receive *after* August 1980?"

"Approximately nine million dollars," Woodall replied.

* * *

Harold Smith tried to use Muhammad Ali one last time. He convinced the Champ to come down to court the day that the defense attorneys gave their closing arguments to show his support. In summation, Howard

Moore gave an impassioned presentation, clearly modeled after Reverend King's "I Have A Dream" speech. The only problem was that most people in the courtroom paid little attention to Moore. They were too busy watching Ali in the gallery.

"I want to talk to you about the dream, a dream of Harold Smith, my client, a dream that is now deferred," Moore intoned loudly. "I believe that Harold's dream, and what he worked for, was best expressed by one of his athletes. I believe it summarizes that feeling in character, that virtue of hard work, that spirit of free enterprise, that spirit of 'Let's do something, let's not curse the darkness, let's light a candle.' " Moore then read a poem by one of the MAAS amateur boxers. It was a tearjerker.

Allison wanted to sober the jurors back up. He began his rebuttal argument sharply. "I want to bring you back from the land of poems and dreams to the facts of this case." He recited the facts, the details of the conspiracy and the involvement of all three defendants in the scheme. To more than one courtroom observer, the evidence was overwhelming.

The jury went into deliberations the next day after lengthy instructions from Judge Marshall on the law.

Eight days later, after poring over the voluminous evidence, the jurors returned guilty verdicts against both Harold Smith and Sammie Marshall. Smith was convicted on thirty-one charges—all the counts in the indictment but one. (The jurors later explained that they couldn't find one of the embezzled checks among the hundreds of exhibits and didn't want to spend any more time looking for it after convicting Smith of so much already.) Marshall was found guilty on three of the four charges against him—the conspiracy count, the false entry charge and the embezzlement count based on the Telstar cashier's check. He was acquitted of the embezzlement count based on the February 1979 parking lot incident. Apparently the jurors had not believed Nix and Ortiz.

It was a convincing win for the government. The next day's Los Angeles *Herald-Examiner* headline announced harold smith GUILTY IN WELLS FARGO SWINDLE—$21 MILLION BANK EMBEZZLEMENT LARGEST IN U.S.

EPILOGUE

At his sentencing, Harold Smith tried his usual tactics of flattery and manipulation, calling United States District Judge Consuelo B. Marshall "a beautiful black woman" and telling her, "I love you." Judge Marshall sentenced him to ten years in the federal penitentiary. Harold served his time in the federal correctional facilities at Danbury, Connecticut; Petersburg, Virginia, and Boron, California before being paroled in October 1988. In prison, he reportedly kept a thick book of his press clippings and was quick to explain to his fellow cons how he was "framed." After his release—perhaps even before—Harold went back to the fight game, using the connections he had made during his high-flying scamming days at MAPS. In 1988, prior to his release that year, he was accused of illegally managing one such former associate, heavy-weight Tony Tubbs, from behind bars. In 1990, he became an "adviser" to former heavyweight champion Larry Holmes, who was making a come-back. Early that same year, Harold quietly obtained a California boxing manager's license in Los Angeles with the assistance of State Athletic Commission official Marty Denkin, another old acquaintance, without the usual public hearing before the full Commission. Later on, he continued advising Holmes, former welterweight and middleweight champ Thomas "Hitman" Hearns, and other fighters; dabbled with casino boxing in the South; reportedly promoted the first pro fight in Communist China, dubbed by Smith as the "Brawl at the Wall," and re-ingratiated himself with Muhammad Ali, whom he accompanied on a six-city trip to China in 1994. Whenever he was asked how he could get back into boxing despite his well-publicized fraud conviction, Harold always has a ready, slick answer: "My problem was banking, not boxing."

***

Benjamin Lewis was sentenced to five years in accordance with his plea agreement with the government. Lewis is incarcerated at the federal prison camp in Lompoc, California. A "lead man" in the furniture factory, he has helped build thousands of wooden in-and-out trays that are used in government offices throughout the country. Two months after he entered prison, Lewis's body began shaking uncontrollably one day. When the seizure passed, he felt a new sense of relief. That night for the first time in more than three years he got a good night's sleep. "It was as if all the tension I had been living with left me at once," he says. "While working at the bank, I gave the best acting performance of my life. The role lasted almost three years, and I was on night and day. I still don't know how I managed to pull it off." Lewis was released from prison in 1985. The former bus driver and ex-banker quietly ran a small limousine service in south Los Angeles for a decade until his sudden death from a heart attack in 1995, at age 61.

***

Sammie Marshall received a three-year sentence and is imprisoned at the federal prison facility in Boron, California. To this day, he maintains his innocence of the scheme to embezzle from Wells Fargo Bank.

***

Jennifer King, following her conviction upon retrial on one count of criminal contempt of court, was ordered to serve three hundred hours of community service and placed on two years' probation. As a result of a disciplinary investigation by the California State Bar, she was placed on three years' probation by the State Supreme Court. King is presently practicing law in Beverly Hills, California.

***

Robert Michaels, King's law partner, was found guilty in an unrelated grand theft case and was sentenced to one year in the Los Angeles County jail. Scheduled to be released in late 1984, he was also ordered to pay restitution in the amount of $250,000 and spend five years on probation. Michaels was convicted of stealing the money from a client.

***

Gene Kawakami, as a result of his conviction on one count of making a false entry in bank records, served two months in a halfway house. In addition he was ordered to perform several hundred hours of public service work, a requirement he fulfilled at a public library near his home. His sentence completed, Kawakami is now working fewer hours and making more money than he did at Wells Fargo Bank. A business management consultant in Southern California, he invests other people's money for a living.

***

Brian Feeley found himself blacklisted in banking circles after his termination by Wells Fargo. He owns and operates a nurses uniform store in Hollywood, California—a business he bought with his life savings. "My biggest mistake was that I trusted a friend," Feeley says. "I never thought Ben would do such a thing."

***

Teri Key returned to her native North Carolina following her breakup with Tony Key. She works as a surgical assistant and goes by her maiden name (Godwin). "I learned a lot about life in the fast lane in California," she says. "I came back home because I didn't want to live like that anymore. Things are simpler now."

***

Dean Allison left the U.S. Attorney's Office in late 1982 after six years of government service. He became a partner in the Los Angeles office of Jones, Day, Reavis & Pogue, one of the world's biggest law firms, handling large-scale civil litigation. After 30 years of practicing law, he took early retirement in 2004 to pursue his lifelong dream of coaching high school football. Today, he is still coaching. His teams have won several championships.

***

And Muhammad Ali—well, he'll always be the Champ.

ABOUT THE AUTHOR

Bruce Henderson is the author of more than twenty nonfiction books, including *True Evidence: The Hunt for the I-5 Serial Killer*; *Fatal North: Murder and Survival on the First North Pole Expedition*, winner of a national book award, and the #1 New York Times bestseller, *And the Sea Will Tell*, a true story of murder on a South Seas island that was adapted for a highly-rated CBS miniseries. He lives in Menlo Park, California. Find Bruce on the web at: www.BruceHendersonBooks.com.

ALSO BY BRUCE HENDERSON

Trace Evidence: The Hunt for the I-5 Serial Killer
Fatal North: Murder and Survival on the First North Pole Expedition
And the Sea Will Tell
Hero Found: The Greatest POW Escape of the Vietnam War
True North: Peary, Cook and the Race to the Pole